BRITAIN'S ENCOUNTER WITH MEIJI JAPAN, 1868–1912

*Also by Olive Checkland*

PHILANTHROPY IN VICTORIAN SCOTLAND
HEALTH CARE AS SOCIAL HISTORY (*edited with M. Lamb*)
INDUSTRY AND ETHOS: Scotland, 1832–1914
(*with S. G. Checkland*)

# Britain's Encounter with Meiji Japan, 1868–1912

Olive Checkland
*Honorary Research Fellow*
*University of Glasgow*

MACMILLAN

First published 1989

Published by
THE MACMILLAN PRESS LTD
Houndmills, Basingstoke, Hampshire RG21 2XS
and London
Companies and representatives
throughout the world

Typeset by Footnote Graphics,
Warminster, Wilts

Printed in the People's Republic of China

British Library Cataloguing in Publication Data
Checkland, Olive
Britain's encounter with Meiji Japan,
1868–1912.
1. Great Britain. Relations, 1868–1912 with
Japan 2. Japan. Relations, 1868–1912 with
Great Britain
I. Title
303.4'8241'052
ISBN 0–333–48346–4

For
S.G.C.
in 'love, favour and affection'

# Contents

# List of Tables

# List of Maps

# List of Cartoons

# List of Plates

# Preface

The Restoration of the Emperor at the beginning of 1868 enabled Japan to embark on a course of action which was to bring her, within a remarkably short time, to the status of a world power. During the forty-four years for which the Emperor chose the name *Meiji*, or Enlightenment, Britain was the most influential foreign power. The present study is concerned on the one hand with the extraordinary response of Japan to the industrial, educational and military challenges involved and on the other with the reaction of British entrepreneurs, engineers and educators, to the opportunities afforded them through the Japanese connection. In the background to both was the Japanese state, itself adjusting radically and soon in a position to make itself the arbiter of the whole process. Meanwhile at a more theoretical level there was the continuing philosophical debate as to whether Western individualism could be reconciled with both the traditional values of Japanese society and the seemingly inevitable necessity that the state exert economic control.

Two general frames of reference are applied by recent scholars to the *Meiji* modernisation of Japan. The first is the notion of growth from above and the second that of growth from below. In the West at least the former has tended until recently to be dominant. It stressed the actions of government in its control and sponsorship of the economy, thus liquidating feudal obstacles to growth, seeking the appropriate monetary and fiscal systems, stimulating the industrial base, and using the foreigner but keeping him at bay. This view, of course, emphasised positive action from the government at the centre, and thus focused attention on the young oligarchs who created and manipulated the new regime. Against this is the second view that the real engine of development lay elsewhere partly in the population growth rate – of a people well educated – and partly in the generation of a surplus, especially in rice, a phenomenon established well before the Restoration. There was also a highly active merchant and proto-banking community in whom resided the most important elements of liquidity and business skills.

The present study offers a third perspective, namely growth stimulated from outside, by the adoption of best practice from the West and by borrowing from the Western foreigner. Implicit in the approach from outside, with its aspects of shock (itself a great inducer of change) and of technical and other borrowing, is the tantalising counter-factual question – what would have happened in Japan if the foreigners had stayed at home, leaving the indigenous forces to work things out for themselves without foreign intervention?

But once the American, Commander Matthew Perry – to be followed by Lord Elgin and the others – had broken through Japan's seclusion, change was inevitable. The foreigners demanded treaties which although accepted and signed contained provisions to which the Japanese objected. They disliked the enclaves of the treaty ports in which the foreigners resided and traded, outside the provisions of Japanese law. They objected to the control of import duties, which were limited to 5 per cent *ad valorem*. The foreigners regarded the treaty ports with their foreign consular courts, as a necessary protection for their citizens and the trading controls no different from those imposed elsewhere in the undeveloped world.

The Japanese labelled their treaties as 'unequal'. They believed the clauses relating to foreigners and trading smacked of semi-colonialism. It became the corner-stone of Japanese foreign policy to renegotiate the treaties at the earliest possible opportunity. The treaty ports disappeared in 1899 and tariff autonomy was achieved in 1911. The 'unequal' treaties remain a background to this study, their very existence during most of the *Meiji* era acting as a stimulus to action for a whole class of educated Japanese.

Once the Restoration had been safely accomplished the young *Meiji* oligarchs, almost all with experience of working and studying in the West, embarked on a headlong course of modernisation. This involved wholesale borrowing and an influx of skilled foreigners into Japan. These employees, exceptionally well paid, were on short – usually three to four years – fixed-term contracts. They all worked under the authority of Japanese superiors. In this sense Japan was unique and quite unlike India or other similar countries. Most of the foreigners hired were British although many Americans, Germans, Italians, French and other foreign citizens were employed. Some of the British were engineers, including men with rare specialisms as shipbuilders, ship-designers, and naval architects. Others were educators, bringing Western literacy and advanced scientific and technical education to Japan. The decade from 1872 to 1882 could readily be named 'the experts' decade'.

But the high price of employing foreigners and allowing them to order expensive equipment from abroad, together with the cost of putting down the *Satsuma* rebellion in 1877, caused great difficulties in Japan. Inflation and prices soared and there was much unrest. In 1881 during a political power struggle the liberal Shigenobu Okuma was ousted by Masayoshi Matsukata. Under Matsukata's guidance a deflationary financial policy based on central government control was adopted which, over the succeeding years, brought a new financial order. The establishment of the Bank of Japan by Matsukata in 1882 marked the beginning of the new era. Inflationary pressures were slowly reduced, savings mobilised and channelled into various forms of enterprise. As a result it was possible for Japan not only to set up a convertible currency system but also to finance the war against China in 1894–5. Having won the war Japan demanded a huge indemnity. On the Gold Standard from 1897, Japan could thereafter borrow on good terms on the world money markets. It was the first time that an undeveloped nation had emerged onto the world stage.

But the Japanese always wanted to create a great Japan. At home and abroad they were consumed by a desire to do the best for their country. Although those who took power in 1868 were largely from the clans of *Satsuma* and *Choshu*, in the south-west of the country, in the name of the Emperor men from many clans and many areas were involved in the effort to build a new Japan.

This book is concerned with the way in which the British sought opportunity in Japan and how they coped with Japanese requests for help in gaining modern skills and experience. Although the cross-fertilisation discussed here is set in *Meiji* Japan and Victorian Britain there is much which is as relevant today as it was then concerning the relationship between the two countries. As the process of change accelerated, the Japanese, although continuing and developing their British connection drew more widely on other foreign resources. Interest in codes of law, general education and a modern constitution took them also to France, America and Germany.

Late Victorian Britain, still proud and confident in her industrial supremacy, produced many facilitators who rendered important service to Japan. Not all were motivated by self-interest. British academics enjoyed teaching Japanese students for they found them apt and eager – and they took class prizes. British industrialists, agreed, on signing contracts with the Japanese, to employ engineers and apprentices in the shipyard and on the shop-floor. Such Japanese 'workmen' – in reality highly qualified engineers – proved diligent and competent.

The core of the book relates to the methods by which technical transfer was effected. Three consecutive but overlapping phases can be discerned. The first, the 'experts' decade', was followed by a second stage during which young Japanese men, well-educated and of good potential, were sent overseas for a period of work and experience. During the third phase, which continued until the onset of the First World War and encouraged the continuing exchange of personnel between Britain and Japan, sophisticated engineering products were manufactured under licence in Japan.

Shipbuilding is taken as the leading sector industry through which the Japanese gained access to the advanced technology of the day. Not only did the Royal Navy nurture and encourage the Imperial Japanese Navy but Japanese naval or civilian engineering officers worked in British engineering and shipbuilding concerns being in residence for long years at Glasgow, Newcastle upon Tyne, Barrow-in-Furness or Sheffield. In Britain, by 1911, the legend had grown that vessels for the Imperial Japanese Navy, with identical specifications to those for the Royal Navy, but built in British yards under Japanese supervision, performed better than British vessels built in British yards under British supervision.

But the Japanese recognised from the beginning that scientific and engineering education is an essential prerequisite for any successful transfer. There is much new insight into the remarkable provision and the achievements at the Imperial College of Engineering in Tokyo which had an independent life for thirteen years before being amalgamated into the Faculty of Engineering of the University of Tokyo. Nor can the role of the Scots as educators be overlooked. In engineering and in naval architecture they occupied important positions in Britain and Japan.

There were also those who, without intent, by their writing or teaching, assisted the movement of ideas from Britain to Japan. These influential figures rarely visited Japan. Men like Herbert Spencer and John Stuart Mill and at a humbler level Samuel Smiles (whose *Thrift* and *Self Help* struck a sympathetic chord in Japan) were widely read in translation among the Japanese. Others like Lord Kelvin willingly accepted foreign research students, including Japanese, into their classes and laboratories and admitted them to the fellowship of advanced scholarship.

An early pioneer of research in this field was Grace Fox with her *Britain and Japan, 1855–85* (1969). Her work remains indispensable. Much, however, has since come to light concerning the complex relationships between Britain and *Meiji* Japan, and there has been serious consideration, deriving from development studies, of the processes involved in the interaction between an advanced economy and an aspiring one.

The notes and references provided aim to develop ideas and interpretations which could not easily be incorporated into the text. It is hoped that students and researchers, in both Britain and Japan, will find these helpful and informative but that they will not hesitate to amplify inadequacies and in so doing share their learning with me.

In the early phase of this study I was indebted to Masami Kita who, as research fellow in the University of Glasgow, first aroused my enthusiasm for his discoveries of Scottish links with *Meiji* Japan. In the spring of 1984 Masami Kita brought his work to fruition by publishing *Kokusai Nippon wo kiri hiraita hitobito: Nippon to Scotland no Kizuna* (*Pioneers of Making Japan International: Linkage between Japan and Scotland*).

The archives of the University of Glasgow have proved particularly fruitful for two reasons. Because of the way in which the University retained its records at this period it is possible there to trace in detail the academic careers of Japanese students. In addition the Business History Archive in the Adam Smith Record Store, the University of Glasgow, set up by the late Professor Sydney Checkland, makes available a wide range of shipbuilding and other engineering firms' records. The assistance received over several years has been much appreciated.

In Japan, in 1981, the generosity of the Japan Academy enabled me to pursue research interests in Tokyo, Sapporo, Nagasaki, Osaka, Kobe and Yokohama. I am indebted to Masaji Arai, Akira Hayumi, Kenji Imazu, Akio Ishizaka, Masaaki Kobayashi, Yoshitaka Komatsu, Mataji Miyamoto, Keiichiro Nakagawa, Akio Okochi, Takuji Sakamoto, Chuhei Sugiyama, Sakae Tsunoyama, Yukio Yamashita, Yasukichi Yasuba, Mine Yasuzawa and Tsunehiko Yui for organising research visits to archives throughout Japan.

Three years later in 1984 thanks to an invitiation from the Faculty of Business and Commerce at Keio University, a longer study period was spent in Japan. This enabled further work to be done on many English language sources in Japanese archives. But, in addition, Japanese friends and colleagues have been supportive of all endeavours and have never failed to give generously of their time and expertise. The series of lectures which my husband and I gave at Keio in the autumn of 1984 brought further valued contacts including those with Eiichi Aoki, Takeshi Hamashita, Heita Kawakatsu, Norikazu Kudo, Tetsuro Nakaoka, Shunsako Nishikawa, Reiko Okayama, Osamu Saito, Yoko Sano, Shinya Sugiyama, Terumi Tabata,

Kazuhiko Uejima, Yoko Wake and Naoki Watanabe. Their assistance has been much appreciated. My greatest debt in Japan is to Norio and Setsuko Tamaki who with much kindness and affection permitted their lives to be dominated by Checkland research preoccupations during the latter half of 1984.

In the West Alec Cairncross, Douglas Farnie, James Galbraith, Edwin Green, Simon Hanna, Margaret Lamb, Sylvia Lewis, David Lyon, Tam Mito, Michael Moss, Ian Nish, Margaret Pamplin, Erich Pauer, Regine Matthias Pauer, Robert Phillifent, Richard Potts, Alan Reid, Jean Robertson and Robin Spencer have responded in full measure to many queries.

The book benefited greatly from the insights of my late husband, Sydney Checkland. After March 1986, the loving care of our five children has encouraged the completion of this work. Isabel Burnside, ably supported by Bill and Craig, has continued to provide not only the efficiency for which she is well known, but also the freindship which has made the creation of this book easier.

*Ferry Path, Cambridge* OLIVE CHECKLAND

# Author's Note

Japanese names are rendered with given name followed by family name.

Dates are in Western style.

# List of Abbreviations

| | |
|---|---|
| AA | Armstrong Archives, Tyne and Wear County Council |
| AINA | Associate of the Institute of Naval Engineers |
| AMB | Armstrong Minute Books, Tyne and Wear County Council |
| ASRS | Adam Smith Record Store, Glasgow University Archives |
| AUL | Aberdeen University Library |
| *BA* | *Report of the British Association for the Advancement of Science* |
| BE | Bachelor of Engineering |
| *BEM* | *Blackwoods Edinburgh Magazine* |
| *BH* | *Business History* |
| *BHR* | *Business History Review* |
| *BJHS* | *British Journal for the History of Science* |
| BM | British Museum |
| *BSOAS* | *Bulletin of School of Oriental and African Studies*, University of London |
| CE | Certificate of Proficiency in Engineering Science |
| CR | Commercial Report |
| *DNB* | *Dictionary of National Biography* |
| *EcHR* | *Economic History Review* |
| EL | Elgin Letters, Broomhall, Fife, Scotland |
| EUL | Edinburgh University Library |
| FO | Foreign Office |
| FRS | Fellow of the Royal Society |
| FRSE | Fellow of the Royal Society of Edinburgh |
| GUA | Glasgow University Archives |
| GUL | Glasgow University Library |
| HBM | Her Britannic Majesty |
| HIJM | His Imperial Japanese Majesty |
| HC | House of Commons |
| HL | House of Lords |
| ICE | Imperial College of Engineering, Tokyo |
| ICERD | International Centre for Economics and Related Disciplines, London School of Economics |
| IJN | Imperial Japanese Navy |
| *ILN* | *Illustrated London News* |
| *JAS* | *Journal of Asian Studies* |

| | |
|---|---|
| *JCH* | *Journal of Contemporary History* |
| JM | Jardine Matheson Archives, University Library, Cambridge |
| *JRIBA* | *Journal of the Royal Institute of British Architects* |
| *JSHS* | *Japanese Studies in the History of Science* |
| *JSL* | *Japan Society of London, Proceedings and Transactions* |
| *JWH* | *Journal of World History* |
| LSE | London School of Economics Library |
| *MAS* | *Modern Asian Studies* |
| ML | Mitchell Library, Glasgow |
| *MN* | *Monumenta Nipponica* |
| MP | Member of Parliament |
| *MPICE* | *Minutes of Proceedings of the Institution of Civil Engineers* |
| NBL | North British Locomotive Company |
| NLS | National Library of Scotland |
| NMM | National Maritime Museum |
| NYK | Nippon Yusen Kaisha |
| OM | Okuma Monjo, Papers of Okuma Shigenobu, Waseda University, Tokyo |
| *PGPS* | *Proceedings of the Glasgow Philosophical Society* |
| PP | Parliamentary Papers |
| PRO | Public Record Office |
| *PRS* | *Proceedings Royal Society* |
| *PRSE* | *Proceedings of the Royal Society of Edinburgh* |
| RC | Royal Commission |
| StAUL | St Andrews University Library |
| *TASJ* | *Transactions of the Asiatic Society of Japan* |
| *TIESS* | *Transactions of the Institution of Engineers and Shipbuilders in Scotland* |
| *TLS* | *Times Literary Supplement* |
| *TNASS* | *Transactions of the National Association for the Promotion of Social Science* |
| *TNECIES* | *Transactions of the North East Coast Institution of Engineers and Shipbuilders* |
| *TINA* | *Transactions of the Institute of Naval Architecture* |
| TWAS | Tyne and Wear Archives Services |
| UCL | University College, the University of London |
| ULC | University Library, Cambridge |
| V. and A. | Victoria and Albert Museum |
| WEG | William Elliott Griffis papers, Rutgers University Library, New Jersey, USA |

*Map* 1.1 Japan in Meiji times

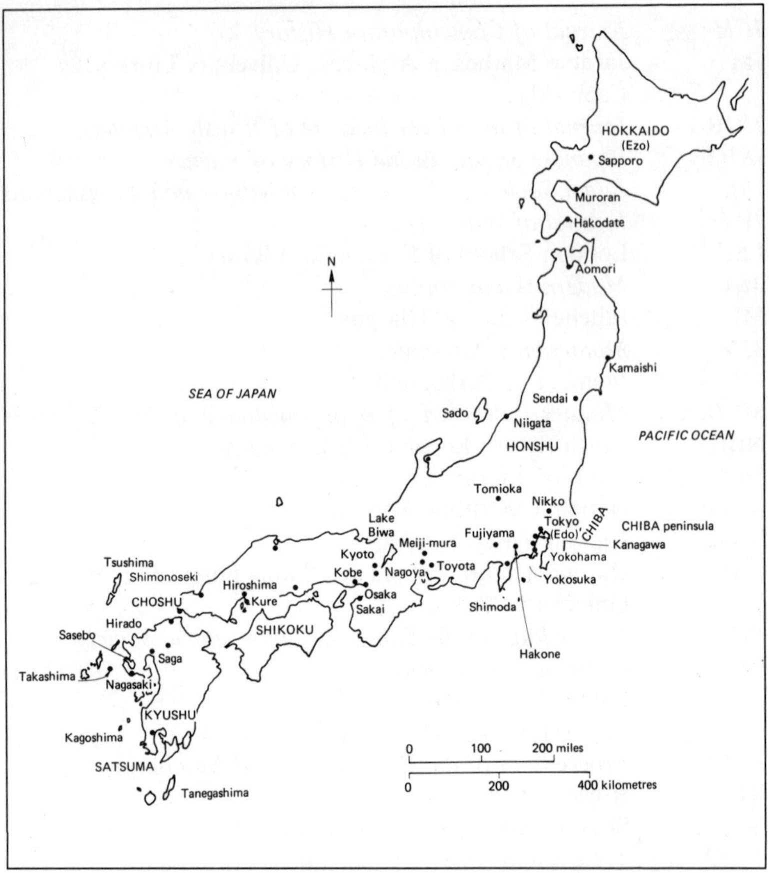

# Part I

# The British in Japan: A Search for Opportunity

# 1 Diplomats and Consuls

## 1 LORD ELGIN IN JAPAN

Whatever diplomatic skills the British were later to deploy in Japan were not, however, available to James, the 8th Earl of Elgin (1811–63),[1,2] the first British plenipotentiary to treat with the Japanese. Having forced the Treaty of Tientsin on the Chinese (26 June 1858) he was authorised to make a quick dash to Japan, to make contact and, if possible, sign a trade treaty there. Elgin's action was perhaps indicative of his confidence in his own skills as a negotiator, for, despite his expostulation, 'How to make a treaty without *time*, *interpreter* or credentials!',[3] he believed he had a fair chance of success. Partly because of favourable outside circumstances and partly due to Japanese complaisance, he did succeed in bringing his negotiations to a speedy and successful conclusion. He arrived in Japan on 3 August 1858 and signed the Treaty of Edo on 26 August.[4,5]

It was the Americans, in the person of their consul, Townshend Harris (1804–75),[6] who had taken the real initiative and borne the brunt of the negotiations for the first trade treaty with Japan (that of Kanagawa), which after much delay was signed on 29 July 1858. The Japanese had been brought to the point of signing the American treaty only by the news – which Townshend Harris ensured was speedily carried to them – that Elgin had signed the Treaty of Tientsin with China and was on his way to Japan. The Japanese were aware that their Treaty of Kanagawa conceded less to the Americans than did the Chinese Treaty of Tientsin to the British.

It was recognised in the Far East from the 1840s that the British, with their lobby of clamant traders, would bring pressure to trade in Japan, although the government in London in the early 1850s showed no sense of urgency. Because of affairs at home, including the demands made by the Crimean War (1854–6) the British were content to follow the American lead. This dilatory approach, whether conscious or not, had much to commend it, encouraging, as it did, the Americans to undertake the initial bargaining with the Japanese. They, having occupied and taken up the land to their own western seaboard, were anxious for a Pacific role, yet offered no immediate threat to the supremacy of the British as traders in the East. The leisurely British response was also useful at home, helping to placate those who had been repelled by the forceful initiatives taken in China and shocked by the exploitation of opium as a means of forcing trade.

The authorities in Japan recognised that the British posed a serious threat. The regular intelligence which they received from China where the British trained and employed a small cadre of their own people as interpreters in the Chinese language gave some idea of British intentions. The Japanese rightly assumed that they would in the fullness of time extend their interest to Japan.

Putting much faith in the promise of Townshend Harris that he would try to persuade Elgin to accept a version of the Treaty of Kanagawa, the Japanese awaited his arrival. Fortunately Elgin, fresh from trials and travails in China and ready for a change, was prepared to like Japan whose people he found 'a most curious contrast to the Chinese, so anxious to learn and so *prévenants*'.[7]

Elgin's instructions had been carefully worded. Before leaving London he had been advised:

> Your Excellency will understand that it is not the intention of Her Majesty's Government to impose a new Treaty on Japan by forcible means. We wish to conciliate the goodwill of the Government and people of Japan; but we have no cause of quarrel with them to justify our having recourse to coercive measures on any account, and least of all in order to compel them to conclude a Treaty the provisions of which might be repugnant to their wishes or interests.[8]

Bearing in mind the constraints of time – for Elgin was needed back in China – as well as his instructions from London, it was not difficult for him to accept Townshend Harris's proposal that he use the Treaty of Kanagawa as a basis for his own negotiations.[9] In order to treat with the Japanese at all, Elgin was glad to accept the services of Mr Harris's Dutch interpreter, Henry Heuskens,[10] for Dutch was then the only European language known sufficiently well in Japan. Elgin also praised the Japanese negotiators, 'I was much struck by the manner in which they did their work; making very shrewd observations, and putting very shrewd questions, but by no means in a captious or cavilling spirit.'[11] Elgin's pleasure at being in Japan continued as the bargaining proceeded harmoniously,[12] and the Treaty of Edo, a modified version of Harris's, was signed on 26 August 1858 at 1 p.m. After suitable ceremony and the presentation of the steam yacht, *The Emperor*,[13] a present from Queen Victoria,

Elgin sailed away 'quitting the only place which I have left with any feeling of regret since I reached this abominable East'.[14]

## 2 THE TREATY OF EDO

The Treaty of Edo was to be the basis for future British and Japanese relations. It was not to be replaced *in toto* for forty years. Its principal clauses related to diplomatic representation, foreign residence and trade regulations. Nagasaki, Hakodate and Kanagawa were named as treaty ports to be opened soon to foreigners; Niigata (or some other port on the Sea of Japan coast) and Hyogo (later Kobe) were to be opened later. Foreigners were to have rights of residence in Edo (from 1 January 1862) and in Osaka (from 1 January 1863). Diplomatic representation was to be established in the treaty ports and in Edo. Consular jurisdiction and extraterritoriality were stipulated. Trade regulations between the two countries allowed for exports from Japan to be taxed at 5 per cent. Imports of gold and silver together with the personal effects of foreign residents were to be imported freely while a list of items including 'supplies for rigging and repairing ships, coal, timber, steam machinery, zinc, lead, tin and various foodstuffs, cotton and wollen manufactured goods' could be imported paying a 5 per cent duty.[15]

For the British the treaty was satisfactory, giving them the sort of rights and privileges to which they were accustomed in undeveloped countries. For the Japanese matters were more complex. They knew they were fortunate to have escaped from a more onerous treaty but nevertheless they were conscious that some of the clauses gave foreigners rights and privileges which, to them, were deeply offensive. These concerned the concessions of extraterritoriality and consular jurisdiction which permitted foreigners to live in Japan in their own communities and to be tried for alleged offences by their own consular officials in consular courts. Not only was judicial authority over the foreigners denied to the Japanese, so too was fiscal autonomy. They were in effect denied the right to operate a tariff other than the 5 per cent. Although nothing could be done about these in 1858, the Japanese resolved to put an end to these practices in course of time. To renegotiate the 'unequal treaties', as they were called in Japan, became the cornerstone of their foreign policy.

Once the treaty arrived in London the British government began to consider setting up a Japanese diplomatic and consular service. There was still no sense of urgency about what appeared to the Foreign Office in London to be so minor a matter. In the Far East however merchants awaited expectantly. Ships were being loaded with merchandise for Japan well before the opening day of 1 July 1859.

## 3 THE DIPLOMATIC ESTABLISHMENT

To put things on a proper footing Sir Rutherford Alcock[16] (previously in service in China) was appointed Consul General to Japan (1859–65)[17] and he and his staff prepared themselves to take up their posts. Alcock was nervous about his reception. He guessed that the Japanese would not necessarily interpret the treaty as he would wish. He also knew that elements of the population, notably the *samurai*, 'the two-sworded men', were xenophobic, and he feared for his own safety and that of his people.

The diplomatic and consular establishment in the Far East,[18] or indeed elsewhere in areas distant from Britain was a very different affair from the grand embassies of Europe where aristocratic names graced the diplomatic lists. In these remote places men were chosen to serve who were prepared to live uncomfortably, and perhaps dangerously. Some consular staff had amassed local knowledge, some had been trained as interpreters; consular representation depended upon the successful establishment of trade and it was with the commercial world that the consular officer was closely linked.[19]

Alcock himself, originally an army surgeon, had elevated himself, by dint of hard work, from the ranks of consular officers. Indeed later in his career when Lord Russell recommended him as Minister to China, the Queen initially objected on the grounds that, 'he was not high bred enough for the Chinese'.[20] In the course of his service he had learned, as Elgin had done, that in Japan as elsewhere he must as representative of a great country, exert his authority.

The first problem which arose, virtually as they came ashore, related to accommodation. Two temples were offered (their guest-houses being the only type of building capable of housing even a modest mission),[21] the Japanese preferring one and Alcock choosing the other. He did so partly because of convenience but also to assert the authority of the nation which he represented. The comfort and morale of a mission often depended on the skill and tact of a minister in handling such matters. Other grounds of disagreement threatened. These related to the site of the treaty port itself, the exchange rate for

Japanese currency and access by road between Edo and the treaty port. Of these matters more later.

In 1865 when he had been in Japan for six years, Rutherford Alcock was appointed Minister to China – his final posting before retirement. Although his years in Japan had been full of worry, he had succeeded in establishing the legation at Edo and the consulates elsewhere in Japan.[22] His period of service was but a preliminary to what was to come.

## 4 'THE FORMER CONSUL PARKES'

Sir Harry Parkes (1828–85) was British Minister to Japan for eighteen years from 1865 to 1883. He took full advantage of Britain's superior power to pursue a vigorous policy which was accepted by his government at home and warmly approved by his compatriots in Japan. The Japanese, while appreciating his assistance to them in coming to terms with the modern world, came to resent his overbearing manner and resist his attempted intrusion into their affairs.[23]

Parkes's attitudes had been formed in China where he had entered service as a student interpreter at the age of 14.[24] From 1842 he had been present on many important diplomatic missions in China where British forcefulness had been matched by Chinese equivocation. Parkes responded strongly to what he always believed was Chinese 'vacillation and deceit'. Consul Parkes of Canton retained these attitudes when he was promoted, at the age of 38, to ministerial authority in Japan, apparently allowing free rein to his choleric temper which, although combined with a capacity for 'great personal kindness', produced a strong response from those with whom he came into contact.

In Britain Parkes had a dazzling and well-deserved reputation for bravery. He had been knighted by Queen Victoria at the age of 34 as a token of thanks for his part in Lord Elgin's Mission to China in 1860. Parkes and others had been captured, under a flag of truce, by the Chinese on 18 September 1860. He and his comrades had been subjected to shocking treatment. Throughout the ordeal, Parkes as spokesman had shown spartan courage and indeed defiance in the face of death. On 8 October the senior members of the party were released though other members of the group suffered terrible torture and dreadful deaths.[25]

Although he completed his career in the early days of the ocean telegraph, Parkes was a diplomat of an earlier era. He had been trained to take his own decisions and to stand by them.[26] When Parkes arrived in Japan in 1865 he had no means of judging how affairs there would develop. The *Shogun*'s government had acceded to foreign pressure and opened the treaty ports. This controversial but inevitable decision, coming after 200 years of seclusion, caused dismay in many quarters in Japan. There was an undercurrent of unrest, related to but not necessarily caused by the advent of foreigners on Japanese soil. Some were attacked and several murdered by infuriated *samurai*. But in the south and west Japanese princes were themselves adding to the sense of unease by quietly resisting the will of central government. Despite the remoteness of the disaffected clans Parkes could not remain unaware of the difficulties, technically responsible as he was for the behaviour of his fellow citizens who were themselves the instruments by which clan defiance of central government was encouraged. Some British merchants based in Nagasaki had no scruples, exploiting the disaffection by trading with the clans in proscribed goods, including ships and guns.[27]

At the time Parkes took up his office as Minister, events in London were taking a further turn. The *Satsuma* mission which arrived in London in 1865 was in close touch with Laurence Oliphant,[28] who had made important contacts in Japan while serving there. Under its leaders Matsuki Koan and Tomoatsu Godai,[29] and through the intervention of Laurence Oliphant, the *Satsuma* men were putting pressure on the British government to permit direct trade with the clans. Oliphant prepared a memorandum for the *Satsuma* leaders to present to Lord Clarendon, then Foreign Secretary, advocating a federal system of independent *daimyo* to replace the *Bakufu* government. A copy of this memorandum was sent on to Harry Parkes in Japan.

At the same time Parkes was under some pressure in Japan to reconsider official British policy. Should he continue to support the *Shogun*'s government? In Nagasaki, some, including the young Scottish merchant Thomas Glover, were already implicitly supporting the clans. Ernest Satow, aided and abetted by Algernon Mitford[30] (both on the staff as trainee interpreters), was in close commune with young clan leaders. Satow's mastery of Japanese enabled him to discuss in depth with the young Japanese leaders the political problems facing Japan. He in turn became sympathetic to their aspirations.[31] Parkes, not convinced that the *Shogun* would fall, kept his head and steered a middle course, trying not to antagonise anyone.[32] After the break came in 1868, with Restoration of the Emperor by the clansmen of the south-west, the British were well placed to develop new friendships with the young *Meiji* leaders so well known to Satow and Glover.

The early *Meiji* years were probably the happiest and most successful of Parkes's career. Although the Japanese old guard were hostile to the turn of events there was in general an air of excitement about and a willingness to change. Feudalism and the clan system were abolished and the prefectural system set up in 1872.[33] Parkes and his staff were in constant communication with the new young Japanese ministers and interconnections between Britain and Japan developed rapidly. During these years 'there had been constant travel to collect intelligence and carry the flag of diplomatic activity'.[34] One of Parkes's consular officials summed him up as:

> A man of indomitable courage, both in the presence of physical danger and in the assumption of moral responsibility, of untiring industry, masterful disposition and strong determination in carrying to a successful end whatever he had set his hand to, he represented the most pronounced policy of Lord Palmerston in the advancement and protection of Englishmen and England's interests.[35]

But Parkes, although elevated in Japan to the diplomatic role, had lost nothing of his cunning as the promoter of commercial interests. In 'the former consul Parkes' the British could hardly have found a Minister more likely to stimulate trading connections. He was indefatigable. He understood that if the Japanese hired British subjects for any major enterprise this would produce useful spin-offs, stimulating to British industry and profitable to British banking and finance. With active cooperation from Parkes and his staff major construction contracts for railways, lighthouses and the Japanese Mint were awarded to Britain. Hundreds of British experts poured into Japan. British assistance in helping with the new Japanese Navy and the Merchant Marine ensured important and continuing contacts.[36]

But the Japanese, while recognising their immediate need, 'kept arrangements to a minimum' and spent much time and energy trying to limit British influence and, by involving advisers of other nationalities, preventing too great a reliance on the nationals of any one power. Nevertheless, as a result of much exertion, Britain commanded 75 per cent of the trade with *Bakumatsu* Japan before 1868, and 50 per cent in the *Meiji* era. Parkes regarded this as right and proper.

Parkes was also responsible for the safety of British nationals in Japan, another duty which he undertook with apparent relish. Attacks on foreigners in the early years by xenophobic Japanese (Parkes himself and his entourage had been subject to one),[37] took up a good deal of consular time. Some of these cases reflect no credit on the British. Yet diplomatic exertions had to be made to protect even those disreputable British citizens who got into trouble. It was this sort of incident which so annoyed the Japanese who were powerless under the terms of the 'unequal treaties' to take action against a foreigner however odious his behaviour.

During these years, say until *Meiji* 11 (1878), Parkes was successful in establishing a strong British presence in Japan. At the same time competitors envious of Britain's pre-eminence were launching effective counter-action. Both the USA and Germany were mounting sustained challenges to British influence.[38] The French, Italians and Russians also believed they had particular strengths from which Japan could benefit. The *Japan Punch* enjoyed, as the cartoon shows, international rivalry.

There was constant tension between the British and the Americans as each strove to exert influence, at the expense of the other, in Japan.

*Cartoon* 1.1 The British Minister searches ... (*Japan Punch*, 1874)

After 1880 the excitement of the early *Meiji* years had gone. Parkes himself, no longer so energetic, suffered from poor health and could no longer follow the punishing work regime which he had always set himself and imposed upon his staff. Even more serious, the hectoring style which had so coloured his diplomacy and which had not abated was no longer appropriate. In the early years Japanese politicians had needed guidance and although Parkes's manner was resented, his knowledge of the world and practical commonsense had been useful. By the late 1870s, as Basil Chamberlain explained, 'His outspoken threats earned for him the dread and dislike of the Japanese.'[39] Nor did Sir Harry's high-handed approach go unnoticed. On 24 June 1879 Sir John Pope Hennessy,[40] then Governor of Hong Kong, wrote to the British Foreign Secretary Lord Salisbury, recommending removal of Parkes because 'your representative has been here too long without going home'. Hennessy also wrote to Gladstone, regretting 'the somewhat acrid policy of our Minister here, the former consul Parkes of Canton' and claiming:

> Over and over again members of the Mikado's cabinet have said to me, how different would be the feeling of this country towards England if the generous policy that Mr Gladstone has shown not only in Europe but in distant Borneo was adopted by the British Minister instead of the constant bullying we receive.[41]

Notwithstanding, Parkes, an effective Minister who used his strength to push British interests as far as he could, certainly forced pro-Western interpretations on a weak and inexperienced Japan.[42] Once he had gone, foreign legal advisers assisted Japan to exert her authority. Where the meaning of the treaty was ambiguous Japan held her ground and refused to concede.[43]

The departure of Sir Harry Parkes as British Minister in Japan marked the end of an era. The Ministers who followed were career diplomats and included Sir Francis Plunkett (1835–1907)[44] in Tokyo from 1883–8; Sir Hugh Fraser, who took over in 1888 and died in office in Tokyo in 1894;[45] and P. Le Poer Trench who filled in for one year when Fraser died.[46] The appointment in 1895 of a distinguished Japanologist marked something of a departure.

## 5 INTERPRETER SATOW

From 1895 to 1900 Britain was represented in Japan by Ernest Mason Satow (1843–1929)[47] who had earlier served in Japan for twenty years. He was the British Minister in Japan during the years of international rivalry in the Far East, when Japan was manoeuvring to resist Russia's territorial ambitions in Korea, Manchuria and the Liaotung peninsula. He left Japan in 1900 to take up his last diplomatic post as Minister in China before his retirement.

Satow was unique in his knowledge and understanding of Japan. As a young man, a graduate of the University of London, he had read and been enthralled by Laurence Oliphant's account of Japan in his *Narrative of Lord Elgin's Mission to China and Japan* (1859). So when, in 1861 at the age of 18, he passed out first in the examination for foreign office interpreters he opted for service in Japan.[48,49]

After an interlude in China, Ernest Satow's arrival in Tokyo on 8 September 1862 was to be the beginning of a life-long connection with Japan. The task of learning the Japanese language was difficult and demanding, but by March 1863 he was making remarkable progress as the Minister, Sir Rutherford Alcock, reported:

> Satow is the only man of these sent out east from England who have succeeded in so far mastering the difficulties of the written language up to the present time as to be able to read and translate.[50]

During the exciting decade of the 1860s Satow's influence was significant, for he was the first Englishman 'to enter the underworld of *samurai* politics, and the first to use his pen to influence the outcome of the *Tokugawa* crisis'.[51] A. B. Mitford, commented on 'the extraordinary ability of Mr Satow'. Both Mitford and Satow relished their roles as intriguers. As Mitford wrote 'Satow and myself were very much more under observation than we had been, and it was not easy to keep up our communications with the Daimio's party . . . We managed to defeat them by climbing over the walls of the legation building at night.'[52]

If the young men had had their way British policy would have become one of cautious encouragement for those in Japan who believed that the *Shogun* should withdraw, thus permitting the reinstatement of the Emperor. In the event, despite the potential for violence, the Restoration of the Emperor was accomplished reasonably peacefully in the first days of 1868.

Satow's life at this time was certainly fulfilling, 'Those years, from 1862–1869, were my life.' From January 1868 until 1884, he served formally as Japanese Secretary – 'the real motive source of the legation, [who] occupies a position of greater importance than that of the nominal head, but, with an irony, which is not uncommon in government administration, he is the least appreciated member'.[53] When Satow returned to Japan as Minister in 1895,[54] at the age of 51, he found those young Japanese with whom he had talked politics in the heady 1860s, and whose aspiration for a new Japan he had shared, now transformed into senior ministers. It was a fortunate posting of 'an important and experienced diplomat to the country which had shaped him as much as he had shaped Japan during his previous twenty years of service there. No other European was so qualified or able as he to observe and evaluate conditions in Japan.[55]

## 6 RENEGOTIATING THE UNEQUAL TREATIES

Although renegotiation of the treaties was unimportant to the foreign powers it remained an urgent priority for the Japanese. Foreign residents in Japan strongly resisted any talk of new treaties, although neither their interests nor indeed Japanese affairs generally commanded much attention at home.

In 1893, Munemitsu Mutsu (1844–97),[56] then Foreign Secretary, decided to attempt once more to renegotiate for the removal of extra-territorial rights. His approach to Britain drew a cautiously encouraging response. Perhaps the cries of the opposition parties demanding that Japan unilaterally denounce the treaties, which might have generated instability, were heard in London. Negotiations were successful and the Anglo-Japanese Commerical treaty was signed on 16 July 1894.[57] Under its terms extra-territoriality was to remain until 1899 and there was to be a new *ad valorem* tariff. As Ian Nish has explained, this treaty 'gave Japan an incentive to proceed with the introduction of a revised civil code and that portion of the commercial code which remained incomplete, and thus to proceed further with her modernisation'.[58] The negotiations of 1894 and the resultant treaty were important, enabling Japan to assert her nationhood. In some senses the commercial treaty of 1894 represented a turning-point. As Sir Edward Grey remarked 'the time had come when dealings with Japan might be put on the same equal terms as existed between the nations of European origin'.[59] The Treaty served as a model for the other foreign powers, including Russia, Germany and the USA.

The final victory for Japan came on 1 July 1899 when the revised treaties came into force, freeing her from the earlier offensive and inhibiting provisions. It had taken Japan just over forty years to reverse the treaties of Harris, Elgin and the rest. The British and other foreign nationals thereafter had to accept that they no longer had privileged status. There were strong reactions from those treaty-port residents who feared for their 'perpetual leases' and disliked having to pay Japanese municipal taxes. In course of time the furore died down and life continued much as usual.

The Japanese who were responsible had reason to be proud of their achievements. Despite setbacks and false starts, the programme of modernisation on which Japan had embarked had proved remarkably successful. Once Japan was accepted as a responsible power she could be considered as a possible partner. This led in course of time to the Anglo-Japanese Alliance.

## 7 THE ANGLO-JAPANESE ALLIANCE

But Japan as she in her turn asserted herself against other peoples of mainland Asia, was not to be free from Western intervention. After she had defeated China in 1895 she was forced at the insistence of Russia, France and Germany to accept modifications on the subsequent Treaty of Shimonoseki, in which China had conceded much. The power struggle over the vacuum created by the break-up of the Chinese Empire had been building for years. This coincided with a new-found Japanese assertiveness. Although the manoeuvrings of the great powers may have been based on economic imperatives, strategic considerations were also compelling. In some senses the decade 1895–1905 marked a watershed in that for the first time Japan, a power from the East, was exerting pressure and taking the initiative. Previously such forceful behaviour had always come from America or Western Europe.

It was a bitter blow to Japan to have to bow to foreign pressure. Though Britain, the USA and Italy stood aside, Russia, France and Germany were able to insist that Japan should return to China the newly conceded Liaotung peninsula. The affront which Japan believed she had received from these powers may have temporarily discouraged any thoughts of alliance with Russia, France or Germany. And yet Japan, as a new and rising force in the world, felt weak and vulnerable. Some Japanese believed that Britain was the logical ally and several started working to this end.

Perhaps the most influential figure in Japan who supported the idea of an Anglo-Japanese Alliance was Yukichi Fukuzawa.[60,61] As editor of the newspaper *Jiji Shimpo* (founded 1882) he published, in the summer of 1895, articles advocating such an alliance. These were probably written by Tadasu Hayashi,[62] an ardent anglophile. Later Hayashi, as Minister for Japan in London, was to play a major role in the negotiations. The second of the two articles for *Jiji Shimpo* (July 1895) claimed that an alliance between Britain and Japan could bring a settlement to the Far East. The author concluded 'England and Japan together can control China and ensure the maintenance of peace in the Orient.'[63] Another supporter of the idea of an alliance was Takaaki Kato (1860–1926)[64] who had had a career in business and government before coming Minister for Japan in London between 1894 and 1899. He pressed the Foreign Office to agree in principle to the idea of an alliance with Great Britain. Perhaps Kato was over-eager, at any rate he left London in April 1899 empty-handed.[65] He may also have felt frustrated by the lack of response of successive governments in Tokyo to his pleas. On the other hand, Kato must be given credit for keeping before a wide variety of politicians in Japan the *idea* of an Anglo-Japanese Alliance.

On the British side there were those who recognised the possibility that an active Japanese presence in the Far East would be convenient as a block to Russian plans for further expansion. Lord Kimberley, Foreign Secretary in Rosebery's government (which fell on 24 June 1895), believed that Japan might prove a useful friend in the Far East. The appointment of Sir Ernest Satow as Minister to Japan, was opportune for Satow was certainly able to interpret the Japanese to his government.[66]

When Satow was appointed as British Minister to China in 1900 Sir Claude MacDonald (1852–1915) took over in Tokyo where he was to serve until 1912. Satow and MacDonald together made a powerful team. MacDonald, although officially posted to Tokyo, was to spend some time as an informal negotiator in 1901. He had conversations in London concerning Japan and its future relations with Britain with many influential people from the King downwards. The Earl of Salisbury, as Prime Minister, was not too enthusiastic about any special link with Japan, although he did have a high regard for MacDonald and was therefore prepared to listen. Over these months in 1901 MacDonald was able to discuss in detail the possibility of an alliance with Hayashi in London. There were also others who were working to create a climate of opinion favourable to an alliance.[67]

The actual negotiations were carried on in London by the Minister,

Hayashi,[68] and Lord Lansdowne, the Foreign Secretary. It is possible that Hayashi's keen sense of purpose succeeded both in winning Lansdowne (and the British Cabinet) over to the idea of an Anglo-Japanese Alliance, as well as in carrying along the Japanese government. The British, with world opinion ranged against them over the South African War, felt isolated and had reasons for wanting an ally and may have preferred to make the link with Japan themselves rather than allow the Russians or the Germans to do so. For the Japanese such an alliance with Britain would give them much-coveted world status. They were aiming at a balance of power in the Far East which would safeguard the rights they had already assumed to interfere in Korea and China. The bargaining continued and was successful.

The Treaty was signed by Hayashi and Lansdowne in London on 18 January 1902, and the text released in Tokyo on 12 February and in London on 11 February.[69] The core of the Anglo-Japanese Alliance related to the possibility of war between one of the contracting policies and a third party over Japanese or British 'special interests' in China and also (in the case of Japan) in Korea. In these circumstances, the endeavours of the non-warring member of the alliance would be to maintain a strict neutrality and to ensure neutrality in all other powers. If another power should intervene then the second of the alliance signatories would also go to war with that power. The alliance was to run for five years and was to be renewable. It was continued throughout the war years of 1914–18. Under the alliance the British gave – indeed guaranteed – Japan a free hand in Asia, in return for a restraint upon Russian ambitions in the East.[70]

The Anglo-Japanese Alliance was well received in Japan and encouraged Japan's yearning for international status. It ended British isolation, which had been made painfully apparent during the difficult days of the Boer War, and ensured an easement of Britain's self-appointed role as policemen in the Far East. The alliance was renewed in 1905 and renegotiated in 1911 despite the reservations of Sir Claude MacDonald and his staff at the embassy in Tokyo, who were concerned about the Japanese potential for aggression in Manchuria. Pressure for renewal in 1911 did come strongly from Japan although 'the profound importance of the alliance to Great Britain's foreign and strategic policy in the world' was also well understood at the Foreign Office in London.[71]

## 8 A DIPLOMATIC ROLE MODEL FOR JAPAN?

The signing of the Anglo-Japanese Alliance in 1902 marked the emergence of Japan as a power of potential world status. In just over thirty years she had transformed herself. No longer a nation in retreat, a mysterious unknown shrinking behind outmoded defences, she was now a nation bent on becoming ever stronger. Despite the importance of Americans, Germans, French and Russians in Japan Britain remained the most powerful foreign influence.

In one sense the British had taught well. The aggressive diplomacy of Sir Harry Parkes and his ilk had had its effect. As he noted:

> To the *Meiji* mind, international relations in the second half of the nineteenth century were based on a predatory system of might . . . international law was followed only insofar as it benefited a nation to do so and the strong ignored the law when it was to their advantage.[72]

While held in check by the foreign treaties the Japanese could not hope to assert real international authority. In any case would not a soft approach have been equated with weakness?

James Bruce, the 8th Earl of Elgin and his brother Fred, later Sir Frederick Bruce,[73] who spent their working lives on remote diplomatic missions, both reluctant imperialists, were particularly sensitive to the threatening behaviour of their compatriots in Japan. Elgin had worried greatly about the effect of his intervention in Japan in 1858. Sir Frederick Bruce, when British Minister in China, was forthright in his condemnation of what he called 'the arrogant tone of our communities' in the East. He had been particularly incensed by the Richardson affair which was a *cause célèbre* in Japan, in 1862, writing:

> Mr Richardson rides out for pleasure, he meets the procession of a Japanese Noble accustomed from childhood to certain marks of respect – If Mr Richardson objected to paying them why did he not do as he was urged by his more sensible companions and turn back or leave the road? I knew the unfortunate man, for I had to support the Consul in Shanghai in inflicting upon him a heavy fine for a most brutal and unprovoked attack upon an unoffending coolie in his employ. He was a type too often found among our middle class, with the brutal courage of a prize fighter, unchecked by a single chivalrous instinct. The instincts of these men are developed

> among the debasing incidents of a life in the East. They acquire a taste for inflicting suffering and practising it upon people who don't resist.[74]

Despite Sir Frederick Bruce's words both he and his brother, Lord Elgin, were ambivalent, deploring some aspects of British policy and yet, as British representatives, forced to carry them out. They both admired Sir Harry Parkes, with whom they worked in China before his appointment to Japan, and yet Parkes, the pre-eminent Palmerstonian, epitomised a world in which might is right. After Parkes and the Bruce brothers has passed from the scene the Japanese, taking full advantage of unpleasant lessons, painfully learnt, became themselves well able to combine subtlety and threat to gain their own ends.

And so Japanese diplomacy came of age. The Japanese had little to learn from British or any other Western diplomats for Japanese negotiating skills had been well honed not only by early contacts with foreigners but also by centuries of internal politics. In one sense however Japan was forced to learn from the West. She needed to understand how the Western powers viewed matters of international concern. In theory her foreign treaties could have been renegotiated any time after 1872; in practice the Western powers had to be convinced that Japan's internal structure, especially the legal codes, conformed to the standards of a civilised country as understood by the world powers. Japan's apprenticeship ended, in diplomatic as well as other senses, when treaty renegotiation was successfully concluded.

# 2 Traders and Bankers

## 1 THE SEARCH FOR MARKETS

By the second half of the nineteenth century Britain believed that as a mature industrial economy, she required the stimulus of further demand for her manufactured goods from ever wider markets. Lord Clarendon, the Foreign Secretary, in writing to Lord Elgin prior to his departure for the Far East, recognised the importance of trade, writing 'the object to be kept in view by your Excellency is to establish commercial relations with Japan... We desire no exclusive advantage ... are anxious that other countries should reap the full benefit of our exertions for the promotion of civilization and commerce.'[1] The attitudes expressed here accord ill with the actual behaviour of British merchants in the Far East.

Many of those who appeared as traders in Japan had already been in business in China, 'opened' since 1842.[2] These men waited impatiently for access to another Far Eastern market. They expected to be able to buy tea, silks, lacquer-ware and other luxury and exotic items from Japan, and were keen to supply in return Lancashire cottons and other manufactures. By the terms of Elgin's Treaty a wide range of foreign goods were to be allowed into Japan at a nominal duty of 5 per cent.[3] In addition merchants expected that an initial advantage could be gained by the manipulation of the currency exchange, for gold in Japan had long been undervalued.

British traders, however, were vulnerable in Japan for trade remained precarious and profits uncertain. Before the age of the telegraph, lines of communications between Japan and Europe were long and hazardous.[4] McMaster has deduced that 'By greasing the necessary wheels of commerce they were often able to make profits of more than 400 per cent on their exports.'[5] Even so the turnover of merchants, for example in Nagasaki in the 1860s, suggests that such profits could be accompanied by daunting losses. Many went out of business.

Initially, trade with Japan required an extra leg on the journey to China. In the course of time Japan was drawn into a trading network, which consisted of a triangular trade with China and south-east Asia, and a long linear trade-route via India and the Middle East to Europe. Trade goods leaving Japan were mostly raw materials of one sort or another or semi-manufactured goods. Sea foods from around Japan's coast found a ready market locally in China. For the European markets, tea, silk, thread and cloth, which had been partly processed, filled the holds of trading vessels, together with Japanese art products, such as porcelain and lacquer-ware. The trade in goods was sometimes less important than the trade in coins and currencies. In an imperfect market traders were not slow to reap rewards by manipulating unequal exchange rates.[6]

## 2 TREATY PORT TRADERS AND CONSULS

By the terms of the Treaty of Peace, Amity and Commerce between Great Britain and Japan (26 August 1858) trade was to be permitted, through treaty ports,[7] the first of which – Nagasaki, Hakodate and Kanagawa (later Yokohama) – were to be opened on 1 July 1859. Later, in effect on 1 January 1868, Hyogo (now Kobe) and Niigata, on the coast of the sea of Japan were added. In addition Tokyo and Osaka were to be designated 'open' towns where foreigners could also live and work.

It is not clear why these five sites (later accepted by the Americans, British, French, Russians and Dutch), were chosen by Townshend Harris, or conceded by the Japanese. Nagasaki, selected originally for its remoteness, was, pre-*Meiji*, the point of Western contact; Kanagawa (or Yokohama) was controversial, for it was to be the link to the largest conurbation, that of Edo, later Tokyo; Hakodate, far distant in the north, was a base for foreign fishing and especially for whaling vessels. The choice of Hyogo (Kobe) meant an entrée, at some distance, to the other great population and trading centre of Osaka, and was sufficiently distant from the ancient capital of Kyoto to be acceptable. The choice of Niigata is something of a mystery.[8] Each of the five sites required the building of a new settlement for foreigners, each with a handful of foreign consuls. It was at Yokohama and Kobe that the West really plugged in to the economic potential of Japan. It was at Edo (Tokyo) and Osaka that the forces of growth from below, in response to the market had found their focus in Japan. And yet Edo had been created from above, brought into being in the seventeenth century as his capital by the iron will of the first *Shogun*.

Nagasaki, in the south-west, on Kyushu Island, had been for centuries the only gateway to Japan for it had housed in its harbour, first a handful of Portuguese and then Dutch traders, confined to their 'factory' on the tiny artificial island of Deshima. Hakodate, on the as-yet-undeveloped north island of Yezo (now Hokkaido), had become a necessary stop-over for whaling and fishing vessels. It was important for servicing and supplying such ships but offered few attractions to mercantile enterprise, and was never to be more than a convenient outpost.

The opening of Kanagawa as a treaty port was the most significant of the European intrusions for it brought the foreigner right into Edo Bay and almost to the gates of Edo itself. Indeed in the ten months between the signing of the Treaty and the opening of the port the Japanese authorities had already had second thoughts. They came to believe that Kanagawa, situated astride the Tokaido Road along which then passed endless processions of *daimyos* with their countless servants and baggage escorted by their two-sworded men, had been wrongly designated a treaty port. They feared armed clashes between *samurai* and foreigners. The Japanese decided therefore to shift the foreign settlement to Yokohama, then an insignificant fishing village on the mud flats of Edo Bay.[9]

Alcock was furious with the Japanese for varying the Treaty in this way. Both he and Townshend Harris, the American Consul General, were suspicious, believing that the Japanese, if they succeeded in holding the foreign merchants in Yokohama might, by controlling the causeway, create another Deshima and keep the foreigners in virtual imprisonment. Matters were promptly and effectively taken out of diplomatic hands by merchants who were not prepared to stand off with their valuable cargoes packed in expensively leased ships. Led by William Keswick (1834–1912) of Jardine Matheson, the merchants accepted Yokohama; came ashore with their cargoes, occupied the lots prepared for them and announced themselves ready for trade.[10]

Yokohama, although destined to become one of the great ports of the world and the largest port of Japan, in the early days produced a low level of mercantile behaviour. Ernest Satow described British merchants as men 'who came without much capital, to make a livelihood, or if possible, something more, hastened to the attainment of their object without being troubled with much scruple',[11] while in Satow's view the Japanese merchants were 'adventurers, destitute of capital and ignorant of commerce'.[12]

Paske Smith suggests that by 1868 there were over fifty British firms in Yokohama but very few of them were to survive.[13] Jardine Matheson & Company were the most important and they set up on the Yokohama Bund at Lot No. 1. Their rivals were Butterfield, Swire, although W. R. Adamson & Company and Aspinall, Cornes & Company were in Yokohama from an early date. All of these survive in some form today. The small foreign settlement was served by the Peninsular & Oriental Steam Navigation Company which started a Shanghai–Japan service in the summer of 1859.

After 1858 there was a leisureliness about trading which belonged to a pre-industrial age.[14] Once the Suez Canal was opened in November 1869,[15] the old trade, carried earlier in sailing ships around the Cape, gave way to steamships following the more direct canal route.[16] The opening of the canal was followed soon after by the completion of the telegraphic link – originally via Russia – with the West. As the modern world encroached the old trading ways receded; poorly funded merchants tended to disappear and merchanting relied on firms with a stronger financial base.

Until 1868, in the interval between Elgin's visit and the Restoration, the atmosphere in Nagasaki was rather different from that in Yokohama. At Nagasaki it was possible for Japanese and foreigner to develop a degree of rapport as the port attracted those Japanese who wished to borrow the learning of the West. Indeed Nagasaki's remoteness became an advantage; distance gave protection and allowed both Japanese and foreigner a freedom of action unparalleled elsewhere in Japan. Nagasaki was Japan's window on the West, with European culture refracted through Dutch and later English language and learning.

The European merchants were mostly British, Jardine Matheson & Company and Dent & Company being two of the first arrivals. As Grace Fox remarks 'By the end of 1861, 37 of the total 57 foreign merchants who rented land in Nagasaki were British'.[17] Between 1859 and 1867 the feudal clan leaders based near Nagasaki, largely ignoring central government, worked through their own agents and through foreigners, to trade on their own behalf and set up business enterprises. In law, foreign trade and the profit accruing therefrom was claimed as of right by central government. But the British knew well how the great clan chiefs resisted these claims.[18] Many clans, particularly those of the south and west, including *Satsuma*, *Choshu*, *Tosa* and *Hizen* were eager traders buying and selling as far as their resources would allow.

Local clan offices in Nagasaki were staffed by well-educated men, usually *samurai* of good standing, used to dealing with foreigners. The foreign traders in Nagasaki welcomed approaches made to them by *daimyos*' agents and hurried to oblige as far as they could. The presence of active *samurai* agents as well as eager foreign merchants led to an exciting period which increasingly undermined the Shogunate.

Although Marcus Flowers, the British consul in Nagasaki, wrote confidently (in 1868) 'of the opening of the new ports in Hyogo and Osaka' producing 'a beneficial effect upon this place';[19] after 1868 Nagasaki lost ground. The young Japanese moved to Tokyo. The port of Nagasaki, although important as a coaling station and shipbuilding centre, was never to regain its former position.

The third of the early pre-*Meiji* treaty ports, Hakodate,[20] remained basically a fisherman's town, specialising in providing supplies for transient vessels and exporting a variety of fish products. For the curious foreign traveller it was the gateway to the distant world of the 'hairy *Ainu*', the original indigenous people who were even then being squeezed into the more forbidding parts of the remote island of Yezo (Hokkaido). But for the reawakened Japan Hakodate was to have great strategic value against the threat from tzarist Russia. As a contemporary wrote: 'Guardians of Hakodate beware, this is not the kind of an age, when only waves wash ashore.'[21] After 1870 the Russians made some concessions but the Japanese remained deeply concerned about Russian intentions.

The opening, at the beginning of 1868, of Kobe,[22] earlier called Hyogo, and of Niigata,[23] coincided with the ending of the *Tokugawa* regime. But even under a new political regime there was little to be done for Niigata which was sited on a river-mouth badly affected by sand-banks. Its hinterland was traditional rice-growing country in which foreign merchants had little interest.

At Kobe it was different for although there was some competition with Osaka nearby, trade could develop. After Yokohama, Kobe was destined to become the second most important treaty port. The opening of Kobe had earlier been strongly resisted by the shogunate, for it was dangerously close to Kyoto, and therefore to the sacred presence of the Emperor. At Kobe, as at Nagasaki, the relationship between the foreign community and the Japanese officials seemed less tense. Kobe, a new settlement, developed trading opportunities, and was soon the centre of a thriving business community which commanded an intense local loyalty from its residents.

Each foreign settlement sustained a British, and other foreign consuls,[24] for although their duties were primarily commercial, checking and supervising foreign ships in the harbour and collecting data for their commercial reports, they were also responsible for administering the law through the consular courts which were a feature of extraterritorial rights which foreigners enjoyed. The consular staff in Yokohama and Kobe were increasingly busy as these two ports expanded to meet foreign and Japanese inspired trade. Elsewhere in Niigata, Hakodate and Nagasaki consuls could easily become men of leisure enjoying much free time. The consul's lot, bedevilled by isolation and other evils, was not an easy one. On the rare occasions when there was trouble, inept or ineffectual action could lead to thunderous disapproval from diplomatic colleagues in Tokyo.[25]

The treaty ports remained, encapsulating foreign communities, until 1899. When they were about to lose their protected status the merchants expressed much indignation.[26] Lord Charles Beresford in Japan, representing a combined Chamber of Commerce Mission from Britain, advised caution. For forty years the Japanese had had to accept, as the price of modernisation, the intrusion of extraterritoriality; after the change-over and in spite of their fears, foreign residents found that their lives continued much as before.

The Japanese had extracted a price for tolerating the foreign settlements. For the open ports were enclosures within which foreign traders were pinned,[27] not commercial bridgeheads over which they could pass to command trade elsewhere in Japan. The limits of the treaty ports enabled the Japanese to reserve 'landward' trade for themselves.[28] The restrictions imposed on the treaty ports allowed Japanese traders and manufacturers a forty-year breathing-space during which they could adapt themselves, their trade and their manufactures to the new world of international commerce.

Originally therefore the treaty ports, of first importance to the foreigners, were of secondary interest to the Japanese. But it was here in the open ports that the foreigners did succeed 'in creating the institutions of a modernised Japan'.[29] Once this had been done the Japanese were able to take over, adopt and adapt the dock and harbour facilities, and develop them further.

## 3 IMPORTED TECHNOLOGY, STEAMSHIPS AND RAILWAYS

Isolated examples of the products of Western technology were brought into Japan from the earliest days of legitimate trading with the West although these items can have had little significance for the

Japanese economy.[30] They did, however, sustain a continuing Japanese inquisitiveness about the products of the outside world. Part of the Thomas Glover legend in Nagasaki after 1859, rested on the belief that he had brought the first steam locomotive to the Bund there, and also had rigged the first primitive telegraph system between his office in Nagasaki and the Takashima coal-mine some seven miles away.[31] The persistence of these tales suggests Japanese curiosity about industrialisation.

During the forty-four years of the *Meiji* period foreign manufacturers, traders and merchants competed to supply the Japanese market. Manufacturers in Britain, Germany, America or elsewhere knew that competition from foreign rivals was fierce. For some years no one considered the possibility that the Japanese would in due course become manufacturers themselves.

The first import trade in Western technology was in steamships. Between 1859 and 1870 some 160 steamships – of which over 100 were supplied by British traders – passed into Japanese hands.[32] These were paddle or screw vessels, basically of sailing-ship design powered by small auxiliary steam engines.[33] Many of the clan leaders as well as the *Bakufu* government bought occasionally new but usually second-, third- or fourth-hand vessels from Western owners. Government purchases included some nine ships before 1868 and a further three between 1868 and 1870.

Merchants were keen to sell, clan officers keen to buy. Perhaps unscrupulous foreign merchants hoped to sell ships unsaleable elsewhere,[34] but clan negotiators drove hard bargains in which cash transactions were unusual. Small down payments were made initially, further payments depending on the successful sale of future trade goods. Clan agents, eager buyers and reluctant payers, greatly complicated the lives of British merchants. After 1868 clan property, clan indebtedness and therefore ship ownership fell to the state.

One of the British traders, who was actively involved with buying and selling ships and much else, was Thomas Blake Glover (1838–1912)[35] who, although associated with Jardine Matheson, operated as an independent merchant in Nagasaki and later in Kobe, in the 1860s. At this time, young inexperienced and something of a freebooter, he became heavily involved in the ship and arms trade.[36] Because of the skills of the Japanese in bargaining, and the sketchiness of Glover's accounting arrangements he did not know whether he was in profit or not, or how his net worth stood. He went bankrupt in August 1870. Glover is a good example of a man who found the excitements of the Japanese trade more hazardous than he had bargained for.

On the Japanese side it is worth noting that Yataro Iwasaki (1835–85) the founder of Mitsubishi, sharpened his bargaining skills during this period in Nagasaki as agent for the *Tosa han*, by 'exploiting the knowledge and connections acquired as a *han* official began to deal in ships of all sizes sold by former *hans* and foreign merchants. Those who were inexperienced and eager to sell became easy prey for Iwasaki, and those who were experienced and shrewd often found themselves outwitted by him.'[37]

Marcus Flowers, British Consul at Nagasaki in 1868 commented on the Japanese thirst for knowledge:

> so anxious are they to learn that there is not a single steamer that enters the harbour but they are sure to visit and take minute copies of everything they see, and such rapid progress have they made with regard to machinery, that they are able to work all the steamers they have recently purchased themselves.[38]

This may have been so, but many of the vessels bought were old and required constant repair and attention which was provided by foreign officers and crews. The acquisition of a fleet of modern steam vessels was in the 1870s, too capital-intensive a project for any Japanese to undertake.

The theme of ships and shipbuilding is a recurring one. Japan used the services of many Britons as she strove to teach her own people to be 'the makers and operators of ships' (see Chapter 4). Many Japanese were also sent to Britain to work 'in the shipyards' (see Chapter 10).

Another export market which Britain claimed but for which there was later strong competition from both Germany and the USA was that of supplying railway building equipment. Rails, railway engines, rolling stock, signalling systems and engine turntables were all imported. In the case of railway equipment, as with everything else, the Japanese in their railway workshops sought to learn from their imported equipment. Railway locomotives particularly, from the 1890s brought in in kit form, were assembled by eager engineers and technicians (see Chapter 3, Section 2 below).

The nascent Japanese railway industry was particularly fortunate in having at its head Masaru Inoue (1843–1910) who, for over twenty years from 1872,[39] acted as Railway Commissioner. It was William Walter Cargill (1813–94),[40] employed by the Japanese government as a railway adviser from 1872 to 1877, who suggested the appointment.

Inoue, one of the original '*Choshu* Five' had spent the mid-1860s studying in London. Technical efficiency added to his clan background, together with his management skills (he became adept at handling prickly foreign railway engineers as well as Japanese subordinates) made him an ideal choice for railway chief. Inoue retired in 1893 and died in London in 1910 in the course of an inspection tour of European railways.

Under his guidance Japanese railways passed from the phase of being dependent on the foreigner for all railway supplies to building up their own trained personnel, railway workshops and technical expertise. Before the death of the *Meiji* Emperor in 1912 the Japanese railway system had become independent of almost all foreign imports. The heavy duty imposed in 1911 on imported railway locomotives signalled another lost market for British traders.

But there were no such gloomy predictions of lost markets to mar the excitement of the opening, on 14 October 1872, by the *Meiji* Emperor himself of the first Japanese railway.[41] Thereafter it was possible to travel from Yokohama to Shimbashi and later right in to Tokyo 'each way on the hour, every hour' being pulled by a tank-type steam locomotive made by the Lancashire–Yorkshire Engine Company, one of the ten original British engines imported.

Despite the success of the Yokohama–Tokyo railway and the later Kobe–Osaka railway progress was slow and demand for railway products modest until the late 1880s when a greater financial stability was achieved. From 1885 the British had a near-monopoly of supplying iron, and later steel rails (see Table 2.1 for details of the tonnage supplied). The market was effectively supplied by the Barrow Haematite Iron and Steel Company of Barrow-in-Furness. Later Charles Cammell and Co. Ltd, manufacturers of steel rails, armaments and heavy castings at Sheffield, Penistone and Grimethorpe were also successful in the Japanese market.[42]

*Table* 2.1 British rails exported to Japan

| | *tons* |
|---|---|
| 1886 | 7305 |
| 1887 | 21106 |
| 1888 | 105313 |

*Source:* P. J. English, *British Made*, p. 15.

The main suppliers of steam locomotive engines were the North British Locomotive Company based in Glasgow, see Table 2.2. The Vulcan Foundry (of Newton-le-Willows) also supplied twenty-three; Nasmyth Wilson of Patricroft, Manchester, 138; Kitsons of Leeds, twenty-seven; and Beyer Peacock of Manchester who supplied 194[43] shows their purchasers.

*Table* 2.2 North British locomotives exported to Japan, 1903–11

| *Railway* | *1903–11* |
|---|---|
| Nippon | 6 |
| Kansai | 4 |
| Imperial Government Railway | 210 |
| Hokkaido Railway (Kansan) | 11 |
| Imperial Taiwan Railway | 9 |
| | 240 |

*Source*: Compiled from original figures in NBL, GUA.[44]

Signalling systems for the Japanese railways were originally supplied by Saxeby and Farmer (Westinghouse) of London and Liverpool Railway Signals Ltd. Coles of Sunderland supplied early steam cranes and shovels, extensively used for tunnelling and excavating for railway work. Ransomes Rapier of Ipswich, who were suppliers of a variety of machinery, including items for irrigation and flood control, were commissioned by Nippon Railway Company to provide engine turntables, fifteen heavy-duty turntables of 50′ diameter, capable of handling 95-ton engines, were ordered in 1897. All were delivered in the same year. These turntables continued in use into the electric traction era.[45] The *Meiji* Emperor's own railway coach epitomises the remarkable grip which British industry had on Japanese railways, for 'his personal, custom-designed, walnut-pannelled, Birmingham-built coach, enclosing Lancashire cotton cushions, adorned with finest Nottingham lace, smoothly spring-supported on Fox (Leeds) bogies, which sped safely over Barrow- and Sheffield-rolled rails, hauled by Manchester fabricated motive power'[46] illustrated well the remarkable achievements of British trade in this area.

## 4 MANCHESTER COTTON

Perhaps the greatest commercial pressure which lay behind Britain's decision to sent Lord Elgin to Japan, came from the Lancashire cotton men, whose cotton exports have been regarded as the classic vehicle of free-trade imperialism. In Japan, Elgin joked that judging by the nakedness of many in August 1858 'it does not seem likely that there will be any great demand for Manchester cotton goods'.[47] Others were more sanguine: by 1866 Sir Harry Parkes was confirming the development of trade, writing:

> The great expansion of the import trade is attributable to a steadily increasing demand for foreign manufactures in this country, which . . . can obtain clothing more cheaply from foreigners than from its own cottage looms. Under this aspect, Japan promises to furnish a very satisfactory market for British manufactures.[48]

Was this optimism justified? Initially it would appear to have been so for as much as 50 per cent of a relatively small total of goods being brought into Japan before 1868 was of cotton cloth from south Lancashire. Between 1868 and 1877 only a quarter of cotton products was in the form of manufactured cotton cloth. After 1877, the emphasis shifted to imports of cotton yarn, much of which came from Lancashire. During the third phase, from 1891, Japan concentrated on importing raw cotton direct from the countries in which it was grown. The exclusion of Lancashire cotton products from Japan in less than thirty years was followed even more ominously by threats from Japanese cotton manufacturers in third markets in the Far East.[49]

This rapid rejection of Lancashire's cotton products was due to the way in which the Japanese cotton textile industry, although initially alarmed by foreign imports, rallied to protect itself. As early as 1878, Japanese producers had succeeded in rejecting imports of foreign cloth preferring cotton yarn which could subsequently be worked up by local cotton-weavers. The acting British Consul, Dohmer, at Kanagawa, reported in 1879 that 'the enormous consumption of yarn suggests that native wants are rapidly being supplied by native woven cloth, and travellers in the interior of the country report that in various places attempts are being made to foster cotton-weaving'.[50]

By the 1890s, using the traditional hand-loom weaving industry as a base from which to expand, there was an integrated manufacturing process developing, using the 'backward linkage effect'.[51] The pioneer was the Osaka Cotton Mill (1882) and its success was followed rapidly by the establishment of other similar units. By 1890 although Japan continued to import some cloth and some yarn from Lancashire, she was primarily interested in supplies of raw cotton, which came from semi-tropical suppliers and not from Britain. In 1887 the British Vice-Consul noted that 'almost the entire cotton weaving in Japan [is] carried on by means of the old traditional loom'.[52]

Modern research suggests that although initially threatened by competition from fabrics manufactured abroad, the Japanese textile industry soon rallied. It was able to remain competitive and later to squeeze British cotton goods out of the Japanese market-place, because its products although dearer were closely tailored to Japanese demand. Foreign cottons were of a thinness and texture markedly different from the Japanese product and so appealed to different markets.[53] If the home industry remained competitive it could not only retain but increase its market share. To do this it required modern machinery. Much of this came from Lancashire. As in Britain and the West the Japanese cotton industry was first mechanised through the spinning process. Lancashire spindles helped to bring about the first phase of modernisation. The firm which above all supplied mule spindles to Lancashire and the rest of the world including Japan were Platt Brothers of Oldham.

Despite the precosity of the opening of the Kagoshima spinning mill before the Restoration, the first successful implant of cotton-spinning machinery into Japan was that into the Osaka Cotton Spinning Company in 1882. On 29 July 1882 Mitsui and Co ordered 10 500 mule spindles from Platts. Indeed Mitsui were to become the Japanese agents of Platts in future years. Platts were primarily producers of mule spindles; the export of these to Japan reaching its peak in 1885. The Americans were offering strong competition by producing ring spindles and so Platts, at the request of Tata of India,[54] began to manufacture ring spindles and somewhat later exported these to Japan. The peak year of export of ring spindles to Japan was 1896.

Although the spinning process of the cotton industry was mechanised largely by imported Lancashire machinery, the position with regard to the weaving process was more complex. Traditional Japanese material for the various kinds of kimonos was narrow and was best woven on Japanese wooden looms. In 1897 Sakichi Toyoda (1867–1930)[55] invented a wooden power-loom for the traditional narrow fabric. He followed this with a wood and iron machine in 1907. These machines, costing some ¥93 (as compared with ¥782 for a German and ¥389 for a French power-loom), were an immediate success, allowing many small-scale cloth-producers to mechanise and to improve their productivity for a modest outlay.

More heavily capitalised plants could import Western power-looms which wove broader weaves which found some market in Japan. Nevertheless the revolution in the weaving industry was initially based on the narrow Japanese-made wooden power-loom, while Lancashire, traditionally wedded to its wide power-loom made no attempt to produce narrow ones. Platt's pre-war peak year for loom exports was 1909, although the post-war years of 1918 and 1920 were record ones. In the 1920s the trade dwindled to nothing.

There is an interesting sequel to the Platt/Toyoda involvement with the manufacture and world-wide sale of power looms. In 1929 Platt Brothers applied for patent rights on Toyoda's power loom, paying £100 000 for the right to make and sell Toyoda's looms world-wide except in Japan, China and the USA. In the event they only sold 200 looms over a period of two and a half years. It was believed in Japan that Platts had deliberately bought up the patent to foil damaging competition, particularly in India and the UK. This was one of the first recorded reverse technology transfers from Japan to Britain.[56]

Platt Bros were not the only firm manufacturing spindles for export to Japan. Dobson and Barlow were also active in this market. B. A. Dobson (1847–98) visited Japan in 1892 to advise clients there. Special trading links certainly developed between Osaka and Manchester. Indeed by 1891 the *Manchester Guardian* was writing in an article on 'Cotton Spinning in Japan' (14 July 1891) that 'Osaka is the Manchester of Japan'.[57] Because of the strong links between Lancashire and Kansai, the Osaka area of Japan, Japanese firms established themselves in Manchester to do business without the intervention of British traders. The Kansai Trading Co. was set up in Manchester in 1898; two years later Yonekichi Matsumoto established a firm in Manchester under his own name, to carry on import/export trade to Japan, China and Korea. The business links became so strong that in 1907, W. D. Ford-Smith (312 Deansgate) was appointed Honorary Consul (see Chapter 12 below) for Japan in Manchester.[58]

Lancashire received many visits from the Japanese. Such business calls usually passed off with bland complimentary speeches, but on at least two occasions courteous niceties were disturbed by Japanese straight talk. In 1896 the Vice-Minister for Agriculture and Commerce in Japan, Mr Kaneko, is alleged to have said that 'Lancashire is doomed'. While in 1907 Satori Kato remarked in Lancashire, that Japan would establish commercial paramountcy within a generation.[59] These chilling comments did nothing to stem the flow of cotton machinery to Japan. Later when the Japanese cotton textile industry was independently established and competing with Lancashire in world market pessimists could claim to have been right. The British exporters of machinery, as well as of textiles under the competitive system, had raised up their greatest rival.

## 5 BANKERS AND BANKING

Because their financial, and therefore their trading, arrangements with the outside world dependend upon their credit-worthiness, the Japanese ignored foreign advice on these matters at their peril. In accordance with Japanese zeal for independence the story of the development of the Japanese banking system reflects the price Japan paid initially for her hatred of tutelage.[60]

The two men who dominated Japanese banking during the *Meiji* period were Shigenobu Okuma and Masayoshi Matsukata who served successively as Finance Ministers. As they strove to create a modern banking system out of the fragmented confusion they had inherited from an earlier age they were both strongly affected by foreign bankers and foreign banking systems. Although British banks dominated the treaty ports (for several banks had opened sub-offices there) and British bankers were available to give advice and guidance, yet with their usual eclecticism the Japanese examined banking systems world-wide as they searched for a system which would be appropriate for Japan.

As Finance Minister, Okuma served until 1880 handling a most difficult post-Restoration period of much anxiety and uncertainty. He was ousted during a power struggle and replaced by Matsukata who, learning from the financial lessons of the Okuma era, was able to create a banking system, modelled partly on Western ideas, which was to carry Japan into the anticipated industrial age.

The complexities of the challenge are the more clearly understood if a view is taken of the situation which obtained as the foreigners arrived. In August 1858 Sherard Osborn, captaining HMS *Furious* carrying Lord Elgin, gave a graphic account of how the British first experienced the state of Japanese money and banking in Nagasaki when buying souvenirs in pre-*Meiji* Japan.[61] Osborn's account is especially interesting because it tells of a system more remarkable for its complexities and built-in deterrents than for any attempts to encourage and foster trade.

A decade later, with the Restoration in 1868, and the foreigners already resident in the treaty ports, the new government had to face the reality of their financial situation. In feudal Japan the principal domains had themselves issued their own coins and paper money which circulated locally. In attempts to extend their credit, domains had also minted new coins with scant regard for Gresham's Law.[62] The Shogunate had also issued coins, but no paper money. The country was awash with debased coins and devalued paper money. The revenue on which the system ultimately depended was rice, rice taxes being collected in kind. It was hard amidst such confusion to know what 'savings', on which the country ultimately depended for any future development, were being created.

The arrangements in Japan were indeed a world away from those in Europe where by the 1870s Western banking was a sophisticated business based on sound bookkeeping and general managerial skills. Western governments had succeeded in creating strong financial institutions subject to control from the centre. In the case of Britain the government had brought order through the Bank Acts of 1844 and 1845 which raised the Bank of England, as 'the bankers' bank', into a strong if ill-defined, controlling position.

In Japan British and other foreigners put pressure on the authorities to stabilise the currency. At the same time British merchants and bankers were active, not only in providing credit for trading, but also in manipulating the exchanges in any way they could.[63] British traders acted with blatant self-interest in exploiting at great profit to themselves the depreciation of silver in terms of gold, thus helping to frustrate any early Japanese attempts at the gold standard. The Japanese were thus taught some harsh lessons.

The young *Meiji* oligarchs came to recognise that an important element in the success of the West had lain in the ending of monetary confusion. They were earnest in their endeavours to bring monetary stability to Japan. The first task was to replace the depreciated currency, including clan notes and coins, with a uniform coinage readily available and accepted throughout Japan.

Sir Harry Parkes, the British Minister, was keen to help, organising a contract between a foreign bank at Yokohama and the Japanese government to supply a Mint. As it happened an experiment to manufacture silver dollars at Hong Kong had been abandoned and the Hong Kong Mint machinery was for sale.[64] This was bought for Japan and the equipment and British staff established in Osaka where the Imperial Mint was to make its home. Thomas Waters was employed to design and supervise the erection of an imposing building in classic style, part of which remains in the Imperial Mint complex today.

On 4 April 1871 the Imperial Mint was opened;[65] the first modern manufacturing process to be established in Japan. Sir Harry Parkes, acting as spokesman for the foreign Ministers at the opening, holding up a large gold piece that had just been struck off, hoped that the new coins would enjoy a wide circulation 'being a symbol of that honesty and resolve and thoroughness of action which will ever characterise the government of the Sovereign of this realm'.[66] The Japanese government had the difficult task of withdrawing the old coinage and replacing it with the products of the new Mint. Into it flowed old silver pieces, Mexican dollars, Chinese *sycee*, ingots and crude silver, to flow out again as new uniform Japanese coins. By this time the central authority had taken over from the domains and were responsible for clan debts and currency. The new coins gained acceptance first in the treaty ports among the foreigners.

But there were difficulties. As Hazel Jones has noted,[67] the Mint contract ensured that the authority regarding 'the rights and privileges of the Bank,[68] the rigid control of bullion movement, the engagement of foreign employees and the foreign direction of the Mint' remained in foreign hands, notably those of the Oriental Bank,[69] whose manager, John Robertson,[70] shared power with Major William Kinder,[71] the Director of the Imperial Mint. This did not please the Japanese who found themselves responsible only for the running expenses. At first the Japanese worked out a sphere of influence for themselves and one for the foreigners although Major Kinder's own position, entrenched in the contract, and independent of Japanese supervisory control remained an irritant. Kaoru Inoue (1836–1915) had the unenviable task of trying to treat with Kinder who in classic colonial style was working in a spirit of independence disregarding the Japanese officials. Eventually Kiyonari Yoshida argued strongly for the cancellation of the foreigners' contracts. By the end of 1874 this was done and the original agreement broken.[72] This proved an expensive undertaking in more ways than one, but at least thereafter the Mint belonged to the Japanese government 'in name and in fact'.

It was one thing to produce newly minted coins for circulation within Japan and quite another to attempt to launch a Japanese silver trade *yen* to trade overseas at face value. As one commentator has noted, 'the one-yen silver coin was launched in 1871 as a symbol of

The Scot, Mr Robertson, the manager of the Oriental Bank in Yokohama is depicted playing the bagpipes and so calling the tune – determining the exchange rate of the Japanese *yen* and the Chinese *tael*. The Oriental Bank ceased business in 1884 following the founding by the Japanese of the Yokohama Specie Bank in 1880.

*Cartoon* 2.1 The puppet player (*Japan Punch*, 1875)

the modern Japanese currency'.[73] By the nature of things at the time the British, with their connections through Shanghai and Hong Kong with the London money market, were, as the contemporary cartoon shows, the ultimate arbiters of Japan's credit-worthiness and of the acceptability of her currency. The British consuls in Yokohama and Hyogo reported that, since September 1879, 'the foreign banks had accepted the silver yen on a par with the Mexican dollar' which had virtually been expelled from circulation in Japan. Notwithstanding this apparent success in February 1880 the British government refused, without giving reasons, to make the Japanese silver *yen* legal tender.[74] The Japanese thus paid the price for their independence.[75]

While the Japanese were initiating the measures which would bring a uniform currency into being within Japan, modest banking business was being done in the treaty ports. Most of this, including fulfilling quasi-banking functions, conducted by houses like Jardine Matheson, was an extension of their activities in Shanghai and Hong Kong. After some hesitation foreign banks opened offices in Japan including the Chartered Mercantile Bank of India, London and China (later the Mercantile Bank of India) 1863–86; the Central Bank of Western India, 1865–6; Oriental Bank Corporation (later New Oriental) 1865–93; Commercial Bank Corporation of India and the Far East, 1865–6;[76] Hong Kong Bank which opened in Japan in 1866, and the Chartered Mercantile Bank of India, Australia and China which opened in 1880.[77] The Japanese government in the early years did its external business through the Oriental Banking Company. The relationships between the foreign banks in Yokohama and the Japanese government were wary, although they each needed the other.

British banks had four main contributions to make to *Meiji* Japan. They could provide general models for a modern banking and monetary system; they could make available international banking facilities, before the Japanese had had time to develop these; they could promote the Japanese learning process in terms of the internal structure, managerial methods and accounting practice of modern banking, and they could assist in the placing of Japanese loans abroad. At the same time, of course, British bankers were out for profits, to which end they pressed for further scope for their activities against increasing Japanese resistance.

The Japanese learned well the lessons taught by the West. Certainly in banking terms the operation of the currency exchanges against them by traders and merchants reinforced their natural, nationalistic instinct that they were best to do things for themselves.

There were several critical encounters between various Japanese factions as to which banking decisions should be taken. An early one occurred in 1871–2 between Hirobumi Ito and Shigenobu Okuma. Ito favoured the American system of national banks, with no central control on the nation's note issue, while Okuma, having sent his protégé, Kiyonari Yoshida, to London to study the Bank of England, favoured centralising the note issue and using a central bank in Japan as lender of last resort: Ito won. The national banks, which freely issued paper money in the 1870s, plunged the country into an ever-deeper inflation crisis. In 1880 Okuma, fearing for the privation to be imposed on ex-*samurai* and peasants alike, pitted himself against the severe deflationary policy advised by Masayoshi Matsukata. Matsukata won. Okuma resigned from government.[78]

The most notable British banker who helped to train the Japanese in modern banking techniques was Alexander Allan Shand (1844–1930),[79] probably trained in a Scottish bank, who arrived in Yokohama in the late 1860s and by 1870 was acting manager of the Chartered Mercantile Bank. Within a short time he was working for the government, bringing to Japanese banking the kind of care and attention, combined with an innate caution, which gained him great respect. Resident in Japan until 1878, he greatly helped his employers to respond to the urgent banking needs of a country requiring to adapt quickly to rapidly changing circumstances.

His work was primarily to bring British standards of accountancy and systematic inspection to Japanese banking. He became closely associated with Okuma who had himself had wide experience of currency problems in Nagasaki before the Restoration period. Later, as one of Okuma's former secretaries, Shand took great pride in the fact that while he had served Japan's greatest liberal his youngest brother had served Mr Gladstone in a similar capacity.[80]

As Secretary to the Comptroller of the Currency Shand established in Tokyo a school of banking administration where he trained in Western methods of bookkeeping, employees of both the ministry and the First National Bank (*Daiichi Kokuritsu Ginko*). He produced a *Detailed Bank Bookkeeping Manual* which the Ministry published in 1873 and which influenced a generation of young Japanese bankers.[81]

Following the bankruptcy of the finance house, Onogumi, in 1874 Shand was requested to make an inspection of its affairs. He discovered violations of the Bank Law as well as a great deal of confusion. His recommendations on this occasion commended him to

Shibusawa Eiichi (1840–1931).[82] Shand's firmness in recommending sound practice gave him status and prestige in Japan. In 1878 Shand returned home, becoming London manager of the Alliance, later Parr's Bank.[83] He remained an important contact and source of information for his former Japanese employers as well as helping to organise the international loans which the Japanese government took out between 1899 and 1914.

Prior to 1899 Japan took a characteristically sober view of borrowing abroad, sensing that such action could induce a kind of colonial status. Her instincts over this were greatly helped by the first foreign-borrowing experience. The young *Meiji* oligarchs saw the railway as one great engine of modernisation. Money was needed to build the first line from Yokohama to Tokyo. A specious Britisher, Horatio Nelson Lay,[84] offered his services in placing a loan in London. His plan was to charge the Japanese 12 per cent while paying the bondholders 9 per cent. On discovering this near-fraud, the Japanese were very indignant. Though the matter was renegotiated on better terms through the Oriental Banking Company, the Japanese had learned one more lesson from foreign financiers. Thereafter the Japanese government did not borrow abroad until the end of the century.

A. A. Shand had been employed by the Alliance Bank, later Parr's Bank, at home in London and out of Japanese service for over twenty years when the Japanese next borrowed on the London money market. Nevertheless he could be trusted, and in the early years of the twentieth century when several Japanese loans were negotiated Shand was much involved. Mr Shand's 'services in the matter of the recent Japanese loan and generally in maintaining for the Bank the Japanese connection' were frequently noted and Parr's Bank were suitably grateful to the manager of their Bartholomew Lane branch,[85] the Head Office of the Bank.

Not for the last time was the determination by the Japanese to place their country beyond the opinion of the foreigner confirmed. Practical steps were taken when in 1880 the Yokohama Specie Bank was established,[86] to be followed in 1882 by the Bank of Japan.[87] The Specie Bank was deliberately created to handle Japan's foreign export trade. As a result the foreign banks, especially the Oriental Bank,[88] which had done its main business for the Japanese government, were severely affected. The Yokohama Specie Bank had a hard time of it at first, requiring repeated injections of government cash, but the official determination stood firm and the Bank gradually moved to the position of chief financier of Japanese foreign trade.

The Central Bank, the Bank of Japan, was founded by Masayoshi Matsukata on the model of the National Bank of Belgium with the sole right of issuing convertible notes.[89,90] The Bank of Japan began the process of sorting out the paper money which the National Banks had in the 1870s issued almost discriminately. By the end of 1885 paper money was on a parity with silver. By 1897, after the payment by China of the indemnity extracted by Japan after winning the 1894–5 war, the Bank of Japan was able to announce that Japan was on the gold standard.[91]

The final act for Japan of joining the great powers of the world as a reliable member of the international financial community was achieved in the year *Meiji* 30 – that is, thirty years after the upheavals which signalled the Restoration. As one reviewer has noted 'British banks never penetrated Japan, which never really lost control of its banking (or its industry); it frustrated European expansion by a determination to minimize foreign trade until Lord Elgin's Unequal Treaties of 1858 had been revoked'.[92]

## 6 THE MUTUAL RESPONSE

European merchants trading in Japan accepted the complications, caused by language barriers as well as by profound cultural differences, as an inevitable part of business in Asia. Difficulties were exacerbated by the low status of merchants in Japan. The lack of common ground nurtured the belief that the Japanese were unscrupulous and shifty, while the Japanese judged the British to be thrusting and greedy. This was due in part to the fact that the British started from the idea of a specific contract binding both sides in all significant aspects: this was not the Japanese way, in which so much was left intangible to be adjusted as matters proceeded. As a result there was a tendency among British merchants to believe that Japanese merchants lacked commercial integrity. The risks of trade and fear of failure produced a British merchant who, though admired by his compatriots for his resolution, was disliked in Japan for his aggression.

Freed from the modest constraints imposed earlier by the East India Company on its members and released from the subtle discipline exerted at home by fellow-traders and by society generally,[93] the behaviour of foreign merchants in Japan and China was often unscrupulous. It was labelled by Lord Elgin as 'commercial ruffianism'.

When, to this freedom to behave badly, was added the contempt which most felt for the men and societies with which they were dealing, it is clear that foreign-merchant behaviour left much to be desired. The general context in which foreign merchants operated was, in the early days, intrinsically of a 'brutalising' nature. In this atmosphere there was no room for the 'gentility' or the 'Quaker conscience' in the markets of the East. In other aspects of life Japanese women were used; the civilising influence of their own wives and daughters, who in the early years were still living in Britain, was not available to them.

For the Japanese unfamiliar with the invasive foreign presence the opening of the treaty ports was dramatic and frightening. It was explained:

> For long years the trade with Holland and China had been conducted in a nook of Nagasaki on an insignificant scale, a fact known at that time to only a limited number of people. By far the larger section of the nation had no knowledge of what foreign trade was like and the huge majority had never seen a foreigner.[94]

Initially indigenous industry found that demand for its traditional and old-fashioned products dropped, with resultant widespread unemployment. The shock thus administered to Japanese society was strengthened by the reciprocal demand for Western products. These could vary from 'costly implements of modern warfare and expensive machinery down to trifling foodstuffs and toilet articles'. Everyone who had the means hastened to dress themselves in European clothes and those unable to do this 'satisfied their pride by using European underwear beneath their Japanese clothes'.[95]

Although the collapse of native Japanese industry was of no direct concern to the foreign traders in the treaty ports, who welcomed increased demand for their foreign manufactures, the sequel was. For the Japanese people aided and abetted by the government, faced with a serious trade imbalance, made strenuous efforts to modernise their industries so that their own products could recapture the Japanese market.

During the first thirty years of the *Meiji* era Japanese exports valued in *yen*, increased seventeenfold, while imports increased twenty-seven times. For thirteen of the thirty years they had an excess of exports over imports which reflects the great efforts which were made to reverse the trade imbalance. Whatever they achieved in these years was done despite the denial of tariff autonomy.

Although in 1898 exports from Japan were still modest, they demonstrate a favourable trend on which Japan intended to build.[96]

In the course of the fifty-three-year period, between 1859 and 1912, the British had used the treaty ports through which to channel their manufactures. Initially Japanese trade had been badly affected by the activities of the invading foreign traders. By 1912 the year in which they achieved full tariff autonomy, the Japanese had made great progress reorganising their own industry and making determined efforts to seize hold of the direct trade with foreign countries and themselves buy and sell with little help from European middlemen resident at the old treaty ports.[97]

# 3 Engineers for Lighthouses, Railways, Telegraphs and Mines

## 1 THE ROLE OF THE FOREIGN ENGINEER

Once the decision had been taken to modernise there were good openings for the qualified foreign engineer to work in Japan.[1] The Japanese needed railways with permanent way, signalling systems and rolling stock, electric telegraphs with a system of offices and wire connections, tarmacadamed roads and iron bridges, modern harbours and docks as well as lighthouses, lightships and buoys with good and efficient lighting equipment. Although the Japanese themselves had traditional skills in managing water systems,[2] especially for the irrigation of paddy fields, they came to recognise that modern engineering techniques for the large-scale supply of pure drinking water for the cities,[3] the control of water courses, building of canals and the organisation of water-borne sewage were necessary. It was also vital to use modern methods to exploit their mineral resources, especially of coal and copper, and finally, they aspired to establish their own engineering and manufacturing sectors.

All this was to be organised through the new Public Works Department which by law had responsibility for the following bureaux: Mines, Railways, Lighthouses, Telegraphs, Engineering and Manufacturing, Buildings, Accountant, Stores and Secretariat.[4] Foreign engineers were employed in the new departments. They had little or nothing to do with those traditional craft industries which the Japanese themselves attempted to modernise.[5]

The British engineers recruited for these tasks were one of two classes, highly trained manager/engineers – occasionally graduates – and technicians, competent in the practical application of engineering skills. Individual British technicians were employed in Japan for relatively brief periods, particularly during the 'experts' decade' (1872–82), often being offered a contract of some three or four years.[6] Such men trained their Japanese successors. There are few accounts of their work, although a few kept journals and wrote up their experiences after they returned home.

The engineers involved were usually in their early twenties with good training and experience. By working in Japan they could hope to achieve earnings and responsibility far in excess of what they could command at home. Conditions of work may have been strange but most showed flexibility and resource. As the cartoon indicates some believed that over ambitious schemes were foisted on to the Japanese.

It was felt by some that foreign experts recommended elaborate and expensive schemes in advance of Japanese needs.

*Cartoon* 3.1 White elephant (*Japan Punch*, 1875)

The difficulties arose when foreign engineers, however senior, had to work under the authority of Japanese officials. In the early *Meiji* years some of these native officers, ignorant of the new techniques, could be obstructive. In most other developing countries foreign engineers could expect to hold ultimate authority, command the natives, organise the supply of raw materials, whether from local sources or ordered from their home country, and act as paymaster. Often several officials in Japan, with varying degrees of authority, had to give permission for any action. Foreign engineers longed to work with a single Japanese official who had the experience, usually gained by travel in the West, to understand the objective.

Foreigners working on engineering projects also had charge of Japanese as trainee apprentices. The young men seconded for this purpose, often of *samurai* stock, had their own views on the propriety of the work they were called upon to do. Apprentices working on construction projects were required to get their hands dirty; some found this demeaning. British construction engineers working under difficult conditions found this sort of hauteur especially hard to deal with.

In general the engineers who came to Japan fell into one or two broad categories. There were those who came to resent and resist the Japanese hierarchy,[7] and those who, personally self-confident and imbued with gentlemanly forbearance, accepted the *status quo* and worked happily with their Japanese colleagues.[8] For some it was relatively easy, with 'humility and accommodation' to accept with equanimity a Japanese way of doing things. For others, the overwhelming missionary impulse to bring enlightenment brought on a haughty truculence which accorded ill with their status as hired persons and was much resented by their Japanese employers. Those positively minded enjoyed great success and warm approbation; others, despite impressive achievements quickly left, temperamentally unsuited to the conditions of work in Japan. None could know their response to the test to which they were subjecting themselves until they had entered upon the task.

In general the British did prove satisfactory employees for, as one scholar has written:

> British contacts were perhaps more significant and more amenable to future enlargement than those of any other nationality owing to their *laissez faire* spirit . . . their obvious competence in technology and efficiency in business. These were qualities which brought British diplomatic leadership to the fore and may help to account for the fact that 50 per cent (perhaps 2000 persons) of all government foreign employees in the Meiji era would be British.[9]

Each area of engineering presented its own distinctive challenge. In this chapter consideration will be given to lighthouses, railways, telegraphs, and mining. The subsequent chapter is devoted to marine engineering and shipbuilding. These six sectors cover the main British contribution.

## 2 THE JAPAN LIGHTS

The Japanese government were required to provide at the treaty ports 'such lights, buoys or beacons, as may be necessary to render secure the navigation of the approaches to the said ports'.[10] As a result of Sir Harry Parkes's initiatives the Japanese government requested British help, and through the good offices of the Board of Trade, the enquiry eventually arrived at the offices of David and Thomas Stevenson, in Edinburgh.

The Stevensons were engineers to the Commission for Northern Lights,[11] who were responsible in law for the lights and lighthouses around the Scottish coast. They had shown particular ingenuity as well as advanced engineering skills in erecting lighthouses on dangerous and inaccessible sites in Scotland. In 1861, they had broken new ground when they had accepted an invitation from the Indian government to design a lighthouse 'for the notorious Alguada Reef off the South-west tip of Burma'.[12] The approach by the Board of Trade on behalf of Japan, a foreign government, brought a positive response. The extensions of their overseas commitment to encompass Japan was apparently welcomed despite the fact that, at so great a distance, the partners, David and Thomas, would not be able to work as they did in Scotland, on the site. By 15 November 1867 the arrangements, made through the Board of Trade, for Stevenson's to build the 'Japan Lights' were completed.[13]

By 24 February 1868 Richard Henry Brunton (1841–1901)[14] at the age of 27 had been appointed as engineer for the project. Brunton was not a lighthouse engineer (none such came forward when the job was advertised) but Stevenson's brought him to Edinburgh for a period of training.

Brunton spent the spring of 1868, together with his two assistants, Messrs Blundell and McVean, learning the work. It was a complicated process, for Stevenson's, as contractors, undertook all stages of the job, choosing a site and then planning a lighthouse for it, making up equipment to the specifications they had prepared, providing plans and ordering custom-built gear from specialist suppliers, then raising the supporting building and installing the light. Permission was obtained for Brunton and his assistants to spend some time on the east coast of Scotland, resident at Girdle Ness and St Abb's Head lighthouses, learning the lighthouse routine and seeing the keepers in action. The three lighthouse engineers embarked for Japan on 13 June 1868. Even before their arrival in Japan Stevenson's were despatching letters to Brunton about possible technical problems which could arise.

Brunton reached Japan on 8 August 1868. He could have been forgiven for thinking that his coming was inopportune. The lighthouse-building project had been initiated by the old Tokugawa regime. But the Restoration of the Emperor had already taken place and the arrangements were now the responsibility of the new *Meiji* government. Fortunately Brunton had allies. These included Sir Harry Parkes, who intervened in various crises; the new young leaders of Japan who facilitated his work; and the governor of Kanagawa, in whose area at Benten, Yokohama, the headquarters of the Japanese lighthouse service was to be sited. Munenori Terajima,[15] the governor, newly returned from three years residence in Britain and America, spoke good English and was conversant with the West.

The first task was to explore the coasts of Japan to choose sites where lighthouses could best be placed to guide the sea traffic approaching the treaty ports. Sir Harry Parkes's support ensured that the British Admiral, Sir Henry Keppel, agreed to escort Brunton and his colleagues on HMS *Manilla*, under Captain Johnson, on a winter journey. Brunton donned the mantle of authority effortlessly, and perhaps with relish.[16] He was under pressure of time to provide the first modern lights around the coast, for the masters of foreign vessels were clamant in their demands for efficient working lights.

Once Brunton had made his preliminary survey,[17] he worked out a list of lights needed urgently and ordered material from Edinburgh. Stevensons provided the bulk of the structure, other than that made locally, on site in Japan, using 'feeder' firms in Edinburgh with whom they had worked closely and continuously for many years. As Craig Mair reports 'Milne's of Edinburgh would invariably make the cast metal frames and pieces of machinery, while Chance's of Birmingham prepared the lens and prisms, and Smith's of Blair Street ... provided the wicks and burners. Dove's of Edinburgh usually made the lantern glass.'

From the beginning there had been concern over the possible effect of earthquakes on the Japan lights. David Stevenson set himself the task of designing a structure flexible enough to meet this difficulty. He perfected the 'aseismatic joint' by which the upper light-holding platform was balanced on a series of ball-bearings which would allow a certain pliancy during earth tremors. It was a brave try, rarely if ever tested, for lighthouse keepers preferred to fasten the platform down rather than roll from side to side while performing their cleaning duties.[18]

There was an active dialogue between Brunton and Stevenson's, plans passed to and fro, crates containing manufactured parts for specific lights were constantly arriving at the new lighthouse headquarters.[19] Brunton was constantly searching for local raw materials. Near some sites he found granite 'of excellent quality' which could be worked, as in his home town of Aberdeen, into ashlar masonry. He was constantly looking for good wood and discovered a valuable hardwood called *keaki* (*Planera Japonica*). For interior work he used soft woods such as *shinoki*, *sugi* and *matsu*. He was able to use Japanese craftsmen, with their fine traditions of working in stone and wood, although some Scots workmen were also employed.[20]

Wooden lighthouses had foundations of stone,[21] topped by wooden structures and also iron 'straps and bolts'. In these early days all the iron was imported from Edinburgh. There were four, very expensive, iron lighthouses, at Haneda, Yebosishima, Iwoshima and Satamomisaki. Lime was burned as near the site as possible and mixed with sand to form mortar. The indefatigable Brunton also set up brickworks.

Brunton was fortunate in securing the services of Captain A. R. Brown as master of the lighthouse tender the *Thabor*.[22,23] The efficient management of this ship was absolutely essential for the smooth running of the lighthouse building and servicing programme. After 1873 the *Meiji Maru* was in service.[24,25]

Stevenson's relationship with the Japanese was cordial. In 1871 the Government of Japan, in the person of Sano Kobu Shojo, chief of the Lighthouse department, wrote requesting direct contact with Stevenson's, thus cutting out the intermediary, the Board of Trade in London. Brunton for his part requested that Stevenson's, 'will use your every endeavour to make the material sent out as low in price as possible consistent with good quality in the articles'. Stevenson's received payment through the Oriental Bank in London.[26]

From an early date the young *Meiji* Emperor was encouraged by the young oligarchs to visit industrial and other sites,[27] symbols of the new era, to give his approval to the new developments. In March 1874 the Emperor and his party paid a visit to the lighthouse department, 'tastefully decorated with flags, banners and evergreens' where he was received by the Japanese Chief and Brunton, as engineer-in-chief.[28]

From his arrival in August 1868, to his departure from Japan at the end of 1875 Brunton built and put in place thirty-four lighthouses, two lightships, thirteen buoys and three beacons. The bases of the lighthouses, the lightships, the buoys and the beacons (all but the first built at the workshops of the lighthouse authority) were built to Brunton's plans. The superstructures including lanterns, machines, reflectors, reflector-frames and many other items came from Scotland.

It was an astonishing achievement, reflecting Brunton's own inner drive.[29] But there was friction. Though Brunton had generally good relations with high officials, he resisted the authority of lesser functionaries who, according to Japanese custom, were empowered to supervise all his work. There can be little doubt that Brunton had burdensome responsibilities and that sometimes Japanese officials behaved obstructively. Notwithstanding Brunton's extraordinary energy it was probably with some relief that the Japanese parted with so prickly a man. During the Brunton years Japanese lighthouse keepers and engineers replaced the Scots lighthouse men. And as Basil Hall Chamberlain reported 'the instructions for lighthouse keepers remain, as in the past, those of the Scottish Board of Northern Lights'.[30]

## 3 RAILWAY BUILDERS

From the outset there was strong pressure on the *Meiji* regime to establish a railway network. The new young leaders and their advisers had appreciated and enjoyed railway travel overseas.[31] The first railway to be built, commenced in 1870, was Shimbashi (Tokyo) to Yokohama, some 18 miles. In a sense this was an experimental line which reflected partly the needs of the foreign community who wished reliable and quick travel between the capital and the treaty port.

Edmund Morell (1841–71)[32] at the age of 29 was appointed as construction engineer for the railway. As a result of working on New Zealand railways Morell chose a 3′ 6″ gauge. All rails, locomotives and other gear were imported from Britain. It is believed that Morell oversaw as many as 100 foreign engineers as well as large numbers of Japanese. He also had his problems. The young *samurai* who were to assist him wore their two swords and their sandals: the swords disturbed the magnetic measuring instruments and, in violation of law and custom, had to be laid aside, and the sandals were hopeless in the mud of a construction site.[33] The railway was opened on

14 October 1872 by the *Meiji* Emperor himself. The fares were high for the ordinary Japanese so that the 53-minute journey was initially enjoyed mostly by the foreign community. Morell did not live to see the triumphant opening. He died in September 1871 of tuberculosis probably brought on by worry and overwork, at the age of 30.[34,35]

The next railway project was planned on an altogether grander scale being from Shimbashi (Tokyo) to Kobe. It was eventually to become the main line passing from Tokyo through Kyoto to Osaka although there were many difficulties, some of them financial, before this line became a reality in 1889. In Japan, as in Britain, the costs of railway building were consistently underestimated. Japanese land speculators soon saw a new opportunity, buying and selling land through which the railway was to pass. The short Osaka to Kobe link was built, again partly at the behest of the foreign communities who were based in these centres.

Railway building in Japan was difficult. The mountainous landscape with many short fast-flowing rivers rushing to the sea called for complex and expensive engineering. Lines were subject to sudden flooding following heavy rain either during early summer or during the autumn monsoon season. In many places mountain spurs jutted out to the sea, making passage difficult. Railway builders were faced with all manner of engineering problems which caused delays and further expense.[36]

In 1874 there may have been ninety-four British railway engineers working in Japan, out of a total of 104 foreigners. Almost all of these had returned home by the 1880s, although a few remained giving longer periods of service. Two grandsons of Richard Trevithick (1771–1833) – Richard Francis Trevithick (1845–1913) and Francis Henry Trevithick (1850–1937) – served for many years on the Japanese railways.

The Trevithicks, and other British railway engineers, were an important part of the process of 'learning by making' as practised in Japan. The railway industry could not function without the constant maintenance and repair not only of track but also of locomotives and carriages. This encouraged technical competence;[37] the first railway carriage was manufactured in Japan at the Kobe works in 1875. R. F. Trevithick is credited with designing the steam locomotive, model B6, some of which were made in the Kobe factory in the 1890s. At the same time engines, in kit form, were imported from Britain, Germany and the USA, and assembled in Japan. The use of the assembly process as learning experience was very important. Table 3.1 shows

*Table* 3.1 The supply of locomotives to Japan

| | *Manufactured in Japan* | *Imported* | *Percentage of total locomotives* |
|---|---|---|---|
| 1872–1881 | — | 45 | 0 |
| 1882–1891 | 25 | 231 | 0 |
| 1892–1901 | 122 | 959 | 2.6 |
| 1902–1911 | 1254 | 975 | 11.0 |
| 1912–1921 | | 85 | 93.5 |

*Source*: T. Nakaoka, 'On Technological Leaps', p. 16.

how imported locomotives were in time replaced by those of Japanese manufacture.

The Japanese were well served by their own Director General of Government railways, Masaru Inoue, who held the post until 31 March 1893 (see Chapter 2, Section 3 above). During the course of his education in Britain he is believed to have studied railways and railway engineering. Inoue had the gift of bringing together British and Japanese railway engineers. By 1878 he was able to embark, as Director General and Chief Engineer, on the construction of ten miles of railway line from Kyoto to Otsu without using foreign engineers, though he did employ them to make plans for the tunnels and iron bridges.[38]

The British railway operating staff, which included engineers, locomotive drivers, firemen, signalmen and others, served in Japan over a period of great change. There can be little doubt that for the most part they gave loyal service. Perhaps the worst that can be said of them is that they insisted upon using the standards and principles in which they had been trained and were unwilling to depart from these. This allowed their employers to think of them as inflexible and unyielding and encouraged the Japanese to get rid of them as soon as possible. There were also sound economic reasons for terminating the employment of so expensive a group.

The task of the British railway engineers was made more difficult because railways were extrinsic to Japanese experience. During the *Satsuma* rebellion of 1877, the military value of the railways for moving troops became apparent for the first time and gave added impetus to their construction. For the ordinary Japanese citizen an appreciation of railways took much longer.[39] In 1904 after thirty years service in Japan, Consul Longford claimed that 'in Japan it costs more to carry a bale of goods a hundred miles into the country from the port at which it is landed than to send it . . . from Europe to Japan'.[40] In terms of the present Japanese railway system, dominated by the famous and prestigious *Shinkansen* network, the contribution of the early British railway engineers was a modest one. But the honour in which Edmund Morrell is still held is a reminder of the impact which railway engineers made in a Japan struggling to emerge into the modern world.

## 4 TELEGRAPH ENGINEERS

The laying of ocean cables between continents and the opening of telegraphic communications within countries led to extraordinary changes in expectations in the speed of human contact. Governments could make direct and rapid links with their diplomatic representatives and their military forces at home and abroad. Merchants could learn of market conditions and prices, world-wide. The Japanese, especially those who had been abroad, were aware of the importance of these developments. Members of the Iwakura Mission in London in 1872, expressed their astonishment at the business transacted by the telegraph office there. A national telegraph system therefore became part of the desired modernising package for Japan.

British scientists and engineers were well to the fore with the pioneering development of both submarine cables and telegraphy. They had succeeded after some set-backs in laying a successful Atlantic cable in 1866. Two years later Malta was united with Alexandria and then in 1869 the submarine cable system between Suez and Bombay via Aden and the Arabian Sea was completed. By 1870 Indian government telegraphs were also linked to England via Germany and part of Russia and Persia. Japan's turn to be joined to the rest of the world came in 1871 when the Great Northern System was completed from England to Denmark and over Russia and China to Tokyo.[41,42]

As early as 1869 two Japanese telegraph lines had been developed: one between Tokyo and Yokohama and the other between Osaka and Kobe both using Breguet alphabetical instruments. But neither the government nor the public were familiar with the novel gear and it was not maintained.[43] A new beginning was made in 1871: in a short time British engineers erected 900 miles of line which was provisionally opened to traffic. As early as March 1871, Takayoshi Kido was marvelling on 'the miracle of the telegraph'. A Telegraphic

Correspondence Regulation was passed in 1873 and the Telegraph Law in 1874. But the value of the system, although appreciated by foreigners, seemed remote from most Japanese lives. It was not until the *Satsuma* rebellion of 1877 that the government appreciated the potential of telegraphic communication.[44]

The Rules and Regulations applicable to Telegraphic Correspondence on Japanese government lines, appear to have been taken over from British practice. Messages could be sent 'in any of the principal living languages that can be transmitted by the international Morse telegraph alphabet, or in Latin'.[45] Although equipment for setting up the Japanese telegraph service was originally imported, use was soon made of Japanese material where this proved practicable.[46]

The British staff were responsible for laying the necessary submarine cables across the Straits of Shimonoseki, at Inageri Inlet, as well as those connecting Shikoku island with the mainland and linking Hokkaido with Honshu under the Tsugaru Straits. The *Meiji Maru*, the lighthouse service's steam tender, helped to make the Shikoku connection while the HC *Oltsted* belonging to the Great Northern Telegraph Company undertook the northern connection with Hakodate.

As was customary the Japanese were anxious to replace their British staff with their own nationals as soon as possible. To this end steps were taken to train their own people. From 1871 a school was available for telegraph operators. They received education in writing and speaking English and some French and were trained as Morse operators. A course of advanced telegraphy was also available at the Imperial College of Engineering, which some of the graduates supplemented by further study and experience overseas.[47]

The telegraph service in Japan, like the railways, was introduced initially at the urging of foreigners, somewhat to the puzzlement of many Japanese. Only with the *Satsuma* rebellion in the tenth year of *Meiji* did its value become apparent and only a year later, in 1879 did revenue exceed working expenses, when total receipts amounted to £108 323 while running costs were £101 674. In the same year 1 272 756 telegrams were sent of which some 96 per cent were in Japanese; 22 695 international messages were also recorded.

As with so much of the new Japan, expenditure had to be made on the telephone service over several years, as an act of faith, for few Japanese appreciated the value of such facilities. The ruling oligarchs were willing to do this, accepting the recommendations of their British advisers. British telegraph engineers and technicians were happy to set up the system, appeared to show resourcefulness in using local raw materials, and trained their successors to take over.

## 5 MINING SPECIALISTS

The new *Meiji* government was as keenly interested in the mining potential of their country as anyone,[48] but perhaps being better informed made a more realistic appraisal of the potential than the foreigners who, eager to use the modern mining techniques of the west, believed they might have found 'a second Eldorado'. Numbers of foreign mining engineers were to bring the skills of Western mining technology to the industry but in this area the British remained a minority.[49] The confusion which could stem from the employment of mining specialists from more than one nationality in any one mine can be readily understood.

The main minerals available in Japan were copper, silver, gold, iron and coal. Mining these posed fresh challenges at every mining centre for drainage and ventilation proved to be common problems.[50] Foreigners worked for the government and for private owners in all the main mines of Japan at this time. By 1885 they had generally been replaced by Japanese nationals.

Without doubt the mining methods used in Japan until the *Meiji* period were primitive and wasteful. At this time knowledge of the earth's strata was limited and the help which the geologist could give not available to them. Even when good ore was found, methods of extraction were inefficient and wasteful. Ores were dirty when brought to the surface, much good ore was left behind and extraction processes resulted in spoils which contained quantities of metal which primitive processing had failed to release.

The foreigners brought many necessary mining specialisms to the country. In addition to mining engineers there were at the managerial level, geologists; ore preparation, instrument and excavation experts, and smelting engineers. Under the general heading of technicians there were forge workers; ore washing foremen; bricklayers; mine foremen, mechanics and miners.[51]

Both state-owned mines (*Jikiyama*) and private concessions (*Ukeyama*) were recognised, but in 1873 the first mining law 'established state ownership of all unmined ores, and the states' power to direct private activities on the basis of the *berg royal* (mine royal) principle'.[52] In 1890 a Prussian-inspired ordinance was enacted establishing *berg-baufreiheit* (freedom of mining enterprise) and the allocation of mining rights by *priorité de demande* (first-come, first-served basis). This 1890 statute has remained basic despite minor amending legislation.

The prime function of the foreign mining engineer was to apply new techniques, usually involving new machinery, to Japanese mines. The introduction of gunpowder and later dynamite blasting, greatly improved methods of rock-breaking. The resultant deeper tunnelling required modern systems of ventilation and pumping. The more general use of 'over-hand stoping' which involved more efficient extraction of the ore-body was also a major step forward. Equally important was the treatment of the ore and the improvement of refining techniques which produced a larger quantity of usable ore.

As mine manager the foreigner's position was even more difficult. Besides the problems of communication due to the language barrier there were serious organisational tensions stemming from the lack of any unified management structure.[53] Labourers and unskilled workers, illiterate and ignorant as they were, were always discontented. Prisoners were sent to work in the mines, which remained a brutalising work environment even for free labourers.[54] If conditions of work for foreign mining engineers were difficult, so too were their daily lives, isolated as they were in remote and inaccessible places.[55] No doubt the generous salaries compensated for many discomforts.

Perhaps it was at Takashima that British involvement was initially greatest.[56] The existence of good-quality steam coal on Takashima island, barely seven miles from Nagasaki, combined with the very high price of good imported steam coal, encouraged both Japanese and British to seek to exploit the potential. The expansion of the mine and the introduction of modern mining methods involved British mining engineers.[57]

The foreign mining engineers who served in Japan between 1868 and 1880 did make a substantial contribution to the ultimate establishment of a modern mining industry. They and their senior Japanese colleagues were equally affected by the lack of a unified chain of command in mines where 'the contractors and middle men enjoyed a rather far-going authority in most cases not to the advantage of the mine'. In addition to all the built-in problems, mining specialists, particularly foreign ones, did take short-cuts in an attempt to reach profitability quickly. These rarely worked. Most mines did not become profitable until after 1885 when the foreigners had gone. Only the Japanese themselves could, over time, force changes which would allow effective management. When they did so they were then able to take advantage of and develop the machinery, training and techniques introduced by foreign mining specialists.

## 6 THE FRUITS OF TUTELAGE

The 'experts' decade' from 1872 to 1882 saw an astonishing increase and then a sharp decline in the numbers of British engineers, of all ranks, employed in Japan. Contracts were deliberately kept short although some were renewed. After 1882 the British engineers had, in general, gone, and the Japanese filled most of the posts themselves. Until about 1900 a handful of British were invited to stay on and one or two remained in senior and responsible positions in the Railways Bureau and Lighthouse Bureau and probably in several other areas. In this way the Japanese retained sufficient foreign expertise to serve their purpose. For the British engineers and the young *Meiji* oligarchs, the one conditioned by their training, the other by their appreciation of modern engineering wonders in the West, it was easy to understand the importance of the new infrastructure to Japan. For others it was more difficult.

Perhaps the sequence of the new engineering may have been determined by a combination of demand and supply. Only with the outbreak of the *Satsuma* rebellion in 1877 did the Japanese recognise the importance of telegraphs, railways and steamships. Previously the demand had come mostly from the foreigner who needed lighthouses to help him to reach the treaty ports safely, coal to power his steamships, and railways (between Tokyo and Yokohama and Osaka and Kobe) to make his life as a resident in Japan pleasanter.

There were many complex reasons for the Japanese decision to discard most of their foreign engineers. Of these financial pressures were important. Almost 50 per cent of the money spent by the Ministry of Public Works between 1872 and 1880 went to employees, most of them engineers or (in the case of ICE) teachers of various engineering subjects. 1070 British man-years were spent on Japanese railways during the *Meiji* period and all of them were expensive.[58] The most costly of all was W. W. Cargill,[59] employed as 'Railway Director' from 1872–7 at $2000 a month. This is an astonishing figure.[60]

The disappearance of British employment opportunities in later *Meiji* Japan did not go unnoticed. Disgruntled foreign employees were critical. *The Engineer* between 1896 and 1898 ran a series on 'Modern Japan – Industrial and Scientific'[61] lamenting the early insistence of the Japanese on using their own people. It complained:

> There was little to say of the chances of the foreign engineer, for there is none, there being no field for his employment, whether civil, mechanical, or operative, in Japan at the present day. This may no doubt be considered by some as a disappointing state of affairs, and there can be no question as to the fact that Japan is suffering terribly in the quality of her engineering work, the price she is paying for it and the hindrance in turning it out, owing to her exaggerated longing to carry out in practice her theory of 'Japan for the Japanese'.

Notwithstanding, the series ended with a reluctant implied compliment:

> The Japanese are accredited – and perhaps the criticism is a fair one – with possessing an exaggerated amount of self-confidence. Whether such is the case or not, I am afraid that in common justice we, as Englishmen, must admit that it was not precisely a want of confidence in ourselves that caused Great Britain to become the first engineering and industrial country in the world.[62]

Notwithstanding the disgruntlement of the foreign engineer – cast off as he believed, before his time – the Japanese, stimulated perhaps by being forced to face their own errors and do their own problem-solving made extraordinary progress. It was Henry Dyer, always an admiring observer of Japan, who noted with approval at the time of the Sino-Japanese war in 1894–5, the role of the Japanese engineer.[63] His tribute may reflect favourably on the efforts of British engineers who served in Japan, as well as those Japanese-born.

# 4 The Makers and Operators of Ships

## 1 MAHAN'S LAW

The parallel position of Japan off the east coast of the Asiatic land mass and that of Britain off the west coast of Europe has been widely observed.[1] Britain's domination of the seas and consequent imperial achievement offered an obvious paradigm for the Japanese. The American, Captain A. T. Mahan had by his writing,[2] focused attention on the stimulus given to a home-based industry of seafaring power by a strong naval and mercantile shipping presence in the oceans of the world. It was reflected in the early recognition of Britain as a role model for Japan in matters connected with ships and seafaring.

The British were not averse to advising the Japanese on maritime matters. Individuals, whether naval officers, shipbuilders or members of the merchant marine willingly accepted contracts from the Japanese enjoying the increased status and prestige, as well as the generous salaries, which such employment offered. It was also recognised, as Captain Mahan had demonstrated, that when equipment and material had to be imported British employees in Japan would naturally recommend British-made goods. This paradigm was particularly powerful in the case of ships and shipbuilding.

The shipbuilding industry was changing at an astonishing rate. At every level it was being developed along innovatory lines.[3] The sophisticated machinery and equipment developed to make war vessels quicker and more manoeuvrable was soon adapted for merchant vessels. The increased speed and manageability of trading ships led to a more dependable service, faster voyages, quicker turn-round and greater profits.

The rate of change, offering challenge and excitement to committed men, did much to encourage cooperation between British and Japanese shipbuilders in Japan. Although the British regarded the Japanese as pupils, they showed themselves as gifted and willing, keen to apply themselves to scientific and technical questions.[4] In general terms the interrelationships between the makers and operators of ships in Britain and Japan led to a constant traffic between the two countries, generated substantial business for British industry, and opened up a wide range of employment opportunities for the British in Japan.

## 2 OFFICERS, BLUE JACKETS AND THE IMPERIAL JAPANESE NAVY

On 26 June 1897 there was a Grand Review of the Royal Navy to celebrate the sixtieth anniversary of Queen Victoria's accession.[5] 104 British ships of the line steamed proudly past. Among the foreign representatives were ships of the Imperial Japanese Navy. Could any of the British naval officers, who had struggled to train personnel and ships of the infant Imperial Japanese Navy, a mere twenty-five years earlier, have guessed that their protégés would be considered fit to join so distinguished a gathering?

In the 1860s the *Bakufu* government had requested aid from Britain to assist in the establishment of a modern Japanese navy; Commander Richard E. Tracey, RN, was appointed to head the British Naval Mission to Japan. When Tracey and his team arrived in November 1867 the Shogunate was toppling; with the change of government the mission withdrew. The new *Meiji* government also requested British naval aid. In July 1873 Commander Archibald Lucius Douglas and thirty-three other officers and men of the Royal Navy were engaged on three-year contracts. They arrived in Japan in the autumn and set about their task. The work went reasonably well although there was little understanding between the two groups. Teaching was given in English through interpreters. The Japanese willingly adopted British-style uniforms, and British methods of naval training including the firm naval discipline which conformed with Japanese expectations.

By the early 1880s various groups of Royal Navy personnel had fulfilled their contracts and left. They were not replaced. In 1887 Captain John Inglis, RN, was hired as an adviser to the Imperial Japanese Navy. Inglis was reasonably complimentary about much of what he found. He approved of the 'good order, discipline and cleanliness at the training establishments' and praised the 'active and prompt manner in which the sailors go about their business'. Of the ships at sea he was more critical, making suggestions as to improvements in manoeuvres and in gunnery. Inglis recognised the advantages which accrued to the Imperial Japanese Navy in not being encumbered, as was the Royal Navy, with elderly officers who, themselves trained under sail, could not tolerate change.

Inglis proved himself invaluable. He not only answered questions, but obtained much information. As one writer commented, 'Equipment, training manuals, and copies of instructions flowed in a steady stream from England to Japan.'[6] Later, after Inglis, other Royal Navy officers served as Naval Attachés with the Imperial Japanese Navy, often serving on board British-built warships.

The training of naval officers was undertaken in Japan at the Naval Training College (later, in 1876, renamed the Naval Academy)[7] originally established at Tsukiji in Tokyo. In August 1888 the College moved to its present location on 'the charming bay of Etajima, which is nearly land-locked and sheltered by high mountains', near Hiroshima and Kure on the Inland Sea. Here, according to British practice the cadets lived on a training-ship until the red-brick buildings which were to house them were completed in 1893.[8]

Although British material aid to the Japanese navy was 'substantial and significant' there is no evidence to suggest that intellectually Japanese and British naval men understood one another. In civil and military matters or indeed politics there was little common ground. Even so the relationship remained friendly, for the Japanese maintained their interest in Britain's technical skills in warship building, at least until the beginning of the First World War.

## 3 CHARTING JAPANESE WATERS

Between 1854 and 1883 British naval vessels were active in charting the waters around Japan.[9] The pace of work quickened after the official opening of the treaty ports in July 1859 after British traders assured consular staff that 'unsurveyed coasts and harbours are terrible obstacles to the safety of navigation and to the development of trade'. The official British hydrographer, Admiral J. Washington explained that 'the very ports with which by treaty we are allowed to trade are not only not surveyed but [that] we do not know the position of one of them, Niigata, within 20 miles'.

Before the comprehensive survey began in 1868 various naval vessels had made some exploratory journeys. Most notable among these was the preliminary surveying voyage of HMS *Actaeon*, a sailing vessel, drawing 16–18 feet. On leaving Yokohama she proceeded through the Inland Sea by the northern shore. She was towed through the Shimoneseki Straits by HMS *Leven* and then proceeded to Nagasaki. This voyage allowed an assessment to be made of likely problems. When, in 1868, HMS *Sylvia* under Commander Booker was sent to make a 'planned comprehensive survey', economy was recommended; where Japanese plans existed they were to be used; if French and Russian officers engaged on surveying were to be met with, 'information should be exchanged'. It was considered a matter of international concern to make access to the designated treaty ports easier and safer. The work was hazardous. Commander Booker was invalided home after a serious accident crossing the bar of the Osaka river. Commander St John, who replaced him, remained in the area until 1876, making the largest individual British contribution to Japanese marine safety.

The Japanese government welcomed the Royal Navy's assistance as the British hydrographer reported in 1870:

> It is gratifying to relate in connexion with this survey the very great interest which has been manifested in the work by the government of Japan: everywhere the greatest possible attention and civility have been extended to the surveying parties and assistance in the way of guides, interpreters, etc., freely afforded.

The interest of the Japanese was more than academic for they were about to set up their own hydrographic survey which they did in 1871. Several Japanese officers served on the *Sylvia* to learn how to use the various instruments and the art of nautical surveying. Commander St John was encouraging, appreciating as he did, with how little of the coast – that adjacent to the treaty ports and the main shipping lanes – he was directly concerned.

In the course of her operations in 1871, the *Sylvia* surveyed the northern island of Yezo (now Hokkaido) at the request of the Japanese government. The harbour at Muroran was charted and the strength of the current through the Tsugaru Strait experienced. In 1872 the *Sylvia* was on the Pacific coast searching for good harbours. She also examined the access to Kobe. The *Sylvia* was repaired and reboilered in 1873 in England but then set sail again for Japanese waters, subsequently being based at Nagasaki (1876) and off South West Korea (1877).[10] The *Sylvia* was finally withdrawn in 1880 to be replaced by HMS *Flying Fish* and HMS *Magpie*. British work on Japanese hydrographic survey work ceased in 1883. The Japanese Admiralty Survey Office was well established and responsible for producing their own coastal surveys and charts.

Although the pioneering work around Japanese coastal waters was invaluable there had been serious technical difficulties. Until the laying of the submarine telegraph cable from Vladivostok to Nagasaki, completed in 1882, the basic longitudes of Japan could not be exactly confirmed. In the early years secondary meridians were established at Nagasaki and Kobe by calculating from Hong Kong and Shanghai. After 1883 when telegraphic signals could be taken from Madras, via Singapore, Manila, Hong Kong, Shanghai, Nagasaki and Yokohama it was possible to establish final longitudes for the Japanese islands. These were checked by separate calculations done via the trans-Siberian railway telegraph and Vladivostok.

The British contribution to the Japanese hydrographic survey, during the first fifteen years of the *Meiji* period, was substantial. The Japanese appreciated the importance of such surveying work and moved quickly to take over the service. With their commitment to the expansion of naval and merchant shipping, and their early involvement with lighthouse building (see Chapter 3, Section 2 above) it was a priority for them to set up an efficient and comprehensive hydrographic service.

## 4 WARSHIP BUILDING

By 1912 Japan had four imperial dockyards.[11] They were at Yokosuka (1864), Kure (1886), Sasebo (1886) and Maizuru (1901). The oldest and best-equipped was at Yokosuka on Tokyo Bay, where, by 1900, with three dry docks opening into an outer basin, the site was crowded.[12] At Kure on the Inland Sea, south-east of Hiroshima, 'almost impossible of access by an enemy' two large dry docks had been built. The hilly site was also reported as congested. There the Japanese armour-plate works had been established, turning out, in 1905, guns, naval ammunition and torpedoes.[13] Sasebo, in a magnificent setting near Nagasaki, consisted of 'a narrow but deep entrance leading into an asbolutely landlocked harbour'.[14] Maizuru, on the Sea of Japan coast facing Korea, was also a good sheltered site.

Modern Japanese shipbuilding began with small wooden sailing ships at Yokosuka in the 1870s, and from 1890 the Japanese were building larger and more complex vessels although until the First World War some raw materials, machinery and personnel had to be imported. Matters were complicated by major developments in warship building. The new iron and later steel hulls, with larger and more efficient marine engines, together with armour-cladding and more powerful guns, led to repeated revolutions in the industry. Shipyards had to be larger, with much greater capitalisation. To build these required greater management skills. The naval architect emerged as a key figure, who gradually assumed responsibility for the design of all new ships. More draughtsmen were required to prepare plans for vessels of increasing complexity. Workmen – trained to a particular trade – became specialists in a narrower range of skills.

At all Japanese shipyards during the *Meiji* years there was a strong foreign presence. Originally the French had been invited by the *Bakufu* government to establish the Yokosuka yard but after the Restoration British shipbuilders were prominent. There was a constant traffic of British naval architects, ship designers, draughtsmen and shipwrights travelling to Japan. Some stayed a life time, some, contracted to design and supervise the building of a particular ship, soon left; others, like Henry Napier, came as visitors to advise.

In the naval dockyard cruisers were developed,[15] including fast unprotected cruisers (replacing frigates), 'protected cruisers' with a partial armour deck, and 'armoured cruisers' with a complete armour deck. Armour-plating became standard on naval vessels by the 1890s. Originally made of rolled wrought iron backed by teak it was later usually either Harvey or Krupp armour,[16] that is, steel plates toughened with nickel and chromium, made under licence in several countries.

The British First Sea Lord, Admiral Sir John Fisher, appointed on Trafalgar Day 1904, adopted the revolutionary design of the dreadnought and refashioned the British fleet around these vessels.[17] The dreadnought made earlier capital warships obsolete. The consequent expansion of the world's navies was based on a dangerous rivalry. As international battleship fever took hold, navies competed to provide themselves with these vessels. Much of this demand was met from British yards. The signing of the Anglo-Japanese Alliance in 1902 confirmed the friendly relations between the Royal Navy and its newest competitor and encouraged a close professional cooperation. British naval officers were seconded to serve in the Imperial Japanese navy and of course Japanese naval engineers and architects were very active in Britain.

Rapid obsolescence in some sense aided the Japanese and in some senses hindered them. Because of the pace of change they had no choice but to enter the industry at an advanced stage. Counterfactually,

*Table* 4.1 Ships built for the Imperial Japanese Navy in 1901

| *Class* | *Where built* | *Number of ships* | *Total HP* |
|---|---|---|---|
| Warships | Home | 45 | 573 617 |
| | Great Britain | 47 | 376 540 |
| | Elsewhere | 32 | 254 652 |
| | Total | 124 | 1 204 809 |
| Destroyers | Home | 45 | 306 000 |
| | Great Britain | 16 | 95 050 |
| | Elsewhere | 5 | 23 000 |
| | Total | 66 | 424 050 |
| Torpedo Boats | Home | 58 | 77 029 |
| | Great Britain | 10 | 19 217 |
| | Elsewhere | 25 | 39 804 |
| | Total | 93 | 136 050 |
| Submarines | Home | 6 | 3 400 |
| | Great Britain | 2 | 1 200 |
| | Elsewhere | 5 | 1 500 |
| | Total | 13 | 6 100 |
| | Grand Total | 296 | 1 771 009 |

*Source*: The Progress of Naval Engineering in Japan, *TINA* Jubilee Meetings, 1911, Part II, p. 194.

could the Japanese have entered the industry more easily had it remained static?

In the years from 1890 Japanese naval dockyards shared the warship building. Yokosuka took the lion's share, building cruisers and protected cruisers. The establishment of the Japanese armour-plate works at Kure gave the edge to this dockyard which built three of the four Japanese built armoured cruisers each at around 14 000 tons.[18]

As can be seen from Table 4.1, Japanese yards became very much busier in the 1890s and 1900s. Until 1900 foreign designs and designers were 'bought in', each being responsible for a specified ship or group of ships. Although the British were important especially in the commercial yards of Nagasaki and Kobe, the old connection with French yards remained strong, Emil Bertin designed the 1584 ton cruiser *Yaeyama* which was built as Yokosuka between 1887 and 1892.

Under the 1903 warship building programme the *Satsuma*, of 19 700 tons, was the first large warship built in Japan largely from Japanese materials. She was a 'semi-dreadnought' or 'intermediate dreadnought' and carried Krupp Steel Armour, a belt of 9″ to 4″. Under the 1907 programme, the first two dreadnought battleships were built in Japan. They were the *Kawachi* and *Settsu* – one out of Yokosuka and one out of Kure dockyard. These vessels were the first of independent Japanese design although Armstrong provided the guns and mountings. In the years immediately before the First World War, under the warship-building programmes of 1911 and 1913, the *Fuso*, under construction at Kure between 1912 and 1915, and the *Yamashiro*, at Yokosuka between 1913 and 1917, were the first battleships built in Japan using not only Japanese material but also Japanese weapons, although the armour was imported Krupp steel.

Because of the First World War the Japanese were forced to continue their naval shipbuilding without outside aid. That they did so is much to their credit although, without any guidance from British personnel there were aberrations, for left on their own, they suffered from 'an excess of originality rather than slavish copying'.[19]

## 5 MERCHANT MARINERS

The idea that Japan should take to the sea and develop a merchant marine in order to compete for the carrying trade in world markets had been independently formulated in Japan by Toyo Yoshida (1816–62) of Tosa *han* who argued that Japan, like any other country prospecting for power, must 'positively carry out trade with foreign countries'.[20] Yoshida's views were embraced by his clansman, Yataro Iwasaki[21] (1835–85), the founder of Mitsubishi, through whose enterprise the shipping line of Nippon Yusen Kaisha (NYK) was founded in 1885.

Although no foreigners were involved in the internal struggles from which NYK emerged, British sea captains and seamen were the instruments by which Japanese merchant ships were kept working and at sea. Occasionally, as with the expedition against Taiwan in 1874, foreigners played a crucial role. But in the shipping industry as elsewhere in the Japanese economy it was the task of the British sea captains and other officers to train their Japanese successors.

Iwasaki Yataro entered business life before 1868 by serving in the *Kaiseikan* or Industry Promotion Agency by which the *Tosa* clan pursued an active policy of business opportunism. In handling domain finances Yataro is believed to have 'resorted to numerous questionable loans' (some foreign) and various 'unscrupulous practices'.[22] After the Restoration the experience thus gained eventually led him to assume ownership of the *Tosa* domain's business.[23]

Yataro, throughout these unsettled early *Meiji* years never lost sight of the fact that the ultimate goal for Japan was 'to revive its shipping and trade'. He also succeeded in recruiting others who, especially after his early death, were to become important contributors to the Mitsubishi business empire. His two leading *Tosa* associates were Shichizai Ishikawa and Koichiro Kawada. The two non-*Tosa* recruits were Rempei Kondo and Heigoro Shoda. Kondo was in his mature years to serve as president of NYK, between 1895 and 1921, while Shoda, originally recommended by Yukichi Fukuzawa, for whom he had taught at *Keio* school, entered Mitsubishi service in 1875. In addition Iwasaki's brother Yanosuke, came into the firm bringing from the USA, where he had studied between 1872 and 1873, modern ideas of professional management.[24]

The early problems over Japanese mercantile shipping came to a head in 1874 when, after the murder of over fifty shipwrecked Japanese sailors on Taiwan, the government decided it was necessary to launch a campaign against the Chinese-owned island. The physical difficulties of securing ships well-enough built, engined and manned to make the voyage to Taiwan revealed the Japanese plight. In the end the government awarded a contract to Mitsubishi to transport men and supplies to Taiwan. With the funds made available, the government, through Iwasaki, was able to buy well-founded modern steamships to carry the expedition.[25] Foreigners like the ubiquitous Captain Albert Brown and others came to the rescue,[26] captaining ships and ensuring that supplies reached Taiwan.[27] The role of Iwasaki in rescuing the Taiwan expedition and saving from political embarrassment those leaders who had earlier committed themselves to a campaign against Taiwan, may have given him an important boost.[28]

On 15 September 1875, the government issued the First Directive. Under its terms Mitsubishi was granted the thirteen steamships bought for the Taiwan expedition, 'without charge', together with an annual subsidy of ¥250 000. For Mitsubishi this was a remarkably favourable outcome although the firm was specifically prohibited from 'selling or using the ships or subsidies as collateral without advance permission'. This was intended to prevent the 'wheeler-dealer' tactics which had been perfected earlier.

During these years the Japanese government recognised that it needed skilled seamen. In 1875 schools of navigation and engineering were set up to train Japanese personnel to run an efficient merchant navy. Many Britons were on the staff. Captain G. Ramsay became instructor in navigation until his death at the age of 47 in 1886, while Messrs A. F. McNab and James Ellerton were employed as instructors in engineering. As the anonymous author of the *Golden Jubilee History of NYK* remarks 'The most influential among them were Mr A R. Brown (British); Mr Alexander MacMillan (British); Captain Thomas H. James, RNR (British); Captain Richard Swain (American); Captain J. W. Ekstrand (Danish); Captain E. W. Haswell (British); Captain Hector Frazer (British); Captain Francis Edgar Cope (British); Mr James Blair (British), etc.'.[29] Initially, as Table 4.2, shows, large numbers of foreigners were employed as captains, mates, engineers and pursers. Soon after its foundation, in 1866, NYK was employing about one-third foreign staff to run its fleet; but these numbers steadily fell in the following years as more Japanese qualified for senior positions.

The favoured position of Mitsubishi as monopolist in the 1870s enabled the firm to win two battles against competitors. In the first

*Table* 4.2 Japanese and foreign officers employed by Nippon Yusen Kaisha

| *Year* | *Captain* | | *Mate* | | *Chief Engineer* | | *Engineer* | | *Pursuer* | | *Total* | |
|---|---|---|---|---|---|---|---|---|---|---|---|---|
| | *J* | *F* | *J* | *F* | *J* | *F* | *J* | *F* | *J* | *F* | *J* | *F* |
| 1886 | 37 | 26 | 141 | 55 | | | 104 | 78 | 153 | 12 | 435 | 171 |
| 1889 | 30 | 27 | 119 | 54 | | | 105 | 91 | 155 | 13 | 409 | 185 |
| 1891 | 29 | 22 | 108 | 49 | | | 111 | 74 | 144 | 11 | 392 | 156 |
| 1893 | 27 | 21 | 103 | 46 | | | 105 | 54 | 135 | | 370 | 121 |
| 1895 | 38 | 27 | 129 | 82 | | | 172 | 101 | 207 | | 546 | 211 |
| 1897 | 43 | 27 | 104 | 76 | 36 | 25 | 146 | 50 | 180 | | 509 | 178 |
| 1899 | 31 | 21 | 129 | 43 | 39 | 22 | 178 | 33 | 176 | | 553 | 119 |
| 1901 | 45 | 21 | 108 | 27 | 46 | 25 | 205 | 21 | 173 | | 577 | 94 |
| 1903 | 48 | 28 | 220 | 27 | 54 | 26 | 286 | 13 | 174 | | 782 | 94 |
| 1905 | 55 | 29 | 196 | 31 | 58 | 22 | 284 | 8 | 210 | | 803 | 90 |
| 1907 | 58 | 26 | 251 | 28 | 70 | 23 | 286 | 6 | 207 | | 872 | 83 |
| 1909 | 63 | 27 | 272 | 16 | 69 | 19 | 302 | 1 | 131 | | 837 | 63 |
| 1911 | 66 | 16 | 272 | 5 | 75 | 9 | 272 | | 140 | | 825 | 30 |

*Source*: N. Takeshi 'The Contribution of Foreigners', *JWH*, No. IX, 2, 1965, p. 308.

The struggle between the shipping companies in the mid-1870s was reflected in absurd offers to intending passengers.

*Cartoon* 4.1 The rivals (*Japan Punch*, October 1875)

they successfully competed against and subsequently purchased, the American Pacific Mails Shanghai Line. The cartoon 'The Rivals' shows how they forced the British P. & O. Line out of Japanese waters. In the latter struggle the Japanese government materially assisted by directing, in 1876, that any Japanese travelling on a foreign vessel be required to purchase a pass costing 25 *sen*. This example of Japanese 'flag discrimination' showed ingenuity, giving protection to a Japanese concern without violating the terms of the 'Unequal Treaties' which at this time remained in force.

By the end of the 1870s there was some anxiety about the strength of Mitsubishi's monopoly.[30] In July 1882 the government, anxious to curb Mitsubishi, launched Kioda Unya Kaisha. This incorporated a number of older ventures, had a capital of ¥6 000 000, five steamers and twenty-two sailing ships. In the ensuing struggle, which took place early in 1883, fares between Yokohama and Kobe, a journey of some 48 hours, fell from ¥5.00 to ¥0.25. There was a brief pause in the battle when, in February 1885, Yataro Iwasaki died. He was succeeded by his younger brother, Yanosuke Iwasaki. The increasing damage which the two rivals were doing to one another forced the government to intervene. The two companies were ordered to unite.

The new company Nippon Yusen Kaisha (the Japan Mail Steamship Company) established in 1885, received twenty-nine vessels totalling 28 010 gross tons, from KUK and twenty-nine vessels totalling 36 599 gross tons from Mitsubishi. In later years Mitsubishi began to distance itself from NYK which became an independent shipping line. In course of time NYK became powerful in world trade and eventually the leading shipping line.

British mariners, although not directly involved in the power struggles to establish a Japanese merchant marine, were an important part of the industry and rendered valuable service. The omnipresent Captain A. R. Brown performed a multitude of tasks.[31] Brown was the first General Manager of NYK. He had toured extensively in the UK, ordering and supervising the building of ships for Mitsubishi. In the summer of 1886 he made an extensive tour of Korea, Northern China and Russian ports recommending many changes and developments in the service which NYK were offering. He commented on harbours, suggesting that NYK buy or develop better facilities at places like Chemulpho, Chefoo, Shanghai and Vladivostock. He recommended that services to some ports, which were likely to prosper, should be increased and counselled caution where he felt that trade might decline. He also advised the company on what issues to do with shipping they should lobby the government. Brown's report was made to M. Morioka the President of NYK. In terms of numbers involved the British merchant mariners employed in Japanese service were small.[32] Yet men like Captain Brown brought to Japanese service a professionalism and Western expertise which was not immediately available in Japan.

## 6 MERCHANT SHIPBUILDERS

The modernisation of the Japanese commercial shipbuilding industry was effected slowly during the *Meiji* period. Small local shipyards at many places around the coastline continued to produce traditional wooden vessels although in course of time they gave ground, losing business to newer yards building iron and later steel ships.[33] The new industry was concentrated at Nagasaki, Kobe/Osaka, and Uraga, on

Tokyo Bay. The large-scale capital investment required the involvement of entrepreneurs willing to commit considerable resources over a long period not only to set up and equip the site but also to buy the imported technical know-how which was required.

Until the First World War there was a continuous British presence in Japanese shipyards. At the managerial level naval architects from Britain were frequent visitors, some working on contract for periods of a year or more. Ship-designers and draughtsmen and engineers were also present, perhaps to supervise the design and construction of one particular ship, or to take a more general part in improving ship design. British shipwrights and other workers were also recruited to the industry. Some of these men settled in Japan and gave a lifetime's experience to their Japanese employers.

The Japanese government had stepped in, and in 1896 had launched a scheme of subsidies and bounties. The stimulus which these provided for the home-based industry was of great importance, although, as the subsidy laws were designed to encourage yards to embark on building larger ships, only the major yards, like Mitsubishi at Nagasaki,[34] could benefit from the financial assistance offered.[35]

The Shipbuilding Encouragement Law (1896) granted bounties to Japanese subjects for the construction of vessels of over 700 tons. If the ships' engines were built in Japan a further payment was made. This financial support had a dramatic effect on the industry. More tonnage of the larger ships was built by Japanese yards in 1898 alone, than in the whole of the previous twenty years; and within five years of the act, annual production was topping 20 000 gross tons. The achievements of the industry after 1896 were quite startling. Later, in 1910 the law was changed, only vessels made of steel and of over 1000 tons gross qualifying for the bounty, which was also changed to allow '22 *yen* per ton on passenger vessels and 11 *yen* per ton for ordinary cargo vessels'.[36]

By 1916 the Japanese Diet had decided in theory to phase out shipbuilding bounties, but the only immediate result of the relevant act (24 July 1916) was to remove grants for those vessels which were sold to foreign owners. By the end of 1916 over 15 million *yen* had been paid out in subsidy. Over half of this sum went to Mitsubishi for work done at Nagasaki:[37] this produced 182 vessels of over 700 tons totalling 637 230 gross tons. Some 98 per cent of the subsidies were paid 'to the three yards capable of producing ships of over 700 gross tons, these were the Nagasaki yard of Mitsubishi, Kawasaki and the Osaka Iron Works'.[38]

The Japanese government in allocating their financial support for the shipbuilding industry were primarily concerned to encourage a home-based industry. The entrepreneurs involved were largely Japanese but in subsidising the products of the Osaka Iron Works the *Meiji* government were supporting an Irishman, Edward Hazlitt Hunter (1843–1917) who had set up the Osaka Iron Works in 1881 on the delta of the Ajikawa River.[39]

Throughout the *Meiji* years there were British shipbuilders, of various grades and expertise, working side by side with local craftsmen or draughtsmen in Japanese yards and effectively giving advice at many levels including that of naval architecture. Some of these men came as visitors to advise for relatively short periods, others settled in Japan for life.[40] As the industry gained momentum there was recruitment of senior management, often on contract for short periods.[41]

British naval architects were frequent visitors to Japan. Percy A. Hillhouse (1868–1942)[42] was the first appointee to the Chair of Naval Architecture at the Imperial University of Tokyo in 1897 where he served for three years. Earlier Francis Elgar (1845–1909)[43] later director of HM Dockyards in Britain and an expert on the stability of ships, served in Japan as a young man from 1880 to 1881. Professor (Sir) John Harvard Biles (1854–1933), perhaps the most distinguished naval architect to hold the Glasgow chair, was a frequent visitor.[44]

The transfer of shipbuilding technology from Britain to Japan proved to be a long and difficult process.[45] The ultimate objective, the development of a competitive home-based shipbuilding industry in Japan did not come until the later 1930s. In 1912 when the *Meiji* period ended, out of a total world shipping tonnage of almost 3 million gross tons, Japanese yards were producing some 58 000 gross tons. In 1925 out of a world output of over 2 million gross tons Japanese tonnage had remained almost the same at some 56 000 gross tons. Despite the contraction of the industry Britain was, in both 1912 and 1925, producing over 50 per cent of world tonnage. Only by 1935 was the relative position of the Japanese shipbuilding industry altered; in that year British yards launched more than a third of new tonnage while the Japanese produced some 8 per cent of the world's total.[46]

## 7 THE RAISING OF A RIVAL

The onset of the First World War effectively ended any job opportunities in Japan for British citizens as makers or operators of ships. The Japanese had supplanted them.

Indeed during the war years there was an astonishing expansion of the shipbuilding industry as everyone turned to Japan for supplies. As one scholar has noted:

> Between 1913 and 1918 the number of builders capable of producing ships over 1000 tons increased from 5 to 52, the number of yards from 6 to 57 (45 of them steel-using yards) the number of slipways from 17–57 . . . the number of workers from 26 000 to 95 000 and capitalisation from ¥15.5 million to ¥163 million.[47]

There were some problems, for the Japanese iron and steel industry could only supply about 50 per cent of industrial needs and machinery previously imported was no longer available. And yet great technological progress was made as reciprocal engines, turbines and boilers were made by Japanese in Japanese yards. The expansion of the industry was such that the Ship Encouragement Laws, in force since 1896, were suspended in 1917 and abolished in December 1919.

In naval matters the Imperial Japanese Navy's success at the Battle of the Sea of Japan, or Tsushima, in May 1905, had heralded a further change.[48] The Japanese satisfaction in their naval triumph ushered in a new era although they were at pains to keep on good terms with their British allies.[49] Notwithstanding such expressions of cordiality the roles had changed. No longer could the Imperial Japanese Navy be considered as pupils. After May 1905, officers of the Imperial Japanese Navy had successful battle experience which officers of the Royal Navy could not match.

The positive steps which the British had taken to raise a rival in Japan may have been inevitable but they did not go unnoticed. There was a sharp exchange during the discussion in May 1895 following Francis Elgar's lecture on 'Japanese Shipping' to the Japan Society of London. Mr Martell, chief surveyor of Lloyd's Register, remarked that 'eventually we should have in Japan a difficult competitor'. He added that at the present time they were laying thesmelves out, not only to build ships of their own but to build ships for the world . . . he knew that at the present time they were organising an enormous shipbuilding establishment and an enormous steel manufacturing works. He had been told that a ship of some 3000 to 4000 tons could be built in Japan for something like £4000 less than the amount for which we could produce such a ship in this country. Sir E. J. Reed, himself a naval ship-designer who had been in Japan in 1879 and who took a keen interest in Japanese progress in shipbuilding, was irritated by Martell's publicising the possible differential between

Japanese and British production costs. The chairman, His Excellency Takaaki Kato, the Japanese Minister in London, must have listened to this exchange with some interest, especially as Captain Inglis who had been naval adviser to the Imperial Japanese Navy (see Section 2 above) agreed with Mr Martell that 'we had better beware of Japan'. In closing the discussion His Excellency thanked Dr Elgar 'for the sympathetic way he had dealt with the aspirations of the Japanese people'.[50]

But how could the British have done other than assist the Japanese? Had the British declined their aid then the French, the Germans or the Americans would have stepped in gladly. In any case it was inconceivable that the British government, imbued with Gladstonian liberal non-interventionist values, could ever have considered hindering those of its citizens who chose to work in Japan. And of course until, say 1890, it never entered anyone's head that the Japanese might become effective rivals.

Despite the irrevocable changes which had taken place, George Curzon, later Viceroy of India and Foreign Secretary, had no doubts when in 1899 he wrote 'Friendly relations between ourselves and Japan will assist her in that mercantile and industrial development in which she is following in our own footsteps, at the same time that it will confirm to us the continued command of the ocean routes.'[51] Curzon's views would have been echoed by virtually every patriotic citizen.

# 5 Educators for Engineers

## 1 'HONOURABLE FOREIGN EMPLOYEES'

During the 1850s, before the Restoration, the government, despite its exclusionist policies, was hiring some foreign teachers. The Japanese were anxious to improve their own defences and hoped to learn more of military subjects in Nagasaki through the medium of *Rangaku* or Dutch studies.[1] After 1868 foreign instructors were hired in large numbers to teach many subjects including English, mathematics, physics, chemistry and engineering. The specialists were called *oyatoi gaikokujin* or 'honourable foreign employees', and were generally referred to as '*oyatoi*'. They brought expertise, enthusiasm and youth; but the princely salaries which they were paid became a great drain on Japanese resources. As one observer notes, 'The salaries of the *oyatoi gaikokujin* employed by the University of Tokyo in 1877 made up as much as one-third of the entire budget of the Ministry of Education, a financial burden that hastened the replacement of the *oyatoi gaikokujin* by Japanese in government institutions.'[2]

Although English became the first foreign language for many, other Japanese students learnt German or French. Necessity forced Japanese students to become competent in the foreign language, for without good understanding little advantage could be taken of the teaching by foreign masters.[3] German was and remained important for those studying science and medicine.[4] The foreign teachers at the Imperial College of Engineering taught in English. Most of these men were lecturing on scientific and technical subjects. The Japanese insistence on basic science teaching indicated an awareness that the new industrial processes required managers well-grounded in science.[5]

When the University of Tokyo was first established in 1877, by incorporating elements of various other older colleagues,[6] it had had four faculties, law, medicine, literature and science. From 1886, under the Imperial University Ordinance, the University of Tokyo, designated *Teikoku Daigaku*, or Imperial University, became the most important educational institution in Japan. In the same year the *Kobu Dai Gakko*, School of Engineering, hitherto the responsibility of the Ministry of Works, lost its independent status and became a fifth faculty, that of Engineering in the University. The existence of a

Faculty of Engineering so early is remarkable; in Western universities such developments were consistently blocked by the old guard of the *Senatus Academicus*.[7] It was in the field of engineering that the British with 78 per cent of the imported teachers, were pre-eminent. It is with the role of these men as educators that this chapter is concerned.

## 2 THE IMPERIAL UNIVERSITY OF TOKYO

The list of fifteen Professors in the Science Faculty of the University of Tokyo in 1877 included five Americans, three French, two Germans and two Britons as well as three Japanese. The Japanese were Dairoku Kikuchi, Pure and Applied Mathematics; Ryokichi Yatabe, Botany, and Imai Iwao, Metallurgy and German. The two British were Robert H. Smith, Mechanical Engineering, and Robert W. Atkinson, Analytic and Applied Chemistry.

Robert Henry Smith (1851–1914)[8] was the first Professor of Engineering to be responsible for the organisation of the whole Engineering Department of the College, as Smith himself reported, 'to the great satisfaction of the Principal, Yoshinari Hatakayama'. In 1874, as Smith explained, 'on the recommendation of Professor Fleeming Jenkin and others, I was selected by Professor Williamson, of University College, London, on behalf of the Japanese government for the post of Professor of Civil and Mechanical Engineering in the Imperial College in Tokyo, Japan . . . I had to organise the whole course of engineering instruction in the University.'[9] Smith served from 1874 to 1878 when he returned home, later becoming Professor of Engineering at Birmingham.

Robert William Atkinson (1850–1929) was the first Professor of Chemistry in the University of Tokyo who took up his appointment in 1874 and remained in Japan for some seven years. Although born and brought up in Newcastle upon Tyne he received his advanced education in London, first at University College School and then at the Royal College of Chemistry and the Royal School of Mines. He graduated BSc in 1872 and was assistant to Professor Williamson who no doubt recommended him for his Tokyo appointment.[10] He was elected a Fellow of the Chemical Society in 1872 before his departure for Japan and a Fellow of the Institute of Chemistry in 1878 during his time in Japan.[11]

James Alfred Ewing (later Sir Alfred) (1855–1935) arrived in

Japan in 1878, as successor to Smith, and served as Professor of Mechanical Engineering until 1883. The College at this time had some 200 students all told, although Ewing's class of sixteen was relatively small. But they were 'a happy family, singularly intelligent and pleasant, courteous, attentive and capable of receiving anything and everything their professor was able to impart'. Ewing lectured on mechanical engineering and thermodynamics to engineering students, and mechanics, electricity and magnetism to physics students, instilling into the minds of his students, 'the discoveries of Thomson (Kelvin), Joule, Carnot and Watt'.[12] In 1883 Ewing returned to Scotland to take up the Chair of Engineering at the newly established Dundee University College although in 1890 he was successful in his application for the Chair of Engineering in the University of Cambridge (see Chapter 9, Section 5 below).[13]

Ewing was followed in Tokyo by another Edinburgh graduate, Cargill Gilston Knott (1856–1922) who in 1883 left his assistantship to the Professor of Natural Philosophy at the University of Edinburgh to become Professor of Physics in the University of Tokyo. In Japan he had undertaken the *Magnetic Survey of Japan* with Aikitsu Tanakadate (see Chapter 9, Section 6 below). For his work in Japan he was awarded the Order of the Rising Sun, fourth class. Knott remained in Tokyo until 1891 when he returned to Edinburgh as Reader in Natural Philosophy.[14] At the time that these men were serving in colleges of the University of Tokyo an even stronger British presence was established in the Imperial College of Engineering.

## 3 THE IMPERIAL COLLEGE OF ENGINEERING, 1873–86

The Imperial College of Engineering,[15] a privileged institution,[16] set up, organised and sustained by the Ministry of Public Works, was provided with first-class facilities making it a model of its kind. Its sponsors, men of the former *Choshu* clan, who had themselves travelled and studied in the West, appreciated the importance of the engineering profession in the developed world.

The generosity of the Ministry resulted in a remarkable college,[17] the building and equipment of which became one of the wonders of early *Meiji* Japan. Before teaching began in 1873 the British staff were involved in ordering materials and machinery and planning model laboratories and workshops. It was an extraordinary opportunity for the young British teachers on the threshold of their careers.

In 1873 as they prepared to receive their first intake of students they must have wondered about the generous provision in Japan and compared it with that in the United Kingdom where resources for technical and scientific education were so grudgingly given.

In the course of its independent existence, the College trained 211 men, many of whom, after graduation in Japan, proceeded to further education in the West. These, together with the graduates of the other two colleges, made up the engineering élite of *Meiji* Japan. They were chosen as students of ICE by competitive examination, 'for which all Japanese subjects are eligible who are under the age of 20, are of sound constitution, and can produce satisfactory testimonials of good moral character'.[18] Successful candidates were offered Government Exhibitions which covered fees; in return they were required after graduation to serve the government for seven years. In the event of there being a shortfall of government-sponsored students then the College could accept suitably qualified men as private students whose families paid 'seven *yen* monthly towards their expenses'.[19] The *Japan Punch* featured this famous College in 1874.

Though the foreign teaching staff employed at ICE were at the outset British, and, until 1881, there were no Japanese in senior teaching posts, ancillary and domestic positions in the residential college were always occupied by Japanese. Officials from the Ministry of Works filled supervisory roles. These college teachers appear to have been able to prepare their courses and teach without interference.

During the thirteen years of the College's independent existence there were two principals. Henry Dyer (1848–1918) opened the college as its first head in mid-1873 and remained until July 1882 when he returned to Glasgow. Edward Divers (1837–1912) Professor of Chemistry from 1873, took over as principal in 1881, and so remained until 1886 when the College as a separate unit disappeared.

Henry Dyer was an ideal choice,[20] for he combined the attributes of the practical engineer as well as the academically qualified technologist. He had served a full engineering apprenticeship, and so knew how to use his hands and how to function on the shop floor. His degrees of MA,[21] CE and BSc from the University of Glasgow marked a man broadly educated. The Glasgow MA required a facility in Latin and Greek as well as modern languages and philosophy; the Certificate of Proficiency in Engineering and the BSc covered a wide range of scientific and technical work.

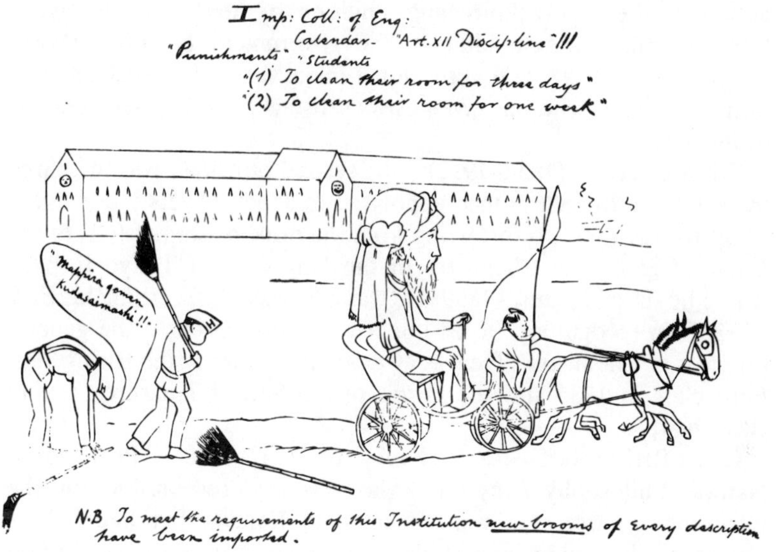


Henry Dyer, with his British colleagues the 'new brooms' at the Imperial College of Engineering, is featured being driven along in a small barouche while Japanese students, who disliked menial work, are despondently cleaning up.

*Cartoon* 5.1 Imperial College of Engineering (*Japan Punch*, June 1874)

Dyer, aged 25, responded with determination and resource to the challenge presented by the College. He negotiated with the Minister, consulted with the other British staff, organised the six-year course, introducing a 'sandwich' course which combined theory and practice as well as supervising the building and setting up of the workshops at Akabane where the necessary practical work was to be done. It would appear that he brought the best of Scottish education to Tokyo. His standards for both staff and students, requiring hard work and earnest application, were demanding, but then morale was high with both students and staff keen to do their utmost to justify the confidence placed in them.[22]

When Dyer left the College in July 1882 he received warm testimonials of appreciation. He was honoured by his Imperial Majesty the Emperor with the Order of the Rising Sun, third class. The Acting Minister of Public Works (A. Yoshikawa) referred in his address to the 'highly flourishing condition' of the ICE due to Dyer's 'utmost ability and assiduity'. The government accepted Dyer's resignation 'with regret that the government should lose such an able, faithful servant, who has given every satisfaction in the performance of his duty'.[23]

Edward Divers (1837–1912)[24] the second principal, was in charge from 1882 until 1886. Once appointed to Japan Divers made every effort to stay there, transferring from the principalship at ICE to the Chair of Inorganic Chemistry in the Unversity of Tokyo in 1886 where he remained until 1899. He was a fine scholar, earning his FRS in 1885 'in recognition of his important contribution to the general progress of Chemistry'. He was awarded the Order of the Rising Sun, third class in 1886 and the Order of the Sacred Treasure, second class, in 1898.

Other British staff were: W. E. Ayrton (1847–1908),[25] Professor of Natural Philosophy (physics), who was also responsible for the telegraphy course. He was educated in London but had held a one-year scholarship as a student of Kelvin's at Glasgow. Ayrton arrived in 1873 and remained at the College until 1878 when he returned to London. David H. Marshall, MA (Edinburgh 1869) Professor of Mathematics, also served as Professor of Natural Philosophy for a time after 1879, although he too left the college in March 1881. Edmund F. Mundy was Professor of Engineering and Technical Drawing. William Barr, AINA (Associate of the Institute of Naval Architects) succeeded Mundy in June 1878.

*Table* 5.1 Staff at the Imperial College of Engineering, Tokyo, in 1873 and 1881

| | *1873* | *1881* |
|---|---|---|
| Minister of Public Works | YAMAO Yozo | YAMAO Yozo |
| Principal | Henry Dyer, MA, CE, BSc, Glasgow | Henry Dyer |
| *General and Scientific Course* | | |
| Professor of Natural Philosophy | W. E. Ayrton, London and Glasgow | |
| Professor of Mathematics | David H. Marshall, Edinburgh | |
| Professor of Chemistry | Edward Divers, MD | Edward Divers, MD, FCS, FIC (Assistant – NAKASHIMA Katsumasa) |
| Professor of Drawing | Edmund F. Mundy, ARSM, London | SUGI Koichiro, Edinburgh |

*Table* 5.1 Continued

| | *1873* | *1881* |
|---|---|---|
| Professor of English Language and Literature and Secretary to the College | William Craigie, MA, Aberdeen | James Main Dixon, MA, St Andrews (Assistant Secretary – INOMATA Masatake) |
| Instructors in Natural, Philosophy and Mathematics | | ‡FUJIOKA Ichisuke, ME; NAKANO Hatsun, ME; ‡ASANO Osuke, ME |
| Instructors in Chemistry | | KOIDE Hidemasa; ‡NAKAMURA Teikichi; ‡KAWAKITA Michitada, ME; ‡HAGA Tamehasa |
| Modeller | Archibald King | |
| General Assistants | George Cawley; Robert Clark | |
| *Technical Course* | | |
| Professor of Civil and Mechanical Engineering | | Henry Dyer, MA, CE, BSc, Glasgow |
| Assistant Professor Engineering | | Thomas Alexander, CE, Glasgow |
| Instructor, Civil Engineering and Surveying | | ‡TSUJIMURA Yokichi |
| Instructor, Mechanical Engineering | | ‡HARADA Torazo; MANO, Bunji |
| Professor Technical Drawing | | SUGI Koichiro, Edinburgh |
| Instructors, Telegraph Engineering | | See Instructors, Natural Philosophy and Mathematics |
| Professor of Architecture | | Josiah Conder, ARIBA |
| Professor of Practical and Applied Chemistry | | Edward Divers |
| Professor of Mineralogy, Geology and Mining | | John Milne, FGS |
| Instructor of Mineralogy | | NAKANO Toshiwo |
| Instructor of Mining | | ‡KUWABARA Masa, ME |
| *Practical Course* | | |
| Workshop Foreman | | George Samuel Brindley and Instructors of Technical Course who also work in Practical Course |

Those marked ‡ were graduates of ICE

*Source*: Compiled from *Historical Materials on the Imperial College of Engineering* and Annual Reports of ICE.

*Table* 5.2 British Staff at the Imperial College of Engineering, 1873–85

| *Name* | *Duty in College and subject taught* | *Salary per month* ¥ | *Date of taking up appointment* | *Date of leaving Japanese service* | *Length of service* |
|---|---|---|---|---|---|
| 1. Dyer, Henry | Dean, Engineering | 660 | 3. 6.1873 | 1. 6.1882 | 9 years |
| 2. Divers, Edward‡ | Dean, Chemistry | 500 | 1. 7.1873 | ?. 7.1885 | 12 years |
| 3. Ayrton, W. E. | Physics, Telegraphy | 500 | 30. 6.1873 | 29. 6.1878 | 5 years |
| 4. Milne, John‡ | Geology | 350 | 8. 3.1876 | ?.12.1885 | 9 years 9 months |
| 5. Marshall, David H. | Physics | 350 | 3. 6.1873 | 26. 3.1881 | 7 years 9 months |
| 6. Brinkley, Frank | Mathematics | 350 | 1. 7.1878 | 31.12.1880 | 1 year 6 months |
| 7. Conder, Joseph | Architecture | 350 | 28. 1.1877 | 28. 1.1882 | 5 years |
| 8. Alexander T.‡ | Civil Engineering | 350 | 19. 3.1878 | ?.12.1885 | 7 years 9 months |
| 9. Thomson, A. W. | ,, ,, | 234 | 4. 8.1878 | 30. 6.1881 | 2 years 10 months |
| 10. Perry, John | ,, ,, | 333 | 9. 9.1875 | 31. 3.1879 | 3 years 6 months |
| 11. West, Charles D.‡ | Engineering | 350 | 16. 8.1882 | ?.12.1885 | 3 years 4 months |
| 12. Angus, W. M. | ,, | 234 | 4. 8.1878 | 30. 9.1881 | 3 years 1 month |
| 13. Cawley, George | ,, | 200 | 19. 6.1873 | 18. 6.1878 | 5 years |
| 14. Dixon, J. M.‡ | English | 300 | 1. 1.1880 | ?.12.1885 | 5 years |
| 15. Dixon, W. G. | ,, | 250 | 20. 8.1876 | 31.12.1879 | 3 years 4 months |

| | | | | | |
|---|---|---|---|---|---|
| 16. Craigie, William | English | 208 | 1. 7.1873 | 29. 2.1876 | 2 years 7 months |
| 17. Brindley, G. S. | Superintendent of Engineering Workshop, Akabane | 230 | 14.12.1875 | ?. 6.1881 | 5 years 6 months |
| 18. Gray, Thomas | Telegraphy | 234 | 5.10.1878 | 3. 6.1881 | 2 years 8 months |
| 19. Mondy, Edmund F. | Drawing | 208 | 1. 7.1873 | 30. 6.1878 | 5 years |
| 20. Barr, W. | ,, | 234 | 4. 8.1878 | 30. 6.1881 | 2 years 10 months |
| 21. Clark, Robert | ,, | 150 | 19. 6.1873 | 18. 9.1878 | 5 years 3 months |
| 22. King, Archibald | Model-making | 141 | 3. 6.1873 | 18. 6.1875 | 2 years |
| 23. Jones, R. D. Rymer | Surveying, Preliminary Course | 250 | 1. 7.1874 | 30. 4.1877 | 2 years 10 months |
| 24. Hamilton, G. | Preliminary Course | 250 | 1. 7.1874 | 30. 4.1877 | 2 years 10 months |
| 25. Sandeman, F. | ,, ,, | 130 | 20. 1.1874 | 30.11.1874 | 10 months |
| 26. George, | ,, ,, | 130 | 5. 2.1874 | 30. 6.1874 | 5 months |
| 27. Luckden, ? | ,, ,, | 130 | 1.12.1874 | 30. 4.1877 | 3 years 5 months |
| 28. MacRae, | ,, ,, | 130 | 11. 1.1875 | 30. 6.1877 | 2 years 5 months |

‡ were re-employed later by the Ministry of Education

*Source*: Tokyo University (ed.) *Historical Materials on the Imperial College of Engineering, 1871–1886* (Tokyo 1931) pp. 353 and 354; H. J. Jones, 'The Meiji Government and Foreign Employees, 1868–1900' (PhD, Michigan, 1967) and *Live Machines, Hired Foreigners and Meiji Japan* (Tenterden, 1980).

Three further appointments, of a modeller and two general assistants, were made in the persons of Archibald King, George Cawley and Robert Clark.

The teaching of English was undertaken by William Craigie, MA (Aberdeen) who was also Secretary to the College.[26] His successor was William Gray Dixon, MA (Glasgow),[27] who after some three years service, gave place to his brother James Main Dixon, MA (St Andrews).[28] J. M. Dixon remained in Tokyo for some thirteen years and (after the transfer of ICE) served in the University of Tokyo.

For the first two or three years the College staff did not change, but in 1876 there were developments, for Dyer, originally appointed as Principal and Professor of Engineering, was able to recruit John Perry as Professor of Civil and Mechanical Engineering.[29] In the same year John Milne (1850–1913),[30] Fellow of the Geological Society (FGS), and formerly of King's College and Royal School of Mines, London, was appointed Professor of Geology and Mining. Milne was to become 'the father of modern seismology'. For his work on earthquakes in Japan he was appointed FRS in 1887. Josiah Conder (Soane Medallist of the Royal Institute of British Architects) arrived in 1877 to teach Architecture. He was to make Japan his permanent home. In bringing Western Architecture to Japan, he won an honoured place among Japanese architects (see Chapter 14, Section 4 below). All in all, the College attracted a powerful team. Three of the six original professors (including Dyer) were Scots educated solely in Scotland.

It was College and Ministry policy to appoint Japanese to senior posts as and when qualified men became available (see Table 5.1). Although Japanese were teaching as subordinates in several departments, no senior appointment was made of a Japanese, until 1881, when Koichiro Sugi became Professor of Engineering Drawing. He had served a long apprenticeship. In 1873 he had travelled with the Iwakura Mission until they reached Edinburgh, where he remained studying at the University under Professor Fleeming Jenkin.[31] On his return to Japan in 1876 he became assistant to Edmund Mundy, and then to William Barr, from whom he took over on the latter's departure from Japan in June 1881. The staff lists of the College show a steady filling of posts by Japanese nationals, although new appointees from Britain (see Table 5.2 for British staff) were still arriving for senior posts.

Thomas Alexander (CE Glasgow)[32] became an Assistant Professor of Engineering in 1878 and then Professor in 1879. Arthur Watson

Thomson succeeded as assistant.[33] Thomas Gray (CE Glasgow)[34] came as instructor in Telegraph Engineering in 1878. After Ayrton's departure in June 1878 David Marshall taught physics and mathematics until he left in March 1881. The College was waiting for Rinzaburo Shida who, having graduated brilliantly from ICE in 1879, was in Glasgow under Kelvin from 1881 to 1883. He was appointed to the Chair of Natural Philosophy on his return.

Every member of staff had heavy teaching duties, covering a wide range of courses. In many cases classes required extensive preparations of the practical demonstrations and laboratory experiments judged necessary for a successful presentation. Staff were also heavily burdened by administrative and other duties.[35] Nothwithstanding the work-load the young professors undertook their various tasks with relish. Students were to work for six years before graduating, progressing through three units of two years each. As Dyer explained 'The whole course of training may be thus divided (1) The general and scientific course – taught during the first and second years; (2) The technical course – taught during the third and fourth years; (3) The practical class – taught during the fifth and sixth years.'

The first- and second-year courses which all students attended included, English (language and composition), geography, elementary mathematics, elementary mechanics (theoretical and applied), elementary physics, chemistry, and drawing (geometrical and mechanical).[36]

At the beginning of the third year each student chose to specialise in one of six options – civil engineering; mechanical engineering; telegraph engineering; architecture; chemistry and metallurgy, and mining engineering. At this stage theory and practice were roughly equally divided. The final two years were to be devoted entirely to practical work, although special lectures as well as examinations were also organised in the College. The British staff believed that they could create in Tokyo the ideal College of Engineering balancing theoretical teaching and practical experience, laboratory experimentation and workship practice.

As the language of communication between teachers and taught was English,[37] considerable thought was given to the presentation of the subject in the College. The entrance exam, written in English, was designed to ensure a certain competence among the students. Efforts were made to build on this base as effectively as possible.[38] Exercises in dictation, short essays, and other writing exercises as well as 'a careful course in grammatical analysis' were part of the course. The organisation of the English course certainly suggests the development of a culture pattern very different from that to which students were formerly accustomed.

Under the heading of drawing courses, technical drawing as well as plane and solid geometry were demonstrated. Mathematics included studies of algebra, trigonometry and mechanics. Natural philosophy covered a wide range of subjects including dynamics, kinetics, hydrostatics, optics, magnetism and electricity. Chemistry was taught as an elementary course to second-year students and a theoretical elementary mechanics course was also included. These two years of theoretical study provided the first third of the six-year course, making heavy demands on staff and students alike. The second part of the course covering years three and four involved laboratory work while the final two years were intended to be spent in practical work, giving substance to the theory which students had learnt during the previous four years. The provision of the required practical work in the 1870s in Japan, which had no laboratories, or modern foundries, workshops or shipyards posed its own problems. These were solved by some remarkable provision.

## 4 'A MARVELLOUS LABORATORY'

In the early 1870s when the Imperial College of Engineering was set up, the developed world needed to train engineers and scientists in laboratories where scientific and engineering experiments could be demonstrated. Such experimental work was very expensive demanding investment in properly developed space, equipment and manpower far in excess of the usual provision of a classroom for the teacher.

In the Western world money for properly equipped laboratories was rarely available. Until the University of Glasgow moved in 1870 from its medieval central city site to the more spacious Gilmorehill location, Kelvin claimed to do his experimental work in a coal-cellar. The young professors at ICE, in Japan in the 1870s, asked for laboratory facilities for their students. By and large their Japanese employers provided what they wanted.

The students used laboratories during the third and fourth year of study. The provision originally could accommodate between forty and fifty students. Professor Divers so organised the work that the chemistry laboratories were shared between third-year students of mining and telegraphy and fourth-year students of applied chemistry and metallurgy. As Professor Divers reported 'all necessary apparatus and chemicals being supplied by the College to the students, free of cost, with each student having the exclusive use of a complete set of them'.[39] In addition the General Drawing Office and the Architectural Drawing Office were available for trainee engineers and architects.

But it was William Ayrton's laboratories for the teaching of Natural Philosophy which aroused the most surprise and admiration.[40] As John Perry explained:

> When I arrived in Japan in 1875, I found a marvellous laboratory, such as the world had not seen elsewhere. At Glasgow, at Cambridge, and at Berlin, there were three great personalities; the laboratories of Kelvin, and of Maxwell, and of Helmholtz, however were not to be mentioned in comparison with Ayrton. Fine buildings, splendid apparatus, well-chosen, a never-resting-keen-eyed chief of great originality: these are what I found in Japan.[41]

Laboratories[42] were of great value but engineers needed more. Because there were in Japan no modern factories, workshops or shipyards yet further provision was made.

## 5 THE AKABANE ENGINEERING WORKS

The Ministry of Public Works made a major commitment to the provision of engineering workshops,[43] built on a site separate from the college, at Akabane,[44] to service the department of Public Works. These were initially attached to the college and under Dyer's personal direction. The Ministry was generous with finance; British and Japanese staff and the students themselves contributed much effort to the Works.[45]

The engineering workshops were to play an increasing role in the establishment of engineering industries in Japan. In later years they were transferred to the navy. But in the early years as an adjunct of the College they had several very important functions. They enabled the College students to have practical workshop training, and they also housed large numbers of workmen and apprentices, who were to become the nucleus of a new generation of technician engineers in Japan. Once the workshops were fully operational it would appear that between 320 (in 1876) and 370 (1884) 'workmen and apprentices' were being trained.[46]

For Dyer at Akabane these were the golden years. In 1881 an illustrated catalogue was produced under the title of *Akabane Engineering Works*.[47] It featured a large number of engines, including steam engines, marine engines, locomotive boilers, pumps of various kinds, fire engines, cranes, sugar-cane-crushing mills and many mechanical engineering tools, as well as ironwork and ornamental railings and gates.

The catalogue contains descriptions of each machine in Japanese and English together with a scale drawing of the machine. The book is similar to many such produced by manufacturing engineers and their agents in the Western world to illustrate what was available. The catalogue, perhaps prepared by Brindley,[48] the workshop superintendent, on Dyer's instructions, was a demonstration of the range of machinery which could be used. It is not suggested that all these machines could be made at the Akabane works although in the case of a number of items this claim was made.[49]

Japanese sources report 'The Workshops ceased to operate in March 1880.'[50] Times were changing, the Ministry of Public Works was being urged to hand over the College to the Ministry of Education, *Mombusho*, which planned to make the college the Faculty of Engineering in the reorganised University of Tokyo. It was also felt that the Akabane Works should pass to other hands. From 1880 therefore, until the Akabane Works emerged, as they eventually did, as 'the Ordnance Department of the Navy', there was an interregnum, a period of uncertainty and indecision. Although as far as is known the reorganisation at Akabane did not affect the students in the College.

## 6 JAPANESE STUDENTS

It is instructive to look at the map which shows the places of origin of the students at the ICE in 1877. For, with the exception of the north-east (*Tohoku*) of mainland Japan where the pro-*Bakufu* domains had been thoroughly beaten in the 1868 struggle for power, the men were drawn from all areas. There were many students, as would be expected, from *Satsuma* and *Choshu* areas. Both Yamaguchi, formerly *Choshu*, and Mitsuma (*Uwajima*) were headed by forward-looking *samurai* leaders. But there was a strong cohort also from Tokyo, Shizuoka and Okitama, formerly bases of the Shogunate guards. It seems likely that these men, or rather their sons, applied for places at ICE believing the way forward lay in becoming technocrats under the new regime. Students from Miye and Tsuniga, also well-represented in the College, from formerly *fudai* clans, would probably feel the same.[51]

The students at ICE or other advanced Colleges were for the most part of the *samurai* class although one professor commented that the students included 'a few *Kawazoku* (*sic*) or nobles, one being the son of an ex-*Kuge*, and two or three the sons of ex-*Daimyos*, and a considerable number were of the *Heimin* or commonality'.[52] This generation of aspiring engineers and scientists had all received the early traditional education of a *samurai*, consisting of some seven years training in the Chinese Confucian classical texts, an education devoted to learning by rote, which was intended to induce strict physical and mental self-control. Military training normally began later at the age of 11 or 13 years. Even senior students to whom the classical texts were 'explained' received only dogmatic assertions. Debate or interruption by the student was not encouraged. Subjects such as writing Japanese or doing arithmetic were considered matters for merchants rather than *samurai*.

On top of this traditional training came Western education, emphasising practical utility and staying silent on any moral stance. Not only that but everything which the West taught, and for which the government were paying, was delivered to the Japanese student in English. Soseki Natsume elaborated this point writing 'It would be more accurate to say that in my student days we had to learn everything in English rather than to say that we learned English for so many hours.'[53]

The stresses to which these Japanese students were subjected in the early *Meiji* years is well illustrated in the case of Aikitsu Tanakadate, who ultimately became one of Japan's first distinguished physicists, but who in his youth still hankered after traditional learning and was bewildered by the thrust of Western education.[54]

Most of the students who first applied to ICE were sons of army or navy officers or of government officials. Students who were accepted, after guarantee by two sponsors, were supported by the government so that some fathers, alive to coming changes, could place their sons satisfactorily.[55] It was initially difficult to fill the college places. The entrance exam, entirely in the Western idiom, included papers on reading in English; writing to dictation; arithmetic; elementary

*Map* 5.1a Movements of students from place of origin to Tokyo to attend the Imperial College of Engineering, 1872–86

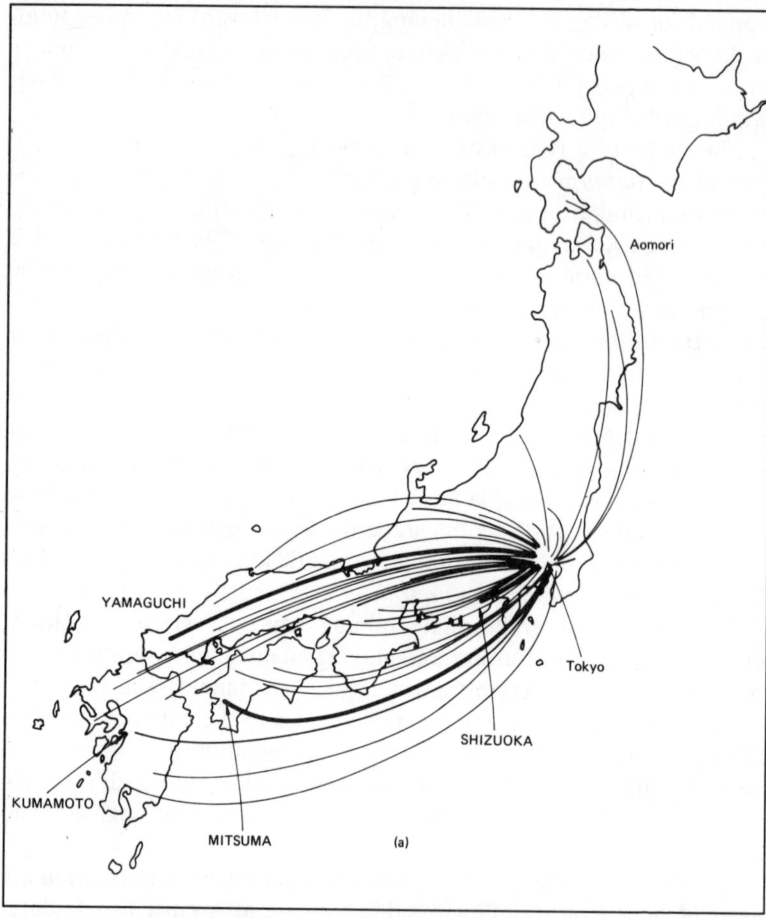


geometry; elementary algebra; geography, and rudimentary physics. In 1874, when teaching had been going on for one year, the College reported that 'the examination in these subjects, will, for a session or two, be of the most elementary kind, but the standard of admission will be raised year by year, till it attains that of European schools'.[56] The college itself instituted a preparatory school in an attempt to prepare young men for the college entrance exam.

The staff had nothing but praise for the 'respectful demeanour' and 'earnest attention' of the students. Indeed the students were believed to be consistently overworking.[57] Professor Ayrton, who taught

*Map* 5.1b Place of origin of students who attended the Imperial College of Engineering in Tokyo, 1873–86.

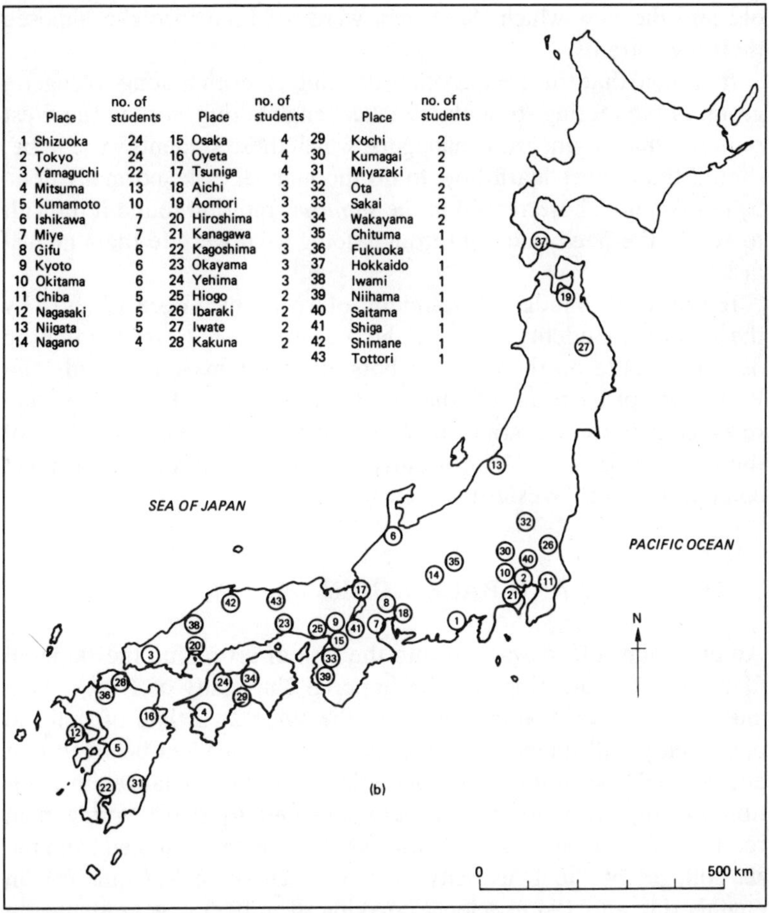


| | Place | no. of students | | Place | no. of students | | Place | no. of students |
|---|---|---|---|---|---|---|---|---|
| 1 | Shizuoka | 24 | 15 | Osaka | 4 | 29 | Kŏchi | 2 |
| 2 | Tokyo | 24 | 16 | Oyeta | 4 | 30 | Kumagai | 2 |
| 3 | Yamaguchi | 22 | 17 | Tsuniga | 4 | 31 | Miyazaki | 2 |
| 4 | Mitsuma | 13 | 18 | Aichi | 3 | 32 | Ota | 2 |
| 5 | Kumamoto | 10 | 19 | Aomori | 3 | 33 | Sakai | 2 |
| 6 | Ishikawa | 7 | 20 | Hiroshima | 3 | 34 | Wakayama | 2 |
| 7 | Miye | 7 | 21 | Kanagawa | 3 | 35 | Chituma | 1 |
| 8 | Gifu | 6 | 22 | Kagoshima | 3 | 36 | Fukuoka | 1 |
| 9 | Kyoto | 6 | 23 | Okayama | 3 | 37 | Hokkaido | 1 |
| 10 | Okitama | 6 | 24 | Yehima | 3 | 38 | Iwami | 1 |
| 11 | Chiba | 5 | 25 | Hiogo | 2 | 39 | Niihama | 1 |
| 12 | Nagasaki | 5 | 26 | Ibaraki | 2 | 40 | Saitama | 1 |
| 13 | Niigata | 5 | 27 | Iwate | 2 | 41 | Shiga | 1 |
| 14 | Nagano | 4 | 28 | Kakuna | 2 | 42 | Shimane | 1 |
| | | | | | | 43 | Tottori | 1 |

natural philosophy at the College from its opening until 1878, was also full of praise, commenting that his Japanese students were 'much quieter in their manner, more earnest in their studies and have greater application' than those of the West. But he also sounded a note of caution, observing that 'the Japanese boy labours under the disadvantage that he is not observant . . . all his knowledge is formal knowledge as learnt in class, and he is comparatively ignorant of any information that he has not acquired from set lessons'.[58] Ayrton's sensitivity to the responses of his Japanese students is a reminder of the enormous leap which his students were required to make, living as they did in a pre-industrial world without those machines which were part of everyday life in the West. The compromises between the old and the new which these men were required to make imposed their own strains.

It is clear that there were other difficulties, even among so eager a group of pioneering students. Practical engineering work in the West required that engineering managers, which these students were to be, should themselves learn how to do the manual tasks normally done by craftsmen. Those reared in the *samurai* tradition found it difficult to accept the need to learn through doing what were to them menial tasks.

It is difficult to judge the standards of work which were achieved by the Japanese students. Some of the best were able to respond to the demands made on them by teachers like William Ayrton and John Perry. A proportion of the graduates from ICE subsequently received government grants to study further in the West. The best of these won prizes in Western universities where they were in direct competition with Western students.

## 7 TO TOKYO AND BACK AGAIN

An enormous effort was put into the task of setting up the Imperial College of Engineering and the Imperial University of Tokyo. Men and resources were imported from the West at a time of political uncertainty and financial stringency, for *Meiji* leaders believed that educational institutions were necessary engines of change. In addition prestigious scholarships were awarded to those young men recruited for college places. Until 1900, 3126 men graduated from the six colleges of the University of Tokyo. Of these 817 qualified in engineering and 194 in science, making over 1000 new graduates in these fields.[59]

Students were increasingly taught by Japanese staff. From 1880 qualified Japanese staff replaced their foreign colleagues. By 1892 foreign teachers – vital in 1872 – had almost disappeared. Most of them had wished to return home after a period of duty in Tokyo. Few of those who served in Japan were unaffected by their experience.

The Western professors had had the experience of establishing in Tokyo at the Imperial College of Engineering a model college. There was nothing like it in Britain where most young men, intent on engineering as a profession, entered into pupillage, for which they paid a practising engineer, and trained on the job over several years.[60] In Britain and Europe, University senates resisted the idea of technical education as a proper subject for the University, although there were a number of engineering courses – becoming increasingly popular – which could lead to a degree qualification.[61]

Some of the professors who had helped to set up engineering education in Tokyo were keen to establish reverse culture transfer and bring the best of Japanese practice back to Britain. As one commentator has noted 'the shared Japanese experience of Ayrton and Perry was a necessary condition for the success of the Finsbury College venture'.[62] But Finsbury was the blueprint for local technical colleges founded in the 1880s and 1890s. It must therefore be accepted that the wave of broader technical education in the United Kingdom in the late nineteenth century owed not a little to the extraordinary experiment at ICE in Tokyo in the 1870s and 1880s.

It is fortunate therefore, in the light of what happened in Britain which can perhaps be attributed to developments in Tokyo, that the Japanese never argued, given the elementary skills of the students and the limited finance then available, that teaching at a simpler level, with less elaborate equipment would have been adequate. The allocation of generous funds to a college such as ICE placed a severe strain on the Japanese economy. Does the esteem with which engineers in Japan are now regarded reflect the high status of the original foreigners in engineering education? In quantitative terms foreigners played but a minor role in *Meiji* developmental achievement. Nevertheless from this relationship between Western engineering teacher and Japanese engineering student came a fruitful interaction that was critical in Japan's transformation from a feudal, rural economy to one of industry and urbanisation.[63] It is remarkable that so coherent and calculated a response should have been possible. That this was so reflects an appreciation of education, for as everyone had been told in the proclamation of July 1872 'Learning is the key to success in life, and no man can afford to neglect it.'[64]

# 6 British Life in Japan

## 1 TREATY PORT FOREIGNERS

The Britons who sought to make a life for themselves in newly opened Japan attempted as far as possible to establish conditions of living similar to those which they had enjoyed at home. The foreign communities included men of many Western nationalities who sought to create in Japan replicas of the middle class societies in which they had been raised.[1] Many professions and a wide variety of business interests were represented. At the core of the foreign settlements were the commercial men of all ranks who either worked for themselves or for their compatriots.[2] They had come to Japan to further their career prospects, and perhaps for adventure, but they concentrated as far as possible in recreating familiar mores and customs in their new settlements. The missionaries, another identifiable group, lived alongside their merchant neighbours, endeavouring to uphold Christian morals and standards.[3] Those foreign experts who were employed by the Japanese government on short-term contracts were another cadre who lived in tied houses at their place of work, outside the treaty port, but they relied on their compatriots in the foreign settlements for some of their social life. The corps of consuls and diplomats had their own shared concerns and as national representatives commanded a high status. The British Minister and his lady dominated the social scene.

After 1868, armed with a special licence, foreigners could live in the 'open cities', Tokyo and Osaka.[4,5] Some diplomats and missionaries lived in the cities, especially Tokyo, where the Japanese government designated the area of Tsukiji for foreigners' use although Yokohama remained the centre of European and American life. Of Tsukiji, more later.

Europeans in the foreign settlement enjoyed comfortable lives and many may have achieved a higher standard of living in Japan than they could have commanded at home. All had Japanese servants. This master and servant relationship was of course usual elsewhere for British expatriates and was considered normal by them in Japan. But such relationships coloured attitudes; to them the Japanese were not colleagues and equals but 'natives' and subservient. There can be no doubt, as one scholar has noted, that 'treaty port residents might be imperialists without anybody to rule over, but they were nevertheless imperialists for all that'.[6]

At the professional level relationships with the Japanese varied. Those British who were employed by the Japanese, perforce worked closely with them. Relationships were sometimes cordial and sometimes strained. Missionaries could only convert to Christianity those Japanese with whom they had had good personal relationships. Some preferred to minister to the converted in the less demanding atmosphere of the treaty ports. Merchants found doing business with the Japanese difficult for the Japanese code of behaviour seemed different from that of the Westerners. Neither side came out of the early exchanges with credit. In Yokohama the foreigners met 'a rather ramshackle collection of traders' but even a reputable British firm like Jardine's had to be cautioned against 'trying to sell worn-out ships' to the Japanese.[7] Foreign diplomats also found Japanese tactics frustrating, while the Japanese, resentful at the special rights which the foreigners commanded, believed in protecting themselves whenever possible.

Although the Japanese were initially curious about the aliens they remained wary and only a few got to know foreigners really well. Relationships depended on understanding which in turn depended on language. Few of the British could speak Japanese.[8] In time Japanese engineers and officials, many of whom had been partly educated in Britain or America, could speak English. But this did not dispose of the stand-off between the British and Japanese whose cultures and respective assumptions about each other, were often wide of the mark. But there were those, originally 'treaty port foreigners', and opportunists, who later contributed substantially to Japan's progress.[9]

It was in the treaty ports too that the newspaper, hitherto unknown in Japan, was developed. The expatriate communities reported all the activities of their members in the many, sometimes short-lived, English-language newspapers which circulated. These papers were a lifeline, keeping foreigners in touch not only with the affairs of the local community, but also with home and the world outside. If treaty port life was in general dull and isolated, then the newspapers brought a broader view. The first English-language newspaper was the *Nagasaki Shipping List and Advertiser* which appeared on 22 June 1861; when the owner transferred almost at once to Yokohama he transformed his paper into the *Japan Herald* which appeared from 23 November 1861.[10]

The foreign settlements at Nagasaki, Yokohama and Kobe differed widely in character.[11] Nagasaki, having housed the tiny Dutch settlement on Deshima, had a long history of foreign contact: even now the Onchiku Festival features 'Hollanders', men dressed as Dutchmen, and one of the 'props' on these occasions is a bale of tartan cloth. Yokohama, a purpose-built treaty port, created for and by the foreigners grew rapidly as facilities improved and trade increased. Kobe, which acted as an outpost for Osaka and the old capital Kyoto, did not open until 1868 and thereafter flourished, but could not rival Yokohama.

## 2 HOME FROM HOME AT NAGASAKI, YOKOHAMA, KOBE AND TSUKIJI

Nagasaki offered a welcome landfall for those who came to Japan from the climatic extremes of the China Coast. Captain Sherard Osborn, who brought Lord Elgin to Japan in 1858, was effusive about its setting.[12] But Nagasaki had advantages other than those of position and climate. For there, especially in the heady years between 1859 and 1868, the cultures of the East and West met in a more meaningful way than elsewhere. The buccaneering spirit of the British merchant keen to exploit any chance for trade was stimulated by Japanese opportunists in Nagasaki. Despite government laws the region's *daimyos* were willing to trade through their own representatives. Many of the *samurai* who staffed the clan offices in Nagasaki were young, high-ranking officials, and eager business partners, who later came to prominence under the new regime.

After the Restoration foreigners in Nagasaki continued to enjoy friendly relations with their hosts. As became good citizens they illuminated their settlement, in 1872, during a visit of the Emperor, and in 1887 organised a joint reception of themselves and Japanese on the occasion of 'Minister-President Ito's' visit.[13]

Nagasaki continued to be home for some 250–300 Westerners. If Chinese are included there were probably some 1000 aliens in residence. The Westerners lived on the hill, at South Bluff (*Yamate Minami*) or East Bluff (*Yamate Higashi*) overlooking the harbour, with fine views of the port below and the town clustered around it.[14]

By the 1870s, in commercial terms Nagasaki was losing ground. Its residents believed that this was the fault of the Japanese officials there.[15] Japanese officials may indeed have been trying to discourage country merchants from making their way to the foreign settlement but the fact remains that Nagasaki could not hope to maintain its earlier position. But it continued to be an important coaling station and one of the sights for those arriving in Nagasaki was that of the coal barges awaiting the docking ship.[16] Foreign workers employed at the shipyard swelled the ranks of the foreign community, especially after Mitsubishi had taken over.

Yokohama presented a welcoming sight for the foreigners as they arrived by sea as they saw 'the pleasant town of Yokohama with its long line of European-looking buildings extending along the sea-front and its charming residences high upon the Bluff on our left'.[17] But although Yokohama soon became the largest treaty port relations between the Japanese and the foreigners there were rarely cordial. The row over the substitution of Yokohama as treaty port instead of Kanagawa rankled and mutual distrust was hard to eradicate.[18] Japanese sensitivity over the proximity of Yokohama to Tokyo provoked foreign diplomats although many persisted in behaving as if they were colonial rulers. Foreign banks refused to cash cheques presented by Japanese. There was always some fear of violence from Japanese zealots, though this diminished in time.

Yokohama[19] consisted of 'the Native Town, the Settlement and the Bluff'. There was a constant risk of fire, which could spread rapidly in the narrow streets. After 1875, when British and French troops were withdrawn and there was no further need for parade-ground space, foreign residents built homes on the Bluff. One series of houses was known as 'Beato's toothpicks' from the cheapness and flimsiness of their construction.[20] Josiah Conder, the architect, advised his students not to set too much store by the buildings in the European settlements. 'Remember', he said, 'that they are only dwellings in a foreign country and that consequently they have the character of cheap temporary structures.'[21] Others took a longer-term view, for 'Public-spirited Smith' was constantly experimenting with vegetable, fruit and flower seeds in his garden on the Bluff.[22] His triumphs, 'huge cabbages, cauliflowers and what not'[23] were caricatured by Wirgman in the *Japan Punch*. He also 'planted the eucalyptus trees to be found here and there about the Bluff', the ultimate effect was a pleasing one.[24] Christopher Dresser noted that the 'beautiful villas in character half English and half Japanese, nestle in lovely gardens'.[25]

Yokohama prospered.[26] Because of its site close to Tokyo it grew rapidly, docks and harbours were built and an increasing flow of trade brought increasing wealth. It remained the chief centre for the foreigners. In the mid-1870s there were some 1300 (excluding Chinese); from the mid-1880s until 1923 there were always about

2400 foreign residents there. Many missionaries, engineers, and merchant navy officers, not themselves permanent residents, regarded it as their base in Japan. Foreign visitors who would not necessarily visit Nagasaki or Kobe landed at Yokohama and were often entertained by friends and acquaintances on the Bluff. The villas built then were mostly destroyed in the Great Kanto earthquake of 1923, but a few remain, now refurbished to delight the tourist.

Kobe, established (on 1 January 1868, in Hyogo prefecture), simultaneously with the new regime in Japan, seemed to grow in greater harmony with the Japanese, avoiding the friction between the communities which characterised some phases of life in Yokohama. Perhaps the small-scale underfunded merchants had already been weeded out before Kobe opened. At all events Kobe developed as a small, independent and highly regarded foreign settlement. As elsewhere the foreigners preferred to live apart in their own areas. In contrast to Yokohama, for some years they successfully managed their own municipal affairs. Kobe was praised on all sides.[27] In Kobe, as with the other treaty ports, the largest foreign element, apart from Chinese, were British. In 1886, 228 British citizens were resident there out of a total of 390 foreigners.

Kobe flourished as a port partly because its hinterland included Osaka and the rich valley which led to Kyoto. Prosperous foreigners instructed A. N. Hansell, FRIBA, in Japan from 1888 until 1919, and he designed elegant Gothic villas for them. These wooden houses, often of clapboard, were usually on foundations of brick or stone. It is to the great credit of the municipality that these charming houses of the *Ijinkan* which still dominate the hill-slopes above Kobe are now being meticulously restored and brought to life again.[28]

The open cities of Tokyo and Osaka also had their resident foreigners. For example professors at the Imperial College of Engineering lived in purpose-built professorial houses at the College at Toronomon, and other professors occupied premises at the Kaga *Yashiki*, which later became the *Hongo* campus of the University of Tokyo.[29]

In the case of the Tsukiji area of Tokyo, matters were rather different. Tsukiji lies between the Sumida river and the Ginza, on land originally reclaimed from the sea at Tokyo Bay. The enterprise of building the foreign quarter of Tokyo was originally undertaken by the Shogunate on a site sufficiently removed from the centre of Tokyo as to ensure that a safe distance, as well as some canals and gateways, kept the foreigners and xenophobic Japanese in their allotted places. Tsukiji was ready for occupation in late 1867. But it never became popular. Those who utilised the special area of Tsukiji were some of the legations, including the Americans, and the medical missionaries who, as part of their endeavour, established hospitals.[30] Not far away was the Ginza, then rebuilt in foreign mode.[31]

The Tsukiji Settlement in Tokyo might be thought to pose a problem in terms of the response of the regime.[32] One view might be that it represented a Japanese concession to the foreigner and so had a semi-colonial aspect. The alternative view would be that it was part of the general modernising process, along with the *Ginza*,[33] to give Tokyo a modern commercial core. In any case it was no great success, merchants almost to a man preferring Yokohama, and therefore occupies no very important part of the city's life. Nor did its existence have much effect upon the relationship between the Japanese and the foreigner. Dr Henry Faulds, worked for some years in Tsukiji in a mission hospital.[34]

In addition to the three 'successful' foreign settlements there were two other designated sites which never prospered. Niigata (opened 1 January 1868) which lies on the north-west coast of the Sea of Japan, failed primarily because of unsatisfactory port facilities and constantly silting harbour.[35] Hakodate, opened in July 1859, was originally an important supply base for the fishing, especially the whaling industry, but its small community was never able to sustain many foreigners although a few of the elegant Western-style villas which were then built, remain.[36]

## 3 EXPATRIATE SOCIAL LIFE

It was with the organisation of social life in the foreign clubs that the foreign residents came into their own. There were facilities for refreshments, gatherings, dinners and balls. Heavy drinking was common. Games rooms too were provided and in season there were many outdoor activities including picnics and outings. A wide range of outdoor sports including shooting matches, regattas, and hare and hounds were popular. For the more serious-minded the Asiatic Society provided, as the cartoon shows, intellectual stimulus.

The Scots in their kilted tartan ceremonial dress were numerous and intriguingly conspicuous. They certainly attracted a good deal of attention.[37] Annually they feasted St Andrews Day in November, and in January they celebrated the birthday of Robert Burns, their national poet. These occasions gave ample opportunity for fun and games, liberally laced with whisky.[38] Japanese were not included in any foreign social events although horse-racing became 'a joint and prosperous enterprise'. Even at race-meetings the notice read 'No natives will be admitted within the enclosure.'[39]

Personal joys and sorrows were also reported. John Ferguson Dyer was born to Henry and Marie Dyer on 12 July 1875 at the Imperial College of Engineering, Edo (Tokyo), but later the same paper noted that the baby had died 'aged 4 months and 14 days'.[40] Funerals were held in Yokohama thanks to the availability of the railway link with Tokyo. Christopher Dresser also commented on the value of the railway in 1883.[41] The little railway encouraged Yokohama to develop as the main base for foreign residents in the Tokyo area and a little later the Osaka–Kobe railway also granted mobility to foreigners there.

The foreign community was always in transition, the short-term contracts offered by the Japanese ensured that while someone was always arriving others were selling-up and departing. In this way the local small auctions became a special feature of alien life.[42] In addition to the small local social events there were occasions when the *Meiji* government, with a large number of foreign employees present, celebrated in style. For these purposes the premises of the Imperial College of Engineering were often used. Regarded by many in the 1880s as 'the most beautiful building' in Tokyo, it was the scene of the grandest government receptions. On the occasion of the visit of General Ulysses S. Grant (July 1879), the former President of the USA, the reception was held at ICE.[43]

These great receptions were the highlights of the social occasions for the foreign community. Tremendous pressure was put on foreign wives to dress appropriately, while Japanese wives, resplendent either in lovely traditional Japanese costumes or boned and corsetted in European gowns, added to the glamour.[44] In these ways Tokyo established itself as a social centre. Foreign engineers and other employees enjoyed a social life rather different from that which would have been their lot had they been working at home in Britain.

Many expatriates, eager to escape from the almost intolerable summer heat of Tokyo, organised holidays.[45] Favourite places included Hakone, in the hills to the west, Nikko to the north, or Chiba at the sea to the north-east of Tokyo.[46] Such expeditions required major preparations, especially as much food had to be

The Asiatic Society of Japan which was based in Yokohama was a forum for those who wished to read papers and learn more about their adopted country, Japan. Several British mining experts lived and worked on Sado Island in the Sea of Japan, off Niigata, where there were important copper mines.

*Cartoon* 6.1 Meeting of the Asiatic Society (*Japan Punch*, 1875)

carried. Family servants were also of the party so that life could continue as normal once the journey had been successfully completed. Most travelled by *jinrikisha* but occasionally a wooden cart with benches, which was drawn by horses rather than men, was used. Stout hearts were needed for hazards like crossing rivers on flimsy boats. Mosquitoes, fleas and bedbugs were additional worries especially for mothers of small children. Alfred Ewing records a five-weeks stay in Hakone, his wife Annie being 'carried there in a *Kago* which he describes as 'a basket balanced on a pole between the shoulders of two men'. While based at Hakone a favourite trip was to climb the sacred mountain of Japan, the beautiful Fujiyama, some 13 000 feet.[47] This expedition, although immensely popular with devout Japanese, was very demanding. The climb, at first beautiful through the forests, soon became more precipitous; enthusiasts had to clamber up the 'lava-built cone'; as one Cambridge man reported 'You simply walk for hours up a steep and ever steeper heap of ashes.'[48] According to Ewing the climb took 12 hours and he and his wife were pleased to return to Subashiri where they could recover in hot baths.[49]

## 4 WIVES AND HUSBANDS

It was no accident that Puccini should have been attracted to the tale of *Madam Butterfly* for one of his operas in which a beautiful young Japanese girl contracts a 'marriage' with a Westerner temporarily stationed in Nagasaki.[50] The poignancy of the tale involving love, commitment, abandonment, disgrace and death, enhanced by the haunting beauty of the music has kept the opera constantly in the repertoire since 1904 when it was first performed. The romantic story of Cio Cio San or Butterfly was typical. The young men involved, encouraged by distance from home and family, eagerly entered into liaisons with attractive loyal girls which would have been unthinkable at home. The poverty of Japanese families as well as attitudes to women, which expected passivity and selflessness encouraged these unions.

The difficulty was that young men who arrived from the West had little hope of congenial female company from their own societies. In the early days there were fewer ladies 'than could be counted on the fingers of both hands'.[51] Inevitably young men found their way to the *Yoshiwara* where, despite the strictures of the missionaries, the ladies of pleasure flourished.[52] But for young men brought up in the strict Victorian society, this kind of dual life brought its own strains. When urged by his parents to return to live in England in 1864, Satow in confiding his dilemma to his diary, on 'the prospect of marriage and of being able to live a decent life [in England] instead of the immoral one I have led lately [in Japan]',[53] expressed the problems of many in his situation.

Some of the Britons who were living and working in Japan made marriages with Japanese ladies, but to the British communities, cocooned within the treaty ports, these were 'closet' marriages not valid under English law. Frank Brinkley was living with Yaso Tanaka from Ibaraki 'without being legally married because of troublesome intermarriage procedures'[54] although in March 1886 he formally made her his wife. There are several examples of Britons from many professional backgrounds who married Japanese. In the case of

Thomas Blake Glover, his wife Tsuru, from the photographs, rigid and corsetted like any British Victorian matron, had apparently entered the household informally as a girl and only attained public recognition as a wife in Glover's mature years of respectability. Tsuru presided over homes both in Nagasaki and Shiba Park in Tokyo.[55] Thomas and Tsuru are buried together in the Inasa foreign cemetery at Nagasaki. E. H. Hunter the founder of the Osaka Iron Works also took to himself a Japanese wife.[56]

John Milne, Professor of Mining at the Imperial College of Engineering from 1876, met and married a Japanese lady of impeccable family.[57] Fourteen years later on 12 June 1895 when the Milnes were leaving Japan to return to England he married Tone again at the British consulate to regularise her position in English law. Josiah Conder, FRIBA (1852–1920) who arrived in Japan to serve as Professor of Architecture at the Imperial College of Engineering and who, like Hunter and Glover, was based in Japan for the rest of his life, married Kume.[58]

In the case of Ernest Satow there could be no public recognition at any stage in his official diplomatic career that he had a Japanese wife, O-Kane Takeda.[59] Indeed her existence, although acknowledged in Japan, was unknown in the West until G. A. Lensen's book on Satow's latter diaries was published in 1966.

The issue of these marriages usually remained in Japan and embraced the Japanese side of their cultural inheritance.[60] E. H. Hunter's son, Ryotaro, graduated in engineering from the University of Glasgow but on his return to Japan, before taking over his father's firm, the Osaka Iron Works, changed his name to 'Hunta', a Japanese form.[61] Glover's son Tomisaburo ran a fishing fleet out of Nagasaki. In his case the alienation and eventual war between his two countries became a matter of distress.

But the small cohort of men who embraced the culture and life of Japan by marriage were exceptional. Most unmarried young men lived with their fellows in one or other of the foreigners' enclaves. Some lived in dormitories, others 'chummed' with a compatriot and shared domestic accommodation. This 'messing' together was a general custom, each man having separate quarters but eating communally.

Initially in the early unsettled days in *Meiji* Japan there were few wives in residence in the treaty ports but with growing confidence in the new regime, wives and families arrived. The women created a microcosm of Western society, the ladies' own positions being determined by their husband's status. One commentator, who among many, poked gentle fun at the women of these small societies, remarked 'Mr Marshall's residence which was christened and long known as Windsor Castle, because of the fact that Mrs Marshall was the undoubted queen of our society'. During her years in Japan, Lady Parkes, the wife of the British Minister, was the doyenne of such circles. The occasion of Lady Parkes's departure from Japan in 1878, after years of serving as 'a distinguished hostess', was used as an excuse for 'a fabulous good-bye party'.[62]

It is hard to compare those who married in Japanese society with those short-term residents who cocooned themselves in the comforting surroundings of the treaty ports. For the Westerner and the Japanese alike, the foreigners' cemeteries in Yokohama, Kobe and Nagasaki, together with the remaining foreigners' villas – oases amid the constant turmoil of modern urban Japan – are evocative reminders of time long passed.

## 5 THE BROTHERHOOD

For men who lived in exotic places, remote from their homelands, it was important to create as much of the familiar ambience as possible. To this end Freemasons started to organise themselves into Lodges in Japan almost as soon as the treaty ports were open.[63] There were already Lodges in Hong Kong and Shanghai, and members of these who came to serve in Japan lost no time in rallying brothers and potential brothers. In some cases Lodges were set up under the Grand Lodge of Scotland and in others that of England. Those of England predominated and there was some friction from time to time between the two loyalties. There were no Japanese members.[64]

During the forty years in which the principles of extraterritoriality operated, the Freemasons, despite being a secret society (a form of organisation forbidden by Japanese law) operated without let or hindrance in Japan.[65] There was, however, serious concern when it became known that the special privileges of the foreigners in the treaty ports would disappear. In 1899 the District Grand Master in Japan requested an interview with the Japanese Minister for Foreign Affairs.[66]

Notwithstanding reassurances the District Grand Master did decide 'to direct that all public announcements of meetings etc. should be stopped. Under the general acceptance of the term, an advertised meeting is to a certain extent, a public meeting, and that is not our aim.' It seems clear that from 1900 the society, being technically illegal, was circumspect, taking care not to bring itself to public attention.

In Yokohama application had been made in April 1868 for land on which to build a Masonic Hall. Lot No. 170, Yamashita-cho, was allocated and the foundation-stone of the hall laid in March 1869. This hall would appear to have been home for the Yokohama Lodges although those of the Scottish persuasion prepared premises at Lot 61, Yokohama. In Kobe the Rising Sun Lodge No. 1401 (established under the English rules) did succeed in building the Corinthian Hall. Major P. M. Kinder, Master of the Imperial Mint at Osaka, was the first Master of this Lodge and he laid the foundation-stone for the new hall on 16 February 1871. The accommodation included a library, bar, billiard room and an office. The Corinthian Hall was sometimes used by District Grand Lodge and housed the masons' relief efforts after the 1923 earthquake. Many of the headstones in the foreign cemetery at Yokohama have carved into them the symbols of the Order. Japan was in a sense the end of the line, for as the British penetrated the East their settlements tended to produce lodges, around India and the Archipelago to China and Japan. Freemasonry was perhaps the closest and cosiest way of excluding an alien world.

## 6 ENCAPSULATED COLONIALISM

The behaviour of the foreigners in their settlements, with their exclusivism and assumptions of social superiority, was much resented in Japan. As J. Okuda wrote:

> Male adults are in the main composed of young clerks, or unsuccessful men of business. They repair to Japan in the hope . . . of rapidly making fortunes. They have rarely any social position, and trust that assumption will cover their ignorance. Many who would be taken for counter-jumpers in Regent Street, pose as merchant princes on the Bluff at Kanagawa. With their Lilliputian races and regattas, their imitative Chambers of Commerce and their pot-house clubs, they ape the customs, while they ignore the manners of their countrymen at home.[67]

Clearly the continued existence of the treaty ports, including the operation of the foreign consular courts,[68] and the extraterritorial rights which the foreigners enjoyed, smacked of semi-colonialism and remained an affront to Japan.

It had always been a matter of first importance to the Japanese to renegotiate the treaties. In many matters of interpretation of the laws as Dr Hoare has explained,[69] it was relatively easy for a 'strong minister such as Sir Harry Parkes, to push the "rights" of the foreign powers beyond what a strict interpretation of the treaties would allow'. Nevertheless the interpretation of the law in favour of the foreigner was something which the Japanese were bound to take up. It is of some interest to note that non-British foreign legal advisers, employed by the Japanese, were prompt in pointing out opportunities for reinterpretation of the law to achieve an outcome more favourable to the Japanese.

Although the agitation from treaty port residents to maintain their privileges was considerable and they mounted vigorous campaigns to maintain the *status quo*, it was clear by the 1890s that the days of the treaty port enclaves were numbered. Some foreign residents, perhaps not those of the treaty ports, took a more reasonable view, and were not afraid to state the case as they saw it.[70]

Once the privileges had disappeared, with the coming into force of new treaties on 1 July 1899, the foreigners in the treaty ports had perforce to adjust and accept their new position. Despite their anxiety, their lives did not change. As expatriates they still maintained the fabric of their social life, their clubs continued to flourish, their ladies persisted in their little social vanities and their homes remained placidly enclosed in their beautiful gardens. Many indeed after retirement remained permanently in Yokohama, Kobe or Nagasaki knowing that they were in fact more assimilated to society in Japan than they could ever hope to be in an alien England or Scotland to which for too long they had failed to return.

It is nearly ninety years since the treaty ports officially disappeared but the residential areas chosen by the foreigners remain distinct. As a tourist attraction the foreign homes are now being lovingly and expensively restored. The shadowy sense of the foreign presence is perhaps most clearly evoked in the foreign cemeteries, at the erstwhile treaty ports, where, under careful and caring guardianship, the stranger can wander among the graves. At Yokohama, where after the great Kanto earthquake of 1923, Catholics and Protestants were buried side by side, the cemetery is a reminder of the many foreigners who gave their lives in Japan. At the Yokohama Archives of History, where much fine material from the early days is held together with a splendid collection of foreign books amassed over the years by long-stay foreign residents, the present-day visitor can become aware of the importance of the foreigner in historical terms and yet of his tenuous hold on a tradition which was always pre-eminently Japanese.

# Part II

# The Japanese in Britain: A Search for Expertise

# 7 The Iwakura Mission

## 1 AN EXTRAORDINARY JOURNEY

During the year 1871 the men in power in Japan planned to send a strong embassy to visit those countries with which Japan had treaty agreements. Their objectives were threefold, to legitimise the new regime, to initiate a renegotiation of the treaties which had been signed with the foreign powers, and to judge for themselves the industrial achievements of Western societies. Several small missions, under the auspices of the *Bakufu* government, had been mounted earlier.[1] None was as thorough or as comprehensive as this, the Iwakura Mission,[2] named for its leader, Tomomi Iwakura (1825–83). The party included both senior and junior government ministers. The Mission left Japan as a group on 23 December 1871 and some members of it returned as late as 13 September 1873 after an absence of almost two years.

The Embassy landed first in America, on the soil of the USA. After extensive travel and varied experience there,[3] lasting 205 days, they crossed the Atlantic and landed at Liverpool in August 1872. They remained in Britain until December and then crossed the channel to mainland Europe where they visited France, Germany, Belgium, Holland and Russia before sailing east again to return home.

The ambassador, Tomomi Iwakura,[4] one of the ablest of princely leaders, was assisted by four associate ambassadors: Takayoshi Kido (1833–77); Toshimichi Okubo (1830–78); Hirobumi Ito (1841–1909), and Hanzo Yamaguchi or Naoyoshi (1842–94).[5] The willingness of these senior officers, totalling perhaps half of the government strength, to subject themselves to so long and arduous a journey, suggests a remarkable determination. None of these men, apart from Ito, had travelled in the West before.[6] Although thoroughly trained in traditional Confucian learning few of the delegation had received any education in Western studies. The young secretaries who acted as interpreters had previously travelled in the West. The diplomatic party numbered nearly fifty with an average age of about 30. The student group of about fifty, including five girls,[7] gradually dispersed as the Mission travelled, taking up residence at the universities or colleges where they were to study.

The ambassadors and their assistants were responsible for three different sets of enquiries. One was to study the law and government, to examine British political institutions including the House of Commons and the House of Lords. The second was to study economic structure including industry, transport and communications, banking, currency and taxation and how these all affected trade. The third was to examine education in all its aspects together with the equipment and training of military and naval personnel.

The embassy was accompanied by an official reporter, Kunitake Kume (1839–1931) who published in October 1978, *A true account of the tour in America and Europe of the Special Embassy (Tokumei Tenken Taishi Bei-O Kairan Jikki)*. This publication, in several volumes, brought to the attention of a wider public in Japan, the achievements and limitations of the West. The *Jikki* has been hailed as 'quite simply the best work of its genre and deserves by virtue of its literary qualities alone a prominent place in the cultural history of *Meiji* Japan'.[8] The availability of this and other accounts, published by other members of the ambassadorial party, brought the mission's achievements to a wider public in Japan. Perhaps Iwakura's choice of Kunitake Kume, as reporter for the mission, was indeed an inspired one, for Kume came to the task with the traditional training of a Confucian scholar. Throughout his long and arduous journey he was filtering his new experiences through tried and trusted modes of thought. In this way the apparent turmoil of the Western world was reported by a product of traditional Eastern culture.

## 2 TREATY RENEGOTIATION

According to the foreign agreements which the Japanese had signed in the late 1850s renegotiation of various clauses in the treaties was possible from July 1872. When the Mission left Japan there can be no doubt that they hoped to be able to start discussions on renegotiation in America and Europe. This was originally the principal and primary objective of their journey. The ambassadors failed to appreciate the difficulties which would face them on this head.

The Japanese regarded the treaties as 'unequal' because they imposed restrictions on their government both in its treatment of foreign citizens and in regard to import and export tariffs. The Japanese believed that the treaties affected its status as a sovereign state, suggested an element of semi-colonialism and undermined its authority in the eyes of the world.[9]

During the Mission's long visit to the USA much time went into vain attempts to open a dialogue on renegotiation. The USA, in the person of Hamilton Fish,[10] the Secretary of State, although helpful, was not ultimately willing to consider change.[11]

By the time the Mission reached London, in August 1872,[12] the senior ambassadors were coming to recognise that their aspirations for renegotiation were premature and had little or no hope of success. Discussions between the parties took place at the Foreign Office in November. Queen Victoria, who was at Balmoral in Scotland when they arrived, received the ambassadors at Windsor in the late autumn.

When Queen Victoria bade farewell to the Mission on the eve of their departure for the continent, she told them 'We fully appreciate the wisdom of your views in respect of the Treaties and when the proper time arrives We shall be ready to unite with your Imperial Majesty in concluding such new arrangements as may place the relations on the friendliest and most amicable basis.'[13] The Mission had no option but to accept these bland reassurances.

## 3 BRITISH RED CARPET TREATMENT

Although those countries to which the Japanese journeyed were unwilling to renegotiate treaties with a country which was, as they believed, as backward as Japan, they were eager to entertain so influential and distinguished a delegation. Each country visited, including the USA, Britain, France, Germany, Belgium, Holland and Russia mounted a comprehensive programme designed to impress the Japanese with Western enterprise and achievements. In each place the host-country displayed not only the show-pieces of modern industry but also demonstrated their system and method of government, and showed off their cultural achievements. On sea they travelled by modern steamship and on land they were swiftly conveyed by steam trains running along comprehensive rail networks. Efficient post office and telegraph systems enabled them to keep in contact with their compatriots at home as well as with Western friends.

The Mission's experiences in the USA may have enabled them to look more critically and assess more shrewdly what they were shown in Europe. As Kido's *Diary* shows, the members of the delegation were constantly discussing what they had seen and considering what would be best for Japan. Did government or private industry provide the stimulus for economic expansion and development? Who was responsible for the financing and development of trade and industry? Did industrialisation depend on an educated population for its success? Was the educated élite which populated Western universities and colleges responsible in any way for Western industrial supremacy?

Britain received many visitors from abroad at this time prepared to marvel at the industrial wonders displayed before them. Few can have been given so comprehensive and well-ordered a series of tours of Britain's industrial might as was the Iwakura Mission. Despite increasing competition from other European countries and from America, Britain was still regarded, and still regarded herself, as the supreme example of the successful industrialised state. Although the Mission sampled many aspects of British life, it was the industrial grand tour which was organised for them which brought home the strength of the manufacturing base on which British Imperial power then rested.

In the tours of the industrial north of England long days were spent inspecting key factories and being entertained by local industrial barons. Sometimes they stayed in hotels; on other occasions hospitality was offered by landed or industrial magnates. Lord Mayors and Lord Provosts in England and Scotland respectively, were marshalled to give civic welcomes and Chambers of Commerce rallied their members to render welcoming addresses.

It was an impressive performance, made the more so by the continuing presence of a powerful British entourage. Sir Harry Parkes, HBM Minister in Japan, was on leave and he, together with one of his consular officials, W. G. Aston,[14] who acted as interpreter, were in frequent attendance on the Japanese party. The British government seconded General Alexander as its representative to supervise arrangements.[15]

In the west of Scotland, between 9 and 11 October 1872, a large party was based at Erskine House, guests of Lord Blantyre.[16] It was a particularly appropriate location, for as Takayoshi Kido reported:

> From this house one commands a view of the River Clyde as far as Glasgow, while we are more than ten miles from the sea . . . Later with much effort the channel was dug out and today several dozen steamships sail up and down the river daily.[17]

From this base they visited Glasgow where they were welcomed by various civic dignitaries including the Lord Provost.[18] They saw something of the bustle of a great city, visited a cotton mill and locomotive company as well as the Royal Exchange and the Chamber of Commerce. Kunitake Kume was much impressed by his visit to the Glasgow waterworks in the hills to the north of the city, for he saw there how the initiative of the municipal government in bringing a pure health-giving water to its citizens, had exercised self-help and self-reliance.[19] The following day they travelled to Greenock where they inspected Caird's shipyard. They admired the *City of Chester*, a ship then on the slipway and examined some of the shipbuilding processes. They also visited Walker's Sugar Refinery. Lord Blantyre later escorted them around the farm and workshops at Erskine House.

Their time in Edinburgh was rather different for they saw the High Court and the Palace of Holyroodhouse, the Queen's residence in Scotland, and enjoyed some sightseeing before resuming their industrial pilgrimage.[20] In and near Edinburgh they examined a traction-engine works, an india-rubber factory, and a paper mill. On 16 October they were the guests of the Commissioners for Northern Lights and steamed by their ship *Pharos* to the extraordinary Bell Rock Lighthouse,[21] some 40 miles to the east.[22] Unfortunately what might have been a pleasant day's excursion was marred by pouring rain and heavy seas. The delegation were relieved to return to the relatively sheltered waters of the Firth of Forth where they visited the Isle of May dominated by its Stevenson-built lighthouse.

From Edinburgh they travelled through the Scottish borders visiting woollen mills at Galashiels as well as Melrose Abbey before arriving in Newcastle upon Tyne. There they inspected a copper refining factory, chemical works as well as the shipbuilding yards. Sir William Armstrong, the armaments magnate, escorted them around his works himself and later dined them. This was a particularly interesting meeting, for the Japanese had known of Armstrong's armaments in the 1860s and later the Japanese presence on the Tyne was very important (see Chapter 10 below).

The Mission's visit to Liverpool (30 September 1872) was dominated by ships and shipbuilding. They were impressed by the floating dockyard and the five-storeyed grain elevator as well as the yards of Cammell Laird across the river at Birkenhead. From Liverpool they travelled to Manchester via St Helens, seeing Pilkington's glass factory which, established in 1869, was to become world famous. In Manchester (8 October 1872) and the surrounding areas of Lancashire they familiarised themselves with the cotton textile industry, being especially impressed with a nine-storey spinning mill. They also explored Sir Joseph Whitworth's foundry where Kido commented that 'a pressing machine is used there in the manufacture of large guns and other steel products'.[23] The factory also specialised in making heavy tools such as heavy iron-hammers. At the Town Hall in Manchester after the industrial visits, Hugh Mason, the President of the Chamber of Commerce spoke of Manchester, 'renowned for the enterprise of its merchants, for the intelligent energy of its manufacturers, for the ingenuity of its mechanical engineers, for the skill of its artisans, for the industry of its workers and for the law-abiding temper of its people'. The President also spoke of the Manchester school of economists who stood for 'the great principle of the free exchange of commodities with every part of the globe'.[24]

In Birmingham they expressed interest in Chance's glassworks, (Chance's made the glass for Stevenson-built lighthouses in Japan) and later visited some of the firms making small arms, rifles and other specialised guns. The delegation visited Elkington's and admired their Birmingham 'small wares', which made many cheap metal household articles which had a finish which looked like gold and silver. While in the Midlands (of England) they examined china and porcelain being made in Staffordshire, Cash's cotton-spinning firm in Coventry and paid a visit to Warwick Castle.

When they were in the woollen manufacturing area of Yorkshire they spent time in Bradford. From there they travelled to Saltaire (25 October 1872). This was a model village built by Sir Titus Salt (1803–76) centred on his woollen mills,[25] where high-quality woollen cloth, including alpaca, was woven. Sir Titus's sons were on hand to escort them around. For Sir Titus Salt had provided 'healthy dwellings and gardens in wide streets and capacious squares, ample ground for recreation, a large dining hall and kitchens – baths and washhouses, schools, a mechanics institute, a church; these are some of the characteristics of the future town of Saltaire'. Saltaire, set in green fields was a vivid demonstration of Victorian paternalism, for it encapsulated, as one observer later wrote 'the three Victorian ideals of cleanliness, Godliness and adult education'.[26]

While the main party were on their travels, others were following different itineraries. R. H. Brunton, then on furlough from his employment in Japan as lighthouse engineer, himself organised his own industrial tour, for Ito and a number of his 'intelligent young attachés'.[27]

Other members of the Mission were also pursuing their special interests.[28] Takato Oshima, together with K. Nagano and R. Koma, experts in mining and mineralogy, set off for the south-west of England.[29] Armed with 'an introduction letter' from General Alexander, they first visited the Cornish tin mines, at North Levant (19 September) where 'We don't have the match for the machinery and I could not help saying that the condition of the tunnel is good as well.' Oshima not only studied mining techniques, commenting during some of his exhausting visits that 'the noise of carts and explosion was so enormous that I felt that I was in hell' but also studied closely the 'machinery and tin manufacturing industry'. His interest in the tin extraction process reflects his lifelong concern with metallurgical problems. From Cornwall Oshima journeyed to Plymouth, visiting the naval dockyard at Devonport, then on to brick kilns and paper mills before leaving for Bristol. Oshima continued to study mines and mine working, visiting copper and coal mines. By 17 October they were in Cardiff, then the 'coal metropolis' of the Kingdom, where they examined further coal mines.[30]

Members of the embassy were impressed with the busy factories and the large work-force employed and they also understood the importance of the network of transport communications on which the factories relied.[31] They travelled many hundreds of miles by steam train as they criss-crossed the country. Almost all the mainline railways which exist today were already built.

The Japanese delegation were naturally curious about the training and equipment of the British army and navy. During their early weeks in London (in August 1872) expeditions were arranged to see army manoeuvres and equipment. Because of the role of the British in helping to train the Japanese navy there was a particular interest in naval matters. In Portsmouth they watched naval manoeuvres and spent some time at the naval dockyards.[32]

To learn how the British system of constitutional monarchy worked, the Japanese visited a wide variety of institutions, including the Houses of Parliament, Law Courts and prisons. One member of the party, Mr Yasukawa, concentrated upon the work of the Houses of Parliament, paying some twenty visits to the Commons and nearly twenty to the Lords. On his return to Japan he published extensively on 'the General Theory of the British Parliament'. Hirubumi Ito was fully occupied undertaking much independent travel completing a variety of tasks.

Although they had received so much information and guidance during their visit to Britain, as in every other country on their tour, their priorities did not necessarily match with those of their hosts. The British may have been guilty of overkill, certainly in respect of grand dinners and receptions. Members of the embassy must have been exhausted.[33] Innate courtesy carried the Japanese through these occasions, as they continued to respond to speeches of welcome. Despite the innumerable visits to a wide variety of places of interest, the senior counsellors considered many wider problems.[34]

## 4 A SUCCESSFUL MISSION?

How then did the British and the Japanese rate the success of the Iwakura Mission? It seems clear that for the British, pleased to entertain potential customers, the outcome was satisfactory. Wherever they went mine-owners and manufacturers had demonstrated to their guests British efficiency and productivity. In London the Japanese had noted how the checks and balances operated in political institutions to prevent the abuse of power.

Though the British public in general welcomed the Japanese embassy, it was known that Christianity in 1872 was still a proscribed religion in Japan.[35] Prince Iwakura had been warned by the British *chargé* before he left Japan that any discussion of the treaties would be useless as long as this situation remained. The Japanese believed that the recognition of Christianity could cause unrest in Japan because the basic tenets of Christianity were inimical to the received word regarding the divine origin of the Mikado. *The Times* had published damaging reports about the persecution of Christians.[36] Was Queen Victoria's hope 'that the course of Japanese policy may be such as to ensure for the future the lively sympathy of the nations of Christendom with Japan' an oblique reference to this? In course of time the senior members of the embassy, having experienced a similar strength of feeling in several Western countries, put pressure on the government at home and by early 1873 restrictions on those Japanese who professed Christianity were removed.

Sir Harry Parkes who accompanied the Mission on part of the British tour aimed at 'producing an impression which may prove serviceable hereafter to our intercourse with Japan'.[37] He was also conscious of the dangers to Japan of embarking on too rapid a reformation. Too much change too soon, in a society emerging from a kind of feudalism could bring destabilisation in its wake. Reform of education was urgent and important, for society could make greater demands on an educated people.

For the Japanese, matters were more complex. Iwakura himself had been concerned, before leaving Japan, to reaffirm to the world at large the authority of the Emperor at the head of the new government. This confirmation would also serve to abrogate the treaty making powers which the *Shogun* had earlier wrongfully appropriated. This objective, that the Iwakura Mission would reassert the status and authority of the Emperor with the powerful governments of the West, was successfully accomplished.

Although the Mission's ambitions with regard to treaty renegotiation remained unfulfilled the travellers had a better understanding of the reasoning behind Western attitudes. It was more clearly understood that following the upheaval of the *Meiji* Restoration, 'chaos, anarchy and a return to the old feudal system of political sectionalism had to be averted'.[38] Several of the *Meiji* oligarchs on the Mission were interested in the ability of Western societies to effect gradual change.

Toshimichi Kido, who was responsible for the studies of law and government undertaken by members of the Mission, and who had earlier been impatient with the slow progress of the gradualist approach, was deeply affected by his travels. Above all he came to understand and appreciate those 'constitutional processes which limited those in power and provided a sound base for orderly change'. As a direct result of his Western journey Kido 'after 1873 sought to lead Japan towards constitutional monarchy and to do it by keeping peace with the pro-feudal classes in Japan and with foreign nations'.[39] Kido was also particularly concerned with getting a correct balance, as he wrote 'I am deeply concerned for the future of my beloved country and my people if we disregard the evils and abuses of the world past and present and eagerly borrow everything at random.' Sadly Kido died, perhaps of tuberculosis, only four years later.

The Iwakura Mission's journey impressed upon the senior delegates the reality of political power in Western countries, and reminded them of the need to guard against the re-emergence of 'political sectionalism' in their own country. They also understood more clearly the reforms necessary in Japan before the West would renegotiate the 'unequal' treaties.

The return of the Mission also gave an important boost to the programme of industrial modernisation already in train. Even if individuals had only visited a proportion of the industrial visits arranged in America, Britain and the rest of Europe they could not but be impressed with the achievement.[40,41] In these senses the Iwakura Mission's unprecedented journey by affecting the attitudes of an important cohort of powerful and influential Japanese reinforced the spirit of reform then abroad in Japan.

# 8 Towards an Educational Philosophy

## 1 A NATURAL CURIOSITY

By 1850 those Japanese living on Kyushu Island, who knew of the long-established Dutch settlement at Nagasaki,[1] were increasingly curious about the wonders of the outside world.[2] Despite prohibition from central government, leaders of the outer domains, such as *Satsuma* and *Choshu*,[3,4] were happy to send young men abroad to learn directly from the West. In this way various groups, aided by foreign merchants, were temporarily spirited away from Japan to pursue their studies overseas and familiarise themselves with cultures other than their own.

In 1865 the *Satsuma* clan mounted an important mission sending a group of students to London under the care of *Satsuma* leaders.[5] The delegation had several objects; to encourage the young men to undertake various lines of study, to make the case for the clans (as distinct from that of the *Bakufu*), to the British government, and to attempt to make a judgement of the advantages and disadvantages of Western industrial, economic and political development.

Among the young members was Arinori Mori (1847–89)[6] who at the age of 18 first left Japan as a member of this *Satsuma* Mission. Between 1865 and 1884 Mori spent three substantial periods in the West, totalling nearly a quarter of his life. He was away from Japan between 1865 and 1867 mostly in Britain and America; later between 1871 and 1873 he was Japan's first Minister to Washington, subsequently between 1880 and 1884 he was Minister to the Court of St James in London. After his final return to Japan he emerged as an authoritarian figure.[7] Although he had apparently regained his Japanese *persona* in his role as Minister of Education, he was shot, at the age of 41, by a Shinto fanatic, on 11 February 1889, who believed that Mori had betrayed Japan and was a Christian.

Arinori Mori's career illustrates well the challenge posed to the young *Meiji* leaders by the ideas and philosophies of the West. In order to rebut and withstand the threat from the treaty powers Japanese leaders sought to comprehend and interpret. Mori, initially the most volatile of these, himself introduced a strongly centralised education system which owed far more to the Japanese authoritarian principles than to Western liberalism.

## 2 THE CONFUCIAN HERITAGE AND THE SCHOOL FOR WESTERN LEARNING

Arinori Mori was born, in 1847, in Kagoshima to a *samurai* family of the *Satsuma* clan. Although the social grading of his family within the *samurai* class is uncertain, his father, while he may have been subsisting at a level of genteel poverty, insisted on his sons receiving a good Chinese classical education at the clan-operated school.[8] In addition to this, Mori, like every other small boy in Satsuma, was drawn in to the *Gojn*.[9] This was an organisation run, with guidance, by the boys themselves, which absorbed the energy and activities of all the young of the *Satsuma* clan.

Because Satsuma territory was relatively close to Nagasaki where Western ideas entered Japan, there were many who knew of *Rangaku* or Dutch learning although formal education in Western ideas was not available except in a clandestine way until after 1863. In that year the British bombardment of Kagoshima,[10] the Satsuma capital, effected a change of heart. The school for Western learning was opened in the Kagoshima Shipbuilding Office in 1864.[11] The subjects taught related largely to naval and military affairs. Almost all the students worked through the Dutch language; only Mori Arinori and some eight or nine others studied English.

At the same time the influential men of the domain were discussing whether it would be wise to send a representative group to Europe to see for themselves what ideas and technology lay behind the achievements of the West. In the event Mori and thirteen other young men – ten from the school for Western learning – were selected to go to study in England and France. This large party was escorted by Tomoatsu Godai and Munenori Terajima as well as by Ryle Holme, an English merchant associated with Thomas Glover, in Nagasaki.[12,13] The speed with which *Satsuma* organised their party, which set sail on SS *Australian* in April 1865, suggests the urgency of the task. Mori himself can only have been some months into the course for Western learning, although he may earlier have been learning English informally. He and others of his group had been well trained to withstand the hardship of a strange life in England but their natural curiosity must have caused them to wonder about what they would find at journey's end.

## 3 THE WEST OBSERVED

From their arrival in England in June 1865 Mori and some of his group were to remain in the West for almost three years. Two of these years, 1865–7, were spent in London. In the summer of 1867 they removed to upper New York state where, in a rural community commanded by the mystic Thomas Lake Harris, they experienced a daily life of spiritual intensity and hard domestic labour.

This first Western experience was of great importance, especially perhaps to Mori, who, barely 18 when he arrived in London, was nearly 21 when he returned to Japan. During these impressionable years Mori was to receive ideas on which he would ponder for the rest of his days. One Westerner became particularly influential.

Laurence Oliphant (1822–88),[14] an extraordinary character, had early made his mark as a fearless adventurer and writer of racy travellers' tales. He was also an amateur politician as well as a socialite, well known on the London scene. He appears to have been in touch with the *Satsuma* group from their arrival in London in June 1865.[15] He certainly played an important, perhaps a crucial role, in introducing the *Satsuma* leaders to those at the Foreign Office who determined British foreign policy. Before long Mori was writing home to his brothers letters which contained sentiments redolent of Oliphant's teaching.

Despite Oliphant's access to and popularity with those in political power, he was basically a deeply disturbed man distracted by the guilt feelings of the dedicated evangelical. Although he gave his young Japanese friends the benefit of his opinions, including his severe criticisms of Russia and ardent optimism about the USA, which Mori came to share, he also involved them in one of the most bizarre religious and emotional experiences to which any tyro can ever have been subjected.

In the summer of 1867 Mori and some of the Japanese, from the *Satsuma* as well as from other Japanese groups decided to travel to America with Oliphant, to see the settlement of Thomas Lake Harris at Brocton, New York where 'the Brotherhood of the new life' lived and worked.

During the two years prior to their departure for America Mori and his fellows had studied much with Oliphant and F. V. Dickens among others.[16] According to clan instructions they were supposed, in London, to be studying military subjects; naval surveying was Mori's intended field, but guided by Professor Williamson at University

College, London, subjects other than military ones seemed appropriate. Mori himself had a flair for mathematics 'covering the ground from simple arithmetic to spherical trigonometry in two years', he also studied physics, chemistry and history. Most of his fellow-students also followed diverse paths finding much intellectual excitement in fields other than the military.

In the summer of 1866 Mori – perhaps feeling culpable for not following the prescribed course in naval science more diligently – and his colleague, Matsumura, determined on a working holiday. They joined the *George and Emily*, a three-masted sailing barque, at Newcastle, resolved to serve on her as deck-hands on her voyage to Russia with coal. This was certainly an educative trip for the Japanese did not 'even know the name of the mast' but the Captain and the crew 'were most helpful and polite'. On arrival in Russia, they spent three weeks or so making contacts with some of the *Bakufu*-sponsored students and others including Russians before returning to Britain which was for Mori 'with the sensation of having come home to my own country'.[17]

The invitation to join the community of 'the Brotherhood' came at an appropriate time, for *Satsuma* funds to support the young men in London were no longer available. Harris was prepared to pay expenses. Travel to America would take them in the direction of home and so the invitation was accepted by several of the Japanese, including some non-*Satsuma* men.[18]

Thomas Lake Harris (1823–1906)[19] although English and taken to the USA as a child, was a former Swedenborgian who pushed the orthodox meaning of that faith, which hovers between Christianity and spiritualism, towards new interpretations. While denouncing other sects he developed his own peculiar hermeneutics.[20] Laurence Oliphant's mother, with whom Laurence was deeply involved, became a discipline of Harris in America and there Laurence followed her.[21] Harris himself wanted to believe that in Japan he would be able to set up as a charismatic avatar with an Asiatic following.

When Mori's group arrived in upper New York Harris was enthusiastic, writing:

> I have thus solved the problem of Japan. Its successful outcome depends on finding a *Daimyo* who will carry it out . . . The policy is this: that *Daimyo* will declare himself neutral and a peacemaker in all Japanese conflicts. He will accept the New Life, take the advanced Japanese who are receiving the truths and establish a Military College.[22]

In this way Harris held out golden opportunities for the Japanese as disciples. During the year that Mori was in the community, he worked hard on exhausting physical tasks as well as having long sessions with Oliphant and Harris. During the early months of 1868 there were as many as thirteen Japanese in residence. As the biographer of Mori has explained, the Brotherhood was 'a baffling concoction of the earnest and the eminently sensible with the fanciful and downright preposterous'.[23] How then did Mori and his fellows cope? They probably made little of the finer refinements of Harris's doctrine but they could understand the general Christian and socialist predilections of members of the community, including Oliphant, and they learned much from their daily contact with other residents.

Members of the Japanese contingent left Brocton and the T. L. Harris community in 1868. There had been disagreements. The Restoration had taken place; some, including Mori, believed that they should be in Japan. They sailed from New York, crossed at Panama and arrived back in Yokohama in July 1868.

The three years had provided an extraordinary range of experiences. During the first year in London they had absorbed a thousand impressions of Western life and civilisation, the journey to Russia had given them another base-line from which they could begin to establish comparisons. The second year in London thus found them more aware and more critically conscious. The third year in America had given them, through the curious vehicle of Harris's and Oliphant's teaching, a deepening awareness of the moral problems involved in creating a modern Japan.

Back in Japan Mori found it difficult to adjust. His companions may either have had fewer problems, or have been more circumspect. It was only after he had re-entered Japanese society in August 1868 that Mori was forced to face the inconsistencies of his position as a good Japanese on the one hand and as an apostle of the West on the other. For a time he responded in Western terms. Almost at once he was plunged into active politics. The pressures quickly manifested themselves. After the years in Western suits Mori reappeared in Tokyo in traditional *samurai* garb wearing his two swords reversed so that all could see they were not available for use. On 6 July 1869 he insisted on introducing a debate 'that persons other than civil and military officers should be permitted to dispense with the wearing of swords'. Mori argued that 'our land is now at peace with the prosperity of our Imperial Throne waxing day by day'. His course of action provoked an outcry and instant notoriety. He was at once stripped of his official status in the foreign ministry and dispatched forthwith home to Kagoshima. Mori had touched a raw nerve. Not for another seven years would the government follow Mori's lead and order *samurai* to abandon sword-carrying.

During the succeeding 18 months of 'exile' in Kagoshima Mori had time to consider his position and ponder the future. He spent his time living simply and frugally, teaching English and imposing strict moral standards on his pupils. He was brought into public life again in 1870.[24] The government required his services for the new diplomatic service which it had been resolved to establish. Mori was restored to his former rank and appointed as *chargé d'affaires* in Washington, while his friend, Naonubu Samejima, was appointed to cover London, Paris and Berlin.[25]

## 4 THE JAPANESE INTERPRETER

During the remainder of 1871 Mori, in Washington, enjoyed learning the diplomatic ropes from the 'avuncular Hamilton Fish'.[26] There was plenty of time for reading, making notes and conversation. This comparatively leisurely life ended abruptly when, on 29 February 1872, the Iwakura Mission arrived. The Mission remained in America until the end of July. The pace of life changed as Mori strove to deal with a demanding diplomatic schedule.

The Iwakura Mission's original and primary objective of treaty renegotiation proved more difficult than the Japanese had believed. Hamilton Fish (1808–93), the US Secretary of State and a lawyer by training, believed that the Japanese did not have the correct credentials. Later it became clear that despite Japanese persistence there would be no renegotiation until Japanese laws had been remodelled in modern mode. Although Mori had a difficult part to play, one senior member of the mission, and a leading *Choshu* statesman, Takayoshi Kido (1833–77), was critical of his behaviour.[27]

Once the Mission had sailed for Europe Mori in Washington reverted to his earlier studies trying to discover how to interpret Western philosophy in Japanese terms. He prepared a paper on *Education in Japan* (1 January 1873) in the course of which he proposed the abolition of the Japanese language and the adoption of English as an alternative. In making this extraordinary recommendation he abandoned the half-way house suggested by others, that the

Japanese vernacular should be retained, and a Romanised script substituted which would take the place of the Chinese characters previously used. Mori's own proposals received a universally hostile reception.[28] Many – including scholars and the Press – rallied to the defence of Japanese.[29] The final irony came when in 1873 David Murray, the American adviser on education in Japan, in his report for the Ministry of Education (*Mombusho*) dismissed Mori's idea as impracticable.

After his term of office in Washington Mori returned home for the second time on 23 July 1873. Although he was older and better informed about the West, he still had the ability to shock. His paper on *Education in Japan* had been issued only months before his return so that his notoriety continued. After returning home he published his famous 'Discourse on Wives and Mistresses' discussing with refreshing candour alternatives to the Japanese traditional views of women in society. It was a subject which was to interest him throughout his life. On 26 February 1875 Mori made a 'contractual marriage' with Hirose Tsumeko in 'a Western-style civil ceremony without precedent'.[30]

But Mori did more. He brought to Japan the Western tradition of the academic society and the learned journal and founded the *Meirokusha* (the *Meiji* Six Society) and *Meiroku Zasshi* (*Meiji* Six Journal).[31] These were based on the learned societies and journals common in America and Europe.[32] The group met in the upper rooms of the *Seiyoken*,[33] a Western-style restaurant in Tsukiji. The *Meirokusha* became renowned in Japan as a forum for public lectures. Fukuzawa particularly encouraged members to prepare formal speeches which were often delivered to large audiences. The *Meiroku Zasshi* published as articles, papers already given as lectures and other critical responses to the lectures (see Appendix C).[34] Mori wrote for the first few issues but his role primarily was as organiser or promoter. Within months he was dispatched as minister to China where he became involved with the resolution of the Korean crisis.

After the period in Peking Mori was promoted to Vice Minister (27 June 1878) and shortly thereafter (6 November 1879) as Minister to the Court of St James in London. He was 32 years of age when he arrived in London for his last extended period of service abroad. His metamorphosis was well advanced, no longer only the *enfant terrible*, he was rapidly becoming the senior diplomat with particular interests in education and politics.

## 5 THE IMPACT OF WESTERN PHILOSOPHIES

Mori's arrival in the USA for his second visit coincided with the beginning of his studies of mainstream Western philosophy. From February 1871 he was attempting to understand current ideas in the West. Inevitably as he studied he became aware of the problems, as well as the inconsistencies and controversy which surrounded them.

In 1859 Charles Darwin (1809–82)[35] had published *On the Origin of Species by means of Natural Selection, or The Preservation of Favoured Races in the Struggle for Life*. This book together with Darwin's *The Descent of Man, and Selection in Relation to Sex* (1871), created consternation in the Western world because of the implied challenge to the fundamentalist beliefs embodied in the Christian text, the Old Testament of the Bible. Although in some senses these debates were of no direct concern to the Japanese, as non-Christians, the sequel was. Herbert Spencer (1820–1903)[36] became involved in the study of the development of the ideas of evolution, as they related to society and especially to the ideas of sociology. He published *Social Studies* (1851) and *The Principles of Psychology* (1855). Later (1857) he published, *Essay: Scientific, Political and Speculative* and then (1862) as *First Principles* part of his last major work, *A System of Synthetic Philosophy*, which was not completed until 1896. In most of his writings he adumbrated theories relating to the 'Survival of the fittest through a process of natural selection'. His volume on *Education* (1861) was also translated into many languages and had a world-wide influence.

Spencer's views were strongly focused on the individual, his rights and his duties. Despite the fact that the cult of the individual was neither known nor understood in Japan the application of 'Social Darwinianism' to human society was of interest to many. The philosophical problems in reconciling the rights of the individual with those of the majority had been posed many times but most recently and effectively in the mid-nineteenth century by John Stuart Mill (1806–73).[37]

Others whose ideas reached Japan included Adam Smith (1723–90) whose exposition of the evolutionary and allocative power of the market system was particularly appealing.[38] In addition the ideas of Thomas Babington Macaulay (1800–59) whose Whig theory of history, built on ideas on continuous optimum, could be very attractive. At a more popular level the Victorian ideas of *Self-Help* and *Thrift* brought the Scotsman, Samuel Smiles (1812–1904) to the attention of the Japanese public. All these ideas were introduced to Japan by men who felt the excitement of new modes of thought but who were baffled by the challenge of synthesis.

Throughout these Western philosophies ran ideas concerning the rights and duties of individuals. These were being popularised in Britain where education for all, universal manhood suffrage and secret ballots were the current demands. How far could the cult of the individual be taken in *Meiji* Japan where individual rights were usually subservient to the desired objectives of conformity and consensus?

If Herbert Spencer is taken as epitomising the Western philosopher of the day then it can be seen that his ideas were influential in Japan among three main groups. These were the popular rights movement – most active between 1874 and 1889; the *Meiji* government itself, and Tokyo University. Those who demanded greater individual rights in Japan found Herbert Spencer's ideas much to their liking for he attacked central government power and 'asserted that the least government was the best government'. The government model condemned by Spencer seemed to some to fit only too well the power-hungry government in *Meiji* Japan. Many of Herbert Spencer's works were available in translation in Japan; the work of Ko Matsushima in producing *Social Statistics* between 1881 and 1883 was particularly useful.[39]

Naohiro Sakamoto, earlier called Namio Sakamoto (1853–1911) showed a deep understanding of Spencer's ideas. He worked on Spencer in the original English and proved himself an intelligent and respected scholar. He later retired from active politics and became a Christian missionary but not before he had used Spencer's ideas effectively in opposing the centralised educational policy and the government's determined efforts to suppress the popular rights movement. Another interpreter was Tokutomi Soho (1863–1957)[40] whose dangerous ultranationalism of the 1930s should not be allowed to obscure his earlier enthusiasm and understanding of popular rights. Tokutomi's idea of *Heiminshugi*, which can be translated as 'populism' or 'democracy' was an important concept in *Meiji* Japan.

Arinori Mori and Kentaro Kaneko (1853–1942)[41] both important figures within the *Meiji* government itself, also made serious studies of Spencer's work. Mori Arinori had an active friendship with Spencer which blossomed during Mori's years in London as Japanese Minister.

With both Kaneko and Mori, Spencer advocated none of the

theories for which he had argued so persuasively in his works. For Spencer Japan was a backward society and therefore the policies which were advised for Western societies were not applicable to Japan. When Spencer met Kaneko in London in 1890 he reported that Spencer argued:

> If the Japanese constitution and laws have not the same spirit and nature as have Japanese history and customs, future difficulties will be numerous; and you will not attain the aims of constitutional government. I had advised Mr Mori to use the principles of gradualism and conservatism ... My principle of politics is to reduce government activities and let the people themselves do their own business ... But, this presupposes a future perfect world. Instructions to reduce government interference must be gradual.

Spencer's ideas also entered Japan through the teaching at the University of Tokyo. From 1877 when teaching started at the university, Professors Edward Sylvester Morse (1838–1925) and Ernest Francisco Fenellosa (1853–1908), both Harvard graduates, began to teach Western ideas. Morse was Professor of Zoology and so soon came to Darwin's theories. Fenellosa, later famous as a discerning student of Japanese art, started his career in Japan teaching the history of philosophy (1877–85), political economy (1877–83), political science (1877–80), and logic (1877–85). Some of his teaching seems to have been related to Spencer's sociology. Some of his pupils at Tokyo were destined to become government ministers and in this way brought their interpretation of Spencer's ideas directly into government circles.

## 6 IN LONDON, WITH HERBERT SPENCER

Mori's appointment to London in 1879 brought him into direct personal contact with those who managed the affairs of Britain, then the greatest world power. In diplomatic terms he was frustrated by the unwillingness of the second Gladstonian government (1880–5) with the ageing Lord Granville as foreign secretary, to view with anything other than marginal interest the problems of Japan. The Japanese sense of urgency and their determination to renegotiate the 'unequal treaties' met with no response.

But despite the slighting way with which his diplomatic demands were met at the foreign office, Mori quickly settled into enjoying life in London. He appreciated from the beginning of his London sojourn the privilege, to which his diplomatic rank entitled him, of being an honorary member of the Athenaeum Club in Pall Mall. There he found men willing to talk, exhort and explain and it was at the Athenaeum that Mori based his social life.

By coincidence Herbert Spencer was also a member of the Athenaeum. He practically lived there. Spencer in the early 1880s was deeply engaged in the preparation of Part V, Political Institutions, of his *Principles of Sociology*. His long-term interest in Japan caused him to cultivate the company of the new Japanese minister, Mori Arinori, whom he had met previously in 1873. The resultant exchanges affected both men, Spencer taking Japan as an example of the undeveloped country in working out his own theories, and Mori and other Japanese leaders taking Spencer's views into consideration when discussing what ought to happen in Japan.

The overwhelming thrust of Herbert Spencer's views regarding Japan were conservative in the extreme. In 1873 when he first met Mori in London, Spencer confided to his diary 'He came to ask my opinion about the reorganisation of Japanese institutions. I gave him conservative advice – urging that they would have eventually to return to a form not much in advance of what they had and that they ought not attempt to diverge widely from it.'[42]

Between 1873 and 1880 when Mori arrived in London as Japanese Minister Mori's views were moving steadily towards statism. He and Ito were in general agreement, both becoming reluctant to make any fundamental changes as they personally moved into middle age.

Mori gave a great deal of thought to the development of a successful civil service through which good government could be effected. He saw entrance examinations with stiff academic standards to pick out the best candidates, together with good pensions on retiral, as essential to the development of a highly competent and unbribable group of administrators.

During the early 1880s in London Mori worked hard to produce *Representative Government*. Almost certainly Spencer found even this too radical. In 1892 when Spencer was in touch with Kentaro Kaneko he referred to Mori's draft which he had seen remarking 'I gave him very conservative advice, contending that it was impossible that the Japanese, hitherto accustomed to despotic rule, should all at once become capable of constitutional government.'

Perhaps Spencer rightly interpreted the difficulties for Japan in moving from the 'militant' phase of the *Tokugawa* regime, which

Spencer saw as 'an organisation completely militant, under which political freedom was unknown', to the 'industrial' society. Spencer's fears caused him to recommend that, in line with the Japanese system of family organisation, 'popular' political power should be vested in the patriarchs, heads of families, or groups of families. These men should be entitled to make *'statements of grievances'*. After *three or four generations* this body might 'suggest remedies' or eventually might be given 'a full power of legislation'. As a result he gave to those Japanese leaders with whom he was in direct contact, advice which was so far removed from his public liberal persona that he felt it necessary to write to Kaneko 'I give this advice in confidence. I wish that it should not transpire publicly, at any rate during my life, for I do not desire to rouse the animosity of my fellow-countrymen.'[43]

Mori's involvement with Herbert Spencer, as well as with ex-President Ulysses S. Grant, who also gave guarded advice, resulted in Japanese leaders having the increasingly conservative views of their middle years reinforced. In this frame of mind Mori left England for the last time saying, 'I am Japanese by blood I cannot be impartial'.[44]

## 7 THE IMPERIAL SOLUTION

By 7 May 1884 Mori, back in Tokyo, had been appointed to various important offices, including that of commissioner in the Ministry of Education (*Mombusho*). From this time he devoted himself almost entirely to education, being appointed – on 22 December 1885 – as Minister for Education.[45] But Mori did have an advantage over many others, he was a committed educationalist and his wide and varied experience enabled him to bring to the task enthusiasm and dedication. His educational inspection journeys to various parts of Japan were a *tour de force* for, with his well-developed gift for public speaking, he addressed teachers, administrators and local government officials as well as students, impelling them to consider educational objectives and standards.

What then were the ideas that Mori carried with him to the Ministry of Education and around Japan as he toured the schools? How had this travelled man interpreted the concepts with which he had become familiar during his years in the West? In the end did the Japanese inheritance produce its own answers? Were Western ideas introduced into Japanese education in any measure?

It was Kowashi Inoue who after Mori's death described his policy as 'a philosophy of education based on the national polity'. As Mori frequently stated 'The goal of our educational administration is likewise purely and simply the service of the state.' Teachers and administrators were exhorted to make the state their *honzon* or main image. In November 1887 Mori was even more specific, 'Reading, writing and arithmetic are not our concern in the education and instruction of the young . . . Education is entirely a matter of bringing up men of character . . . who are the good subjects required by our Empire.'[46]

In 1886 in order to bring the education system into line Mori promulgated various School Ordinances. At the top of the educational pyramid was the Imperial University of Tokyo.[47] At an administrative level the Imperial University was strictly tied in to the Ministry of Education, the Minister himself being responsible for senior appointments.

The Imperial University was supplied with its students by the higher middle schools to which only a few could aspire. Here the curriculum was planned along professional lines, students studying law, literature, science, medicine, engineering, agriculture or commerce. The best students in these schools were expected to proceed to university and graduate to a high rank in the civil service. By 1900 the higher middle schools had become a forcing ground in the preparation for entry to the Imperial University. Only five (later seven) such schools were authorised. They were the responsibility of the *Mombusho* which paid for everything.

The next level, was the ordinary middle school which was to have courses on Japanese language, the Chinese classics, two Western languages, history, geography, mathematics, natural history, physics, chemistry, agriculture, calligraphy, drawing, singing and gymnastics. There were some fifty-eight ordinary middle schools after 1886 (although the number had risen to 217 by 1900). Originally Mori only permitted each prefecture to establish one such school for the full maintenance of which it was responsible.

It was Mori's ambition to make the four-year ordinary primary school course compulsory, with the option of another additional four year course in a higher primary school. But there were loopholes and parents themselves were required to provide tuition fees for their children's attendance at these schools. Approximately half the eligible children attended in the early years. By 1900 80 per cent of children were at school. By 1907 the attendance rate had reached over 98 per cent. The overall achievement of the education system in getting children to attend school was remarkable.[48]

For the training of teachers Mori introduced 'normal schools' and through these the most controversial part of his educational regimen. On his return to Japan from London in 1884 he had been displeased by the behaviour of those attending Tokyo Colleges where many, fresh from academic triumphs in far-distant prefectures had won places in prestigious education institutions in Tokyo. These students themselves, challenged by the hectic pace of life in Tokyo, showed their unease by arrogant and aggressive behaviour.

Mori, like some educationalists in the West, was attracted by the idea of military-style physical training which, it was believed, would introduce physical fitness and discipline into otherwise disorderly lives. In May 1885 military drill was introduced into Tokyo Normal School. A year's experiment so convinced Mori of the value of this system that 'normal-school' life was increasingly organised along military lines.

The objectives of teacher training according to the Normal School Ordinance of 1886 were 'obedience, trust and affection and dignity', echoing the Confucian doctrines from which Mori had started. Mori himself explained what he hoped to do as follows,

> This military-style physical training is something to be used entirely as a means for promoting the three qualities of character I have just mentioned ... The things we hope to achieve by means of this training are: first to instil – with the sense of urgency possessed by actual soldiers – those habits of obedience which are appropriate in the classroom. Secondly as you know soldiers are always formed into squads, each squad possessing its own leader who devotes himself, head, mind and soul, to the welfare of his group. And thirdly, every company has its commanding officer who controls and supervises it, and who must comport himself with dignity. By the same token, our students by trading off the roles of common soldier, squad leader and commanding officer will build up the traits of character appropriate to each of these three roles.

Mori's enthusiasm for military drill encouraged him to seek to transfer responsibility for this from the *Mombusho* (the Ministry of Education) to the military authorities. Some good no doubt resulted from the general improvement in health and well-being of Japanese students but organising the dormitory, refectory and study-hall along military lines left the nation open to abuses which would in time corrupt Japanese society.[49]

It has been suggested that Mori's inspiration came from the English 'public' school where the Arnoldian themes of personal discipline and moral uplift were strong. The difficulty with this analogy is that the pupils of the English 'public' schools – aristocratic or upper-middle-class youths – were being taught how to behave as Christian gentlemen with responsibilities as well as privileges. These 'public' schools have always encouraged, within a class framework, a strong sense of individualism amongst their pupils.

It seems reasonably clear that Mori developed some of his ideas on physical education, social ethics, constitutionalism and commerce either from reading Spencer or from talking to him. The conservative advice which Spencer gave reinforced Mori's cautious approach. Mori was assassinated on 11 February 1889, at the age of 41. His work at the Ministry of Education had lasted for four years. During this brief time Mori set the Japanese education system along an orthodox and authoritarian path. As Ito remarked, his image as 'a Westerner born of Japan' can hardly fit the man who re-established Japanese education on such traditional lines.

# 9 Students

## 1 AN EDUCATED ELITE

Seldom can a people have obeyed an Emperor's injunction more faithfully than the Japanese, who, advised in 1868, that 'knowledge shall be sought throughout the world',[1] promptly set about their search. They quickly found their way to Britain. Throughout the *Meiji* years Japanese students were to be found in various parts of the United Kingdom working long hours, sometimes following two courses at once, and always trying to better themselves for the ultimate benefit of their country. The young men involved were usually of *samurai* stock whose education had been sufficiently comprehensive to include a study of English. Of these, some had ambitions to serve in the upper management of developing Japanese industries. Others, of impressive academic attainment, hoped to command high positions in the university structure of the new Japan. Yet others, the sons of former princes, and desirous of learning the ways of Western gentlemen, came to the ancient English universities.

It is virtually impossible to trace all the Japanese who studied in Britain during the *Meiji* period, but some general estimate should be attempted. There were perhaps as many as 100 men studying in one way or another in Scotland, of whom the majority were in Glasgow and the west. Possibly 100 attended in various capacities and at various places in London, with perhaps up to 100 working for a time as students in Oxford and Cambridge. Civic universities in the rest of Britain accounted for a further group, although (except in the case of Birmingham after 1900) only in ones and twos. If students, apprentices, naval cadets and other categories, like student engineers, are included, a tentative figure might emerge of some 500 young men studying in Britain, mostly between 1890 and 1914. These represented a cohort of intelligent highly trained Japanese who pursued at least part of their Western education somewhere in England, Scotland, Ireland or Wales.

There are formidable difficulties in tracing them.[2] Students in Victorian days, whether British or foreign, did not necessarily appear in University lists of graduates following the successful completion of a comprehensive degree course. Many signed on for a single course covering a single term. Few university records are sufficiently detailed to trace these 'casual' or 'private' students. By methodical study it might be possible to locate short-term students in college registers at Oxford or Cambridge. Fortunately, some Japanese students, who did not graduate, give details, in their autobiographies, of their university study.

Japanese students in Britain can usefully if arbitrarily be divided into two groups: those who came before 1880 and those who came after. Pre-1880 students had many difficulties. Their English may not have been good and their education in Japan may not have been either comprehensive or advanced. This group did perform very useful pioneering functions, familiarising themselves with British academic institutions, learning about teaching methods and laboratory work, as well as examination standards and procedures. Post-1880 students were better educated in Western modes, had often distinguished themselves during their university or college courses in Japan and knew more clearly what they were looking for in Britain.

In choosing, Oxford, Cambridge and London, prestige was more important than expense. Other universities and colleges were preferred for their known excellence in technical work, applied science teaching and industrial training. Japanese were often awarded government studentships; although those at Oxford, Cambridge and London were more usually privately financed.

Expense was always a consideration. Throughout the *Meiji* period the Japanese were forced, in difficult financial circumstances, to consider value for money. This accounts for the large numbers of Japanese students who registered for single courses, costing £3 or so, and who hoped in this piecemeal way to make up an education.[3] On the practical side, Japanese students also worked in shipyards, factories and engineering workshops thus again forwarding the process of technical transfer. Young professional engineers from Japan also served as juniors in a wide variety of capacities. Some were assistants with civil engineering firms, helping to build roads and bridges, others worked for railway engineers and yet others for hydraulic and electricity concerns. Almost all references to these men's probationary years in British service have come from their biographies or from their families.

## 2 AT OXFORD AND CAMBRIDGE

The Japanese who were studying at the ancient English universities, and who were members of colleges, were usually from high-ranking families.[4] They often brought with them intelligent young clansmen, who studied seriously, as advisers or 'guardians'. Most Japanese students in Oxford and Cambridge attended after 1880.

At the ancient English universities they were offered high-quality instruction and membership of colleges patronised by the British ruling class. Young Japanese whose rank and family background entitled them to expect to represent their country in the diplomatic service or who hoped to serve in the Japanese government found it appropriate to learn something of British society at this level. These young men were highly regarded.[5]

At Oxford Japanese students were of the highest rank. The Iwakura family patronised Balliol.[6] Maybe the Balliol connection was encouraged by John Harrington Gubbins,[7] one of the early Japanologists, who, after a career as interpreter, was appointed to a lectureship in Japanese,[8] based at Balliol, where he was a Fellow from 1909 to 1912. When Gubbins retired in 1912, the appointment was not renewed.[9]

In Cambridge between the 1880s and the early 1900s there was an active Japanese Club composed of Japanese undergraduates supported by senior members of their colleges. The Club met 'to study the training and character of the English gentleman'.[10] A senior don took the chair and another acted as speaker, seeking to convey an understanding of the mores of the upper-class Englishman. Many aspects of the life of an English gentleman were adverted to in the lectures. Sir John Seeley, then Regius Professor of Modern History, Master of Gonville and Caius College, lectured on 'History and Ethics', and the Master of Pembroke College, discoursed on 'The Comity of Nations' (see Appendix D for list of lectures given). Although some of the material – especially that relating to Christianity – was alien, the intelligent Japanese undergraduate could learn a good deal of the objectives and motivation of British society at this level. That the society was aristocratic and exclusive is attested by Lady Macalister whose husband, Sir Donald, was an active supporter. She mentions that one man suggested as a member was refused on the grounds that 'only those with eight generations of nobility in their ancestry were eligible'.[11] Those Japanese who supported this society were not the same persons as those whose names graced the lists of students who had excelled in, for example, pure mathematics, which was taught with distinction at this time in Cambridge.

Cambridge offered the most advanced teaching of pure mathematics then available, making it necessary for all wishing to excel in the subject to take further training there.[12] Otherwise, Oxford and Cambridge were in a kind of scientific doldrums being slow to respond to the challenges of the new science and technology.[13] There were however some signs of change, perhaps encouraged by the Prince Consort, who as Chancellor of Cambridge from 1847 to his death in 1861, was keen to introduce new topics in the moral and natural sciences.[14]

In 1875, Cambridge set up a Chair in Mechanism and Engineering,[15] although the department did not really take off until 1890 with the appointment of James Alfred Ewing (1855–1935) to the chair.[16] Ewing had already served with distinction in Japan (see Chapter 5, section 2 above). He quickly found the money to establish proper engineering laboratories. At Oxford, hesitant steps were taken with the introduction of Schools of Natural Science, Physics and Mathematics. The world of social science was represented by law and modern history. But engineering as an academic discipline proved unacceptable at Oxford until 1908, when it became the last major university to institute a Chair in Engineering. Frewin Jenkin, son of Fleeming Jenkin (the first Professor of Engineering at Edinburgh in 1868), was the first incumbent. Oxford's unwillingness to come to terms with scientific and technical education did not go unnoticed. John Perry (1850–1930) complained 'She has always ostentatiously held herself aloof from manufacturers and commerce' and said that the 'absence of scientific method is evident everywhere'.[17]

A small but impressive gallery of Japanese Cambridge graduates stands out. Dairoku Kikuchi (1855–1917) became 19th Wrangler in Mathematics in 1877.[18] Kencho Suyematsu (1855–1920) graduated LLB in 1884, LLM in 1888, and was later honoured with the DLitt.[19] Manjiro Inagaki (1861–1908)[20] graduated BA in 1889, having been much influenced by Seeley whom he regarded as his master. Inagaki in 1890, published *Japan and the Pacific*, a truly precocious achievement in which he showed a strongly independent cast of mind. Inagaki based his argument on the assumption that Britain and Russia must inevitably come into conflict in the Pacific, and that 'without doubt Japan is the key to the Pacific'. The book is dedicated to Seeley; would the prevision of its author have disturbed the dedicatee? Inagaki later made his career in the Japanese foreign service, serving as ambassador to Spain.

The economics teaching which was being developed in Cambridge by Henry Fawcett and Alfred Marshall also attracted the Japanese.[21,22] Juichi Soyeda (1864–1929) came to Cambridge in 1884 after graduating at the Imperial University of Tokyo in 1884.[23] He remained as a non-collegiate student until 1887, attending Alfred Marshall's lectures. Soyeda was reported by C. R. Ashbee (of Kings) as 'a future Japanese statesman . . . a fine intelligent being and emphatically a gentleman, full of information and greed for knowledge'.[24] He became President of the Cambridge Economic Club in the Easter term 1887.[25] The debate on bimetallism which was then raging in Cambridge, was of great interest to the Japanese.[26]

Not all Japanese at Cambridge were successful,[27] but all – whatever their intellectual achievements – straddled two worlds. The frontispiece of the report of the fourth meeting of the Japan Club (November 1888) reads:

> Look at the winding course of the Ke, with the green bamboo so luxuriant! Here is our elegant and accomplished gentleman (the princely man of Confucius!) as we cut and then file; as we chisel and then grind, *so has he cultivated himself*. How grave is he and how dignified! How majestic and distinguished! Our elegant and accomplished gentleman can never be forgotten.[28]

Nor has the ambivalence disappeared in the succeeding century. 'English public school virtues of independence, self-discipline and courtesy' are still considered important. As Father Tagawa Shigeru, the principal of the Catholic foundation which owns the 'Japanese Eton' at Willen Park, Milton Keynes, said recently, 'We want the children to be good English and Japanese gentlemen.'[29]

## 3 IN LONDON

Tracing Japanese students in London from British sources has presented special problems: because of war damage records at London's colleges are scrappy, and the surviving fragments, though valuable in themselves, do not permit a comprehensive picture to be drawn. Japanese students can be traced at University College,[30] King's College, the School of Chemistry, the Royal School of Mines and the Royal School of Science which were the forerunners of Imperial College. It is likely that they attended at other Colleges. From Japanese sources it is sometimes easier because more family and clan records remain. In several cases Japanese scholars have pursued these matters and have brought together much material.

University College, London became something of a Mecca for Japanese students even before the restoration of the Emperor in

1868. One of the most interesting groups of students to register at UCL was the famous '*Choshu* five' who left Japan secretly in 1863 on a mission to see the West for themselves. The five were Hirubumi Ito, Kaoru Inoue, Yakichi Nomura,[31] Yozo Yamao and Kinsuke Endo. All were to attain high government rank and become national leaders in the new Japan. In 1864 when Alexander Williamson, Professor of Chemistry at UCL, first befriended them they were unknown.

Some fifteen *Satsuma* students, also left Japan secretly in April 1865 and landed at Southampton in June 1865.[32] They also applied to Alexander Williamson and were registered in the Faculties of Arts and Laws at UCL.[33] None of these men remained long enough in London to follow degree courses; while attending one or more courses they pursued other interests in a bid to inform themselves about the West.[34] It is believed in Japan that perhaps fifty Japanese had studied at UCL before 1880.

Japanese students were to be found studying a wide variety of subjects although most opted for science and engineering studies, including physics, chemistry and analytical chemistry, geology and mineralogy, mechanical and geometric drawing and engineering. The engineering teaching at UCL was well established, the Chair having been set up very early in 1840.

One of the most successful students, at UCL from 1876 to 1881, was Joji Sakurai (1858–1939).[35] His main subject was chemistry but he also took courses in geology, mineralogy and physics. Sakurai, later Baron, became Professor of Chemistry in the Imperial University of Tokyo, President of the Imperial Academy and National Research Council of Japan.

But it was not for scientific teaching that University College, London, became attractive to the Japanese. In 1876 the economist, W. S. Jevons moved from Manchester to London where he taught at UCL. At least seven young Japanese presented themselves as his students.[36]

Although very many Japanese students passed through the gates of the Colleges of the University of London during the *Meiji* era, in some senses those who registered in Scotland are more 'visible' because of the full archival records still available there.

## 4 AT SCOTTISH UNIVERSITIES AND COLLEGES

Japanese students discovered very early the merits of the parallel, but different, university structure which existed in Scotland at the four ancient universities there.[37] Indeed Scotland may have attracted the largest contingent of all. From 1880 to 1914 some sixty Japanese registered at the University of Glasgow. Others studied at the University of Edinburgh and at the Andersonian (now the University of Strathclyde). It is not known how many of these were also shipyard apprentices but certainly some spent time working in the shipyards. The Japanese studying in Glasgow were usually sponsored by the Japanese government who paid their fees.

From the early days in the 1860s when Thomas B. Glover, trading in Nagaski, sent Japanese pupils to schools in Aberdeen,[38] Scots merchants in Japan ensured that Scottish/Japanese university links were strong. Nor was the Japanese confidence in the promise of Scotland misplaced. As has been explained:

> Lord Kelvin (Sir William Thomson)[39] succeeded to the chair of Natural Philosophy in Glasgow in 1846 and began his great electrical researches leading to his successful scientific and business exploits in cable laying in the 1860s and after. Around Thomson clustered a galaxy of professors, as pupils, teachers and business partners – Lewis Gordon, Fleeming Jenkin, P. G. Tait, Alfred Ewing – active in university science in Scotland and entrepreneurship in the electrical industry. Products of the Scottish universities, and usually of the Cambridge Mathematical Tripos also, were amongst the finest flower of Scottish Victorian culture, and in their presence the Scottish universities were confident enough to hold to the traditions.[40]

This 'Golden Age' in the Scottish Universities was known to and appreciated by the Japanese.[41]

The Scottish universities since the days of the eighteenth-century Enlightenment had taught a wide range of subjects including science, political economy, political science and philosophy. Adam Smith, formerly Professor of Moral Philosophy at the University of Glasgow, published *The Wealth of Nations* in 1776. At the same time, the distinction brought by Joseph Black by his work in chemistry and on latent heat and James Watt, innovative in engineering, had coincided with the enormous expansion of Scotland's industrial base and eventually, in 1840, brought a Regius Chair of Engineering to Glasgow University.[42,43] Initially few students opted for engineering courses, but soon there was increased demand. The second University in Glasgow, the Andersonian,[44] which had earlier served as a Mechanics Institute, organised popular, cheap, day and evening classes for mechanics and technicians. Between 1866 and 1868 both Yozo Yamao,[45] and Henry Dyer were registered at evening classes there.[46] Is it possible that Glasgow was initially favoured by the Japanese because of the low fees required by university and Andersonian alike?

The academic advantage which made Glasgow a desirable centre for the Japanese was the presence of teachers, including Kelvin, whose research interests lay in the problems of Clyde industries especially shipbuilding – applied science and technology. Despite the availability of the naval architecture course in London,[47] there was strong demand for such specialisms to be available in Scotland. The University of Glasgow was memorialised in 1880 by a large number of shipbuilders, marine engineers, shipowners and others who wished to establish a lectureship in shipbuilding and marine engineering. Thanks to the generous intervention of Mrs Elder, widow of John Elder, Shipbuilder, the Chair of Naval Architecture at the University of Glasgow, the first in the world, was set up in 1883.[48]

Glasgow's Chair of Naval Architecture confirmed for the Japanese Glasgow's supremacy as a place to study. One Japanese student invited by the Japanese government to attend at the Massachusetts Institute of Technology in 1912, 'gave a flat refusal' because 'MIT was a second-rate university at that time'. The same student came willingly to Glasgow University a year later 'because the University of Glasgow was in the highest class in the world for naval architecture and marine engineering'.[49] This man graduated BSc Glasgow in 1915.

The first student to make the move from London to Glasgow had been one of the original '*Choshu* five'. In 1866, after his time studying in London at UCL, Yozo Yamao moved to Glasgow where he spent a further two years. There he succeeded in working at Napier's shipyard by day and studying at the Andersonian University by night.[50] Yamao never forgot his Scottish experience and his understanding of the facilities available in Glasgow may help to explain Japanese preferences later.

The Japanese who came to Glasgow to study were primarily scientists and engineers. Natural philosophy (physics), mathematics, engineering, chemistry and naval architecture were the subjects for which the Japanese were registered. Some came for full degree courses and were resident in Glasgow for several years, graduating BSc and CE. Many came for shorter periods. A few came as research students (see Section 6 below) – a category then undifferentiated in the University's records. As with any group of students the Japanese varied in competence. It is noteworthy however that the prize lists of the University of Glasgow from 1880 are peppered with Japanese names. Perhaps the most interesting list is that of 1881–2 when 'for general eminence', the members of the natural philosophy class voted three Japanese, first, second and seventh.[51] These men were Rinzaburo Shida, Naomoto Takayama, and Kyoshi Minami. Rinzaburo Shida is among those whose name appears more than once in the University records. Perhaps his most notable achievement was to win, in session 1881–2, the Cleland Gold Medal in Natural Philosophy 'for the best experimental investigation of Magnetic susceptibility'. Naomoto Takayama and Kiyoshi Minami were also regular prizewinners. Another Japanese student, Sampachi Fukazawa, created a precedent in 1901 when he requested, and was granted, permission to present himself for an examination in Japanese,[52] as his necessary foreign language for entrance to the university. Sampachi Fukuzawa graduated BSc in 1904.

Although the aristocratic Japanese names graced the College lists of Oxford and Cambridge the men who came to Glasgow could also be from important families. In addition to the third son of Yukichi Fukuzawa, the grandson of Yataro Iwasaki, Taizo Shoda was a student of Glasgow. Taizo Shoda later had a distinguished career in Japan as an aero engine designer.[53]

From the 1880s onward Glasgow University continued to employ an impressive range of teachers headed by Kelvin himself in the Chair of Natural Philosophy (Physics).[54] Kelvin's brother James Thomson was Professor of Engineering until 1889 when Archibald Barr took over. John Harvard Biles (Sir John from 1914) occupied the Chair of Naval Architecture from 1891. Kelvin, Barr and Biles were all involved in industry, Kelvin's many patents are well known, Barr was senior partner in Barr & Stroud, the new thriving optical range-finder firm (see Chapter 13, Section 5 below) and Biles worked as consultant with various shipbuilding firms. It was this marriage of theory and practice which attracted the Japanese to Scotland.

## 5 THE ENGLISH CIVIC UNIVERSITIES

The civil colleges were founded in England at Manchester (as Owen's College, 1851),[55] Newcastle (as Armstrong College, 1871),[56] Leeds (1874), Bristol (1876), Sheffield (1879), Birmingham (as Mason's College, 1880), Liverpool and Nottingham (1881), partly in response to feelings of local pride and partly to fill the gap caused by the failure of Oxford and Cambridge to broaden their curriculum to include science. The reluctant development of science and engineering teaching at Oxbridge,[57] and the needs of a great industrial nation, helped to bring to fruition a long-overdue local University College movement. The colleges, all to become Universities in due course, found their *métier*, not in competing with Oxford and Cambridge, as they at first intended, but in building on the strength of the local industrial base. Thus Manchester (Owen's College) in appointing (Sir) Henry Roscoe to the Chair of Chemistry 1857,[58] succeeded, perhaps inadvertently, in bringing college and industry into close harmony. Roscoe undertook widespread industrial consultancy as part of his professional work.[59] Roscoe's work at Manchester attracted Japanese students. Roscoe himself commented that all he met with were 'one or all extraordinarily persevering, painstaking men'. He also recounted how a Japanese student, who had taken the first-year prize at Owen's College, from a class of 150 to 200, considered himself disgraced, when in the second year he was placed only second.[60] Manchester, as the centre of the cotton industry, was used by some Japanese who wished to do advanced work in textile science, which included chemistry.[61]

At Newcastle, the College of Science,[62] was strongly linked with local industry. There was an extraordinary preponderance of engineers, especially mining engineers, reflecting the primary interests of the north-east coal industry. These strengths were high priorities for the Japanese so that the College and the nearby shipyards attracted numbers of students.

In the University of Birmingham in October 1902 innovation came with a Faculty of Commerce under W. J. Ashley.[63] It was Joseph Chamberlain's express intention to systematise and develop 'the special training which is required by men of business'. The courses under the general heading of 'business management' proved especially attractive, to foreign students. By 1906–7 there were fifty-seven students, including some six Japanese, among whom was Takakiyo Mitsui. The House of Mitsui recognised the merits of the Faculty, not only by providing students in the early days, but also by funding in the 1920s the Mitsui Chair of Finance.

## 6 RESEARCH STUDENTS

Throughout the *Meiji* period Japanese students already educated at home were sent overseas for further education and research.[64] Most who travelled chose to work in America, Britain or Germany. For those whose fields related to government and constitutional matters there were few problems, other than those of mastering their chosen subject, for these were the subjects traditionally associated with the educated *samurai*. Science was a different matter. Could a life's work dedicated to science be justifed? The matter was of considerable importance for the programme of technical transfer, upon which Japan was pinning so much, was dependent, at least in part, on the successful implantation of hard scientific knowledge.

The struggle of the first generation of Japanese scientists to come to terms with the new learning is illuminating. Initially Aikitsu Tanakadate (1856–1952) was determined to train himself for the traditional *samurai* duties of 'governing the country'. But, interested in the early scientific education he had received and after much heart-searching as to whether science was an honourable calling, he resolved 'to study physics, which is the basis of all science so as to make up in full measure for our country's deficiencies'.[65] Tanakadate did his post-graduate study (1888–91) on ammeters (which he had originally started in Tokyo) at the University of Glasgow working under Kelvin. He had been trained in Tokyo by Cargill G. Knott (DSc, Edinburgh) (see Chapter 5 above). Subsequently Tanakadate became Professor of Physics at the Imperial University of Tokyo and Director of the Physical Institute. He was the foremost Japanese physicist of his generation. As a geophysicist he is sometimes known as 'the father of Japanese seismology'.

Kaichi Watanabe (1858–1932) graduated from ICE in 1883 before proceeding to Scotland in 1884 for further study at the University of Glasgow. He later worked for the civil engineering firm, Benjamin Baker, then designers for the proposed Forth Railway Bridge. Watanabe features as the central figure in the well-known picture demonstrating the cantilever principle used in making the Forth Bridge.[66] On his return to Japan he was appointed chief engineer of Japan Public Works Company (*Nippon Doboku Kaisha*). Watanabe was later director of Sangu and Narita railway companies and Tokyo and Kyoto Electric railway companies.

On the occasion of Kelvin's 80th birthday on 25 June 1904, six of his former Japanese research students sent 'hearty birthday greetings'. The telegram was signed by Masuda, Taniguchi, Watanabe, Mano, Goto and Tanakadate. Kelvin carefully preserved the telegram in the notebook he was then using. These men also spent research time in Germany.[67]

Another promising physicist was Rinzaburo Shida (1855–92) who, a first-class graduate from the Imperial College of Engineering in 1879, had worked with W. J. Ayrton at the laboratories in Tokyo, specialising in telegraph engineering.[68] Shida was based in Glasgow in the early 1880s working under Kelvin on electromagnetism and telegraphy. He travelled widely carrying introductions from Kelvin to German scholars. On his return to Japan in 1883 he became Professor of Natural Philosophy at ICE, a post which had remained vacant since 1879 when Ayrton had returned to London. Shida was also much involved with the technical development of telegraphy in Japan. He died in 1892 at the age of 37. The loss of young men like Shida, after heavy investment in his education to an advanced level, from diseases such as tuberculosis, was not uncommon in Japan at this time.

## 7 CAN WE COMPETE?

The young Japanese who were sent to study in Britain during the *Meiji* era were a talented group chosen to spearhead Japanese attempts to affect the transfer of scientific as well as philosophic and literary ideas to Japan. Those who studied here took back with them the skills they had learnt, some understanding of Western society and perhaps a strengthened determination to compete with the West. Their first duty was to attempt the difficult and time-consuming task of operating in English. They were thereafter required to make continuous contact, to live in Britain, to study day by day, to work in a subordinate capacity, to accept instruction and, if necessary, rebuke, and to endure the hardships of being strangers in a strange land.[69]

The young Japanese at Oxford and Cambridge were rather different, living as they did in college rooms with their servants, and those of the college, in attendance. Coming often from the upper classes with its various grades and its partly archaic values, were they looking for a new concept of élitism which would supersede or modify their own? Is it possible that at a certain level of consciousness these young men were seeking an alternate view of self more consistent with that of Britain's ruling groups? Were they testing the British model for fit? Or were they merely playing, enjoying a mode of life and a means of learning which was not available to them in Japan?

For the rest, the tiny majority of students sent, and financed, by the

Japanese government, matters were very serious. They needed to learn as much as they could as effectively as possible for transfer back to Japan. Yozo Yamao, the oldest of the original *Choshu* five, showed a deep understanding when he wrote 'if no industry exists one need only train people, for they will develop industry themselves'.[70]

For the scientists and engineers seeking advanced scientific and technical knowledge success in the research laboratory was all-important. Japanese research students were bound to seek to work with the best teams in the best research laboratories.[71] It was James Alfred Ewing who, in 1891 himself striving to establish university engineering laboratories in Cambridge, spelt out their function.[72]

For Japanese research students the questions were even more compelling. Can we compete in terms of scholarship in world terms? The generation of young men first trained as scientists and engineers by men like Dyer, Ayrton, Perry, Milne, Ewing and Cargill Knott were encouraged in Japan as undergraduates to work in laboratories as part of the research team. But did any of the Western teachers envisage a world in which Japanese would be supreme in their own laboratories turning out world-class research work themselves?

Western professors spoke highly of their Japanese students. Their endeavours were commended. But did Western scientists, while encouraging the Japanese as research colleagues, doubt the 'seed and the soil' of Japan? Would it be possible for Japan to grow an indigenous scientific tradition which would enable her to make an original contribution? Erwin Baelz, the German medical doctor who worked in Japan for twenty-five years deplored what he took to be Japanese attitudes.[73] The greatest compliment Baelz could say of a Japanese was that 'he is just like a German'. Did Baelz's remarks echo the feelings of others?

The man who took these matters most to heart was Hantaro Nagaoka (1865–1950) who entered the university of Tokyo in 1884 to study physics where he was taught by Cargill Knott. Later between 1893 and 1896 he studied further in Germany with Helmholtz, Boltzmann, Planck, Fuchs and Schwartz.[74] Fortunately Nagaoka's own work in physics was distinguished. As one Japanese commentator has written, 'That Professor Nagoaka was the first to propound the nuclear structure of the atom will ever stand to his credit in the history of science.'[75] Notwithstanding such an accolade Nagaoka was right to be concerned. Japanese scholars always had the problem of writing and presenting the results of their researches in a foreign language. Even then they could not assume international recognition.[76] Was Nagaoka's belief that the West underrated the achievements of the Japanese justified?[77] When, in 1949 Hideki Yukawa won for Japan the Nobel prize in physics for the first time on the 'theoretical prediction of the neson' both Aikitsu Tanakadate and Hantaro Nagaoka were still alive. Yukawa himself attributed his decision to study physics 'to the fact that one could find among the Japanese on the path such a great physicist as Hantaro Nagaoka'.

The way of all Japanese students abroad in Britain or elsewhere was hard. Some became enamoured of the foreign country to which they were assigned; all were changed to some extent by their experiences. It was Ogai Mori (1862–1922) who left the most eloquent note of his responses to studying abroad writing:

> Among my fellow-students residing abroad those who came with prepossessed ideas could achieve but little in learning whereas those who humbled themselves in learning and took time to form their opinions achieved good results after coming home. If I may speak of my own case when I took my first step in Europe I felt just like a *muku-dori* (grey starling) flying into a great city. And up to now I have never regretted this attitude I assumed.[78]

# 10 In the Shipyards

## 1 STRANGERS IN OUR MIDST

While the shipbuilding industry was being slowly and painstakingly built up in Japan further steps were being taken to learn more advanced shipbuilding technology from Britain for importation to Japan. The Royal Navy,[1] the 'Mother of Navies', was in close cooperation with the Imperial Japanese Navy, from which came many shipbuilding orders. British shipyards were also successful in tendering to build commercial shipping for the Japanese,[2] stipulating, when signing contracts for such ships, that their own personnel help with construction.

Japanese apprentices, university-trained engineers, naval cadets, naval engineering officers and high-ranking naval officers were all frequently in attendance at British shipyards. Some served for years, working on or supervising the production of a ship. Others made state visits to enjoy the hospitality provided at the ceremonial ship-launch. Visitors' books of industrial firms testify to the regularity and frequency of such visits.

In Britain the steamship revolution caused greater centralisation of the shipbuilding industry which was relocated in the industrial north especially on the Clyde,[3] the Tyne,[4] the Mersey,[5] and in Belfast.[6] The reason for the dominance of these centres was originally the proximity of cheap supplies of iron and coal and later the availability of steel plates and bars. These factors, together with a low-paid and docile labour force proved decisive. All the new centres were dependent either on artificial dredging or on purpose-built docks and harbours.[7] The new shipyards were larger, on more spacious sites and so could accommodate larger vessels. After the 1870s few wooden sailing vessels were built, although with older seamen the disciplines of sail-seamanship remained compelling.[8] The concentration of shipbuilding on the River Clyde can be seen from the map, 10.1.

But the new generation of ships were of iron and very shortly thereafter of steel. Steel was preferred because it enabled the ship-designer or naval architect to design a lightness of hull which gave both speed and strength.[9] Unfortunately with a relatively thin hull the problems of sea-water corrosion became more pressing, requiring the use of various protective and preservative measures.

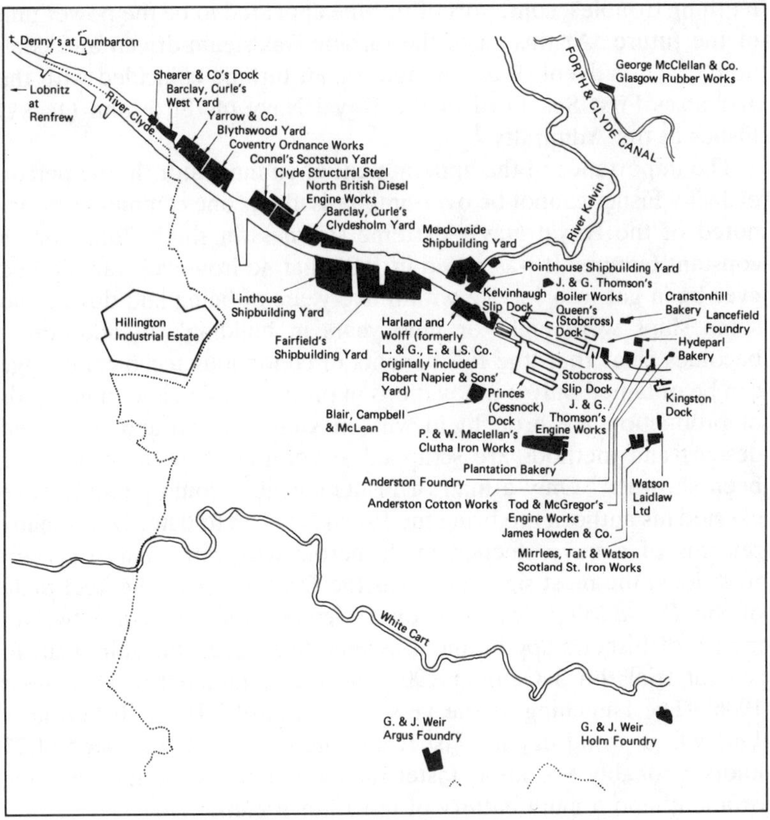


*Map* 10.1 Shipyards on the Clyde, Scotland

Engines for ships were also improving very quickly.[10] About 1850 the earlier paddle-wheel drive had been replaced by the propeller which had been successfully harnessed to the drive shaft. The compound steam engine and the triple expansion engine were both used. The reciprocating coal-fired steam engine remained,[11] until the end of the century in some form, the motive power for all modern ships.

But an even more radical change was coming. In 1897 Charles Algernon Parsons (1854–1931)[12] at the naval review at Spithead, held to celebrate Queen Victoria's Diamond Jubilee, demonstrated in the *Turbinia*, speeds of over 30 knots, and 'showed the experts of the world her superior speed and power resources compared with contemporary boats and destroyers'.[13] The *Turbinia* had three propeller-shafts each with three propellers in series. Although there were teething troubles, some sort of turbine appeared to be the power unit of the future. At this stage the turbine was steam-driven and coal-fired.[14] The advent of a workable steam turbine coincided with the arrival as First Sea Lord of the Royal Navy of (Sir) John (Jacky) Fisher at the Admiralty.[15]

The importance of the appointment of an innovator, in the person of Jacky Fisher cannot be over-emphasised. As one commentator has noted of the Royal Navy 'extreme slowness in shipbuilding was a constant feature. It was noted in 1885 that no iron-clad warship had ever been got into service within five years of being laid down, and some ships were eight or nine years in building'. In addition it becomes clear that 'the full benefits of continuous technical change can be obtained only if innovations in product design and in methods of production are brought in with maximum speed and if the old designs and methods are scrapped as soon as their inferiority has been shown'.[16] Only a man of Fisher's calibre could possibly have exerted his authority to bring the Royal Navy up to date. Of his many reforms of a navy steeped in its heroic past with many outworn traditions, the most significant was the *Dreadnought*. The keel-plate of the *Dreadnought* was laid on 5 October 1905, within a twelve-month of Fisher's appointment as First Sea Lord: 'the ship went to sea for trials on 3 October 1906 and was completed in December 1906'. The launching of the vessel by Edward VII on 10 February 1906 was a proud day for Fisher and the navy. It had a speed of 21 knots, probably two knots faster than any other battleship 'building or afloat' and a main battery of ten 12-inch guns.

The rapid adoption of the turbine principle to the naval vessels of the world should not obscure the parallel progress made with screw-driven commercial vessels.[17] The *Mauretania* and her sister ship the *Lusitania* were built in 1906 by Cunard. The *Mauretania*, powered by four propellers, had a driving power of 54 000 kw (73 000 HP) an increase of some thirty times on the engine power of the *Turbinia*. The *Mauretania* made up to 27 knots during her trials and won the Atlantic Blue Riband in 1907, a title she retained until 1929.

The radical changes taking place in shipbuilding, whether naval or commercial, provided great stimulus for those engaged in the industry. Japanese personnel, whether naval cadets, engineer officers, naval inspectors or apprentices, all had a great deal to gain from working in British shipyards at this time. Their achievement was to be measured by their ability to transfer what they had learned to the shipyards at home in Japan.

## 2 APPRENTICES

During the *Meiji* years the Japanese government were keen to place apprentices in British industrial enterprises so that they could learn practical skills in the shipyard or on the shop-floor. It is not easy to trace these men. There are two main sources of information. Families in Japan treasure recollections and biographical memoirs which record details of the life and work of grandfather or great-grandfather, and the original apprentice and business records of individual firms give particulars of negotiations which led to the Japanese presence in the British work-place.

The agreement to accept Japanese apprentices was arranged at the highest level. It was part of the package discussed by the firm's directorate when bargaining for orders from Japan. Japanese names rarely appear in the ordinary apprentice books, preserved in the business records of many British firms, for of course the Japanese apprentices were different.[18] They were not as others, young men signing on for a period of years to learn a single trade; they were often highly educated, well-trained young engineers who needed to sample a wide variety of processes within any one firm. The Japanese pressed hard to have their men accepted.

Pride of place to the first Japanese to serve as an apprentice must go to Yozo Yamao who in Glasgow between 1866 and 1868 served in Napier's Shipyard on the Clyde by day and attended the cheap, popular working-men's classes at the Andersonian University in the evenings.[19] His family treasure the simple tools which he used during these years. The Kawada family developed a long-standing connection with Lobnitz and Co., Shipbuilders, at Renfrew on the Clyde. Kawada *père* was an apprentice in the yards, to be followed by his son.[20] The long period of Riokichi Kawada's apprenticeship, from September 1877 to May 1884, with Lobnitz reveals how great a commitment of time and money the Japanese were prepared to invest.[21]

Kawada's apprenticeship is especially notable because of his family's role in the Mitsubishi firm and at the Nagasaki shipyard. Koichiro Kawada, Riokichi's father, was like his master, Yataro Iwasaki, Mitsubishi's founder, a *Tosa* man who became General Director of Mitsubishi in 1883, and was regarded with Ishikawa and Iwasaki as one of the 'three rivers' or originators of the firm.[22] A man with such connections and as thoroughly trained as Riokichi could expect to make a considerable impact on his return to Japan.

Another with strong Mitsubishi connection who spent years in Glasgow was Taizo Shoda, who graduated at the University of Glasgow (BSc, 1916) and at the same time served his apprenticeship with David Rowan.[23]

In 1890 Messrs Armstrong Whitworth on the Tyne received Motoreru Haramiishi (1870–1934), who had studied at Tokyo Technical School, as a shipbuilding 'apprentice'.[24] He remained on Tyneside for nine years before returning to the ship design and drawing office of Mitsubishi Shipbuilding and Engineering Co. Ltd.

The negotiations between the Japanese and British engineering firms included discussions about engineering apprentices. The Japanese pushed to have larger numbers of their people employed, the British stalled, claiming that it would be difficult to keep production going with untrained Japanese as part of the team. Both sides compromised; the Japanese placing a reduced number of trainees, the British promising to give those selected broad experience of a wide range of processes.

Mr Douglas Vickers in writing to Mr Komura at Mitsui (34 Lime Street, EC) from Vickers River Don Works, Sheffield, noted that he had had representations from the Japanese, from both naval and civil personnel, to get Japanese into various works including the Sheffield Steel Plate Works.[25] Another firm who were persuaded to accept Japanese in the works was J. & G. Weir of Cathcart, Glasgow, makers of sophisticated pumps and other gear for warships and merchant ships.[26,27] Weir's relationship with the Japanese naval authorities in Britain was very close and indeed from 1912, their equipment was being made under licence in Japan by Kawasaki and Mitsubishi (see Chapter 13 below). A.R. Brown, the honorary consul for Japan in Glasgow reported in 1895 on five students from the Tokyo Nautical School 'who are now serving as apprentices on board ships owned in Glasgow'.[28] There is also a legend that in Japanese steel works cries of 'Awa Parkhead' 'Awa Camlachie' resounded as Japanese, trained in Glasgow at Beardmore's Parkhead Forge, gave the traditional workmen's cries as they coaxed heavy steel plates into position.[29]

## 3 NAVAL CADETS

Once the Japanese had decided to take the Royal Navy as their model they were anxious for their midshipmen or cadets to have the benefit of British naval training. One of the first reports relates to a Lieutenant Etzaki who had served with the Royal Navy about 1870.[30]

In 1872 a group of young men destined for high office in the Imperial Japanese Navy landed at Southampton. This group is of particular interest because it contained Heihachiro Togo (1848–1934), the future Nelson of Japan.[31] The cadets were registered at the Thames Nautical Training College. Here the instruction was carried on on HMS *Worcester*, permanently moored, and run according to RN service regulations. After their theoretical training, the young men were posted to the sea-going training ship *Hampshire*. By the end of February 1875 they had navigated around the Cape of Good Hope and arrived in Melbourne. They returned to the Thames at the end of September 1875.

After this Togo was sent to Cambridge to study higher mathematics under the guidance of the Rev. A. D. Capel who lodged him in his own home. After the completion of all their training, Togo and the other cadets were appointed 'inspectors' for ships then being built in Britain for the Imperial Japanese Navy.[32] This cohort of young Japanese naval officers were destined to become the first generation of modern Japanese admirals.

## 4 NAVAL CONTRACTS AND NAVAL INSPECTORS

In contracting for ships from builders in Britain the Japanese initially required the services of British intermediaries (see Chapter 12 below). They needed to employ men sufficiently skilled to set out the required specifications, negotiate with a detailed knowledge of Japanese requirements, supervise the ships as they took shape on the stocks,[33] check the performance of the ships at their trials, and on completion arrange for a captain and crew to steam the ship to Japan. In addition agents had to be found both in Yokohama and London who would handle the complex finances of such transactions, for according to contract, monies were payable at various stages during the course of construction.

Later, especially for ships under construction for the Imperial Japanese Navy, the Japanese were determined to use their own trained naval personnel. The role of the Engineer Naval Officer, so long a Cinderella figure in the Royal Navy, was acknowledged in the Imperial Japanese Navy as of great importance.

The building of the *Great Eastern* was a straw in the wind,[34] demonstrating the value of scientific and engineering principles in ship design. With the establishment on 16 Janury 1860 of the Institute of Naval Architects (INA) the way was clear for real advancement.[35] Even with a new professional body the Admiralty remained cool to the idea of scientific ship design. In course of time the Admiralty conceded; the Surveyors' Department of the Royal Navy was re-organised. In 1883 the Royal Corps of Naval Constructors formalised and professionalised a group of properly trained ship-designers.[36]

Traditionally the Royal Dockyards had built ships for the Royal Navy; most private shipbuilders had not been involved with this work. After the 1860s, with the feared aggression of Louis Napoleon in France, there came a determination to maintain naval strength. The Ravensworth Report of 1884 suggested that the government should award naval contracts to private firms, but they also recommended that the Royal Yards should continue to be involved with experimental work.

Naval contracts, the legal agreement between builders and the commissioning purchaser, were prepared by the shipyard concerned after consultation with the Admiralty. Each contract included all possible details of technical requirement, price, methods of payment and the arrangements for the supervision of the vessel while building. When the Japanese started to award naval contracts to British yards these were basically the same as those signed by the Royal Navy and contained clauses giving the Japanese similar supervisory control. How valuable were these facilities? Did the use of these opportunities by Japanese naval officers in British shipyards encourage the process of technical transfer?

In a contract prepared for Sir William Armstrong, Mitchell and Co. (on the Tyne) in 1884 entitled 'Japanese Contract' for 'one swift unarmoured ship of war to carry the armament specified', the statement is made that it is to be 'built, equipped and fitted similarly and in all respects equal to the best ships of corresponding type in the British Navy'.[37] The contract gave the inspector rights to ask for any information and to see 'all drawings of details' and to examine all construction material. Further detail was given relating to engines and equipment as well as the trials of the completed vessel. The wording of the contract suggests a shipbuilder keen to satisfy a demanding customer. In this way the Imperial Japanese government was substituted for the British Admiralty.

It seems clear that the clauses regarding inspection were put in by British contractors as a matter of habit and custom. Perhaps they did not expect the Japanese to provide their own inspectorate? Did Armstrong's believe that a British inspector or inspectors would be appointed? There is as yet no evidence from which to judge the relationship between the shipbuilder and the Japanese inspector on the Tyne, but there are hints of difficulties on the Clyde.

In 1890 J. & G. Thomson (later John Brown & Co.) built at Clydebank, for the Japanese, the *Chiyoda*, a protected cruiser of 2439 tons. There were difficulties with the ship's boilers. In 1895 Professor (Sir) John Harvard Biles (since 1891 Professor of Naval Architecture at the University of Glasgow) visited Japan. He did report (in October 1895) on the result of his visit to the *Chiyoda* advising that in his view 'the boilers would not steam with the Japanese coal on account of the small diameter of the tubes, these tubes being readily choked with the sooty deposit from the Japanese coal'. He also found that:

> a considerable amount of prejudice had been created in the minds of several of the officials by statements which had been made by some of the Japanese people who were at Clydebank during the building of the *Chiyoda*. These statements were generally of the nature of complaints that the wishes of the Japanese officials had not been attended to in many matters, and that they had been treated as if they knew very little of the subject of construction.[38]

Biles was himself chief designer at J. & G. Thomson at the time of the building of the *Chiyoda*.

During the 1890s the Japanese made new and more comprehensive arrangements for supervising ship-ordering and shipbuilding. They employed British firms and agents to some extent (see Chapter 13 below) but they also used London-based Japanese firms.

Messrs Mitsui & Co. had had an office in London since 1877 and by 1903 were acting as agents for Vickers, Son & Maxim.[39] With the planned extension of Japanese naval requirements in 1903, tenders were invited from Messrs Vickers, Son & Maxim Ltd, Sir W. Armstrong Whitworth, Thompson & Co, the Thames Iron Works, the Fairfield Co., and Messrs Laird & Co., although 'the [Japanese] authorities do not think much of these two firms anyway'. Even if one of the less favoured firms succeeded in quoting keenly enough to get the order it was the opinion of the (Japanese) Naval Construction Department that the question of armament 'will be entirely one of competition in price by Vickers and Armstrong'.[40]

Another active firm was Messrs Takata & Company (of 88

Bishopsgate Street Within, London) who from the early years of the twentieth century were available to negotiate between Japanese shipping concerns and British shipbuilders. The contract envelopes remain showing the agreement between William Denny and Sons of Dumbarton, and *Nippon Tetsudo Kwaisha*.[41]

In the same contract there is a separate statement on the 'power of inspectors':

> The Inspector or Inspectors appointed by the company are to have access at all reasonable times to the yards and workshops of the Builders where the various parts of the steamer are being prepared and executed. No obstacle whatever to be put in the way of their seeing that the work is carried out in accordance with the requirements of this specification.

One of the Japanese naval engineers who filled the role of supervisor was Dr S. Yokota (of 30 St Vincent Crescent, Glasgow)[42] who wrote to William Denny's (9 September 1907):

> I have duly received your letter of yesterday informing me the price for the extra winch with copper piping. I ask you to give me a little more detailed estimate, about this, as my own estimate comes out to be different from yours, and I like to be a correct reporter as advised by your good Mr John M. Denny. Perhaps my own estimate may be wrong, but I would like to see the cause of the difference.

There is however a notable difference in tone between this letter and the frustrations which the Japanese had experienced in trying to supervise the building of the *Chiyoda* in 1890.

Despite some of the difficulties which the Japanese may have experienced in British shipyards they were in general terms satisfied clients. Although Vickers, Son & Maxim had taken the precaution of making the Japanese firm Mitsui their agents it was believed 'that the Armstrong has extremely firm hold at the [Japanese] Admiralty most assuredly on account of their longer connection with the Japanese Navy'.[43]

Vickers being the newcomer, knew very well the hazards of the arms trade, and made a special effort for the Japanese .[44] In so cut-throat a market the British were prepared to go to a great deal of trouble for their Japanese customers. The report from Mitsui concluded with the following reminder: 'The Krupps are still keeping up their efforts claiming their capability to make battleships exactly like the English design of best type in both ships and ordnance.'

## 5 A RELATIONSHIP 'LACKING IN WARMTH'

Following the battle of Tsushima in the Sea of Japan in May 1905, there was a sharp change in the relationship between the Royal Navy and the Imperial Japanese Navy.[45] By their achievement the Japanese had passed their initiation test brilliantly. With their victory they removed themselves from tutelage at a stroke. After May 1905 the officers and men of the Imperial Japanese Navy had battle experience with which none in the West could compete.

Prior to 1905 there was close cooperation. Members of the Imperial Navy were keen to learn, those of Royal Navy keen to teach. The closeness was underlined by the Admiralty itself, which in 1900, in handling naval orders, in giving 'statements of dimensions' and 'estimates of weights' and other technical particulars, would group vessels with identical specifications in this way: 'HMS *Drake*, Japanese cruisers *Idzumo* and *Iwate* and HMS *Monmouth*'.[46]

Cooperation between the two navies was especially close after 1902 when, after the signing of the Anglo-Japanese Alliance, the Royal Navy encouraged the Imperial Japanese Navy to undertake patrol duties in Far Eastern Pacific waters. But in 1905, in naval officers' minds, the Japanese success against the Russians replaced the previous trust with a nervousness which time did not dispel.[47]

In the light of these changes, attitudes hardened.[48] The British view was 'No information should be given which in any way anticipates accomplished facts. For instance, details of ships which have not yet been laid down or improvements in guns, machinery etc which are still at the experimental stage.' Similarly as regards fleet exercises, tactics etc., the British became guarded: information should not be given until changes are carried so far that they must be looked upon as definitely established and consequently as a part of the war organisation with which it would be important that the two fleets, if allied in war, should be fully acquainted.[49]

The London government, however, did not lose sight of the implications of a failure to renew the Anglo-Japanese Alliance.[50] Earl Grey had a strong feeling that renewal would be advantageous to Britain. In the course of a compelling passage the Committee for Imperial Defence concluded 'in the interests of strategy, in the interests of naval expenditure and in the interests of stability, it is essential that the Japanese Alliance should be extended'.[51] It was officially renewed on 13 July 1911. At the same time Anglo-German relations deteriorated sharply. As Marder concludes 'It was fortunate that there was no Japanese problem to divert naval strength from home waters.'[52]

Notwithstanding the value of the continued Anglo-Japanese Alliance which, renewed for ten years, was to remain in force until July 1921, the coming of the First World War effectively marked the end of an era. Neither British or German shipbuilders could continue to supply Japan. The Japanese returned home to be reabsorbed into their home yards, where they attempted to put to good use all that they had learned abroad.

In the British shipyards throughout the *Meiji* period everyone cooperated with Japanese requests for help and training. For a country believed so undeveloped, there could be no harm in such assistance. The battle of Tsushima in the Sea of Japan in May 1905 came as a shock not only to the Royal Navy but also to the British government. The latter could congratulate itself on its prescience in making the Anglo-Japanese Alliance in 1902, but for the Royal Navy the raising of a rival caused discomfiture.

# 11 Japanese Life in Britain

## 1 COMMITTED TO LEARN

Those Japanese who arrived in Victorian Britain to work or study required to be adaptable and flexible. Not only was the pace and mode of life in Britain different from that in Japan but they were forced to live and work by communicating in a language other than their own. It is true that there were those in Britain who would be helpful and supportive but even so the shock of life in a strange country offered many challenges to all Japanese living here.

These men came at this time primarily in learning roles and so were dependent on the good will of those who accepted them on to the shop-floor, for study courses, allowed them to follow apprenticeships, permitted them to work in shipbuilding yards and took them in as lodgers. Training at home in Japan had encouraged the necessary deference.[1] Diplomats as official representatives of their government may have behaved and been received differently.

The reception accorded to Japanese depended in large measure on the view of Japan taken in Britain and the image of Japan projected here. Certainly there was great curiosity which was neither knowledgeable nor well informed. The comic opera, *The Mikado*, the best-known of all the Gilbert and Sullivan works, was first presented to the British public in 1885.[2] It was an immediate success. The presentation of Japan given there shocked those Japanese who knew of it. Although, as the opening chorus sings, 'We are the gentlemen of Japan, On many a vase or jar, On many a screen and fan, We figure in lively paint, Our attitudes queer and quaint';[3] the lyrics were laced with British 'in' jokes of the day, such as the reference to the 'parliamentary trains'.[4] Nevertheless the parody of the Mikado with his court, as comic characters, was in Japanese eyes grossly insulting to Japan.[5]

Although these attitudes were a world away from the engineering and shipbuilding industries in which many Japanese came to work, nevertheless the '*Mikado*' view of Japan had an important place in British society producing, in the work-place and elsewhere a tolerance and a patronage based on a widely held view of British superiority. But even here the Japanese may have benefited. Had the Japanese been seen as competitors rather than as curiosities, they might then have been subjected to greater hostility.

Many Japanese lived in the industrial centres. Glasgow, Newcastle upon Tyne, Barrow-in-Furness, and Sheffield became their temporary home. In Glasgow and Liverpool from 1890, Manchester 1907, and Middlesbrough 1898, the presence of Englishmen appointed as Honorary Japanese consuls (see Chapter 12 below) may have made things easier by providing a base and some support. In London, too, the Japanese diplomatic presence may have been of help. It was possible for those in London to constitute the beginnings of a Japanese community. The men in London were businessmen and diplomats rather than young engineers.

It was never easy for the Japanese to live and work in Britain.[6] Success or failure in mastering the English language determined the response of each individual. Some arrived well-prepared, others, with little facility, struggled constantly with what proved to be an intractable problem. Maybe those with practical objectives, who worked in workshop, laboratory or shipyard, overcame the language barrier by constant and zealous application to the tasks in hand.

## 2 STUDENTS, NAVAL OFFICERS, ENGINEERS AND BANKERS

The pressures of living in Britain are most readily seen in the early years. Then, overt signs of strain, which would by later generations be suppressed, were apparent. Arthur Lloyd gives a graphic, if unflattering account of the appearance of his first class in Tokyo in the early *Meiji* years, writing 'Before me, on rude benches, sat a motley crowd of ruffians – unkempt, unshaven, I had almost said unwashed, with bare legs and short gowns.'[7] These were the men who arrived in Britain, or France, or Germany or the USA, newly imprisoned in their stiff dark Western suits to absorb not only some of the manners and customs of the West but also the technology which underpinned Western society.

The first few students to arrive from Japan came sponsored either by the *Bakufu* government or by their clan. Sir Edmund Hammond, then Permanent Private Secretary at the Foreign Office, took an interest in their arrangements, writing to Sir Harry Parkes:

> I have seen Mr *X*, a Japanese student and like him. We have accepted him and have given him a letter to Professor Williamson of UCL, who has charge of the Satsuma's lads, and who I have no

doubt will give him the best advice. I have recommended him to make use of University College rather than King's College,[8] as their locality is better and there would probably be greater facility for obtaining suitable lodgings in the neighbourhood.[9]

Later Hammond referred to difficulties writing:

Lloyd will have written to you about a *quasi* mutiny among some of his flock. I understand he is now satisfied. I sent a message ... to the refractory students, saying that if they did not behave well and obey their teachers they would at once be sent back to Japan and they must judge for themselves what reception they would be likely to meet with on their return home.[10]

It seems likely that the problems to which Hammond refers were related to the attitudes of Japanese students, as *samurai*, to their foreign teacher. The behaviour of these men, government-sponsored, and 'Such an unruly lot' as Hammond commented, seemed to be in marked contrast to the '*Satsuma* youths, who have on the contrary ... conducted themselves well'.

But 'poor Lloyd's' difficulties reflect the novelty of the position of the early *samurai* student in Britain faced with so many challenges. Provocative behaviour was one way of providing an outlet for men defiantly Japanese in the face of culture shock. Rebellious and inconsiderate behaviour was self-defeating, denied the prime objectives of the Japanese students and later became completely atypical of Japanese behaviour abroad.

Naval officers came to the United Kingdom for two main purposes, either as a group of officers of the Imperial Japanese Navy to take over a new ship from a British shipyard or as inspectors to supervise the building of Japanese naval vessels in British yards. Men in the second group were often resident in Britain for several years while the former stayed only briefly.

Those officers who were to take command of vessels on completion, spent some time visiting, prior to the take-over. It was a kind of busman's holiday, officers taking the opportunity of being shown around specialist firms. The visitors' book of Barr & Stroud, in Glasgow, whose range-finders were much in demand for naval vessels, is peppered with lists of the names of Japanese officers from ships of the Imperial Japanese Navy including those from the *Takasago, Kasagi, Asahi, Izumo, Akebono, Azuma, Hatsuse, Iwate, Kurama, Kongo, Tone* and *Mikasa*.[11]

Naval Engineer Officers supervising the building of vessels for the Imperial Japanese Navy were resident for long periods. At Newcastle upon Tyne they worked each day at Armstrong's Elswick Ordnance Works and Naval Shipyard or at Barrow-in-Furness, working at Vickers, or Glasgow working at one of the shipyards there. There were also officers resident at Sheffield where the steelworks made much of the fine grade steel for ships' plates and for armour-plating.

They were single-minded; their work also dominated their leisure. Fred T. Jane described the typical behaviour of a naval officer whose ship was 'in an elementary stage at Elswick' writing 'The working at his profession . . . consisted in spending the day pouring over naval books. I generally found him deep in Mahan with halma-pieces on sheets of paper to work out the tactics.' Jane also commented that 'his idea of a holiday appears to be to come to Portsmouth, spend the day going over the dockyard, with a visit to my house to play naval war games to the small hours as a kind of subsequent dissipation and relaxation'.[12]

Other young engineers served as employees of British firms in a variety of capacities. Some of these men undertook short periods of service 'in the field', after studying some aspect of engineering work at colleges in this country. Others came expressly to widen their experience after their education in Japan. Tsoji Ishiguro was one of the latter group proceeding directly into the service of a civil engineer, Mr Edward Easton (11 Delahay Street, Westminster, London), after graduating from the University of Tokyo in July 1878. For the three years from 1879 to 1881 Ishiguro served Mr Easton in a variety of capacities before returning home to a distinguished career as an engineer for the Imperial Japanese Government. He explained that he:

> was engaged upon the Herts and Essex Water Works (extension); Grays Water Works, Faversham Swing Bridge, etc., etc., and helped to design the Gas Holder of East Grinstead, a Bridge over the river Naver, a Bridge over the Halladale, Casheldue Bridge, together with Pumping establishment at Khatatbeh in Egypt and Irrigation works in Behara District; Iron-Roof for the circular tank of Alexandria Water Works. Carried out – Deal Water Works; Behere Irrigation Works at Khatatbeh, Egypt; Installation of experimental electric lighting at Stafford House (Duke of Sutherland) with Gramme machine in 1881. Engineer to a new Manufactury of 'Insulite' with Dr Fleeming (of Cambridge). An inspector

for pumps and irrigation plants made at the Firth Iron Works (then Messrs Eaton and Anderson) to be sent out to Egypt, on behalf of Mr Ed East etc. etc.[13]

Kaichi Watanabe was another student engineer who served in private industry. After a six-year course, at the Imperial College of Engineering, and further study at the University of Glasgow, he was employed as a junior engineer by Sir John Fowler and Mr Benjamin Baker. This firm had just won the contract to erect the projected Forth Railway Bridge and Watanabe became one of the assistant engineers on that project. When the engineers rigged up a 'living model' of the cantilever principle on which the massive bridge was to be built, Watanabe was the central of the three figures featured on the photograph taken.[14]

It seems certain that Japanese were also present in several industries other than shipbuilding and engineering. Mr K. Tatsumi, the manager of the Yokohama Specie Bank in London, introduced Mr. K. Suzuki, 'a very influential man' from the Bank of Japan, to the Midland Bank in 1904. It was arranged through Sir Edward Holden, the Chairman of the Midland, that Mr Suzuki be 'allowed to go through our Sparkbrook, New Street, Dale End branches (all in Birmingham) and afterwards Threadneedle Street and Head Office, in London, to see our system'. It is not known how long Mr Suzuki spent working in the various branches of the Midland Bank although as was explained the Japanese was of sufficient importance to warrant the attendance of Mr Mare, our Chief Inspector, who 'took Mr Suzuki down to Birmingham to introduce him to our officer there'.[15]

That Japanese demand brought relief in unexpected quarters is made clear by the manager of the Ossett Branch of the York and County Bank who, in 1904, reported on 'the large orders placed by Japan in Dewsbury and district' which have 'given us a spurt, a considerable quantity of our speciality (Mungo) being required'.[16]

## 3 JAPANESE IN LONDON, AN OFFICIAL AND AN UNOFFICIAL PRESENCE

When the Japanese Foreign Office was established in 1869 in Tokyo it had in all twelve members of staff. The first *chargé d' affaires* in London was Naonobu Samejima who arrived in October 1870. He also had responsibility for what Japanese presence there then was in

Paris and Berlin. In the succeeding years the service was expanded, Ministers resident in London, included Munenori Terajima, Kagenori Ueno and Arinori Mori (see Chapter 8 above).[17] By the 1890s the office in London, and the numbers of staff to support it, became increasingly important as efforts were mounted by the Japanese to renegotiate the foreign treaties. The diplomats were always keen to emphasise the honour and dignity of their country. They disapproved heartily of the efforts to popularise and indeed trivialise the image of Japan.

Tannaker and Buhicrosan conceived the idea of introducing a Japanese village to London.[18] They planned to bring Japanese street performers as well as Japanese craftsmen and create as much of the atmosphere of 'old Japan' as they could. A site was obtained opposite Albert Gate at Knightsbridge and they proceeded to hire 'over one hundred persons including twenty-six women and children'. As *The Times* reported:

> on entering the hall the visitor finds himself in a broad street of shops and houses, from which rows of smaller shops forming narrow lanes are laid out to the right. These are not mere painted fronts but well-built apartments of various appearance, each with its own characteristic ornamentation of parti-coloured bamboo, on solid panels, with shingled or thatched roof and with sliding trellis, shutters and translucent screens.[19]

But the village was a spectacle, the craft-made items were not for sale: 'it has been thought best not to make the affair a bazaar'.[20] The Japanese village was officially opened on 10 January 1885 by Sir Rutherford Alcock under the royal patronage of Princess Christian and Princess Louise. Between January and May, the 112 days it was open, 250 000 people paid the one-shilling admission fee. After a tour of Germany the exhibition was reopened on 2 December 1885 under the name of 'Japan in London'.

The Japanese government and the diplomatic community in London, disapproved of the Japanese village. They feared that the display trivialised Japan and brought the nation into disrepute. The official view was that such showmanship perpetuated the notion of Japan as a comic, backward and undeveloped country. Passports were denied to those Japanese who made up the population of the village, who therefore left Japan unofficially. Neither the Japanese business nor diplomatic community in London wanted to be associated with Japanese street life which they regarded as low and vulgar.

Despite the official view in London, the village was regarded as 'very bold and successful'. A whole host of industrial processes were featured including:

> the lacquering of wood, pottery making and decoration, *cloisonné* work on a copper foundation, carving of ivory and wood, the inlaying of ivory, mother of pearl and metal, the carving of hardened clay, lantern-making and painting, fan-making and umbrella-making. In addition textile and allied manufacturing, spinning and hand-loom weaving and embroidery, as well as sandal-making, pipe-making, block-making and coopering were demonstrated.

Several of these processes were pictorially featured in the *Illustrated London News*. The publicity given to all this must have provided a useful stimulus to the demand for cheap Japanese-manufactured art objects. In addition to the village itself there were exhibitions of Japanese 'Amusements and Athletic Games' including wrestling. Unfortunately there was a serious fire on 2 May 1885. The pictures show the Kensington entrance and a view of the side entrance to the Humphries Hall 'after the roof fell in'.[21]

Buhierosen and Tannaker's Exhibition projected a view of Japan which fitted in well with British preconceptions of what Japan was like. The Japanese government, the main aim of whose foreign policy was to renegotiate the 'unequal' treaties, deplored a demonstration in the British capital of what they judged to be Japanese backwardness.

## 4 THE HAND OF FRIENDSHIP

Although there was a lot of ignorance and misconception about the Japanese there was also kindliness offered to those who experienced life for a time in Britain. Some of those who had served in Japan understood the motivation and determination of the Japanese visitors. Some made great efforts to assist the Japanese and extend the hand of friendship.

It is possible to examine in detail the role of A. R. Brown, the Honorary Japanese Consul in Glasgow (1890–1913) in assisting those Japanese who for professional reasons came to live temporarily in Glasgow. Brown, a very active man, certainly did act as a focus for the Japanese in Glasgow. One photograph remains, suitably bedecked with the flag of the rising sun, showing gatherings of Japanese to whom he played host. Brown left one list giving the names of young men who had studied in Glasgow in the later *Meiji* years, who subsequently occupied important positions in Japan.[22] These included: Mr Taizo Shoda, later Vice President, Mitsubishi Shipbuilding Co., Kobe; Mr Kyohei Kato, later President, Mitsubishi Shoji Kaisha; Mr Yamaki, later President of Tokyo Marine Insurance Co. (all related to the Iwasaki family); Mr S Kondo, son of Baron Kondo, NYK; Mr N. Matsumura, later President, Yonei Shoten; Mr Chozo Isono, later President, Meidi-ya (his son, Mr Keizo Isono also studied later in Brown's office). On the occasion of A. R. Brown's death in 1913 a letter of condolence arrived from 'The Glasgow Society' in Tokyo signed by a representative eleven members who included A. Tanakadate and S. Terano, physicists, as well as several important businessmen such as C. Shiba and Y. Yamamoto.[23]

There were other friendships which grew out of joint professional interests. Professor D'Arcy W. Thompson, FRS, of University College, Dundee, was in correspondence between 1896 and 1901 with Professor K. Mitsukuri of the University of Tokyo.[24] They were both zoologists. They visited each other's countries and also exchanged specimens of crustacea, giving both scholars access to species new to them. Professor Mitsukuri was glad to receive several papers and 'photographs of molluscan radulae' which would, he hoped, help him to sort out his specimens in Japan. Mrs Mitsukuri repaid the kindness offered to her husband while in Scotland by sending Professor Thompson 'a suit of Japanese Kimono for a young lady'. In order that the dress should be correctly arranged a Japanese doll was made and 'dressed as it should be', the pattern for the material was chosen 'to be not loud and yet withal to be gay'.

Another long-stay engineer who spent his training years on Tyneside was Motoreru Haramiishi.[25] He had arrived at Armstrong Whitworth's Shipyard in 1890 after his studies at the Tokyo Technical School. On his return to Japan in 1899, he entered the ship-design and drawing office of the Mitsubishi Shipbuilding and engineering Co. Ltd. Haramiishi earned his spurs during the Russo-Japanese war of 1904–5 during which he concentrated on ship-repair work. He gave a lifetime's service to Mitsubishi Shipbuilding working not only at Nagasaki but also helping to set up new shipbuilding and engineering plants at Kobe and Shimonoseki. He was an authority on electric welding which he had espoused in its early days. He organised and presided over the Japan Welding Society founded in 1926.

At Cambridge the collegiate system ensured that most students would be registered at and have rooms in one of the Colleges, although some including distinguished Japanese, like J. Soyeda and K. Noda, were non-collegiate students. Even with the backing of their colleges it was noted that 'As strangers in a strange land, the Japanese cling closely together, and may generally be met with in twos and threes.' Indeed 'a faint film of reserve' was observed as 'the friendships which the Japanese form at Cambridge, though natural and cordial ... rarely develop into real intimacies ... because few confidences are given or invited'.[26]

> Indeed the reservations in Cambridge went somewhat further for Cambridge teachers are unanimous in declaring the Japanese to be pleasant to work with and most of them have evinced a genuine desire to learn ... but unless the work of students has been submitted to the test of public examination, the most conscientious teachers have found it extremely difficult, almost impossible to determine how far the instruction given has taken root in the mind of the pupil.[27]

For those Japanese resident for brief periods local hospitality was ample. But what of those in Glasgow, or elsewhere for the long years of an apprenticeship? One rather sad correspondence remains as evidence of a friendship between a Glasgow girl and a Japanese student.[28] Reading the letters of the girl, which survive, it is clear that she, a shop-girl, was neither well-educated nor of good family. Her letters reveal shaky arithmetic, 'how many inches are there in a foot?', and poor spelling, although the sentiments they convey are blameless. She deplored the 'rough uncultivated boors' with whom her young Japanese friend had to work at the shipyard. There is talk of marriage. The girl's mother, although receiving weekly visits and weekly bunches of flowers, appears to have taken fright. Jeanie was despatched to work in a shop in Sunderland. The correspondence ceased in the spring of 1884 when the young man returned to Japan.

Other young Japanese were perhaps more fortunate, meeting girls from families of professional men. After the *Meiji* period had ended Masataka Taketsuru,[29] later the founder of Nikka whisky company, in Glasgow as a student at the end of the First World War, met and married a doctor's daughter, Rita Cowan. Taketsuru seems to have first met Rita's sister Ella, but he was subsequently invited home where he met Rita. They were married in 1920, with Ella the only family witness, at one of the Station Hotels in Glasgow. Dr Samuel Campbell Cowan, her father, practised medicine at Middlecroft,

Kirkintilloch outside of Glasgow but died in 1918.[30] Taketsuru was, when registered as a chemistry student at the University of Glasgow for the summer session of 1919, resident at Middlecroft. Taketsuru spent several years in Scotland, visited and worked at several whisky distilleries including those at Campbeltown and Glenlivet. He returned to Japan with his wife, although they had no children a son was adopted.

Another long affair, not consummated, was that between Marie Stopes and Professor Kuyiro Fujii. Dr Stopes, a brilliant young scientist, met Fujii in Munich in 1903; subsequently he lived in England where their relationship deepened. She was awarded a grant by the Royal Society to pursue her scientific studies in Japan and to Japan she followed him. There is no doubt about the depths of their feelings. In the end he, a married man, although much troubled, allowed the relationship to lapse and Marie Stopes returned home.[31]

The records of the University of Glasgow give students' addresses both at home and in Glasgow. Many lodged in the Hillhead area close the University.[32] Others including Taizo Shoda (BSc, 1916), the son of Heigoro Shoda of Mitsubishi, lived rather more grandly with the Finlays (of Finlay & Co., tea-merchants) at 276 Nithsdale Rod, Glasgow, while Shigeya Kondo, son of Rempei Kondo, president of NYK, in Glasgow from 1904 to 1950, was resident at Clydeview Cottage, Renfrew, perhaps with the Lobnitz family, whose shipyards were there.

Perhaps 1901 was the *annus mirabilis* for Glasgow. In June the University of Glasgow celebrated its 450th birthday. On that occasion the University awarded many foreign scholars, including Professor Joji Sakurai, of the University of Tokyo, with the degree of LLD.[33] In September 1901 the International Engineering Congress was held in Glasgow.[34] The Glasgow University again welcomed many hundreds of visitors including a distinguished contingent from Japan.[35] In Cambridge the following year Viscount Hayashi, the Japanese Ambassador to the Court of St James, was honoured by the University with the degree of LLD, no doubt as a recognition for his part in negotiating the Anglo-Japanese Alliance of 1902.

## 5 WELCOME GUESTS?

The Japanese who lived in Victorian or Edwardian Britain required fortitude and perseverance. They rarely had their wives and families with them and, except in London, where the Japanese were mostly diplomats and businessmen, had no opportunity to create communities. Those in Glasgow were also fortunate, for the presence there of the Honorary Japanese Consul, from 1890, and of Henry Dyer ensured them of support.

Most of the men were in Britain to assimilate technical knowledge as quickly and effectively as possible. To this end a regime of concentrated work was often adopted to the exclusion of all else. Life was full of stress not only because of the work but also because of the welcome. Were Japanese studying and learning here granted facilities on sufferance? It is hard to tell, depending no doubt on individual personalities. Some like Yozo Yamao remembered their time in the Glasgow shipyards with pleasure, others no doubt fared less well.[36] What is clear is that during this period Japanese were usually regarded patronisingly, and on the factory floor as oddities. This attitude was changing by the 1890s when the competence of the Japanese in the workshop, shipyard or laboratory led some of those who taught them to ponder the ultimate outcome of such a transfer of skills.

It is fair to say that most Japanese had a difficult life in Britain before 1914. They supported themselves with an inner strength derived from their own personal determination to do their best to further the objectives of *Meiji* Japan. These, to achieve independence in industrial and military matters, were not appreciated in the West. Each Japanese was therefore able to further his aims with assistance, willingly or grudgingly given. There can be little doubt that Japan's programme of modernisation was much furthered by the devotion of those who sampled the rigours of living as foreigners in Britain.

1. View of the Imperial College of Engineering, *c.* 1880. This European style building was one of the wonders of early Meiji Japan. It was designed by Charles Alfred Chastel de Boinville.

2. The *Tosa Maru* inaugurated NYK's passenger service from Yokohama to London in March 1896. Note the gala atmosphere, the ships 'dressed overall', the wooden dockside with railway lines, the Japanese in traditional dress and the Japanese Government launch (*front right*).

3. The *Asahi*, *c.* 1899, being visited by a party of some fifteen Japanese officials; note the top hat, several bowler hats as well as cloth caps worn by the various Japanese (John Brown's Shipyard, Clydebank, Scotland).

4. A. R. Brown, the Honorary Japanese Consul at Glasgow, *c.* 1908. Brown is flanked by his partner, George McFarlane (*second left*) and Henry Dyell (*second right*) and eleven Japanese. Most of the men later occupied important positions in Japan.

5a. Shigeya Kondo, later Baron Kondo and wife, *c.* 1912, in traditional Japanese garb.

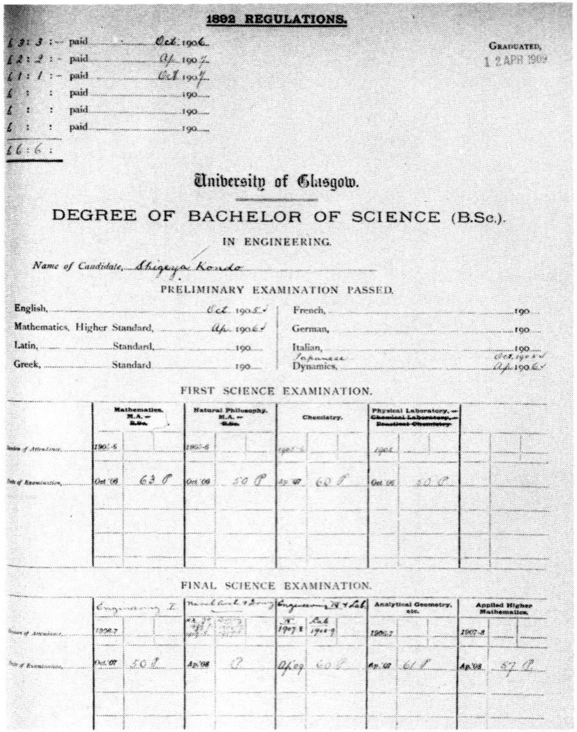

1892 REGULATIONS.

£3:3:– paid Oct 1906.
£2:2:– paid Ap 1907.
£1:1:– paid Oct 1907.
£ : : paid 190
£ : : paid 190
£ : : paid 190
£6:6:

GRADUATED, 12 APR 1909

University of Glasgow.

DEGREE OF BACHELOR OF SCIENCE (B.Sc.).

IN ENGINEERING.

Name of Candidate, Shigeya Kondo

PRELIMINARY EXAMINATION PASSED.

| | | | |
|---|---|---|---|
| English, | Oct 1905 | French, | 190 |
| Mathematics, Higher Standard, | Ap 1906 | German, | 190 |
| Latin, Standard, | 190 | Italian, | 190 |
| | | Japanese | Oct 1905 |
| Greek, Standard | 190 | Dynamics, | Ap 1906 |

FIRST SCIENCE EXAMINATION.

| | Mathematics, M.A. – B.Sc. | Natural Philosophy, M.A. – B.Sc. | Chemistry. | Physical Laboratory. |
|---|---|---|---|---|
| Session of Attendance, | 1905-6 | 1905-6 | 1905-6 | 1906 |
| Date of Examination, | Oct '06 63 P | Oct '06 50 P | Ap '07 60 P | Oct '06 50 P |

FINAL SCIENCE EXAMINATION.

| | Engineering I | Naval Arch. + Drawing | Engineering II + Lab | Analytical Geometry, etc. | Applied Higher Mathematics. |
|---|---|---|---|---|---|
| Session of Attendance, | 1906-7 | [illegible] | 1907-8 / 1908-9 | 1906-7 | 1907-8 |
| Date of Examination, | Oct '07 50 P | Ap '08 P | Ap '09 60 P | Ap '07 61 P | Ap '08 57 P |

5b. BSc Engineering Certificate for Shigeya Kondo, University of Glasgow, 1909. Kondo was one of several men from distinguished Japanese families who studied in Glasgow. The Japanese concentrated on naval architecture, engineering and science subjects.

6. Henry Dyer had served as Principal of the Imperial College of Engineering in Tokyo from 1873 to 1882. After his return to Glasgow he advised and befriended those Japanese resident in Scotland.

7a. The *Meiji Maru*, built at Robert Napier's Yard on the Clyde in 1873, has survived. Now in dry dock at the Mercantile Marine University in Tokyo. It was a steamship but note the elegant sailing-ship lines. The Emperor's cabin was finely decorated. The inset is of A. R. Brown, the *Meiji Maru's* first Master.

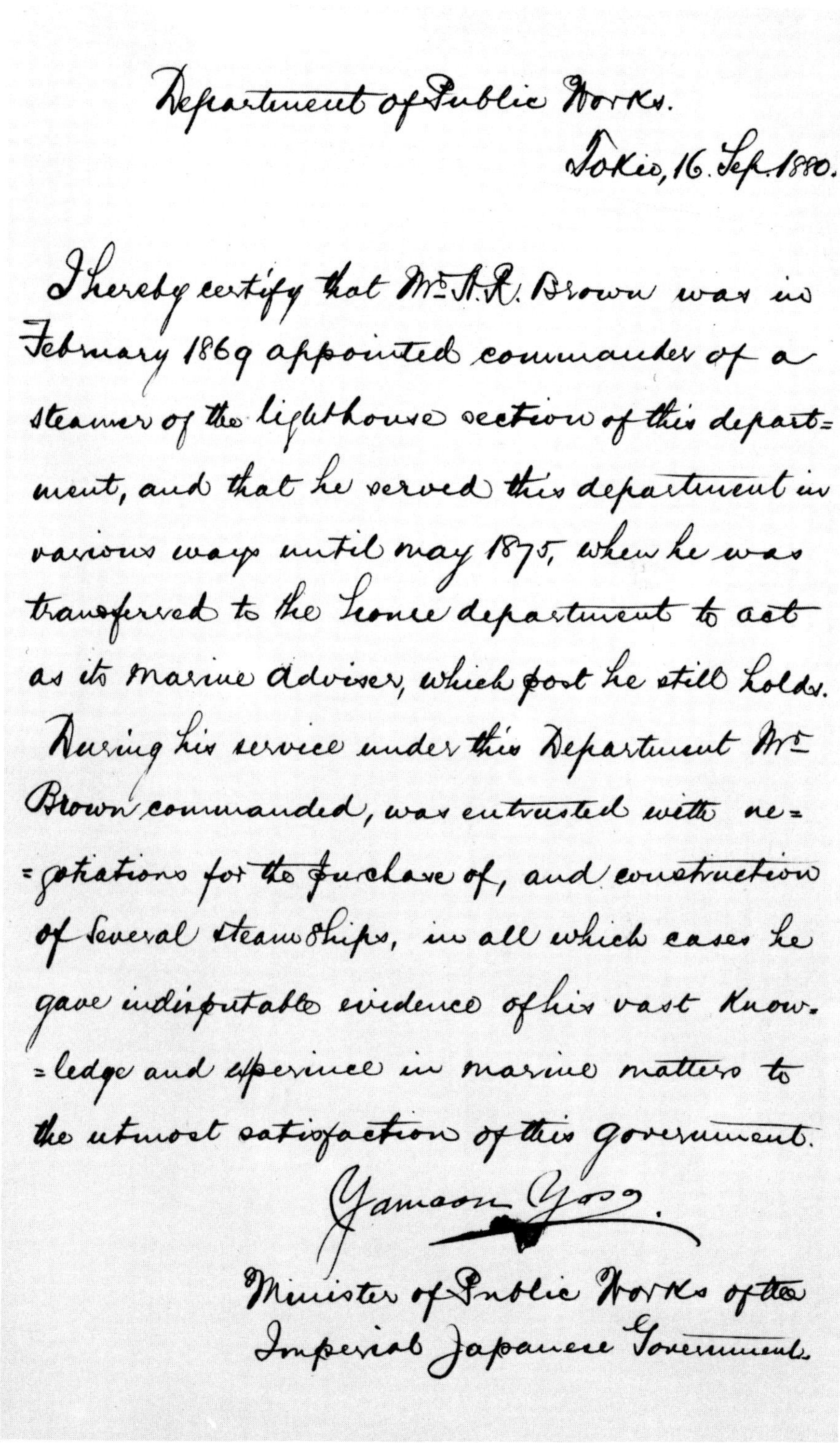

Department of Public Works.

Tokio, 16. Sep. 1880.

I hereby certify that Mr. A. R. Brown was in February 1869 appointed commander of a steamer of the lighthouse section of this depart=ment, and that he served this department in various ways until May 1875, when he was transferred to the Home department to act as its Marine Adviser, which post he still holds.

During his service under this Department Mr. Brown commanded, was entrusted with ne=gotiations for the purchase of, and construction of several steamships, in all which cases he gave indisputable evidence of his vast know=ledge and experience in marine matters to the utmost satisfaction of this government.

Yamao Yozo.

Minister of Public Works of the Imperial Japanese Government.

7b. Yozo Yamao, the Minister of Public Works, recorded A. R. Brown's service. In 1889 Brown became Honorary Consul for Japan in Glasgow.

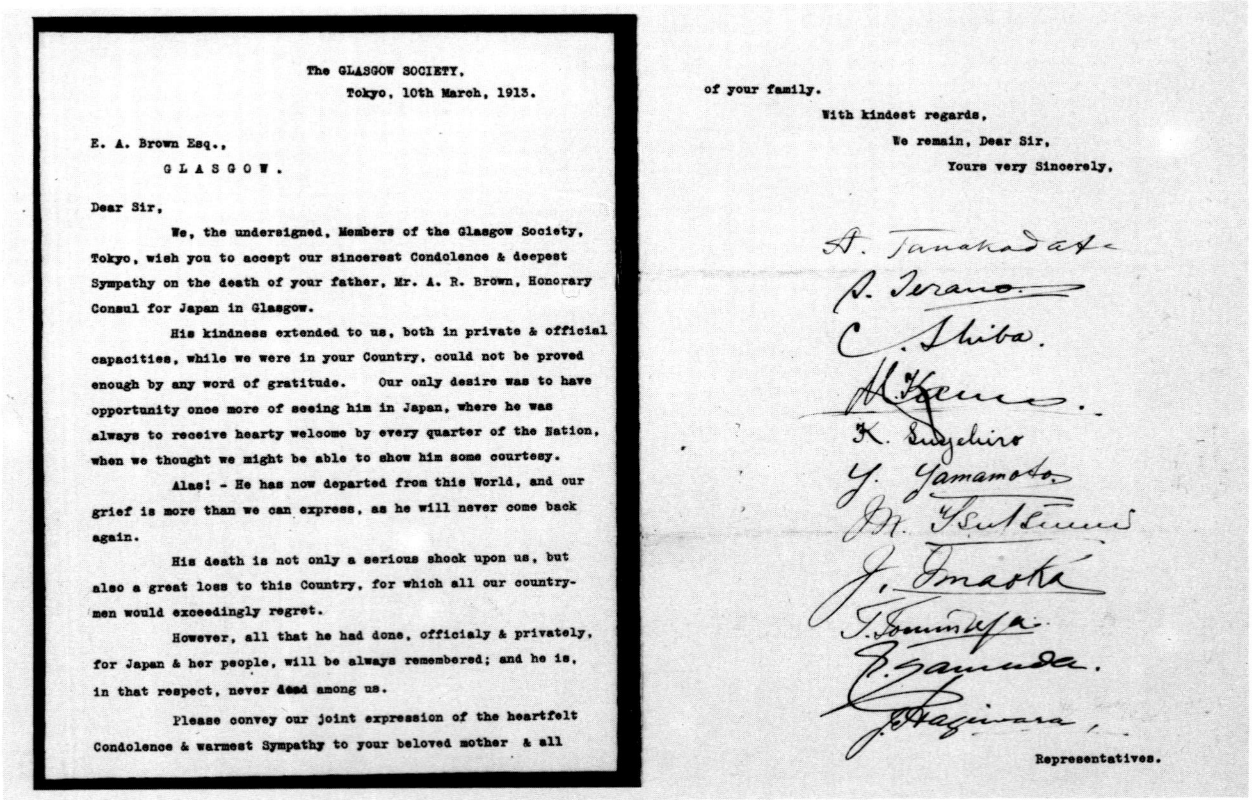
The GLASGOW SOCIETY,
Tokyo, 10th March, 1913.

E. A. Brown Esq.,
GLASGOW.

Dear Sir,

We, the undersigned, Members of the Glasgow Society, Tokyo, wish you to accept our sincerest Condolence & deepest Sympathy on the death of your father, Mr. A. R. Brown, Honorary Consul for Japan in Glasgow.

His kindness extended to us, both in private & official capacities, while we were in your Country, could not be proved enough by any word of gratitude. Our only desire was to have opportunity once more of seeing him in Japan, where he was always to receive hearty welcome by every quarter of the Nation, when we thought we might be able to show him some courtesy.

Alas! - He has now departed from this World, and our grief is more than we can express, as he will never come back again.

His death is not only a serious shock upon us, but also a great loss to this Country, for which all our countrymen would exceedingly regret.

However, all that he had done, officialy & privately, for Japan & her people, will be always remembered; and he is, in that respect, never dead among us.

Please convey our joint expression of the heartfelt Condolence & warmest Sympathy to your beloved mother & all of your family.

With kindest regards,
We remain, Dear Sir,
Yours very Sincerely,

A. Tanakadate
S. Terano
C. Shiba
K. Suyehiro
Y. Yamamoto
J. Imaoka
Yamada.
Hagiwara.

Representatives.

8. Representatives of the Glasgow Society in Tokyo sent condolences to Edward Brown, on the death of his father. A. Tanakadate, the famous physicist, heads the list of names.

# Part III

# The British Facilitators

# 12 Networks, Commercial and Academic

## 1 APPROACH BY PERSONAL CONTACT

Once the Japanese had resolved to make contact with the West they showed themselves skilled at associating with those who, because of their personal and professional status, were able to offer advice and effect useful introductions. In both the commercial and the academic worlds the Japanese in Britain quickly obtained important and influential contacts.[1] As customers they commanded deferential attention. As students their hard work and respectful approach brought them access to distinguished scholars.

By the second half of the *Meiji* period (from 1890) the networks were well established. In commercial terms the Japanese were in continuous contact with firms whose goods they wanted to buy; they could also expect assistance from their trade consuls in London and from their honorary consuls elsewhere. In addition, Japanese firms were themselves soon opening offices in London, offering an agency service to their compatriots. Academically Japanese students had access to the best of higher learning while young Japanese of exceptional ability became known to the most influential scholars in the Universities.

During the early *Meiji* years the Japanese usually had foreign agents who negotiated for them in the purchase of complicated equipment. For these services they used trusted Westerners, including ships' captains, and academic engineers.[2]

Did direct ordering by the Japanese pose problems? Did industrial firms receiving first orders ignore Japanese instructions? There is some evidence that the Japanese may have felt this to be the case.[3] The remedy was in their own hands and they did not again order from that source. Later in the shipbuilding industries, Japanese ship inspectors, highly trained engineering specialists, were believed to exert a strong influence on the shipbuilding process. In a short time the Japanese had a commercial and industrial network in areas like Glasgow and the West of Scotland, Manchester and Lancashire, Newcastle upon Tyne and the north-east where they employed either their own compatriots or known and trusted British citizens.[4]

Academic facilitators either in Japan or in the West encouraged the Japanese to enter the intellectual world of the late nineteenth century. Those Britons who had themselves served in Japan are mentioned in Part I of this work and especially in Chapter 5 above. But there were those in Britain, some of whom never went to Japan, who advised the Japanese government, made recommendations as to courses of study and in general assisted Japanese who came to study here. In connection with scientific, technical and engineering education especially the links were strong. In general it was the senior men in England or Scotland who remained at home and advised; recommending their most gifted juniors for service in Japan.

## 2 THE COMMERCIAL NETWORK

The best-known figure who was involved with young Japanese before the *Meiji* Restoration was Hugh Matheson who, as the head of Matheson's business in London, by chance found himself the doyen of those to whom the Japanese were referred on their arrival in Britain.[5] Because of Jardine Matheson's trading presence in Nagasaki and Yokohama from 1859 and the availability of their ships, passages were booked for young Japanese to travel to London. But the Japanese did not anticipate working indefinitely through such a British firm. They expected eventually to work through Japanese agents who had established offices in London. In the early *Meiji* years there were a number of British citizens who wished to become agents in Japan for British firms. Many offered their services; few were accepted.

There are many snippets of information about agents employed to solicit orders from Japan for British products. One Scottish firm found itself in a mass of complexities following an enquiry, and later an order, from Japan. In 1892, Messrs Glenfield and Co. were approached by John Matthew James of Tokyo, Japan, who offered to act as their agent over possible contracts for 'Sluice Valves, Hydrants etc.' which were required for the 'Tokyo Water Works now about to be constructed'.[6,7] Mr James intimated that business of about £10 000 might be forthcoming, and suggested that the firm would be well advised to appoint him as agent in Tokyo 'to tender for the contract for valves etc. in this company's name and to act for us there, and be paid by commission'. The company's initial reaction was lukewarm; they feared to 'displease merchants' who would 'probably boycott the company for other enquiries'.

Subsequently others, including Mr Meik, CE, a Scottish engineer, wrote from London to Glenfields praising Mr James's 'abilities and trustworthiness', his 'respectability, general business qualifications and his intimate acquaintance with Japanese authorities and language'.[8] Eventually the managing director recommended that Mr James should be appointed as Glenfield's agent. This was agreed.

The main points of Mr James's contract were 'that Mr James should receive £200 in payment of his services for the first two years and if 2.5 per cent on the sales to Japan during that period exceeded this amount the excess to be paid to Mr James. For the third year Mr James was to be paid a commission of 1.5 per cent on the sales. Beyond three years the arrangement was to be subject to revisal.'[9]

The appointment of Mr James was only the beginning of a long and involved saga. The Tokyo Water Works Company required Glenfield to use, in addition to Mr James, an agent in London approved by them. Messrs Mitsui & Co. were suggested.[10] When the valves and other water-works equipment arrived in Tokyo it was claimed that much of it was faulty.[11] This resulted in the Japanese superintendent suggesting 10 per cent off the original price. The problems continued for some time, indeed Mr James retired as Glenfield's representative in Japan although Professor K. Burton at once offered his services. Professor Burton was also 'well-known in Japan' and had been 'in Japan for eight or nine years' and had 'a high position in the University of Tokyo and had designed the Tokyo Water Works and other Water Works in Japan'.[12]

The seemingly endless complications, resulting in the first place from the inexperience of the Glenfield Company in dealing with orders from Japan are a reminder of the costs and frustrations involved in handling new accounts of this kind.[13] By 1900, it was clear that it was useless for British or other foreign firms to appoint their own nationals as agents. Glenfield persisted with the Japanese market, but, from the first of January 1901 their agent was Mr Kawakami,[14] recommended to them by Mr T. Sano, the engineer of the Tokyo Water Works.

In 1903, John Brown & Company, Shipbuilders of Clydebank,[15] who had just been awarded the contract for the *Asahi*, appointed Captain Takayama as their agent for the sale of war vessels to the Japanese government; Brown's acted through Messrs Illies and Co. of Yokohama and Hamburg. The firm's optimism over further orders was not fulfilled and the appointment was terminated in March 1908 when John Brown's 'regretted that business has not resulted' although they 'desired to express our best thanks for your efforts'.

Not surprisingly the Japanese preferred to work through their own compatriots and a Japanese commercial network was soon available to them in London. The first office opened by a Japanese commercial concern in London was that of Shoji Okura, a general trading company, founded by Kihachiro Okura (1837–1928) in the Ginza in Tokyo in 1873.[16] In 1874 he opened in London. Okura's business, concerned as it was with the import and export trade, grew rapidly. Mitsui, who were initially concerned to ship rice to Europe and keen to buy British woollen cloth and blankets, sent Robert Irwin to London in February 1877 to open an agency (raised to office status in 1880) for them there.[17] They made an agreement to carry their rice cargoes on ships which Mitsubishi was sending to England for refitting. This is believed to be the first time that Japanese-owned vessels had carried a Japanese cargo direct to Europe. Later Japanese firms ordering goods from England or Scotland, were glad to avail themselves of the specialist services which Mitsui provided. Messrs Takata & Co. (of 88 Bishopsgate Street Within, London) had also opened a London office.[18] They became expert at ordering ships on behalf of Japanese owners.

In 1907 Messrs Takata was using, and possibly employing themselves, a Japanese inspector, Dr S. Yokota, who, being resident in Glasgow, was able to raise technical queries with the shipbuilder about the costing of items being prepared for the ship.[19] In the specification provided by Messrs Takata (7 May 1906) details are given not only of the machinery and structure of the vessel but also of the homely and domestic items required in the 'Bakery, galley and pantry output' where 'Biscuit tubes, biscuit forcer, Apple corer, Bread Rasp, Backwheat Jug, larding needles and Trussing needles' were itemised.[20]

At the same time that these orders were being agreed, Alexander Stephen's, another respected shipbuilding firm on the Clyde, were trying to break into the Japanese market.[21] But as can be gleaned from the correspondence with Messrs Takata, Stephen's were not, in this case, within the favoured circle. They were clearly disadvantaged, trying (in June 1906) to secure the order while cutting costs to the bone without knowing who else was tendering or at what price. By 2 October 1906 Messrs Takata were writing to William Denny Brothers, who had secured the orders for the *Hirafu Maru* and the *Tamura Maru*, that 'we beg to confirm that we have received a cable from Japan intimating that our friends have secured the order for you'. William Denny of Dumbarton on the lower Clyde, became an important supplier of ships to Japan over many years. Denny's were indeed fortunate; they were part of the network and had a long working association with the Honorary Japanese consul in Glasgow.

## 3 THE CONSULAR PROMOTER

Japan maintained Honorary Consulates in Glasgow (between 1890 and 1941), Middlesbrough (1898–1922), Manchester (1907–41) and Liverpool (1889–1986).[22] The men who served Japan in this way were almost always active business men with good contacts who could not only facilitate business but assist visiting and resident Japanese nationals. In Britain Japanese interests were especially focused on the shipbuilding industry in Glasgow and the West of Scotland, the cotton industry in Liverpool and Manchester and the shipbuilding and chemical industry on the Tees and the Tyne. The Honorary Consuls, themselves promoters, performed a valuable service by acting as agents and giving their Japanese customers the benefits of their skills in operating the local business networks.

Albert Richard Brown (1839–1913) is not only the best-known and documented consular figure but also the one with the greatest commitment to Japan.[23] His twenty-year service for the Japanese government in Japan was followed by a period of over twenty years as Japanese consul in Glasgow. A. R. Brown, McFarlane's business was to solicit orders for ships from Japanese (or other foreign customers) prepare the design, place the order, negotiate the contract with the shipbuilder, supervise the construction, deal with the day-to-day problems, accept the finished vessel and if necessary take delivery and organise a captain and crew to deliver the vessel to its owners.[24,25] Brown's worked closely with the Japanese at all levels.

The firm was responsible for the specifications which were made out for the building of the shell of the ship, the design of the engines, which later had to be fitted, pumps and distilling equipment and other auxiliary machinery to be ordered and installed. Based as Brown's were in Glasgow much of the shipbuilding they supervised was on the Clyde, as was engine building and pump supplying. But the Tyne was equally important, where the Elswick Works and the Walker Shipyard of Armstrongs provided shipbuilding facilities and the armaments for all the British-made vessels of war. Although Brown's had an information-gathering role and acted as a base for the Japanese naval officers supervising the building of naval vessels in Britain, they had no direct responsibility for Japanese naval vessels.

Of these fifty-five vessels, 'designed and superintendented by us' between 1900 and 1912, not counting 'other cruisers and dredgers' twenty-one were for Japan and thirty-four for non-Japanese owners. It was an impressive achievement for a relatively new firm. But Captain Brown had been, from the 1870s, a familiar figure in British shipyards. He had ordered and supervised the building of many ships for Japanese owners.

That the shipbuilding link was important for the Japanese is attested by the existence of an Honorary Japanese Consul in Middlesbrough who held office from 1898–1922. The holder was Waynman Dixon, of Cleveland Dock, the Dock, near Cargo Fleet Lane, Middlesbrough. He and his brother Raylton Dixon were shipbuilders and dock owners from the 1880s.[26] It is presumed that Waynman Dixon acted as agent and adviser for the Japanese in shipbuilding matters in the north-east.

The Lancashire connection as evidenced by the Honorary Consulates in Liverpool and Manchester did not continue the shipbuilding interest. The original holder of the Liverpool office, appointed in 1889, was James L. Bowes, a wool broker by trade who may have had business connections with Japan but who was known particularly as an enthusiastic admirer and collector of Japanese art.[27]

The first Honorary Consul for Japan in Manchester was William Dunstan Ford-Smith (1870–1919), managing director of the firm of Smith and Coventry, an engineering firm of Salford. Ford-Smith himself was trained as an engineer. He was reported to have 'travelled around the world and was well acquainted with both China and Japan'.[28] He was appointed Honorary Consul in 1907 and in 1915 was decorated by the Emperor with the Order of the Rising Sun (4th Class). The next appointment would appear to have been W. Peer Groves (1878–1946) who acted for Japan between 1930 and the outbreak of war in 1941. Groves's credentials included serving in the Great War as liaison officer to the Japanese staff for which he also was awarded the Order of the Rising Sun (4th Class). It is not clear whether the Honorary Japanese Consuls in Manchester and Liverpool had connections with the academic world but Hugh Matheson in London and A. R. Brown in Glasgow, certainly had.

## 4 ACADEMIC INTRODUCTIONS: ALEXANDER WILLIAMSON AT UNIVERSITY COLLEGE, LONDON

The earliest links with academic institutions were made in the 1860s before the Restoration. At this time parties of young men, especially from the outer clans, including *Choshu* and *Satsuma*, arrived in London to study and to increase their knowledge of the West. The *Satsuma* group's presence was noted under the heading of 'Our Japanese Visitors'. *The Times* reported that:

> the party sent to England by the Prince of Satsuma are 14 in number consisting of two officers of high rank, an interpreter and 11 young men of good family and education who are to remain in England for some years . . . to acquire a knowledge of the English language and an insight into the literature, arts and science which form such an important element of European civilisation.[29]

In the early days these parties were often consigned to Matheson & Co. in London, where Hugh Matheson made it his job to introduce them around in academic and social circles. Matheson remained an influential figure.[30] As late as 1880 Rinzaburo Shida in his correspondence requesting that Kelvin should recommend him to attend a certain conference did so 'so that Mr Matheson will agree'.[31]

In the academic world the figure who is best known for befriending the Japanese was Alexander William Williamson (1824–1904), Professor of Chemistry at University College, London from 1855 to 1887.[32] As *The Times* noted the *Satsuma* group 'have been placed under the care of Professor Williamson of London University under whose able government their studies are being prosecuted'.[33] He advised several groups of Japanese, organised their lecture schedules, made arrangements for them to do laboratory work as well as arranging accommodation and taking some into his own home. He also acted as an adviser, recommending possible British professors to appointments in Japan. Williamson's importance was greatest in the 1860s and 1870s. Mrs Williamson recorded in her journal that 'Mr David Murray of the education department, Tokio, wrote asking A to recommend and send to Japan a Professor of Chemistry and a Professor of Technology (Engineering)'.[34]

The most distinguished Japanese student who studied with Williamson was Joji Sakurai, one of the first generation of modern

Japanese chemists. Sakurai remembered his teachers at UCL explaining:

> Dr Alex W. Williamson, renowned throughout the whole world for his classical investigation on the formation of ethers and renowned also for his remarkably keen insight into the atomic constitution of matter, was then Professor of Chemistry, and it is needless for me to say how highly I value the scientific training I received from him. I was taught Physics by Professor Carey Foster and Dr Oliver Lodge, and the knowledge of Physics thus acquired was a great help to me in following the remarkably rapid development of Physical Chemistry which was soon to come.[35]

Williamson, although held by his Japanese students almost in veneration 'for his early teaching and beneficent influence' did not, directly through his scholarship, attract to himself a coterie of Japanese students.[36] Other academics were also helpful. Those like John Milne, William Ayrton and John Perry, all distinguished in their own fields, warmly welcomed former Japanese students who visited them in England long after they had returned from service in Japan. When John Milne had returned to England his biographers have noted that 'travellers from Japan were always made welcome', these included Baron Dairoku Kikuchi and Fusakichi Omori, one of Milne's, protégés and 'many other Japanese who were studying in Britain'.[37] While there were many similarities between the English and the Scottish academic world and then as now scholars moved freely between the two, there were distinct attractions in Scotland at this time.

## 5 ACADEMIC INTRODUCTIONS: LORD KELVIN AND THE SCOTTISH CONNECTION

The most influential of those serving in Scotland who became involved with the Japanese was William Thomson (1824–1907), later Lord Kelvin, Professor of Natural Philosophy in the University of Glasgow from 1844 to 1899, whose academic distinction was such that when he died he was accorded the honour of being buried near Isaac Newton in Westminster Abbey.[38] Kelvin's concerns were international; his friends and students came from many nations. Among his students were British scholars who served in Japan as well as Japanese who studied with him in Glasgow.

When the centenary celebrations of Kelvin's birth were taking place in 1924, a message was received from Japan which stated that

> The National Research Council of Japan specially desires to recall with gratitude the interest he took in developing physical science and in encouraging research in this part of the world. At the time when Japan was remodelling her education on modern lines, she was fortunate to have his eminent disciples as organisers. Dyer, Gray, Ayrton, Perry, Ewing and Knott, personally recommended by Lord Kelvin himself, came to the Far East, and by their personal examples, inspired the young students with the spirit of research and love for the pursuit of truth, a spirit which sprang from the soul of the Great Master. And when these students came to Glasgow to receive direct instruction from Sir William he was their father and friend, guiding them by hand through the untrodden realms of physical research.[39]

Kelvin's strength lay in his ability and enthusiasm in applying scientific theory to practical and useful purposes.[40] Before 1900 Kelvin had taken out fifty-six patents. (Those after 1900 were taken out in the name of Kelvin and White.)[41] Of these eleven relate to telegraphy, eleven to compasses and navigation apparatus, six to dynamo machines or electric lamps, twenty-five to electric measuring instruments, one to electrolytic production of alkali and two to valves for fluids.

In the furtherance of his determination to exploit his patents Kelvin maintained and developed 'our intimate connection with the Glasgow business of James White',[42] the latter providing not only scientific and professional services but also undertaking full-scale commercial manufacture of Thomson's many patented electrical and navigational instruments; indeed in 1870 Thomson cited 'the convenience of Glasgow in getting mechanical work done' as a reason for declining the newly founded Chair of Experimental Physics at Cambridge.[43]

In the early *Meiji* years Kelvin was asked, with others, to recommend young British scholars to go to Japan to take responsibilities for teaching, at an advanced level, the first generation of Japanese students of chemistry, physics, mathematics and engineering. Some evidence remains of Kelvin's role. On 27 January 1883, the Rector of Tokyo University (*Tokio Daigakko*) wrote to Kelvin asking him to nominate 'one of as high scientific talent and standing as possible'.[44] Kelvin's recommendation was of Cargill Knott, a promising young Edinburgh graduate.[45]

After 1879 when the first graduating class from the Imperial College of Engineering qualified, numbers of graduates were sent abroad for further education and some arrived in Glasgow. Four letters from one of the most brilliant, Rinzaburo Shida, survive, giving an insight into Kelvin's involvement. Shida's letters to Kelvin are variously addressed from Scotland and from Japan. They contain explanations of his work problems, relating to electricity, electromagnetics and telegraphy as well as requests for advice and guidance. Shida also travelled widely in Europe before returning home. By May 1883 he was back in Japan where he became Professor of Natural Philosophy at ICE and simultaneously Director-General of the Imperial Government Telegraphs in Tokyo.[46]

Aikitsu Tanakadate (1856–1950), one of the best known of an early generation of Japanese physicists, worked in Glasgow on electricity and magnetism under Kelvin on the recommendation of J. A. Ewing between 1888 and 1890. As Koizumi reports 'To the end of his life Tanakadate spoke of the deep impression Thomson had made on him'. Kelvin's generous treatment of the young Japanese, not only in the laboratory but also by entertaining them in his own home was much appreciated as was Kelvin's parting gesture in giving Tanakadate about ten of his personal cards to use for introductions to other scientists in Europe. This was a particularly heart-warming gesture.[47]

Perhaps Lord Kelvin's position was unique. The letter which the president of the 'Lord Kelvin Association' of Utsunomiya Middle School, Japan, wrote to him on 17 November 1906 reporting on a meeting at which 'Your Lordship's portrait was hung over the platform and some speeches were made in praise of your scientific attainment',[48] gives evidence of the reverence with which he was regarded in Japan.

A colleague of Kelvin's at Glasgow, William John McQuorn Rankine (1820–72), the Professor of Engineering at Glasgow was also, in a different sense, an important figure.[49] Rankine had always emphasised what he called 'the cultivation of harmony between theory and practice in Mechanics'. He noted that there are three kinds of subjects: 'purely scientific knowledge – purely practical knowledge – and that intermediate knowledge which relates to the application of scientific principles to practical purposes and which arises from understanding the harmony of theory and practice'. Rankine continued:

In theoretical science the question is – what are we to think? But in practical science the question is – *what are we to do?* In doubtful cases we cannot allow our machines and our works of improvement to wait for the advancement of science; and if existing data are insufficient to give an exact solution – that approximate solution must be acted upon which the best data available show to be the most probable.[50]

Rankine's application of science and engineering to practical purposes involved him in cooperation and experimentation with shipbuilders then involved in the industry on the Clyde. One of the fruitful partnerships was with his friend John Elder (1824–69) one of the most innovative of shipbuilders who brought new expertise to marine engineering with the invention of the compound expansion steam engine in 1855.[51] The untimely deaths of both Elder and Rankine as comparatively young men deprived the shipbuilding industry of two inspired figures. Fortunately in Henry Dyer, who was to graduate withn months of Rankine's death, Japan was able to secure the services and loyalties of one of the last and most distinguished of Rankine's pupils.

In the summer of 1882, after an absence of nearly ten years, Henry Dyer returned to Glasgow. There he remained until his death in 1918, himself providing a pro-Japanese lobby and making available his knowledge and experience to smooth the way for the many Japanese, whether students, shipbuilders, engineers or trainee managers who temporarily made their home in the area. Dyer had a staunch ally in A. R. Brown, the Honorary Japanese Consul in Glasgow.

There can be no doubt of Dyer's pro-Japanese stance. He had been deepy affected by his experience, admiring Japanese corporatism and approving of a policy of strong decision-taking at the centre, especially as it had encouraged the allocation of substantial resources to technical and scientific education.

Perhaps Dyer did not act with prudence or forethought; he had already publicised a quarrel he had had in 1878 with the Institute of Civil Engineers in London.[52] On his return to Scotland he failed to find full-time paid employment. He seems to have believed that his application to become the first occupant of the Chair of Naval Architecture in the University of Glasgow would be successful.[53,54] He applied both in 1883 and again in 1886, on neither occasion with success. It was an unreasonable ambition. The profession of ship-designer had been developing at an astonishing rate during his absence in Japan. In any case he had had no special training in this field, nor had he undertaken the course in naval architecture organised in London. He had been out of Britain for ten years teaching in and administering a College, the first of its kind in an undeveloped country. He was unlucky in another application, that of Principal of the newly organised Heriot Watt College in Edinburgh, which would certainly have suited his talents and experience.[55]

Failing to obtain full-time paid employment Dyer had perforce to occupy himself with other matters. As a life governor of the Glasgow and West of Scotland Technical College (1886) he was indefatigable, creating an efficient College out of a series of fragmented educational institutions which had included the Andersonian University.[56] Using his Japanese experience he became widely known as an expert and writer on technical education. Dyer became a member of the Glasgow School Board in 1891 and later its Vice-Chairman. In 1918 when he died he was chairman, a post he had held since 1914. None of these posts was paid.

In the thirty-six years during which Dyer lived in Glasgow after his return from Japan in 1882 he performed an invaluable service for Japan. It is possible that the Japanese government paid him a pension. Throughout the period Dyer and his family helped the considerable numbers of Japanese resident in Glasgow.[57]

Dyer was also an unofficial liaison officer for the Japanese in Glasgow. He requested (in 1901) that the Court of the University of Glasgow should accept Japanese as a permitted language for entry to the University. This was agreed. The candidate for whom this concession was granted was Sampachi Fukuzawa, third son of Yukichi Fukuzawa although Tatsuzo Kajima and Kouji Satow also sat the Japanese examination at the same time. In September/ October 1901, Tamochika Iwane was the only candidate taking the Japanese examination. Soseki Natsume, between 1901 and 1902, then resident in London was paid a fee of four guineas (£4 4*s*) for setting the papers in Japanese and examining any candidates.[58]

Dyer also became a prolific author. *The Evolution of Industry* appeared in 1895. But some of the remarks in this book, 'a socialist is simply the opposite of an individualist' and 'property of every kind would be held subject to the ultimate public good' frightened some of his British contemporaries.[59] He was on safer ground when he wrote *Dai Nippon: The Britain of the East* in 1905 after the Russo-Japanese war. In 1909 he published *Japan in World Politics* which discussed Japan's rise as a world power. These three books indicate the way

Dyer's mind was developing, his pro-Japanese stand being mixed with a good deal of idealism.

Dyer's predicament in re-entering Scottish life after almost a decade in Japanese service deserves sympathy. He had been appointed to the prestigious position of college principal as a recent graduate at the age of 25. He had held in Tokyo a position of responsibility and power. He came to admire much in Japanese culture. The problems of 'reverse culture shock' on returning to Glasgow in 1882 were acute. His difficulties were exacerbated by the fact that he had no sponsor to support him in his attempt to enter Scottish academic life. Professor Rankine, who had originally recommended him to Ito, had died on Christmas Eve 1872, before Dyer set out for Japan. It is, however, possible that the Japanese in Glasgow benefited because Dyer had more time to devote to them than would otherwise have been the case had he been in full-time employment.

## 6 NETWORKING

Networking is used by us all in many areas of human life from individual contacts at home and at work to commercial and international relationships in the wider world. In the later nineteenth century the regional character of technology required the Japanese to enter several such networks.[60] If it is accepted that no 'universal best way' existed and that each regional centre could offer pre-eminence in some shipbuilding and or armament making techniques, then these areas became prime targets for the Japanese. In Britain this took them to Glasgow and the west of Scotland, Newcastle and the Tyne, Middlesbrough and the Tees, Barrow-in-Furness and Sheffield as well as to Manchester, for cotton and its ancillary industries. The Japanese were always thorough, their engineers were resident in all these centres for years before the First World War. Because of the availability of material it has been possible to trace the intricacies of the network more closely in Glasgow and the west of Scotland than elsewhere. Clearly the Japanese relied a great deal on the advice and guidance of men like Dyer and Brown, both familiar with Japanese arrangements and sympathetic to Japanese aspirations. Commercially Brown provided an invaluable network of connections for the Japanese, and because they worked through him any friction which might have arisen because of their foreignness was defused. Academically Alexander Williamson in London, Professor Sir Henry Roscoe in

Manchester,[61] and Henry Dyer in Glasgow, all provided valuable contacts with the scholarly world.

It was however a dual approach. Large Japanese concerns like Mitsui and Mitsubishi soon established a Japanese-led commercial network in London.[62] From the references which have come to light Messrs Mitsui and Takata were very active in negotiating orders for Japanese owners in British shipbuilding yards. It is also clear that once embarked upon a series of relationships which worked amicably there was a strong incentive to continue along the same lines. The networks to which reference has been made were strong, valuable both for the Japanese and the British. Although the advent of the First World War in 1914 temporarily brought them to an end, some reasserted themselves even in the increasingly difficult atmosphere of the post-war world.

# 13 Licencers and Licensees

## 1 MANUFACTURING LICENCES

By 1900 the Japanese were poised to enter a third, and possibly final, phase of technical transfer.[1] They planned to negotiate manufacturing licences which would enable them to make up in Japan intricate, and valuable, engines and machinery rather than importing them ready-made from Britain or elsewhere. This process constitutes a third phase of technical transfer coming hard on the heels of earlier borrowing. During phase one foreign experts lived and worked in Japan teaching their Japanese students and demonstrating Western technical skills. In phase two the focus shifted back to the West where Japanese students sought to further their education in the classroom or on the shop-floor. In this cycle, one, two and three are likely to be consecutive although there can be overlap, but stage three is necessarily sequential to one and two. That the Japanese were able to undertake a programme of purchasing technology reflects their own determination to buy as well as the willingness of Western firms – at this time mostly British – to sell.

Each phase was undertaken at great expense to the Japanese economy. The employment of the British and other foreign experts, at princely salaries caused financial embarrassment,[2] the expense of sending hundreds of Japanese abroad for further education was great and during the third phase, when whole new industries were set up, further heavy investment was required. The development of manufacturing under licence was only possible because by 1900 the Japanese economy was healthy, and Japan was able to borrow in London on favourable terms.[3]

Successful manufacture under licence demanded a greater commitment of personnel and resources in Japan than any borrowing which had gone before. The obligation of the Japanese licensee as manufacturer might require that he provide a new industrial site with factory and workshops. Preliminary semi-manufacture of raw materials, before the licencing process began, could itself present difficulties. Even if machines and machine tools were provided by the licencer the use of these in complex processes might result in set-backs. Losses could mount quickly if a product proved unusable. Flaws in manufacture required the scrapping of much expensive material.

The British licencer, despite what may have been written into the contract, had practically no say in the making up of the finished product in Japan. Even if British managers, foremen and workers were on hand on the Japanese workshop-floor there was no guarantee that they would be used. Whether the licencer would have entered into agreements with the licensee had he appreciated Japanese attitudes is a matter for conjecture. At the end of the day the British could exert control only over the supply of money if it were being borrowed in London.

The commitments of a manufacturing licence seem to have varied. At one end of the spectrum the licensee was provided with designs, plans, templates and perhaps machine tools and was then expected to make up complicated machines himself using his own raw materials for semi-manufacture and final processing. At the other extreme the licencer himself manufactured the elements of the construction in Britain which were then assembled in Japan. During the early years of the twentieth century, British and Japanese concerns negotiated contracts involving a variety of methods. There are revealing accounts from the British records of the activities of those who before the First World War did negotiate manufacturing licenses with the Japanese.

## 2 THE JAPANESE GOVERNMENT AS ARMAMENT MANUFACTURER

It is a truism to say that it was the guns of the black ships of Commodore Perry and Lord Elgin which forced compliance on a reluctant Japan. The demonstrations of Western naval armaments in the bombardments at Shimonoseki and Kagoshima proved that the Japanese could not repulse the foreigner. It became an urgent priority for Japan herself to develop an armament industry on her own territory which was at that time an unreal ambition.[4] A generation later, the idea, always in Japanese minds, re-emerged. By this time the Japanese government was an important and highly regarded customer of Armstrong, Whitworth & Co Ltd. and Vickers, Maxim, armament-makers and shipbuilders.[5]

In 1905 the Japanese government approached Armstrong's and Vickers requesting their assistance to set up 'a cordite factory in Japan'. This initiative developed into the Japan Steelworks Co. (*Kabushiki Kwaisha Nihon Seikosho*) and the Japan Explosives

Company.[6] A large green-field site was chosen at Muroran on the southern shore of Hokkaido where Isabella Bird had earlier observed 'the beautiful and almost land-locked bay of Muroran with steep wooded sides and deep water close to the shore'.[7,8] The advantages of the site were that it was close to the coal mines of the Hokkaido Coal Company, near to the growing town of Muroran which had a railway link, and a good anchorage which could easily accommodate the largest ships.[9]

By the time the agreement was drawn up in 1907 it was between the Japan Steel Works Company, the British consortium of Sir W. G. Armstrong, Whitworth & Co. Ltd,[10] Vickers, Son and Maxim[11] and the Hokkaido Colliery and Steamship Co. Ltd. The financial obligation was in proportions of a quarter, a quarter, and an half, 'of the ordinary share capital, each engaging mutually not to part with their respective holdings', thus involving a British commitment of 25 per cent of the original investment. The two English companies undertook 'to give the Japan Steel Works the right to use their various patents in Japan, and the benefit of their designs and experience'. They also authorised them to act as their agents in Japan 'for such of their manufactures as the Japan Steel Works is unable to make'.[12]

By 20 February 1908 the works of the Japanese Explosives Co. were complete and 'now beginning to manufacture'.[13] Two years later, in 1910, the Japanese government had asked the company 'to increase its output from 300 to 500 tons per annum, and a verbal promise of 700 to 800 tons per annum in orders had been given'. The British consortium felt that with the Japanese government as customer they were on safe ground and that 'the prospects for the company were favourable'.

By mid-1909 work on the Muroran site was well advanced and the British sent a deputation consisting of Douglas Vickers and John Noble to consider progress. They linked up in Japan with Count Hirosawa, and Admiral Yamanouchi and Mr Inowye, the latter based at the Muroran site. The British found that the area was being developed 'lavishly', land was being reclaimed to extend the site. The total figure of £2 100 000 was quoted as the cost of setting up the plant, of which £150 000 would go on '"duties" on the material and machines imported'. The British emissaries were alarmed at the rising cost of the project and spent much time negotiating with the Japanese at various levels to ensure that capital was forthcoming. Messrs Mitsui & Co., as advisers and arbiters, attempted to mediate between the anxious Britons and the gracious but immovable Japanese.

Douglas Vicker's report on the Seikosho management leaves no doubt about the difficulties of organising and managing such a project involving men from two cultures. The English, in the person of Captain Boyle and Mr Henson, hoped to have 'their proper say in the management'; the Japanese, represented by Admiral Yamanouchi and Mr Inowye, repeatedly promised cooperation but invariably 'consulted nobody'. All sorts of safeguards were discussed to encourage the men to work harmoniously together. In mid-1909 Douglas Vickers hoped that 'the English interests will not be overlooked in the future'.

At the workshop level matters were even more heated; the British delegation tried hard to insist that the British foremen's expertise be used. Japanese foremen in the machine shops were one of the 'weak parts' of the organisation being either 'men of no practical experience, drawn direct from technical schools, or recruited from Kure'.[14]

Although tributes were paid to the care of the Japanese in seeing that the British managers and foremen were comfortable in Muroran, Japanese attitudes led to dissatisfaction and frustration. Although the British foremen were eager to work 'the services of the forgeman from Openshaw are not being taken advantage of, he is practically ignored by the foremen in the shop and his advice is never taken', while 'Japanese self-confidence' ensured that Baldock, the foreman, had no 'opportunity of working'.

Perhaps the Japanese found the British assumptions of superior knowledge intrusive and British attitudes overbearing. Certainly the engineer's report (that of F. B. Trevelyan) suggests an inefficient and poorly run operation and indeed bafflement at the attitude of the English Board which 'originally prompted them in establishing a Japanese Control over the works'. Trevelyan concludes that 'I do not think that any profits will ever be made as long as the works remain under Japanese control.'[15]

K. K. N. Seikosho depended for its orders primarily on the Japanese government, the English deplored the way delivery dates were staggered so that in the case of the 14-inch guns delivery was not expected until the 'middle of 1915'. It is not known what was the effect of the withdrawal of British personnel in 1914.

## 3 AT NAGASAKI, THE MITSUBISHI SHIPYARD

The Nagasaki Shipyard, until the 1880s owned by the Japanese government, was in 1884 in accordance with government policy, initially leased and later sold to Mitsubishi who had earlier, when operating as a shipping company, had a small repair-yard and engine-shop at Yokohama. Men and equipment were transferred to Nagasaki where Mitsubishi subsequently concentrated their shipbuilding efforts. This yard became the most advanced and innovative, pioneering all the new techniques introduced into Japan. Throughout the late *Meiji* years the Mitsubishi Shipyard employed a small group of British ship-designers, marine engineers and shipbuilders often on short-term contracts.

During the decade from January 1904 Mitsubishi purchased twelve licences to manufacture foreign products at their Nagasaki yard. With the exception of that negotiated with *Elektriska Swetning Aktiebor-lag*, which entitled them to develop a Swedish electric welding method, the permissions obtained were apparently from British firms. From this list it can be seen that Mitsubishi as licensee was interested in the better performance of ships, in their engines and the necessary and increasingly sophisticated auxiliary machinery. They were also concerned with the use of electricity as a more efficient source of power.

*Table* 13.1 Manufacturing licences obtained by Mitsubishi Shipbuilding, Nagasaki, 1904–14

| | | |
|---|---|---|
| 1904.1 | Parsons Marine Steam Turbine Co. | Marine steam turbine |
| 1904.1 | C. A. Parsons Co. | Land steam turbine |
| 1904.1 | Josiah Stone & Co. | Stone's manganese bronze |
| 1906.1 | C. A. Parsons & Co. | Continuous current dynamos and alternator |
| 1907.6 | Contraflo Condenser & Kinetic Air Pump Co. | Condenser |
| 1909 | Nesdrum Co.? | Boiler |
| 1910.6 | Richardson & Westgars Co. | Stoker and superheater |
| 1911.10 | Contraflow Condenser & Kinetic Air Pump Co. | Auxiliary machines |
| 1912.2 | J. & G. Weir & Co. | Auxiliary machines |
| 1914.2 | *Elektriska Swetning Aktieborlag* | Electric welding method |
| 1914.2 | Yarrow & Co. | Torpedo boat, boiler |
| 1914.9 | Joseph William Isherwood | Isherwood method of hull construction |

*Source*: Y. Fukusaku, 'Technology Imports and R&D at Mitsubishi Nagasaki Shipyard in the Pre-war Period'.[16]

From records recently available from two British firms, one Scots and one English, it is possible to understand in more detail the relationship between licencer and licensee. From the papers of J. & G. Weir, especially the letterbooks of Sir William Weir, insight can be gained as to how one Scots manufactuer viewed a Japanese licensee. From material which comes from C. A. Parsons & Co. hints can be gathered of what they were doing to supply their client in Japan.

At the end of 1911 J. & G. Weir's, pump and condenser manufacturers of Cathcart, Glasgow, finalised their agreement with the Japanese by which some of Weir's products would be manufactured under licence by Mitsubishi at Nagasaki.[17] They also made a similar agreement with Kawasaki.[18] This manufacturing licence was the logical culmination of a period of constructive cooperation between Weirs and the Japanese.

The development of the compound steam engine exacerbated problems with those ships' boilers which were fed with salt water. Because of the dangers that corroded and badly scaled boilers would burst there were good reasons for a marine engineer to attempt to tackle the problems posed. James Weir (1843–1900) did so.[19] The essence of the process was to collect as distilled water the steam produced during the expansion of the ships' engines and feed this back. This prevented corrosion.[20] The expansion of J. & G. Weir Ltd, into international markets depended ultimately on the technical efficiency and business acumen of William Douglas Weir (1877–1959) who after apprenticeship became Managing Director in 1902.[21]

Weir's initial breakthrough came after the introduction of the water-tube steam boiler. With this new engine, for naval and merchant ships, came a demand for an improved high-pressure feed pump. The development of the steam turbine stimulated Weir's business. The rapid change-over of fuel from coal to oil-fired steam-boilers for all types of ships did nothing to lessen the demand.[22] The provision of these precision instruments provided Weir's with the gap they required in the market.

With the turbine-driven ship, Weir's were on familiar territory for such engines required feed-heating apparatus and, because excess steam could easily be generated, Weirs could also develop fire pumps, bilge pumps and machines to fulfil other pumping functions and so use the extra steam. There was also a demand for independent air pumps (not driven by the main engine) between the condensers and the boilers.[23,24]

The strength of Weir's hold on the business is well illustrated by a letter written in 1911:

> It may interest your German naval friends to know that apart from the British Navy, in which [*sic*] we design all the condensers, we have supplied the designs for the two Argentine battleships building in America, for the *Wyoming* Battleship of the US Navy, for Courbet and Jean Bart of the French Navy, for the four new Dreadnoughts of the Austrian Navy, for all the Dreadnoughts of the Italian Navy, for all the Dreadnoughts and Battle Cruisers of the Japanese Navy, for the new Battleship for the Brazilian Navy, new Battleship for the Turkish Navy, new Battleships for the Chilean Navy – as a matter of fact, almost all the Warships building except the German battleships.
>
> With kindest regards and the Compliments of the Season.
> PS Also all Russian B'ships.[25]

Weir's links with the Japanese were of longstanding. From the end of the nineteenth century to the First World War Japanese were regular correspondents and frequent visitors to Cathcart, Glasgow. In this instance as elsewhere they were as keen to learn as they were to buy. To this end Weir accepted Japanese on the shop-floor and a fee of '£2500 for the tuition of their men'.[26] William Weir was constantly travelling, particularly between Glasgow and London, always ready to discuss orders with his Japanese contacts. It was demanding work, as he explained, 'I was in London on Sunday and saw Fujii and I can tell you that this job beats anything that I was ever at in the way of diplomacy.'[27]

As the association became closer the Japanese indicated that they might like an arrangement to manufacture Weir's pumps in Japan. Differences arose, as Weir wrote to Fujii 'I cannot see that it is worth while going into details of ships and machinery. When the matter is properly decided and necessary financial arrangements made I will then put one of our best men on to the design of the works and the list of the machine tools'.[28] With Mitsubishi and Kawasaki, as Weir explained,

> our arrangement with each of the two private firms in Japan is that they pay us a royalty of 15 per cent on the British selling price which they build in Japan, and they guarantee to pay us not less than £600 for 10 years. Further, each of these firms agree to give us 2/3rds of all the machinery for their present large cruisers for

> construction here. In connection with the Japanese Admiralty, they give us an order of 2/3rds of the Battleship machinery, together with a sum for the designs of the remainder of the machinery based on 15 per cent of the British selling price.[29]

Weir's equipment was also made under licence in America and Germany.

It was an important principle with Weirs to provide all the auxiliary machinery including main and auxiliary condensers, main and auxiliary air pumps, main and auxiliary feed pumps, forced lubrication pumps, oil fuel pumps, fire and bilge pumps and evaporators and distilling machinery. They had discovered that only by providing a custom-built set of equipment for any one vessel could they guarantee that the various items would function efficiently as a whole.

It is not known from the research material at present available how Weir's contribution worked out on the ground in Japan for Mitsubishi or Kawasaki. Did they send skilled craftsmen and foremen to Japan? Were these men frustrated by Japanese determination to be self-sufficient? Perhaps the records of the Japanese companies involved will cast more light on these matters.

Mitsubishi also negotiated licensing agreements with C. A. Parsons & Co. of the Heaton Works, Newcastle upon Tyne, where Charles Parsons had set up a new factory.[30] Originally he was working on the steam turbine for driving electric generators but in 1894 the steam turbine to drive a ship's propeller shaft was patented.

As is widely known Parsons secured a great personal triumph when he demonstrated his *Turbinia* on 26 June 1897, the occasion of Queen Victoria's Diamond Jubilee, by running his 44.5 ton vessel at remarkable speed up and down the lines of ships not only of the Royal Navy but also of world navies assembled to do honour to the occasion.[31]

Subsequently despite early set-backs the steam turbine proved itself as the motor power of the future. The laying down of the turbine-driven battleship *Dreadnought* at Portsmouth on 2 October 1905 marked the beginning of a new era. Not only naval vessels but also passenger liners and other merchant ships were fitted with the new propulsion.

From 1905 Parsons were supplying both marine steam turbines and Parsons dynamos to Japan.[32] In the case of marine steam turbines these were being fitted to ships for Japan being built on the Tyne.[33] In the case of Parsons dynamos, fitted in Japan, the licensee would require to fit them himself and ensure efficient working in Japan. From their intended locations it is clear that connecting them to the existing plant might prove difficult.[34] The use of dynamos in mines suggests the need for improved lighting and pumping machinery.[35] These ten orders are dated between November 1906 and August 1910.

## 4 A 'SPECIAL RELATIONSHIP'

Although the Minute Books are discreet and Letter Book correspondents circumspect, the manufacture of a company's products in Japan led to the development of a special relationship between the supplying company and the Japanese. It was perhaps inevitable in an age of cartels and price agreements that those closely linked should expect and receive favours.

It worked both ways. The British with strong links with Japanese firms expected to get orders. William Weir in writing to James Latta, his 'supersalesman', wrote 'I do not think you could have properly understood him when you say they may wish to make the engines and pumps in Japan, as it has been understood by Captain Fujii and I that we were to get this contract.'[36,37]

From the Japanese side there were also requests, as Admiral Yamanouchi wrote to Albert Vickers:

> I will be ever grateful to you if you will use your influence as the Chairman of the Anglo-French Nickel Co. and bring the *Nihon Seiko-Sho* within that group of favoured few who can purchase your famous nickel [essential for the making of armour-plate] at a greatly reduced price. As you are aware when I was connected with Kure you were kind enough to supply us with a large quantity at £150 per ton. I sincerely hope that you will kindly bestow on us the same favour and if possible a greater favour you will consent to deliver us 30 tons in the shipment by October and 70 tons more in two or three shipments. I am afraid you will think this too much but it is essential to put *Nihon Seiko-Sho* on a sound basis in which Messrs Vickers are also deeply interested.[38]

The difficulty about these 'favours' was that they very quickly became more and soon stepped over the bounds into something less pleasant. Over the years up until 1914 activity became increasingly fevered as suppliers struggled for profitability in an increasingly competitive world.

While Vickers and Armstrongs were competing at home they also had formidable overseas competition such as the Fore River Shipbuilding Company and the New York Shipbuilding Company in the USA and Krupps and Blohm and Voss in Germany. Mitsui, writing to Vickers, commented that 'Krupps are still keeping up their efforts, claiming their capability to make battleships exactly like the English design of best type in both ship and ordnance.' Mitsui concluded this letter by affirming that 'we will never slack our energies on this side to do our utmost'.[39]

The difficulty was to determine what constituted fair practice and what stepped over the boundaries into unscrupulous dealing. One of the most active and assiduous Japanese working in Britain before 1914 was Engineer Officer Captain, later Admiral, Fujii. He was everywhere and he knew everyone. One of his many preoccupations was the building of the Imperial Japanese Navy warship *Kongo* by Vickers and Co., at Barrow-in-Furness between 1911 and 1913. Unfortunately the line between accepting small gifts and 'commissions' or bribes is a thin one and at the beginning of 1914 the Japanese Minister of Marines announced that Admiral Fujii and Captain Sawasaki had been charged with corruption. By April 1914 the changes had become more specific, that three Directors of Mitsui, as agents of Vickers, had been accused of bribing Vice Admiral Matsumoto with £40 000 through Vice Admiral Matsuo in connection with the *Kongo*.

By May 1914 Admiral Fujii was accused of receiving £35 270 between January 1911 and September 1912 'from contractors'. The judgement in what came to be known as 'the Mitsui Case' came on 20 July 1914 when of those involved seven were convicted of receiving, in connection with the *Kongo* 'commission' of £115 000.[40]

## 5 WHO PROMOTED WHOM?

The Japanese were not alone in the years before 1914, in seeking to negotiate manufacturing licences. For the licensee it became a matter of national pride and honour to undertake intricate manufacturing, especially of arms, on its own soil. For the licencer, fearful of a declining export market and generally over-optimistic about his ability to control the industrial process overseas, it apparently offered an opportunity for expansion. The willingness of the British manufacturers to make licensing agreements was determined primarily by fear of the future; if they did not fall in with Japanese plans then others, competitors in Germany or elsewhere, would.

Did no one stand firm and decline the tempting invitations to allow licensing? The only evidence which has so far come to light of a British firm declining to have anything to do with licensing arrangements with Japan comes from Professor Archibald Barr of Barr & Stroud, Glasgow. Professor Barr and Professor Stroud had entered a War Office competition for range- finders – for use by the army and the navy – in 1888. They succeeded, after some setbacks, in designing a much-improved instrument which enabled the new armament of the period to be used much more effectively. Professor Barr wrote to his partner Harold Jackson in 1907:

> asked Professor Czapski (of Zeiss in Germany) – if the Japs were to offer you an order on condition that you taught them how the whole thing (i.e. the manufacture of range-finders) was done, would you accept it? Certainly not, said Professor Czapski. They have been at the same game with Zeiss. All he would promise would be that they could – when the instruments were finished – take them to pieces if they liked and also he would teach them to adjust them. Professor Czapski also said that if opticians would combine and refine said conditions it would be well, because the Japs are so clever in picking up what they see. This from London and Jena just when we have had the same experience is *very* interesting.[41]

The historian of Barr and Stroud believes that the Japanese did start to make their own range-finders and order transmitters for warships at about this time. It is not known whether they did this using only the range-finders supplied to them before 1905.

But there were no such refusals from most manufacturers. Vickers and Armstrongs, usually operating abroad as one consortium, made several agreements whereby they set up subsidiaries in Spain (1887); Italy (1905); Russia (1912); Turkey (July 1914) and of course Japan in 1907. None of these foreign concerns was out of tutelage by the time the war broke out in August 1914; several of the operations overseas had proved troublesome.

Why then did British and firms from other advanced countries act as facilitators and enter into these agreements which despite initial optimism always seemed to cause trouble. The answer lies chiefly in economic realities, governments like that of Japan were no longer prepared to spend large sums overseas if manufacture could be undertaken at home. British, French or German firms were not in the position to choose; if they wanted the business they had no option but to enter into the agreements.

Although accepted by British firms as a way of outpacing rivals, the involvement in armaments manufacture in Japan, as well as in other countries overseas, was often hazardous. Foreign markets were secured temporarily but such licences caused much complication for British personnel and high risk for the capital involved. It was bound also, while producing short-term gains, to result in the end in the withering away of overseas markets. For the receiving country, such as Japan, it was a device for gaining an implant of advanced technology.

# 14 Exhibitions, Designers and Architects

## 1 EXOTIC YET UNKNOWN

Nothing could have been more likely to encourage the interest of the Victorians than a country which combined the exoticism of the East with the added allure that it had previously remained sealed and hidden from the world. Once 'opened' Japan became the subject of an intense curiosity at all levels of society. As is well known Western artists, intrigued by the techniques of Japanese art and especially the Japanese print, travelled to Japan to seek enlightenment. The term *Japonisme,* coined by the French but widely used elsewhere, indicated the interrelationships.[1] British travellers eagerly collected their Japanese porcelain and *objets d'art* in Japan[2] and then came home and dressed their houses in Japanese style. Thousands of ordinary homes in the United Kingdom boasted their mass-produced Japanese export ware, usually a tea-service. Even more common was 'Japanned' ware, a tin tray or tea-caddy, which, never having been nearer Japan than Birmingham, was painted and decorated in 'Japanese style'.[3]

The ubiquitousness of the Japanese style did not go unnoticed. Rebecca West described a room, seen through the eyes of a precocious child which was:

> completely furnished in the Japanese style, which was then (1900) fashionable. The end of the room was taken up with a gilded extension of the chimney-piece, which rose in tiers to the ceiling, each shelf divided into several compartments, in each of which was a single curio, a Japanese cup and saucer, a vase, a carving in jade or rose quartz or ivory and about the room were lacquered tables and flimsy chairs with cushions of oriental fabric . . . the walls were covered with straw wallpaper striped with fine gold thread.

When Rose, the young narrator, questions her school-friend hostess as to 'whether her father had lived long in Japan', Nancy answered 'It all came down from Maples',[4] acknowledging that the famous London furniture store was as far as they had been.

No one turned opportunity, which this curiosity for 'things Japanese' aroused, to better advantage than Mortimer Menpes.[5] After his second visit to Japan in 1896, he published *Japan: A Record in Colour* (1901) with 100 romantically coloured plates of his own. Menpes himself succumbed to the Japanese craze ordering and supervising in Japan the making of the furnishings and fittings for his newly built house in Cadogan Gardens.[6]

Menpes was part of a growing network of connections between the art worlds of England, Scotland and Japan.[7] These artistic facilitators have been little researched except for the case of men as famous as James McNeill Whistler.[8] Menpes, himself for a time an intimate of Whistler's,[9] brought the work of Kawanabe Kyosai to the master's attention.[10] But the English sponsor who brought Kyosai to the attention of Western artists visiting Japan was Josiah Conder, the most famous Western architect who practised in *Meiji* Japan.[11]

Christopher Dresser, himself in Japan for a relatively brief visit in the early part of 1878, was a very active and important facilitator linking up the art worlds of East and West.[12] He was so involved with fine-quality Japanese porcelain and art work that he, with Charles Holme, set up in London a business which his sons operated at the Kobe end.[13] Mortimer Menpes's letters to London from Japan were addressed to Holme.[14] The reticulations of these men within their own circles were important but it was through their work for and encouragement of popular public displays for the masses that Japan and her artistic achievements were made known to an even wider public.

## 2 EXHIBITIONS AND *HAKURANKAI*

The exuberance of Western industrial society, proud of its inventions and competitive in its attitudes, led to the organisation, in the second half of the nineteenth century, of a remarkable series of 'international', 'world', 'universal' exhibitions or expositions. These, started in 1851 in London, with the Great Exhibition of the Works of Industry of all Nations inspired by Albert, the Prince Consort, became a wonderful show-case for manufacturers world-wide.[15] The Great Exhibition itself was a relevation, as has been explained:

> The organisation of this giant enterprise; the inclusion of every important type and process of manufacture then known; the successful appeal to all classes of the population; the stimulation of trade; the creation of a new habit of excursion travel; and . . . the solid profit . . . all commended the Exhibition.[16]

Later, many other International Exhibitions including those at London in 1862, Vienna 1873, the Independence Exhibition Philadelphia 1876, Paris 1867 and 1878, Sydney 1879–80, and Glasgow 1888 and 1901 attracted a good deal of attention. The nineteenth-century exhibition provided entertainment, information and education for a public proud of the artistic and industrial achievements of the period. The educational element was strong, inventions of new machines drew large crowds and exotic pavilions informed many about far-away countries. The Japanese responded to these exhibitions with interest. Yukichi Fukuzawa adverted to these matters in 1866 when, in *Seiyo Jijo* (*Conditions in the West*) he referred to the way in which:

> arts and engineering in every country are developing rapidly and new inventions are appearing one after another. Therefore they prepare the Fairs in the big Western cities every few years, ask the countries all over the world to send their special products, useful machines, antiques and uncommon articles to the Fairs and display the things to their people. This is called *Hakurankai*.

Fukuzawa also referred to the function of the museum which 'in every country collects for long periods articles and things from all over the world'. But in the 1860s, a period of rapid change, 'it often happens that various articles, which used to be regarded as extraordinarily valuable, soon became old-fashioned ... the necessity of yesterday turns out to be the useless object of today'.[17] Museums and exhibitions, having functions to educate, to inform, to entertain and to amuse were not always easily distinguished one from the other.[18]

After the Great Exhibition of 1851 many items were purchased and at the instigation of Henry Cole, with the permission of the Prince Consort, were placed in hastily borrowed rooms at Marlborough House where 'the Schools of Design and their little museum, the Museum of Manufactures' was set up. Shortly afterwards in 1857, the Commissioners appointed to administer the £186 000 profit from the Great Exhibition opened the South Kensington Museum on the spacious 86-acre site which they had bought. It was the Prince Consort's ambition to assemble 'museums, colleges and learned societies' to make an educational centre which would stimulate the interest not only of students but also of the general population.[19] Out of these beginnings came the Science Museum, several Colleges including Imperial, and of course the Victoria and Albert Museum. It is an important corollary to the work of the colleges and museums on the South Kensington site that they were intended to be intellectual centres from which excellence could spread to other parts of the country. They not only had exhibitions and ran museums in London, but they also organised exhibitions and, until 1977, ran the circulating collections by which good design and artefacts were brought to the attention of people in local centres far from London.

Takayoshi Kido (1833–77), in 1873, when in Vienna with the Iwakura Mission, deplored the 'miscellaneous collection of articles' which his countrymen had brought 'to display at the Exposition'. Kido opined that 'The people of our country are not yet able to distinguish between the purpose of an exposition and a museum; therefore they have tried to display a mountain of tiny and delicate Oriental objects' and he bemoaned that this 'seems to invite contempt for the dignity of our country'.[20] Kido's sensitivity was probably misplaced, for many in the Japanese craft industries, which included ceramics, porcelain, lacquer, silks and other textiles, were keen to use the exhibitions as a show-case in which to advertise their wares.

The Japanese first took cognisance of exhibitions abroad when, in 1862 before the Restoration, Yukichi Fukuzawa and the *Bakufu* mission then in Europe, visited the International Exhibition at Crystal Palace in London. There were no official Japanese exhibits although Rutherford Alcock, the first British Consul-General in Japan, who had shown particular interest in and knowledge of Japanese art work, supplied part of his own collection for display.[21]

From 1862 most exhibitions, whether the grand 'universal' or smaller local displays had an officially sanctioned Japanese section. At the Vienna Exhibition, open from 11 May to 1 November 1873 there were almost 100 Japanese participants some of whom travelled to Europe together in a specially chartered French boat. When Philadelphia celebrated in 1876, with the great Independence Exhibition, open from 10 May to 10 November, there were eighty-four Japanese involved including Yoshio Tanaka. The Japanese government spent ¥360 000 – a large sum, but in terms of publicity and advertisement, money well-spent.

By 1878 the Paris Exhibition was capable of attracting more than 26 million visitors. There were 262 Japanese exhibitors, thirty-nine of whom were present in France in person. The specially built Japanese pavilion involved the government in an outlay of ¥210 000. The Japanese government continued to build light ornamental buildings for the various great exhibitions overseas and also encouraged displays at home. In 1881 the Second National Industrial Exposition took place in Tokyo. This attracted over 800 000 visitors. The Sydney Exhibition, open between September 1879 and April 1890, awarded prizes to 215 Japanese exhibits.[22]

The objects shown at exhibitions and donated by the Japanese government, sometimes in exchange for collections of machines and other technical items for display in Japan,[23] were the finest examples available and they inspired many artists and connoisseurs in Britain. One of these was James Lord Bowes, President of the Liverpool Art Club, who with G. A. Audsley, an architect in Liverpool, attempted in *Keramic Art of Japan* 'to classify all known varieties of porcelain and faience in Japan'.[24] Later in 1889 Bowes became Honorary Japanese Consul in Liverpool (see Chapter 12, section 3 above).

Throughout the period the problem of quality caused considerable concern in both Britain and Japan. Admirers of earlier fine Japanese art work deplored the cheap and shoddy goods which later came to be associated with the Japanese name.[25]

Although Kido had regretted that the Japanese should exhibit only the 'delicate oriental objects', these were at this time the stock-in-trade which Japan had to offer and which the West wanted to see.[26] By 1901 the Victorian craze for 'things Japanese' had been established for almost a generation; although the quality of Japanese 'art objects' available in the West varied, there was a discerning Western public. That this was possible was due in part at least to those Westerners like Christopher Dresser, who, influenced by the forms, shapes, colours, textures and techniques of Japanese art, brought a professional outlook to their studies and good-quality Japanese objects to a wider public.

## 3 CHRISTOPHER DRESSER, 'AN ARCHITECT AND ORNAMENTIST'

Christopher Dresser was a pioneer of some importance in Victorian Britain, being the first to regard himself as an industrial designer.[27] He was born in Glasgow (of Yorkshire parents) on 4 July 1834 and, at the age of 13, entered Sir Henry Cole's School of Design at Marlborough House, London. In this way he came at once, and at an early age, in contact with the ideas of those like Cole, Owen Jones, Richard Redgrave and others, who were enthusiastic about the industrial age and who wanted, as did Prince Albert, to base their design work on 'art applied to industry'. In 1854 Dresser became a lecturer in the Department of Science and Art, South Kensington.

Dresser, an early employee of the South Kensington Museum, now the Victoria and Albert Museum, was in broad sympathy with the original objects of that institution which were, briefly, to form a collection which would 'exhibit . . . the practical application of the principles of design in the graceful arrangement of forms and the harmonious combination of colours' for the benefit of 'manufacturers, artisans and the public in general'. He took as his theme 'utility and beauty are not inseparable' developing his ideas in *The Art of Decorative Design* (1862) and later *The Principles of Decorative Design* (1873). In this way attempting to raise the level of design Dresser embraced new materials and new uses for them.[28] Dresser was not sympathetic to the historicism later more closely associated with the Victoria and Albert, nor with the medievalism implicit in the Arts and Crafts movement even then being launched by William Morris.

At the mid-century, the West had little real knowledge of Japan. Although there were some items from Japan on display at the Great Exhibition of 1851 it was not until a full exhibition of Japanese art was held at the Old Watercolour Society in London in 1854 that a serious view could be taken. After this exhibition almost the whole collection was bought by Henry Cole for the Museum of Manufactures in London.[29]

The Japanese for their part welcomed the interest taken by the Western world and contributed Japanese items willingly to the spate of international exhibitions. For them it was important, on a practical level, to have a series of shop windows in which to display their trade goods. Even during the Shogunate, the *Tokugawa* government, and additionally the clan governments of *Saga* and *Satsuma*, had exhibited in the international fair held in Paris in 1867. For the 1871 fair at San Francisco the government ordered Tokyo merchants to exhibit and seconded Junjiro Hosokawa to supervise the Japanese efforts. At the major fair in Vienna in 1873, with Okuma responsible for the arrangements, the government spent heavily to ensure effective publicity for Japan.

Some Japanese were sent to enquire into the museum world and to discover how best Japan could set up modern museums and exhibitions. Christopher Dresser, who had probably first met those Japanese, members of the Iwakura Mission, who visited South Kensington in the autumn of 1872, was already a well-known supporter of *Japonisme*. In 1876 he was invited to visit Japan. In the official records his visit is discussed as follows:

> The South Kensington Museum asked Dr Dresser to bring their donation of European manufactures to the museum in Japan, and to instruct our Japanese officials how to exhibit the objects. Dr Dresser will also inspect Japanese art industries, with the purpose of giving some advice on European taste, and how we can promote the future trade with England.[30]

Toshimichi Okubo, then Minister of the Interior, also commented on the visit expressing the wish that Dr Dresser be urged to visit factories and other areas of interest to him, to encourage Japanese manufacturers to question him about methods in art and industry.[31]

Officially sponsored as he was he saw collections in Japan unknown to the ordinary traveller. The highlight of his visit was the fortnight he spent in Kyoto and Nara visiting the rare collections of art objects belonging to the Mikado. The governor of the city also arranged a special exhibition of Kyoto art manufacturers for him at the House of Commerce in Kyoto.

But this was not all. Dresser's enthusiasm had him visiting some '75 different potteries and porcelain makers'.[32] It was an extraordinary opportunity for so dedicated a man. Dresser also visited and advised at various metal-work and iron companies in Osaka and Sakai. His itinerary also included visits to bamboo and basket works, furniture lacquer, textiles, embroideries, enamels, *cloisonné*, toys and paper. The official invitation to Dresser, as representative of the South Kensington Museum reflected governmental concern with the Japanese 'craft' market overseas. This allowed Dresser 'to achieve the twofold purpose of giving information about European taste in order to promote Anglo-Japanese trade and advising on new industrial developments'.[33]

Christopher Dresser's visit to Japan, when he was 43 years old, lasted 98 days. During this period he enjoyed, at his own insistence, and to the gratification of his hosts, an intensive introduction concerning those businesses of Japan which come under the general umbrella of craft industries. Because of his sympathy with and understanding of these matters he was able to advise and guide Japanese manufacturers. Because of his status as an industrial designer in Britain he was able to absorb from Japan some of the values of the East and allow them to influence the designs he prepared for his clients in the West. Because of the excitement engendered by his visit to Japan he was, on his return to London, to enter upon the most fruitful years of his career during which he served in a wide variety of capacities.[34] His Japanese interests remained strong. While in Japan he had seriously studied Zen Buddhism and Shintoism, so paying a compliment to his hosts by seeking to understand the ideas and reasoning behind their art and artefacts.

As Widar Halen has written, Dresser 'probably did more for the enlightenment of Japanese art, than any other European scholar and designer during this period'. On the occasion of the visit to England in 1880 of Hideharu Kawase, the then Minister of Commerce, Kawase wrote to Dresser, 'This is simply a mark of respect to you, whose intelligent suggestions, have done so much to promote the art and manufactures of Japan.'[35]

It has been argued that the influence which Dresser effected in bringing ideas of art and nature implicit in Eastern art and design was not maintained because of the increasing importance of the medievalism of the William Morris movement. On the other hand the path taken by Dresser led to the work of Charles Rennie Mackintosh and art nouveau and so into the twentieth century. Dresser, through his knowledge and enthusiasm, had put the Japanese art world on the map. Although Dresser described himself as 'an architect and ornamentist'[36] it remained for another Briton to take Western architecture to Japan. He had no need of the temporary structures of exhibitions in which to display his wares for he and his Japanese pupils and colleagues demonstrated their expertise on the ground by designing buildings which, when built, brought to Japanese eyes examples of many styles of architecture.

## 4 WESTERN ARCHITECTURE AND JOSIAH CONDER

Japan had a fine architectural tradition exemplified by her great castles and temples but for some time the coming of the *Meiji* Restoration brought enthusiasm for embracing Western architectural ideas.[37] Modernisation became synonymous with enlightenment. To this end various western architects were appointed for service in Japan. Among these were Charles Alfred Chastel de Boinville who was French in origin;[38] G.V. Cappellette, an Italian; and T.J. Waters, A.N. Hansell (1856–1940) and Josiah Conder (1852–1920) who were English.

As a result of foreign influence a compromise style of building was initially developed, using the timber-frame construction already basic to Japanese domestic building and adding stone or stucco as infill. Sometimes the outer walls were decorated with semi-circular tiles called *Namako-Kabe*. Japanese builders were particularly adept at these techniques. Hotel Tsukiji (1867–8) was erected by Kisuke Shimizu (1815–81), a director of the large building firm Shimizugumi.[39] This was 'a timber-frame construction faced with stucco, 240′ in length by 200′ in width, with a central tower 93′ high which commanded from its top an extensive prospect of the city'. The area of Tsukiji between the Ginza and the Shimoda river had been designated in Tokyo as an area for foreigners. It had an important concentration of 'semi-foreign' houses, some built especially for incomers.[40]

But despite the charm which is apparent from pictures of buildings like the Hotel Tsukiji (the building itself is long gone) this compromise style was scarcely adequate for the grand buildings of *Meiji* Japan. Foreign architects knew only Western modes and were naturally enthusiastic about their introduction. C. A. Chastel de Boinville's great achievement was the Imperial College of Engineering at Toronomon in Tokyo. There he designed the College Hall, 'the most beautiful building of Tokyo'[41] with its 'handsomely decorated aula' and much used by the government for their official functions. Former President, General Ulysses S. Grant, visiting Japan from the USA in 1879, was splendidly fêted there. Mr de Boinville told Clara Whitney that the hall was capable of accommodating 4000 people. As Clara explained 'Two great galleries run around the hall, supported by 50 or more gilded colonnades . . . Indeed the hall of the Imperial College of Engineering looked unusually gay.'[42]

T. J. Waters arrived in Japan in 1868 he was 37 or 38 years old to work for the Ministry of Public Works. He had a varied career in Japan and is well-known for his work in Osaka and Tokyo.[43] Waters was also fond of building in brick. He used this medium in his reconstruction of the Ginza in Tokyo after the fire of 1872. In addition to the bricks the street of shops known as Ginza Brick Street also had a covered way or colonnade supported by stone pillars. Contemporary pictures, which are all that remain, with trees and gas street lamps, suggest a European boulevard.[44]

Although most of the foreign architects worked in Tokyo and its environs, Alexander Nelso Hansell chose to practise in Kobe and Osaka, where he was very active between 1888 and 1920.[45] In addition to his public buildings, Hansell undertook commissions to design and supervise the building of several of the foreigners' houses at Kitanu on the hilly slope north of Kobe port. Indeed it could be said that Hansell made a successful career out of the foreign community at Kobe.

But neither the semi-foreign style of Shimizu nor the classically inspired buildings of others made more than a marginal impact on Japanese architecture. It was Josiah Conder who was destined to become 'the father of Western architecture in Japan'. On 28 January 1877 he took up his position as Professor of Architecture at the Imperial College of Engineering in Tokyo. Within four years of his arrival he had married Kume-Ko Mayoba.[46]

His career was a distinguished one. He continued to serve the Japanese government, he lectured on architecture, and he designed and built many buildings famous in *Meiji* Japan for both government and private clients. He was also responsible for training a generation of Japanese architects, so that his influence remained even after his death. Although many of the fine buildings which Conder and his pupils designed have gone, it is still possible to enjoy some of their work in Tokyo.

Josiah Conder was educated in Bedford and subsequently studied architecture at the South Kensington Art Schools and the Slade Life Classes at University College, London. He was a student, or apprentice, in London to Professor T. Roger Smith and William Burges.[47] In 1876 he won the Soane Medallion from the Royal Institute of British Architects. On the strength of this he was appointed to the Imperial College of Engineering and he took up his duties there early in 1877.

Conder remained as Professor of Architecture at the College for five years advising his students that they should start 'with a conception of the appearance of your structures' and 'a feeling for good proportion, shape of mass and good disposition and balance of parts'. In designing a palace, students were recommended to 'allow full play to your imagination and patriotic sentiments and you may give a worthy grandeur to your design'.[48] He left the College at the end of January 1882 and although he subsequently lectured at the University of Tokyo he spent the rest of his career in Japan as a consultant architect occupying an influential position as *doyen* of foreign architects in Japan.

Because of his position as professor in the Imperial College of Engineering he was closely associated with the young *Meiji* leaders who were much involved with the Ministry of Public Works. He was therefore well known to the new burgeoning Establishment and as events turned out he rapidly found himself centre-stage. The early

*Meiji* years brought something of a rush towards Western manners and customs. To this end Conder was appointed the architect for the *Rokumeikan*, the state-owned guest-house and club buildings, which epitomised the cosmopolitan outlook adopted by the *Meiji* modernisers. The building was planned for a site, formerly a *Satsuma* estate or *Yashiki*, at Hibiya, Tokyo, and construction began in 1881.

When the *Rokumeikan* was completed in 1883 it was indeed a marvel to behold.[49,50] As a result of his *Rokumeikan* commission Conder became a well-known and indeed fashionable architect. Over the succeeding years he designed buildings for the government including the first permanent museum, the Ueno National Museum, a brick structure built in 1881, and the Navy Department Office. He also designed much of Mitsubishi 'London town' which was built piecemeal from the 1890s in Maranouchi, Tokyo. Unfortunately none of his public buildings survive.

Conder was not an outstandingly original architect by Western standards but he was eclectic and willing to borrow from various traditions.[51] The *Rokumeikan* was Italianate, elsewhere he featured the mansard roofs typical of France as well as some neoclassical styles familiar in Britain. This catholic taste Conder also passed on to his pupils. Perhaps the best known of these was Dr Tatsuno Kingo (1854–1919), himself responsible for a series of important buildings.[52]

When Conder died in 1920 he was laid in the burial ground at Gokokuji Temple, Tokyo.[53,54] The Architectural Institute of Japan also wished to pay tribute. They drew up plans for memorial volumes. Unfortunately the great earthquake of 1923 destroyed much Conder material. Not until 1931 were matters properly advanced when three *Memorial Albums* in full colour, with innumerable plates and drawings of all the work which Conder had done, were published. The albums give a marvellous insight into the variety of Conder's work.[55] Designs were prepared for many buildings not all of which Conder actually built.[56] He also became increasingly involved with the Mitsui family and particularly with the Iwasaki family who founded and owned Mitsubishi. By coincidence some of his private work for the Iwasaki family has survived.[57]

## 5 *JAPONISME*

Josiah Conder and Christopher Dresser both involved themselves with the Japanese people. Conder by devoting his life to designing

Western-style buildings in Tokyo encouraged a school of Japanese architects who although educated in Western architectural modes were also sympathetic to their own heritage. It is worth remembering that Conder, from the very beginning of his years in Japan, recognised and appreciated the merits of Japanese architecture.[58]

Christopher Dresser's position was entirely different. He became involved with Japanese art objects without any first-hand knowledge, then was given a brief opportunity to familiarise himself with Japanese art as it really was in Japan. During his 100 days he worked with an enviable intensity, trying, by studying methods and processes of manufacture from raw material to finished article, to understand. After his whirlwind tour he settled down again in London, and continued to use Japanese art as inspiration in his industrial design work. With the publication of *Japan: Its Architecture, Art and art Manufactures* in 1882 Dresser made his statement about Japanese Art.

In this he set out the grounds for his enthusiastic admiration for much of what he had found in Japan.

Both Josiah Conder and Christopher Dresser responded positively to the art and architecture of Japan. While some Westerners, parochial in outlook and narrow in vision, disliked traditional Japanese houses because of their fragility and inflammability and disapproved of temples and shrines, however marvellously wrought, because they were dedicated to non-Christian gods, Conder and Dresser had the ability to see the beauty of Japanese art and architecture through more cosmopolitan eyes. Dresser based his stance on the belief that 'Japan has had a great architectural history' and that 'Ornament springs from architecture'.[59] Conder's message came more directly through the buildings, which he left in Tokyo.

But *Japonisme* for the British was not ultimately solely concerned with art, a strong commercial element was always present. For the Japanese manufacturers, art products, often designed for the less discriminating Western market, were important trade goods. For the British, with a growing middle class willing to pay for exotic items to embellish their homes, Japanese porcelains and silks were desirable. For them it was the great exhibitions themselves which showed in their wonderful pavilions what Japanese art and culture could provide which popularised subsequent public demand.

# 15 A Copartnery: On Japanese Terms?

## 1 THE BRITAIN OF THE EAST?

During the course of the *Meiji* Emperor's forty-four-year rule the Japanese were successful in establishing the foundations of a modern industrialised nation.[1] The outward sign of their changing status as a potential world power came with their signing in 1902 of the Anglo-Japanese Alliance.[2] This was reinforced in May 1905 when, at the battle of the Sea of Japan, or Tsushima,[3] the Imperial Japanese Navy, under Admiral Togo, annihilated the hastily reassembled Russian Baltic fleet. After the Russo-Japanese War the world looked at Japan through different eyes. How could a nation, before 1868 a *quasi*-feudal society based on a rice economy,[4] with no modern industry, have so reorganised itself during a period of little more than a single generation?

The British would have felt that they knew at least part of the answer. Had they not provided technical and scientific specialists to serve in Japan? Were not Japan's new factories stocked with British machinery? Did not everyone know that the Imperial Japanese Navy was modelled on the Royal Navy? And was not the Anglo-Japanese Alliance of 1902 incontrovertible evidence of the close relationship between the two countries?

Indeed, it was popular at this time to link the Empire of the Rising Sun with that 'on which the sun never sets'. In 1904 Henry Dyer subtitled his book *Dai Nippon* (*Great Japan*), 'the Britain of the East'.[5] Nor did the Japanese disagree. In the middle school geography textbook (published 1896) the author writes:

> Generally speaking Britain can be compared to our Japan. This similarity to Japan is particularly notable in such respects as Britain's character as an island kingdom, its relationship to the continent, the size of its territory and population, its maritime climate and the nature of its coast-line. Should we therefore say that Britain is the Japan of the West? (Englishmen regard Japan as the Britain of the East).[6]

It was left to Lord Curzon to sum up, writing of Japan, placed 'at a maritime coign of vantage upon the flank of Asia'.[7] But both Curzon and Dyer in so romantisising the relationship were deceiving themselves and their readers. Emulation was a prelude to competition and ultimately to confrontation.

## 2 THE PSYCHOLOGY OF ENCOUNTER

The attitude of any two nations towards one another reflects the armed force available on either side. In Britain's case, although there were army units available for deployment overseas, it was the Royal Navy which effectively wielded her power. Indeed at the time of the confrontation, Britain, at the height of her authority, was enabled to keep the peace, not by 'the forceful imposition of a *Pax Britannica*' but by 'the international acceptance of a British monopoly of the seas which Mahan rightly identified with world power'.[8] The only check on the interventionists came in Britain from those liberal elements in British society which deplored the way in which Palmerstonian jingoism encouraged simple foreign adventures, for which they could find no moral justification, to develop into expensive military and naval campaigns.

For the Japanese there was no choice. Their weakness forced complaisance. Japan's position had worsened immeasurably since the sixteenth and seventeenth centuries. Then the countries of the Far East, alternately attracted and repelled by the West, had had the option of closing their doors against the invaders. At that time the guns of West and East were not so different in power and effectiveness. The threatened invasion came in the name of the Christian religion. China, Japan and Korea thankfully rejected Western overtures, closed their frontiers and retired into their 'hermit kingdoms'.

By the mid-nineteenth century a policy of exclusion was no longer possible. The development of Western industry afforded ships and guns of a calibre unmatched in the Eastern world. The encounter appeared to proceed along predictable lines. Lord Elgin came. Those Japanese who took a realistic view of Japan's weakness, negotiated a reasonable treaty. The clamant demands of the foreign traders were to be accommodated. And yet paradoxically much in this encounter was atypical. Lord Elgin was an exceptional empire builder.[9] And the Japanese negotiators, despite the weakness of their position, remained cool and calculating.

Perhaps Lord Elgin should be given greater credit for his achievement in Japan than is usually accorded him. It is true that he followed the American envoy and made a treaty along similar lines to that of the American. But being willing to shadow the American was in itself remarkable. Elgin came as the plenipotentiary of the most powerful nation on earth and might have been expected to have taken a high-handed tone, which could have resulted in more onerous treaty terms. But his non-confrontational approach, in stark contrast to that of contemporaries like Sir John Bowring, then Governor of Hong Kong, sparked off no violent damaging response from xenophobic Japanese. As one midshipman in Lord Elgin's party reported:

> The squadron was a very modest one . . . There were only the *Retribution*, the *Furious* and the *Lee*, a gunboat. The *Furious* was a paddle-wheel steam frigate, rather smaller than the *Retribution* and in order to afford accommodation for Lord Elgin and his staff the greater part of her main-deck guns had been landed at Hong Kong and temporary cabins built on the main deck, so that the *Retribution* represented about five-sixths of the fighting power of the squadron.[10]

The vision of the *Furious* topped by makeshift cabins must have astonished those contemporaries who saw it. Elgin's decision to abandon her guns, left 1500 miles away, was indeed bold.

But there was a price to pay for Japanese defencelessness. By Lord Elgin's Treaty of Edo in 1858 the foreigners were empowered to enforce trade on Japan and permitted to live, protected by foreign consular courts, in designated areas in mainland Japan. Nevertheless these concessions obviated any call for direct invasion and occupation. The treaties gave the foreigners certain limited rights in the treaty ports but inversely protected the rest of Japan.

The Japanese more or less kept their side of the bargain although anti-foreign incidents led to bombardment of both *Satsuma* and *Choshu* settlements. None of the westerners had high hopes of the achievements of the Japanese, or any other undeveloped peoples. In the 1870s James McNeill Whistler copied out in his own hand the English translation of a letter written by a Japanese in the 1850s; one sentence read 'I saw in the distance that the wonder of the world was before me; the Oceans had put forth woods, and high trees were visible, and they told me that was the foreigners' vessels.'[11] This vivid and evocative description fitted in well with the preconceptions of Japan and the Japanese held in Britain – what might be termed 'willow-patterned' Japan. The British and other Westerners accepted this view of Japan and assumed a static society unchanging and unchangeable. These predictable responses led to complacency and the acceptance of a *status quo* which it was assumed would be permanent.

The certainties of the Western view gave the Japanese great advantages. No one expected anything from them. They were free to work towards their own ends without interference. No one linked the xenophobic *samurai*, whose early curiosity about the West often showed itself in overt hostility, with those whose energies were subsequently to be harnessed to more positive ends. It was the achievement of the *Meiji* oligarchs to offer opportunities which would satisfy the ambitions of the former *samurai*. These men, already endowed with an inherited social position and an education, were ultimately able to create a new Japan with market-oriented ambitions which they had seen so ably exploited by the West.

## 3 THE *SAMURAI* FACTOR

The official abandonment of feudalism by the new *Meiji* government left some 400 000 men, the traditional warrior class, the *samurai*, stranded. With their families, this group probably amounted to over a million persons and so constituted about 5 per cent of a total Japanese population of rather less than 40 million. The new government by deliberately removing their rights and privileges, reducing and finally abolishing, their pensions, forced them to reassess their situation. Their only options were to stagnate or adapt. The seal was set on this process by the determination of the authorities to recruit a popular conscript army which would owe allegiance to the Emperor. Although there would be space in the new army for some *samurai* officers, the class as a whole could find no outlet here for its energies and expertise. At the same time as the government was reducing and commuting the pensions on which *samurai* had hitherto relied, the *han*, or clans were being reorganised into prefectures. This not only cut away previous loyalties but also removed the occupations of many.

Some influential figures in Japan were concerned at the cavalier treatment meted out to the *samurai* and argued strongly for the provision of alternative employment for so active and potentially innovative a class. One of these, Tomomi Iwakura, himself a member of the class of court nobles (see Chapter 7 above), spoke strongly of the future need to harness the potential of this class. He was warm in his praise of their past achievements, writing:

> For the past 300 years they have been the natural leaders in society; they have participated in governmental affairs, bringing it to a polished purity and virtue. Because of their military and literary accomplishments, this class alone possesses a character that is both noble and individualistic. It is for this reason that the 400 000 *samurai* of today are the most useful group in society and should be called the spirit of the state.[12]

Others of the young oligarchs, themselves of middle *samurai* rank were conscious of the difficulties facing their fellows. Toshimichi Okubo succeeded in setting up an agency to look into possible alternative sources of employment for them. Takayoshi Kido, one of the most perceptive of *Meiji* leaders, also recognised the necessity of harnessing the gifts of this class.[13]

In attempting to rehabilitate the *samurai* class the government was able to offer some openings. Opportunities occurred in administration, education, the constabulary, the army and the navy. Because of the concern with new industrial activity there were also outlets in science and technology. Most of the students recruited to the Imperial College of Engineering and other colleges were the sons of former *samurai* as were the majority of Japanese professors at the Imperial University of Tokyo. Silberman believed that:

> Since education, government service, military expertise and intellectual speculation were activities traditionally considered the only acceptable spheres of *samurai* behaviour, Western languages, technology, political economy and religious and political thought were areas in which the traditional political élite could seek employment and maintenance of prestige without loss of status.[14]

In seeking job opportunities those *samurai* from the south and west of the country were greatly advantaged. The ferment of ideas current in Nagasaki had alerted them to the likelihood of coming change. Some clan officers were already dealing with foreign traders. Previously rigid rules were already being questioned and in some cases flouted. As Silberman has explained 'Satsuma, Choshu, Hizen, Tosa, Fukui, Hiroshima, Owari, Jumamoto and Tottori accounted for 86, or 82 per cent of all those of *Han* origin who engaged in innovational behaviour.'[15] Some *samurai* from the north and east were less fortunate and less likely to be upwardly mobile in *Meiji* society.[16]

Some became labourers, others had a hard life as farmers, literally breaking new ground, in newly-opened Hokkaido.

Notwithstanding, it must be stressed that *samurai* attitudes were more important than geographical location. There were 192 students attending the Imperial College of Engineering in Tokyo in 1877. They came from some forty domains scattered all over Japan (see Map 5.1). For example, three students came from Aomori, two from Iwate and five from Niigata, all remote in Northern Honshu. Clearly families who were prepared to adapt could encourage their sons to take up engineering as a career. These government-supported opportunities, grasped eagerly by some, led to prosperous and fulfilling lives. Arnold Toynbee suggested that:

> They (the *samurai*) rose to a height of self-abnegation which is almost sublime, when they voluntarily divested themselves of their privileges because they were convinced that this sacrifice was required of them in order to enable Japan to hold her own in the environment of a Westernised world from which she could not longer hold aloof.[17]

Even if this older view seems to take on an air of fantasy as modern scholarship has probed more thoroughly into *samurai* motivation the effectiveness of the movement to harness the energies of this class of potentially dangerous men and channel them into modernisation cannot be gainsaid.

The Restoration of 1868 was effected by 'a vast army' of feudal retainers previously stranded in traditional society and no longer content with a *status quo* which had left them impoverished and under-employed. The leaders of this group emerged as the new generation of government, the *Meiji* oligarchs. Others of similar rank and from the same group of enlightened clans also moved into influential positions in the new regime. Although senior administrative posts were the prizes for some of these men – it has been calculated that 41 per cent of prefectural governors initially came from the ranks of *samurai* from the favoured clans – others found an outlet for their energies and expertise in industrial roles, seemingly far removed from earlier preferred *samurai* outlets.

## 4 THE DOOR OF OPPORTUNITY

The nineteenth-century encounter between Britain and Japan was based on technology, not religion. In any society there is less resistance to technical changes than there would be to new religious ideas and therefore the former can often penetrate more effectively.

Already the trickle of ideas, books and men which had slipped into Japan during the later years of isolation, had disturbed the *status quo* and encouraged seditious thoughts in Japanese minds. As Fukuzawa noted 'the world-wide facility of communication has allowed the wind of civilisation to blow into the East, where not a single grass or tree has been left unswayed by it'.[18] As a result the old regime toppled and fell and the Restoration brought in 1868 the promise of change and modernisation. It could be argued that the move into industrialisation was initially 'a purely defensive measure'.[19]

While it is true that Japan had no modern industry in 1868 when the new regime took power, it was not for want of trying. Between 1850 and 1868 as Professor Erich Pauer has shown there were 'at least eleven sites where the construction of reverberatory furnaces actually started; three further sites reached only the planning stage'.[20,21] Another furnace was planned and possibly five other fiefs and their *daimyo* were also interested in proceeding but were prevented from doing so for lack of funds.[22]

The reverberatory furnace movement in Japan is the more remarkable because the Japanese relied on a copy of a book, *Het Gietwezen in 'Srijks Ejzer – Geschutgieterij te Luik* (*Casting in the State Iron* [*cannon*] *Foundry in Liege*) published in 1826 by a Dutch officer, U. Huguenin.[23] Although it was forbidden by law to publicise such military technology, Japanese translators and copyists worked on it in at least three places. Information about such 'factory' complexes was known locally in Japan and at Nagasaki where *Bakufu* officers discussed naval and military matters with Dutch naval officers.

No effective cannon were produced at these industrial sites. But this cannot detract from the importance of the experiments and the determination of the Japanese to succeed. That a small body of Japanese should come to understand the day-to-day difficulties of technical transfer on the ground was later to prove significant. That this Dutch book should have allowed them to penetrate some of the metallurgical problems of modern smelting, where variation in ore, fuel and flux created their own problems, is in itself remarkable. If the Japanese could make progress under these circumstances it is perhaps not so surprising that, with the strong support of the *Meiji* government, technical transfer should later be effected so impressively.

After the Restoration in 1870 the development of a modern industrial base was entrusted to the newly established Ministry of

Industry or Public Works (*Kobusho*) generously funded by Ito, Inoue, Yamao and other leading members of the Satcho group by then powerful in government.

From the beginning, efforts were made to import Western technology. At the same time, with the opening of the Imperial College of Engineering (see Chapter 5 above), staffed by British professors, a beginning was made in teaching modern scientific and technological subjects. The Japanese did not make the mistake of importing technology without teaching basic and then advanced science to support it. The achievement of ICE was to combine engineering theory with practice. The use of the Akabane Engineering Works for practical and laboratory work, in tandem with the theoretical teaching of civil, mechanical, mining and telegraph engineering as well as architecture, chemistry and metallurgy brought the 'sandwich' course to Japan. It was particularly important, in Japan, where rote learning had been universal, to introduce heuristic education,[24] which required students to do, with their own hands, laboratory work and workshop tasks.

With the British teachers of science and technology came also a flood of experts. These men looked critically at undeveloped Japan through European eyes. They thought in Western ways, often recommending large, expensive schemes to the Japanese in advance of Japanese ability to manage and sometimes to pay. In this way lighthouses, railways, telegraph systems and mining projects were undertaken. Most of these were initially set up, organised and run by the British although the Japanese were constantly replacing the foreigners with their own people. It was relatively easy to train lighthouse keepers, railwaymen, telegraph operators, and miners and so Japanese workmen quickly replaced foreign workmen. More senior posts, requiring greater expertise, remained in foreign hands for rather longer. In exceptional cases foreigners remained in responsible posts until 1912 when the *Meiji* era ended. After 1885 this process accelerated as Japanese students, first trained in Japan at ICE or the University of Tokyo, who had been abroad for further training returned home to replace the imported foreigners.

The use of such comprehensive methods to assimilate Western science and technology were successful although there were damaging and expensive failures. The case of the iron and steel industry is a good example of the problems which arose as mismatched attempts were made to marry Western technology with Japanese experience. In 1874 the Ministry of Industry decided to take over the iron mine at

Kamaishi in Northern Honshu and they appointed Takato Oshima and an Austrian engineer, L. Bianchie, to plan a modern ironworks. The Austrian proposed:

> a large-scale iron works with two relatively large, efficient blast furnaces (with a production capacity of 25 tons per day) and a rolling mill to roll wrought iron prepared from pig iron as the main part of the works, as well as a modern railway to convey iron ore and charcoal by steam-locomotive drawn trains from the mines to the furnace.'

Oshima, the Japanese metallurgist/engineer, on the other hand, 'proposed to build five relatively small-sized blast furnaces and to supply them with iron ore carried by economical horse-drawn carts'.[25]

Despite Oshima's knowledge and experience the Ministry of Industry chose to develop the Austrian engineer's design.[26] Blast furnace and equipment, together with railway lines and engines were imported from England. The plant was set up. It started operating in 1880. It closed in 1881 – a disastrous, and expensive failure. The iron ore used presented problems, the quality of the coke was not uniform, there was not enough charcoal, and the limestone used as a flux was ill-matched. The plant closed itself when molten metal blocked the outflow of the blast furnace.

There is an interesting sequel to this failure. The government accepted defeat, sold the plant to Chohei Tanaka who renamed it the Tanaka Iron Works. Tanaka did not attempt to reopen the old blast furnace but concentrated his efforts on smaller scale operations, like those advised by Oshima, of a kind known and understood in Japan. Later, Tanaka asked Kageyoshi Noro (1854–1932) to help. Noro had been thoroughly educated, first in mining and metallurgy in the Faculty of Science of Tokyo University, then in England and Germany. On his return home in 1889 he became Professor in the Faculty of Engineering at Tokyo University. Noro who believed that the steel industry should be 'the touchstone of industrialisation', deplored the fact that they seemed unable to make their own iron and steel by modern methods, and regretted the necessity for spending so much foreign currency on importing it.[27]

With this in mind he set about re-examining the British blast furnace at the Tanaka Iron Works. A coke oven was designed and built to produce reliable coke from Japanese coal. The roasting ovens were enlarged, changes were made in the shape of the furnace interior, alterations were made to the chimneys. By 1886 the plant was functioning and by the 1890s the Tanaka Iron Works at Kamaishi was producing 65 per cent of the total domestic pig iron.[28] It is difficult to apportion blame for the earlier setbacks. The Western engineers and technicians originally engaged to set up the plant did so to the best of their ability. Nevertheless in this case as in others it was the Japanese who in the end solved their own problems. In this way technological transfer was successfully effected. This process of trial and error, combined with a dogged refusal to accept failure, was to lead, slowly, and with many setbacks, to the establishment of successful industrial ventures in Japan.

In December 1897 two articles on the 'Training of Engineers in Japan' appeared in *The Engineer*.[29] Some eighty-four engineers, together with their occupations, with portraits of the ten most distinguished, are given. From the list it can be seen that most of the engineers worked in shipbuilding, textiles or mining although one is an engineer in a 'watch factory', one was 'in Berlin' and one 'in London'. Several of these Japanese engineers had been early students at ICE and the University of Tokyo and had work experience overseas. Tribute was paid to 'the capacity of the Japanese for absorbing technical knowledge'. The author raises a more general criticism that the Japanese engineer lacks 'practical knowledge' and 'works with his gloves on'. Nevertheless to be able to list so many qualified engineers in positions of authority in Japan in December 1897, exactly thirty years after the *Meiji* Restoration is in itself remarkable. The engineering profession in Britain was impressed and indeed envious of the resources which had been allocated in Japan to achieve this objective.

How did the Japanese themselves view their progress? They may have felt that they were making satisfactory advances in scientific and industrial fields but in at least one case there was resentment at Western attitudes. In 1888 Tanakadate, one of the important early Japanese physicists was in Glasgow, working with Kelvin (see Chapter 9, Sections 6 and 7 above). He had left in his stead at the University of Tokyo the young Hantaro Nagaoka, also destined to become a famous physicist. Nagaoka's irritations were expressed in a letter to Tanakadate:

> We must work actively with an open eye, keen sense and ready understanding, indefatigably and not a moment stopping . . . There is no reason why the whites should be so supreme at everything and

as you say, I hope we shall be able to beat those *yatta hottya* (pompous) people in the course of 10 or 20 years . . . another great prerequisite in beating those whites is to make our own work known. This is a great difficulty. As a first step we cannot write in Japanese and make the Westerners understand our writings. We must borrow their language and make the Westerners understand our writings.[30]

The frustrations which the young Nagaoka expressed so flatly are a reminder of real Japanese feelings in the face of Western complacency. Hirubumi Ito once remarked that while living in isolation the Japanese were 'like the frog that lived in the bottom of a well'.[31] Once linked up with the outside world the Japanese strove effectively to overcome their disadvantages.

A great deal has been written about Japan's success as an industrialising economy. It is accepted that as a latecomer Japan utilised to the full 'the advantage of exploiting modern technologies developed in advanced countries'.[32] The argument here is that the purchase of technology from Britain, in the case of the engineering and shipbuilding industries was, given the nature of the conditions involved for buyer and seller, inevitable. The Japanese were never victims of the 'not-invented here' syndrome which implies a refusal to consider inventions made elsewhere.[33]

## 5 THE BRITISH CONTRIBUTION TO EMERGENT JAPAN

News of Lord Elgin's mission in the Far East was received ecstatically at home. The *Daily Telegraph* was thrilled, writing 'The Earldom of Elgin is just now a new and mighty wonder to the Eastern world . . . All the blazonry of the ancient Bruces has been seen . . . In other words our Plenipotentiary in the Oriental waters . . . has been to Japan and signed a treaty of perpetual amity and profitable trade'. The report went on to praise Lord Palmerston's triumphant Chinese policy which has 'cut clean through the exclusive system and calico batteries of Japan, abolishing the Dutch monopoly, competing with the Americans and even eclipsing Russia'.[34] This sort of jingoism continued to reflect one way of looking at Japan and remained paramount in British minds for many years.

But even so, for the British government, Japan was but one interest among many and official concern was not high. It is true that the Lancashire cotton men maintained a noisy lobby demanding access to more and more overseas markets. But, truth to tell, from the 1870s the export of British manufactured goods was growing but slowly and the British share of visible world trade falling. After 1870 imperialism took on another form as British capital, often through lending for railway building, infiltrated many overseas countries.[35] This did not happen to Japan although the Japanese continued to purchase warship technology.[36]

Messrs J. Thornycroft, were builders of torpedo-boats, destroyers, and '30 knotters', for the Royal Navy and the Imperial Japanese Navy. In 1900 the Japanese had asked about the price of building additional torpedo-boats under licence in Japan. Thornycroft's contacted S. W. Barnaby, their chief naval architect, then travelling in the Far East, to ask him to negotiate in the matter. As Thornycroft's wrote, 'It might be an inducement to the [Japanese] Government to order a larger number of sets of machinery, say for four or six vessels, if we were to undertake to give them frame sketches and other detailed particulars to enable them more readily to build the hulls in Japan.'[37]

There was indeed an historical inevitability about the process by which the Japanese made their claim to be the heirs of the British shipbuilding industry. They persuaded the manufacturers to receive their workmen, ship-constructors and engineers in the shipyard to work alongside British personnel. The shipbuilders were also required to provide 'models, drawings, specifications, and all necessary details to enable them, if they were sufficiently skilled in the art, to produce duplicate vessels'.[38] British shipbuilders were keen to respond to such strong demand for orders, could not afford to antagonise a good customer, and so, in the end sold an industry overseas.

But no other course was possible. In a world of cut-throat competition, with Germany and America waiting eagerly for business the British were caught in a trap the implications of which they understood but from which they had no means of escape.

In July 1911, the Institute of Naval Architects celebrated its Golden Jubilee in London – a grand occasion, supported *in absentia* by several kings and the Emperor of Germany. Japan sent a large delegation, all professionals.[39] Out of a lavish five-day programme of entertainment, three mornings were reserved for the presentation of professional papers by naval architects and marine engineers from around the world. Of the twenty-one papers read, four were by the

Japanese. Rear-Admiral Kondo, offered 'The Progress of Naval Construction in Japan', Dr. S. Terano and M. Yukawa discussed 'The Development of Merchant Shipping in Japan', Dr S. Terano and Professor Baron Shiba introduced 'Remarks on the Design and Service Performance of the Transpacific Liners *Tenyo Maru* and *Chijo Maru*' while Engineer Rear-Admiral T. Fujii charted 'The Progress of Naval Engineering in Japan'.[40] There were also papers from Swedish, French, German, as well as British delegates.

The 'Japanese' papers gave details of the progress of the shipbuilding industry in Japan. It is worth noting that while the Japanese had received much help from Britain (see Chapters 4 and 10 above) they were not afraid of developing their own ideas and using them to improve on what they had learnt. By 1911 they were using Admiral Miyabara's boilers for their vessels which they believed gave a better performance than boilers from overseas.[41]

The way in which the Japanese pushed open the door of opportunity is well illustrated by the information contained in Table 4.1 which shows how, until 1911, Japan was building ships at home, ordering from Britain and also from other foreign non-British yards.

And what is more the Japanese were beguiling students. People enjoyed helping them. One of the most interesting, and honest statements, which sums up much of the argument here, came in 1911 during the discussion following Engineer-Rear-Admiral Fujii's paper on 'The Progress of Naval Engineering in Japan' from Mr A. E. Seaton, a member of the Council, who said:

> It is not perhaps inappropriate that I should open the discussion seeing that 39 years ago there were sent to me two Japanese as pupils, to be taught engineering and shipbuilding. Both ... were my pupils for some years, and I can say that I never had a greater pleasure in life from a professional point of view than in the teaching of these two gentlemen and of the four others who followed them. The first of these is now well-known to all the world as Admiral Sassow, late Chief Constructor of the IJN. In helping to educate those Japanese I can honestly say that they educated me, for the result of my teaching was the production of my first book largely as a result of the crucial questions which my pupils put to me. I also had the pleasure of designing the engines for their first modern warships the *Kongo-go* and *Hei Hei*, belted cruisers, in 1875 and 1876. Even in those days ... the Japanese were smart enough then to have something better than the British ship of the

same class. That class we knew as the *Gem*, but our *Gems* were not very brilliant, because they were all very short of boiler power. They had very big cylinders, but had not got correspondingly big boilers; the result was that with a great deal of very hard and careful stoking something like 12.5 knots could be got out of them. In the Japanese *Gems* the boilers were large enough to give a speed of 14 knots comfortably; the consequence was that while the British *Gems* were struggling along at 12.5 knots the Japanese Ships were going with ease a knot faster.[42]

That the fear of Japanese competition had become a matter for serious concern seems apparent when in December 1905, J. Spencer Phillips, the President of the Institute of Bankers in London remarked, 'We must expect competition, very severe competition, not only from European nations but from our new ally Japan, whose commercial expansion will no doubt be marked by the same thoroughness, the same precision of organisation which has distinguished her military expansion.'[43] Even the cautious diplomat Ernest Satow was writing home 'I am convinced that the Japanese are ambitious of being a great naval and military power and they are confidently persuaded that they possess the necessary gifts.'[44]

That these matters had become a consideration of substance is clear from the election material circulated by William Keswick, the Unionist candidate for Surrey, in the parliamentary election in 1906. Keswick, the first merchant ashore in Yokahama in 1859, had served Jardine Matheson very profitably in the Far East for over thirty years. Notwithstanding his success in selling British goods during his working career he plumped unhesitatingly for industrial chauvinism when he urged his future constituents to elect him on a platform of 'no more foreign goods dumped into England' and 'kick all aliens out of England'.[45] Unfriendly observers might have commented on British hypocrisy. Much is made at present of methods of trading and the Japanese tend to be made the scapegoats for embarrassing the West by their success. But as Humpty Dumpty might have said, comparing Japan's vulnerability to Western trade in the nineteenth century with her unassailable trading position now 'it all depends on what you mean by unfair trading practice'.

Notwithstanding the serious sense of unease in many quarters as Japanese competition became more effective, public opinion in Britain remained ardently pro-Japanese. One observer, a student in 1904–5, wrote:

The Russo-Japanese war was then at its height . . . Like everyone else I was patriotically pro-Japanese, and in the popular pantomime songs of the year, Japanese themes took the place of 'Goodbye my Blue Bell' . . . At the singing after school matches fags favoured a song called 'Farewell Little Yo-san' of which the chorus ran:

Farewell my little Yo-san, Goodbye my sweetheart true,
Over the mighty ocean, There's a duty there to do,
Sometimes will you remember To-Ki your sailor-man,
Who is going out to fight For the cause of the right
and the freedom of dear Japan.[46]

## 6 ON JAPANESE TERMS?

How could anyone consider that the arrangements made by the treaty powers could have been 'on Japanese terms'? They had been required to agree treaties, to grant rights of extraterritoriality, to concede tariff autonomy, all of which affronted their self-respect as a nation. It had taken them immense effort to reverse these measures. They only succeeded in 1899 in abolishing extraterritoriality and not until 1912 did they regain control over their own tariff. Yet despite the severe disadvantages under which the Japanese laboured it is possible to argue that they came to be more in command than would ever have been thought possible.

That this could happen at all depended on those characteristics of loyalty and steadiness of the Japanese people which were used to unify the nation. This was done through the Emperor. Although no one denied the sharp break which took place in Japan in 1868, the 'Restoration' was done in the name of an older unity. By the new constitution of 11 February 1889, the Emperor became not only a constitutional monarch but also the embodiment of all political authority. Before him all were subjects. To him all owed loyalty.[47]

The Japanese as a people remained highly disciplined and work-oriented. It has been argued that Japanese peasants, living in a rice economy which required strict timing in the allocation of water resources, understood time units in a way unknown in the pre-industrial West, and so were more able to adapt to industrial and factory conditions.[48] Japanese merchants soon developed interests in manufacturing, and *samurai* above all, could switch to many fields.[49]

Of course these years were not conflict-free in Japan. The phrase *fukoku kyohei*, 'enrich the country, strengthen the army', was adopted during the *Meiji* years to mean using Western methods to strengthen Japan – against the West. There were many rivalries. The dominant ex-*samurai* group of *Satsuma* and *Choshu* (the *Satcho* group) competing with those of other less favoured *han* who were equally determined to prove themselves. All needed to be effective in order to compete successfully with the Western world.

If the period before 1885 was a preliminary, with much indecision and doubt, the period after 1885 brought cohesion and progress. That this was possible reflected the intervention of Masayoshi Matsukata, as Finance Minister from October 1881. He, appreciating the corrosions caused by inflation which endangered 'the safe economic growth of our country', [50] introduced Western financial orthodoxy in Japan.

Much of this remained hidden from Westerners. Those foreigners who lived in the treaty ports, insulated from real Japanese life, were also ignorant. Only rarely did an outsider understand how the treaties protected Japan from foreign interference. J. H. Gubbins remarked on 'how small a fraction of the country foreigners were admitted to' and how at the places opened 'foreign ships were permitted to visit only four places scattered at wide intervals along Japan's extensive seaboard'.[51] Informed men like Ernest Satow or his successor Claude MacDonald, were certainly able to advise their government. But the British government, like others, had many pressing preoccupations of which Japan was only one.

At the beginning of the *Meiji* period Sir Harry Parkes, representing the British government in Japan, assumed the right to interfere in Japan's affairs. It was a relatively easy matter for the Japanese resenting such assumptions to employ American advisers who soon found ways of frustrating what seemed to them to be unreasonable British demands.[52]

Industrially the British were harder to beat. In shipbuilding and allied engineering industries especially, the British though challenged were not overtaken before 1914. In Japan the process of easing-out British products took far longer than the *Meiji* years. Paradoxically the language barrier provided the Japanese with an effective camouflage when working in the West. As they stood silent, wrestling with the unfamiliar English, foolish assumptions were made of their understanding.

Japan, recognising the good sense of Adam Smith's dictum that 'defence is prior to opulence', set herself the task of creating on her own soil a modern shipbuilding and armament industry. She did this by cooperating with the makers of these items in Britain, America, France and Germany. The three phases of technical transfer, employment of foreign experts in Japan, placing of Japanese experts in Western countries, and manufacturing under licence, foreign products, mostly British, in Japan, before 1914, ensured a steady build-up of these industries. With no older traditions of manufacture to replace, Japan was able to press ahead uninhibited by a workforce, or management, determined to maintain old ways. Given the vigour of Japan, released from earlier feudal stagnation, and the complacency of the West, it was possible for the Japanese to reverse the disadvantages and create a world in which they no longer required a copartnership with Britain, but which was certainly 'On Japanese terms'.

# Appendix A: Glossary of Japanese Terms

| | |
|---|---|
| *Ainu* | indigenous people who lived in Hokkaido, as the *Meiji* government invested in the Hokkaido so the Ainu were pushed into more remote areas. See Isabella Bird's *Unbeaten Tracks in Japan* for her brief experience of living with them. |
| *Bakufu* | the government under the *Shogun*, which ruled Japan until 1868. |
| *Choshu* | the clan or *han*, in present day Yamaguchi Prefecture, which played a decisive role with others, including *Satsuma,* in opposing Shogunal power in the 1860s. *Choshu* men were influential in the *Meiji* government. |
| *daimyo* | Feudal lord who held land assessed at 10 000 *Koku* or more. There were three categories, *shinpan daimyo* who were hereditary vassals of the *Tokugawa* clan, *fudai daimyo* who had no blood ties with the *Tokugawa* family but who had been serving it before it obtained the position of *shogun*, and *tozama daimyo* who fitted neither of the other two categories. Unrest from the followers of the *tozama daimyo* resulted in the fall of the *Tokugawa* Shogunate and the Restoration of the Emperor in 1868. |
| *Dajokan* | the executive council of the early *Meiji* government. |
| *Edo* | the name of the *Tokugawa* capital, renamed Tokyo. |
| *'fukoku-kyohei'* | a slogan meaning 'enrich the country, strengthen the army'. It was used by those who wished to use Western methods to strengthen Japan against the West. |
| *genro* | elder statesmen, name given to those few who became influential but unofficial advisers to the *Meiji* Emperor. |
| *gunken seido* | the prefectural system. |
| *haihan-chiken* | the abolition of the domains, *han*, and the establishment of prefectures, *ken*, a change made by the *Meiji* government in 1871. |
| *han* | land held by a *daimyo*, translated as domain, fief or clan. |
| *hanseki-hokan* | the enforced surrender of *daimyo* lands and populations to the Emperor which the *Meiji* government carried out in 1869. |
| *hatamoto* | *Tokugawa* retainers, upper and middle *Samurai*, ranked immediately below *fudai daimyo*. |
| *heimin* | commoner, generally a person below the rank of *samurai* in the *Meiji* period. |

| | |
|---|---|
| *Hizen han* | also known as *Saga*, contained active reformers (now *Saga* prefecture, *Kyushu*). |
| *hoken seido* | feudal system. |
| *Koku* | measure, especially of rice, the equivalent of 4.96 bushels or 180 litres, used in land assessment. |
| *Kokugaku* | 'National learning' intellectual school emphasising Japanese traditions, especially *Shinto*. |
| *Kuge* | nobles of the imperial court. |
| *naiyu-gaikan* | 'troubles at home, dangers from abroad' suggests domestic unrest and foreign attack simultaneously, a Chinese formula for disaster. |
| *osei-fukko* | 'the restoration of imperial rule', the term used prior to 1868 by those who wished to reinstate the Emperor. |
| *oyatoi gaikokujin* | term used for 'government foreign employees' in the *Meiji* period, the short form was '*Yatoi*', literally 'hired menial'. |
| *Rangaku* | Dutch studies; Western studies through Dutch books and contacts in the *Tokugawa* period. |
| *ronin* | *samurai* who were no longer tied to their feudal lords and were therefore leaderless. |
| *ryo* | unit of gold currency equal to 60 *momme* of silver, replaced by the *yen* after the Restoration. |
| *Saga han* | also known as *Hizen*, q.v. |
| *Samurai* | feudal retainer. There were several ranks within this category, but used here as a generic term; their pensions were commuted and finally abolished by the *Meiji* government. |
| *Sanke* | *Kii, Owari* and *Mito*, the three senior branches (*shinpan daimyo*) of the *Tokugawa* family. |
| *Satsuma han* | led by the *Shimazu* family; became important point of entry, often through the capital Kagoshima, of foreign innovation, eventually played leading role in the *Meiji* Restoration of January 1868 (now *Kagoshima* prefecture). |
| *Satsuma–Choshu* Alliance | a military coalition (1866) against the *Tokugawa* Shogunate by *Satsuma* and *Choshu* domains. As a result of 'Satcho' determination the Shogunate was ended late in 1867. These men became the oligarchs of the *Meiji* government. |
| *Shizoku* | a term used after 1868 instead of *samurai* |
| *Shogun* | properly *sei-tai-shogun*, 'the barbarian-subduing generalissimo', the Emperor's military deputy, who ruled Japan before 1868. |
| *'Sonno-joi'* | 'Honour the Emperor, expel the barbarian'; slogan used after the foreign treaties of 1858 when the foreigner had gained a foothold in Japan through the treaty ports. |
| *Tosa han* | men from *Tosa* supported moves to restore the Emperor (now *Kochi* prefecture, *Shikoku*). |

| | |
|---|---|
| *yashiki* | *han* or clan residences, consisting of land and buildings, often spacious inner-city sites. |
| *yen* | unit of Japanese currency, intended as equivalent of US dollar in 1871, although its value declined. |

# Appendix B: Biographical Details of Japanese Leaders during the *Meiji* Period

ENDO Kinsuke, *Choshu*, one of original '*Choshu* Five'; studied in London at UCL in mid-1860s.

ENOMOTO Takeaki (1836–1908) student of naval science under Dutch at Nagasaki, later in Holland, 1862; held senior *Bakufu* naval post in 1867; resisted Restoration and fled to Hokkaido, 1868–9; pardoned in 1872 and appointed to government office, attained cabinet rank.

ETO Shimpei (1834–74), low-ranking *samurai* of *Hizen* clan, although member of early *Meiji* government-led revolt in *Saga* clan after Korea dispute in 1873; executed.

FUKUZAWA, Yukichi (1835–1901) influential educator and populariser of Western ideas, of *Nakatsu* domain, founder of *Keio Gijuku*, now *Keio* University, of the newspaper *Jiji Shimpo* and of the art of public speaking. Fukuzawa, stifled by the 'narrow stiffness' of clan life, made strenuous efforts as a young man to familiarise himself with Western learning. He not only learnt Dutch and later English, but succeeded in 1860 in joining the first Japanese expedition to America, followed in 1862 by a further mission to Europe during which he visited France, England, Holland, Russia and Portugal. On his return he published *Seiyo Jijo* (*Conditions in the West*) which made his reputation as an interpreter of foreigners and their countries to the Japanese. Throughout his life he continued to educate his fellow-Japanese in the ideas behind Western progress, particularly the importance of science and the spirit of independence.

GODAI Tomoatsu (1836–85) *Satsuma* clan; studied naval science under Dutch at Nagasaki; advocated 'enrich country, strengthen army' (*fukoku-kyohei*); led *Satsuma* mission to Europe with Terajima Munenori, 1865–6; later, entrepreneur who developed interests in transport, mining and textiles; became leader of *Osaka* business community.

GOTO Shojiro (1838–97) *Tosa* clan; related to Yoshida Toyo; became active leader and intriguer in the years leading to Restoration; senior member of early *Meiji* government; later engaged in business enterprises and party politics.

HITOTSUBASHI Keiki, see *Tokugawa* Keiki.

II Naosuke (1815–60); *Fudai daimyo, Tairo* or regent between 1858 and 1860, and therefore responsible for the 1858 treaties with the foreign powers; assassinated.

INOUE Kaoru (1836–1915), *Choshu* middle-ranking *samurai*; one of the original '*Choshu* Five', studied in London, UCL, 1863–4; held senior posts in *Meiji* government, finance expert and later *Genro*; close links with Ito Hirobumi.

INOUE Masaru (1843–1910) *Choshu*; one of original '*Choshu* Five' in London; studied at UCL 1863–4; became Chief of Japanese railways until 1893.

ITO Hirobumi (1841–1909); *Choshu* clan; student of Yoshida Shoin; made *Samurai* in 1863; one of original '*Choshu* Five'; studied in London, 1863–4; regarded as 'Western' expert; became influential as government minister, Prime Minister and *genro*.

IWAKURA Tomomi (1825–83), also known as Tomoyoshi; middle-rank court noble; although initially hostile to change later associated with *Satsuma*, especially *Okubo Toshimichi*; after Restoration, key-member of *Meiji* government; led Iwakura Mission, 1871–3, and later became a senior minister and influential adviser.

IWASAKI Koyata (1879–1945) nephew of Yataro; studied at Tokyo and Cambridge Universities (Pembroke College); returned to Japan in 1906 and became Vice-President of Mitsubishi, then in 1916, President. He separated various parts of the business into Mitsubishi Shipbuilding (1917) (now Mitsubishi Heavy Industries Ltd), Mitsubishi Mining (now Mitsubishi Mining and Cement Co. Ltd) and Mitsubishi Corporation (1918) and Mitsubishi Bank Ltd (1919).

IWASAKI Yataro (1835–85) of *Tosa han*, founder of the Mitsubishi industrial and commercial empire, passed a fruitful apprenticeship manipulating business deals for *Tosa han*, learnt how to take advantage of unsettled early *Meiji* years, founded Mitsubishi Shokai trading company 1873, largely engaged in shipping. His aggressive tactics and careful cultivation of friendships within government paid off.

IWASAKI, Yanosuke, younger brother of Yataro who took over Mitsubishi in 1885.

KAWADA, Koichiro, influential member of triumvirate which took over Mitsubishi in 1885 on founder's death, his son Riokichi served long apprenticeship at Lobnitz shipyard on the Clyde.

KIDO Takayoshi (1833–77), *Choshu*; student of Yoshida Shoin; leader of *Choshu* from 1862; effective leader from 1865; important member of early *Meiji* government.

KOMATSU Tatewaki (1835–70), *Satsuma* ally of Okubo Toshimichi, senior member of early *Meiji* government.

MATSUKATA Masayoshi (1835–1924) *Satsuma*; modest official career in *Satsuma* before 1868; posts in local and central government; became financial expert responsible, after 1881, for severe deflationary policies, later Prime Minister and *genro*.

MASUDA Takashi (1848–1938) leader of Mitsui financial combine; organised trading company with Inoue Kaoru; taken over 1876 by Mitsui.

MATSUKI Koan, see *Terajima* Munenori.

MEIJI Emperor (1852–1912) given name Mutsuhito; chose name of *Meiji* era meaning 'enlightenment'; son of Komei, succeeded to throne, 13 February 1867; originally manipulated by young revolutionaries; later became an influential figure.

MITSUI family, their business concerns had been powerful during the *Tokugawa* period from 1600 to 1868, but reorganised in the *Meiji* period. The Mitsui Company was founded as a general trading company in 1876.

One of the major components in the Mitsui business empire was, and is, the Mitsui Bank.

MORI, Arinori (1847–89), a prominent spokesman for Western ideas; primarily a diplomat and educationalist; as the Minister for education, despite his Western proclivities he imposed an élitist and statist system on Japanese education; assassinated by a *Shinto* fanatic, 11 February 1889 (see Chapter 8).

NABESHIMA Naomasa (1814–71) *Tozama daimyo* of *Hizen* or *Saga* clan; patron of technological change; held senior posts in early *Meiji* government.

NISHI Amane (1829–97) student of *Rangaku*; studied in Leiden, 1862–5; later became *Meiji* bureaucrat, specialist in Western law, military administration and philosophy.

OKUBO Toshimichi (1830–78) also known as Ichizo; *Satsuma*; key figure in early *Meiji* government until assassinated.

OKUMA Shigenobu (1838–1922) *Hizen* clan; student of *Rangaku*, then of English; influential in domain affairs before 1868; cabinet minister and Prime Minister; founder of Waseda University; never travelled abroad.

OKURA Kirachiro, founder of Okura & Co. Ltd in Tokyo in 1873; opened in London in 1874.

SAIGO Takamori (1828–77) *Satsuma* leader before Restoration, *Meiji* leader after, but had stormy career; led *Samurai* revolt 1877; committed suicide on battlefield.

SAKAMOTO Ryoma (1835–67) *Tosa* clan; active in bringing about *Satsuma–Choshu* alliance; assassinated.

SANJO Sanetomi (1837–91) also known as *Saneyoshi*; Court noble; fled to *Choshu*, 1863; later became a senior minister in the *Meiji* government.

SHIMAZU Hisamitsu (1817–87) also known as *Saburo*; effective head of *Satsuma* during 1860s; supported Okubo Toshimichi and Saigo Takamori, but conservative after 1868.

SHIMAZU Nariakira (1809–58) *Tozama daimyo* of *Satsuma*; reformer, encouraging imports of Western technology.

SHODA, Heigoro (1847–1922) originally trained at Keio, under Yukichi Fukuzawa; transferred to Mitsubishi and married one of Yataro Iwasaki's daughters; became general manager of Mitsubishi in 1886; shipbuilding expert.

SOEJIMA Taneomi (1828–1905) *Hizen*; student of *Rangaku*, later English; diplomatic specialist; represented Japan overseas; later became a cabinet minister.

TERAJIMA Munenori (1832–93) earlier known as *MATSUKI* Koan; *Satsuma*; studied medicine and *Rangaku*; doctor and adviser to Shimazu Nariakiri; led influential *Satsuma* Mission to Europe 1865–6 with Godai Tomoatsu; senior diplomatic posts in *Meiji* government; Foreign Minister 1873; Vice-president of Privy Council 1891.

TOGO Heihachiro (1848–1934) *Satsuma*; Fleet admiral in IJN, commanded at Battle of Sea of Japan or Tsushima, 27–28 May 1905 when IJN destroyed Russian Baltic Fleet.

TOKUGAWA Keiki (1837–1913) earlier known as *Hitotsubashi* (q.v.) also *Yoshinobu*; succeeded as *Shogun*, January 1867, fifteenth and last of *Tokugawa* line.

YAMAGATA Aritomo (1838–1922) *Choshu*; outstanding figure of late *Meiji* period; Prime Minister and *genro*.

YAMAO Yozo (1837–1917) *Choshu*, one of he original '*Choshu* Five'; educated in London at UCL, and also at Glasgow; influential in *Meiji* government particularly on technical development and education.

YOSHIDA Toyo (1816–62) also known as *Genkichi*; *Tosa* reformer, influential figure advocating modernisation, assassinated.

# Appendix C: Academic Societies and Journals Founded in *Meiji* Japan

| *Founding dates* | *Names of Societies* *Japanese* | *English* | *Titles of journals* | *Founding dates of journals* |
|---|---|---|---|---|
| 1873 | *Meirokusha* | 6th year of *Meiji* Society | *Meiroku Zasshi* | 1874 |
| 1877 | *Tokyo Sugaku Kaisha* | Tokyo Mathematical Society | *Tokyo Sugaku Kaisha Zaashi* | 1878 |
| | | | *Gakugei Shirin* published by University of Tokyo, translations of articles in Western Journals | 1877 |
| 1878 | *Tokyo Kagaku Kai* | Tokyo Chemical Society | *Nihon Kagaku Kaishi* | 1880 |
| 1878 | *Tokyo Seibutsu Gakkai* | Tokyo Biological Society | | |
| 1879 | *Ko Gakkai* | Engineering Society | *Kogaku Shoshi* | 1881 |
| 1879 | *Tokyo Gakushi Kaiin* | Tokyo Academy | *Tokyo Gakushi Kaiin Zasshi* | 1879 |
| 1879 | *Tokyo Chigaku Kyokai* | Tokyo Geographical Society | *Tokyo Chigaku Kyokai Hokoku* | 1879 |
| | | | Memoirs of the Science Department, University of Tokyo, Japan | |
| 1880 | *Nihon Jishin Gakkai* | The Seismological Society of Japan | | |

(*continued*)

| *Founding dates* | *Names of Societies* *Japanese* | *English* | *Titles of journals* | *Founding dates of journals* |
|---|---|---|---|---|
| (*continued*) | | | | |
| | | | *Tokyo Gakugei Zasshi* intellectual journal; articles mostly by University of Tokyo professors | 1881 |
| 1882 | *Tokyo Seibutsu Gakkai* | (1878) split into – | | |
| | (1) *Tokyo Shokubutsu Gakkai* | Tokyo Botanical Society | *Shokubutsugaku Zasshi* | 1887 |
| | (2) *Tokyo Dobutsu Gakkai* | Tokyo Zoological Society | *Dobutsugaku Zasshi* | 1887 |
| 1884 | *Tokyo Jinrui Gakkai* | Tokyo Anthropological Society | *Jinruigaku Zasshi* | 1886 |
| 1884 | *Tokyo Sugaku Kaisha* renamed *Sugaku Butsuri Gakkai* | Tokyo Mathematico-Physical Society | *Tokyo Sugaku Butsuri Gakkai Kijii* | 1885 |
| 1885 | *Nihon Kiseichu Gakkai* | Parasitological Society of Japan | | |
| 1885 | *Nihon Kogyo Kai* | Mining Society of Japan | | |
| 1886 | *Kenchiku Gakkai* | Architectural Society | | |
| 1887 | *Tokyo Igakkai* | Tokyo Medical Society | *Journal of the College of Science*, Imperial University, Japan. | |
| 1888 | *Denki Gakkai* | Electrical Society | | |
| | | | *Tokyo Butsuri Gakko Zasshi* (published by Tokyo School of Physics) | 1891 |
| 1893 | *Nihon Chishitsu Gakkai* | Geological Society of Japan | *Chishitsugaku Zasshi* | 1893 |
| 1902 | | | Proceedings of the Tokyo Mathematico-Physical Society | 1902 |
| 1904 | | | *Journal of the College of Engineering*, Tokyo Imperial University, Japan | 1904 |

*Source*: K. Koizumi, 'Japan's First Physicists', *Historical Studies in the Physical Sciences*, vol. 6 (1975), p. 104.

# Appendix D: Lectures Given to the Japan Society of Cambridge, 1888–92

| *Date* | *Title of Lecture* | *Lecturer* | *Comments* |
|---|---|---|---|
| 1888 | The Character of the English Gentleman and English Public Schools | Professor Sir Donald Wade KCB (Kings) | |
| 1889 March | The University life of an English Gentleman | Dr Donald MacAlister (St Johns) | |
| 1889 August | The Domestic Education of the English Gentleman | Dr J. S. Reid (Caius) | |
| 1890 February | The Influence of Christianity upon the Character of an English Gentleman | Rev. Professor B. F. Westcott DD (Kings) (now Lord Bishop of Durham) | |
| 1890 December | The Comity of Nations | Dr C. E. Searle (Master of Pembroke) | Mrs Searle entertained members of the Society to luncheon before the meeting |
| 1891 | Ambition | Rev. A. H. F. Boughey (Trinity) | |
| 1891 June | Science as a Training | Professor Alexander MacAlister (St Johns) | |
| 1891 November | Industry, Art and Character | Mr H. S. Foxwell (St Johns) but also Professor of Political Economy at University College, London | |
| 1892 March | Literature as Training | Dr A. W. Verrall (Trinity) | |
| No date | English Gentlemen in the Past | Dr Butler (Master of Trinity) | |
| | The House of Commons | Sir Richard Jebb, MP (Regius Professor of Greek) | |
| | History and Ethics | Sir John Seeley (Regius Professor of Modern History) | |
| | The Sacredness of Property | Rev. Dr Cunningham | |
| | The English Gentleman in English Law | Dr E. W. Maitland | |

*Sources*: *Transactions and Proceedings of Japan Society, London*, vol. VII (London, 1908) p. 49. *Japanese Club at Cambridge*, 7th, 8th, and 9th Meetings, GUL, Stack Education, R5 1916–C.

# Notes and References

Full publication details of authors' works to which reference is made here will be found in the Bibliography.

## 1 Diplomats and Consuls

1. See G. Fox, *Britain and Japan, 1858–1883*, Part I, Diplomatic Relations.
2. The 8th Earl of Elgin was also the 12th Earl of Kincardine. The author is indebted to Andrew, the Right Honourable Earl of Elgin and Kincardine, of Broomhall, Fife, Scotland, for permission to quote from the Bruce family papers. See S. G. Checkland, *The Elgins, 1766–1917*. J. L. Morison, *The Eighth Earl of Elgin*, and L. Oliphant, *Narrative of the Earl of Elgin's Mission to China and Japan*.
3. T. Walrond, *Letters and Journals of James, 8th Earl of Elgin*, p. 263. While in Japan Elgin wrote a long letter-diary to Louisa, his wife, which covered the whole of his Japanese trip. References here are to Walrond, where he quotes, or to the original letter-diary, hereafter *EL*, held by Lord Elgin, at Broomhall, Fife, Scotland.
4. For the text of the Treaty of Peace, Amity and Commerce between Great Britain and Japan, Edo, 26 August 1858, see *Meiji Japan through Contemporary Sources*, vol. 1, pp. 36–44.
5. The only British agreement which pre-dates that of Lord Elgin's treaty had been negotiated by Rear Admiral Sir James Stirling. For the text see 'Convention between Great Britain and Japan for Regulating the admission of British Ships into Ports of Japan', in *Meiji Japan through Contemporary Sources* vol. 1, pp. 4–5.
6. See M. E. Cosenza, *The Complete Journal of Townshend Harris*, and O. Statler, *Shimoda Story*.
7. Walrond, *Letters*, p. 265.
8. PP, 1859, vol. XXXIII (2571) pp. 1–6, Clarendon to Elgin, no. 16, 20 April 1857.
9. As Elgin wrote, 'I found that the Consul had contrived to make a pretty good treaty with Japan, evidently under the influence of the *contre coup* of our proceedings in China', *EL*, 12 August 1858.
10. Elgin sent a watch and chain, 'as a trifling acknowledgement of the very valuable assistance rendered by you to me', *EL*, 27 August 1858.
11. Walrond, *Letters*, p. 268.
12. Elgin was not to know that a bitter power struggle was going on in Japan and that only because Ii Naosuke (1815–60) *daimyo* of Hikone, and regent to the young Emperor, was in the ascendant was his mission so successfully and speedily completed. Ii paid the price for his complaisance, being assassinated in 1860.
13. *The Emperor*, an armed steam yacht of 4 guns built at Blackwall in

1856, was 370 gross tons, 135′ × 22′ with iron paddle; later renamed *Banryu* and *Raiden Maru*, served in Japanese navy as *Raiden* (1877–88). Later a whaler, broken up in Osaka in the late 1890s. See T. M. Milne, *Steam Vessels Sold to Japan*, NMM THS/13/2, p. 76. Admiral Fitzgerald also reported that *The Emperor* 'was a handsome little vessel ... she was also thoroughly sea-worthy and had made her own way out to China via the Cape ... The Japanese took kindly to her and showed great anxiety to learn how to work her themselves without any assistance from foreigners'; see P. Fitzgerald, *Memories of the Sea*, pp. 114–15.

14. Walrond, *Letters*, p. 274.
15. The treaties were basically the same, Elgin had inserted a 'most-favoured nation' clause, which Harris had omitted, see W. G. Beasley, *Great Britain and the Opening of Japan*, pp. 190–1.
16. Rutherford Alcock, 1809–97, army surgeon, Marine Brigade, Portugal, 1832–6; consul at Foochow, China, 1844; Shanghai, 1846; first consul-general Japan, 1859–65; Minister Plenipotentiary, Peking 1865–71. For his response to Japan see Alcock, *The Capital of the Tycoon*, reprinted Greenwood, 1969.
17. See Fitzgerald *Memories*, 1, p. 356.
18. The Far East Consular service (China, later Japan, Siam and Korea) developed into a 'close service specially recruited with its own system of promotion and payment and its own code of instructions', see D. C. M. Platt, 'The Role of the British Consular Services in Overseas Trade', *EcHR*, no. 3 (1963) pp. 494–512.
19. The Consul's function was to 'protect and promote trade, administer shipping laws, act as head of the resident community and generally represent his government'. See P. Byrd, 'Regional and Functional Specialization in the British Consular Service', *JCH*, vol. 7, 1–2, 1972, pp. 127–45. Gibbon wrote of the 'humble station of the agents of commerce in a foreign land'. See R. A. Jones, *The Nineteenth Century Foreign Office* and *The British Diplomatic Service*.
20. R. A. Jones, *British Diplomatic Service*, p. 209.
21. Both Tozenji Temple, and the nearby Senkakuji Temple, at Shinagawa, were used by the British. Both were then close to Tokyo Bay, and – in the event of emergency – to the ships of the Royal Navy. Both temples can still be visited today. See R. Alcock, *The Capital of the Tycoon*, vol. I, and A. B. F. Mitford, *Memories*, vol. I, p. 383.
22. Alcock left Japan 'with the pleasant remembrance of difficulties overcome' but 'there still lingers a weary sense of the trouble that preyed upon the mind', Alcock, *Capital of the Tycoon*, vol. I, p. 150.
23. See B. H. Chamberlain, *Things Japanese*, pp. 360–2, F. V. Dickens, *The Life of Sir Harry Parkes*, vol. II, 1894; G. Daniels, 'Sir Harry Parkes, British Representative in Japan, 1865–1882', thesis, 1967, and H. Cortazzi, 'The Pestilently Active Minister', pp. 147–61.
24. The need for student interpreters in the Far East gave openings to gifted men, including Parkes and Satow, to enter the service and rise in it. The French initially used 'Two Catholic Fathers ... of the Mission Etrangères, who had come to the Ryukyu Islands and studied Japanese

as interpreters and this caused friction with a regime in which Christianity was proscribed. See C. Yamada, *Japonisme in Art*, p. 33.

25. See S. G. Checkland, *The Elgins*, ch. 15.
26. See Parkes Papers, ULC, Correspondence Hammond to Parkes, 15 March 1868. By June 1868 Hammond was writing about affairs in Japan, 'I am glad to find you take so sanguine a view of the general prospect before us' (Parkes Papers, ULC Correspondence Hammond to Parkes, 17 June 1868). See Mitford (Lord Redesdale) *Memories*, vol. I, p. 109. See also M. A. Anderson, 'Edmund Hammond, Permanent Under-Secretary of State for Foreign Affairs, 1854–1873', thesis, 1955.
27. For Thomas Blake Glover (1848–1911) see Mitford, *Memories*, vol. I, p. 377. See O. Checkland, 'Scotland and Japan, 1860–1914' and S. Sugiyama, 'Glover & Co: a British merchant in Nagasaki, 1861–1870' in I Nish (ed.) *Bakumatsu and Meiji: Studies in Japan's Economic and Social History*, International Studies, 1981/2, LSE, and S. Sugiyama, 'Thomas B. Glover: a British Merchant in Japan, 1861–70', *BH*, vol. XXVI, no. 2 (July 1984) pp. 115–38.
28. Laurence Oliphant had been in Japan in 1853, as private secretary to Lord Elgin, and in 1861 as Secretary of the Legation. See A. Taylor, *Laurence Oliphant, 1829–1888*, 1982. A contemporary summed him up as 'a mystic in lavender kid gloves, full of spiritualism, strange creeds, and skits upon society', Mitford, *Memories*, p. 125; see also I. P. Hall, *Mori Arinori*, 1973, pp. 73–4; P. Harrison, *Oliphant*, 1956; and Chapter 8 of this volume.
29. Matsuki Koan, 1832–93, later known as Terajima Munenori, had studied medicine and Dutch studies. He later became a senior diplomatic representative. Godai Tomoatsu, 1836–85, later became an entrepreneur, with interests in transport, mining and textiles. See also biographical notes, in Appendix.
30. A. B. F. Mitford, later Lord Redesdale (1837–1916), had as a young man transferred from the FO to the diplomatic service. He served in Japan from 1866 to 1870, learning Japanese with Satow. In 1871 the publication of *Tales of Old Japan* made him famous. He became Baron Redesdale of Redesdale, Northumberland in 1876. He accompanied Prince Arthur of Connaught to Japan in 1906, and published *The Garter Mission to Japan* in that year.
31. Satow wrote *Eikoku Sakuron* (English Policy) articles for the *Japan Times* (which were widely circulated), in which he argued that the Tycoon should step down and that a confederation of *daimyo* under the Emperor should take his place. The articles were widely believed in Japan to be official British policy, although Satow remarks that 'as far as I know it never came to the ears of my Chief', see E. M. Satow, *A Diplomat in Japan*, pp. 159–60. Satow's intervention, he wrote later, was 'doubtless very wrong, and very irregular' (p. 159).
32. For Parkes policy during the final years of the Shogunate see G. Daniels, 'The British Role in the *Meiji* Restoration: A Re-interpretive note', *MAS*, II, vol. 4, 1968, pp. 291–313.
33. The changes which took place were as follows: August 1871, the

abolition of the semi-independent *han* or clans and the establishment of a military, national administrative framework; September 1872, compulsory education for all children; December 1873 compulsory military service for all males; January 1873, the Gregorian calendar replaced the old lunar calendar; July 1873, the imposition of national system of taxation payable in money, not kind (rice), calculated on value of land rather than its crop.

34. G. Daniels, thesis, p. 370.
35. J. H. Longford, 'England's record in Japan', *JSL*, vol. VII, 1904–7, p. 104.
36. Parkes did not 'recognise any very definite line between our political and our commercial interests', see G. Daniels, thesis, p. 241.
37. After the attack the British moved back to Yokohama for a time. See H. Cortazzi, 'The Pestilently Active Minister', *MN*, Summer 1984, vol. XXXIX, no. 4, p. 152.
38. The Americans stressed the common interests, which, as a Pacific power, they had with Japan. They proffered advice on agriculture and education and their citizens were appointed as advisers to various offices of the Japanese government. The Germans had had a role in developing Japanese science and medicine from the beginning. In the later *Meiji* years the German position became stronger as they made remarkable progress in scientific and technical fields. A. H. House, an American journalist, made a career out of denigrating the British. His favourite target was Sir Harry Parkes, 'a living and breathing thorn in the side of Japan' whose career had been 'one long series of exactions, oppressions, insults and humiliations' practised on the Japanese. He founded *The Tokio Times*, see *Tokio Times*, 7 and 28 December 1878, and G. Daniels, thesis, p. 315.
39. B. H. Chamberlain, *Things Japanese*, 1905, p. 392.
40. Sir John Pope Hennessy (1834–91), Governor of Hong Kong from 1877 to March 1882, had spent his vacations in Japan. At the end of 1882 he was gazetted as Governor of Mauritius.
41. The Okuma Papers, *Okuma Monjo* (hereafter *OM*), are held in Waseda University Library. There are some letters in English. The references here are to *OM* C.300, C.301 and C.333. It is not known how copies of these letters come to be in the *Okuma Monjo*; my thanks to Yoshitaka Komatsu for bringing these to my attention.
42. It is worth noting that by the 'adaptations authorised by the Fugitive Offenders Act' of 1881, Britain grouped together for legal purposes, as if they were British possessions' China, Japan and Korea. See J. C. Tarring, *British Consular Jurisdiction*, p. 109.
43. The case of Luis Campos in 1889 aroused much interest. Consul Longford's consular constable arrested Campos outside the boundaries of the treaty port. The Japanese protested. The Minister, Sir Hugh Fraser, instructed Consul Longford to release the man who was then re-arrested by the Japanese and handed over by them to the British. Fraser's actions aroused the anger of the treaty port residents. Lady Fraser reported, 'the papers were noisy, and British gringoes (of whom the East is alas full) talked of the fine old days and Sir Harry Parkes'; see J. Hoare, in Nish and Dunn, *European Studies on Japan*, p. 127.

44. Sir F. R. Plunkett, an Irish Roman Catholic, was already familiar with Japan, having served there as Secretary of Legation in the 1870s.
45. Sir Hugh Fraser had Far Eastern experience having served in Peking for several years between 1867 and 1879. See M. C. Fraser, *A Diplomat's Wife in Japan*, edited by H. Cortazzi, 1982.
46. P. Le Poer Trench had previously served as Secretary of Legation in Tokyo for seven years.
47. See E. M. Satow, *A Diplomat in Japan*, and B. M. Allen, *Sir Ernest Satow*.
48. Interpreters had been recruited originally by recommendation, later by an examination following recommendation. After 1872 candidates took an open competitive examination. See R. A. Jones, *The British Diplomatic Service*, p. 210.
49. Allen, *Sir Ernest Satow*, p. 5.
50. Ibid, p. 27.
51. G. Fox, *Britain and Japan*, p. 9.
52. Mitford, *Memories*, vol. II, p. 416.
53. A. Michie, *The Englishman in China*, vol. II, p. 363.
54. Satow had left Japan in 1884 to further his career. He became Consul General in Bangkok and later (1888) Minister Resident in Montevideo and (1893) in Tangier.
55. G. A. Lensen *Korea and Manchuria . . . The Observations of Sir Ernest Satow*, Introduction, p. 9. Note also Sir George Sansom's comment:

    > Satow was perhaps a rather dry scholar, but he was a prodigious worker. Besides being a most valuable member of the British legation in Japan at a crucial period, he added to his understanding of Japanese politics a remarkable command of the Japanese language and a scholar's interest in Japanese history and literature. Much of his work is still not superseded. He is one of the founding fathers of modern Japanology'; see Sir G. Sansom, reprinted *JAS*, vol. XXIV, no. 4, August 1965, p. 566.

56. Munemitsu Matsu when ambassador to the USA in 1888 had succeeded in, negotiating Japan's first 'equal' Treaty of Amity and Commerce with Mexico, and a revised Treaty of Commerce with the USA (February 1889).
57. For the text of the Treaty of Commerce and Navigation between Great Britain and Japan, 16 July 1894, see *Meiji Japan through Contemporary Sources*, Tokyo, 1972, vol. 3, pp. 187–200. The Japanese Minister in London at the time was Shuzo Aoki. See also I. H. Nish, 'Japan reverses the Unequal Treaties, the Anglo-Japanese Commercial Treaty of 1894', Papers of Hong Kong International Conference on Asian History, no. 20, 1964.
58. I. H. Nish, *Anglo-Japanese Alliance*, 1966, p. 10.
59. E. Grey (Viscount Grey of Falloden), *Twenty-five Years, 1892–1916*, 1925, vol. 1, p. 71.
60. This section owes much to I. H. Nish, *The Anglo-Japanese Alliance, the Diplomacy of Two Island Empires, 1894–1907*, 1966.
61. Yukichi Fukuzawa (1835–1901) was the principal philosopher and

populariser of Western ideas of *Meiji* Japan, see Fukuzawa, Y., *Autobiography of Fukuzawa Yukichi* translated by E. Kiyooka, and biographical notes in Appendix.

62. Tadasu Hayashi (1850–1913), born Sakura *han*, Shimosa province, son of 'Dutch' trained doctor, studied in England, 1866–8, rebelled against new government, captured at Hakodate, but pardoned and entered government in 1871; Second Secretary to Iwakura Mission, Minister for Japan in London, 1899–1905; Foreign Minister, 1906; see also T. Hayashi, *The Secret Memoirs of Count Hayashi*.
63. Hayashi, *Secret Memoires*, p. 84.
64. Takaaki Kato, 1860–1926, educated Nagoya and Tokyo entered Mitsubishi Company and became protégé of Iwasaki Yataro, whose eldest daughter he married. He entered public service in 1887, and became private secretary to Okuma in 1888; appointed minister to Court of St James in London, 1894. He was an Anglophile.
65. Joseph Chamberlain, in March 1898 (at a dinner in Kato's honour) spoke of 'the readiness of Great Britain to enter into an agreement with Japan for the settlement of relations in the Far East'. See A. M. Pooley, *Hayashi*, p. 83.
66. But Satow although 'he cultivated good will on both sides' never went so far as to advocate an alliance. Nish, *Anglo-Japanese Alliance*, p. 79.
67. Sir Ellis Ashmead Bartlett spoke strongly in the House of Commons, 'I consider the rise of Japanese power in the East has been providential for this country . . . There is a very great and strong power growing up in Japan and by the help alone of Japan we can retain our position in the North Pacific', (Parliamentary Debates, 1 March 1896, 4th Series LIV, pp. 305–306). In the newspaper world there were supporters including Sir Edwin Arnold of *The Daily Telegraph*; Sir Valentine Chirol (1852–1929), foreign editor of *The Times*; Frank Brinkley (1841–1912), proprietor and editor of the *Japan Mail*, and Tokyo correspondent of *The Times* and foreign adviser to NYK, who spoke Japanese well (see *Who Was Who, 1897–1916*). *The Times* Tokyo correspondent (from 1894) was Dr G. E. Morrison, correspondent in Peking from 1897 (see *The Correspondence of G. E. Morrison*, and also H. Trevor Roper, *Hermit of Pekin: The Secret Life of Sir Edmund Backhouse*). These men were actively pro-Japanese.
68. See Ian Nish, *The Anglo-Japanese Alliance*, pp. 131–4.
69. 'The Japanese government insisted on early publication of the treaty, the British government also felt "that it could not be kept secret for long and that as we should certainly have it dragged out of us in Parliament it was much better to make a clean breast of it at once" ', C. F. Chang, *Anglo-Japanese Alliance*, p. 82.
70. The alliance was welcomed in Britain by the Admiralty. In 1903 the Commander of the China Station, Admiral Sir Cyprian Bridge, wrote that he 'got on very well with the Japs.' It was a different matter in the army, where responses to the German-trained Japanese produced critical judgements. Sandhurst-trained, Sir Claude MacDonald, took a more optimistic view writing 'one of the assets . . . in favour of the

alliance was the splendid courage of our allies (then to be)'. See P. Towle, *Estimating Foreign Military Power*, pp. 129 and 116.

71. P. Lowe, *Great Britain and Japan, 1911–1915*, p. 41.
72. S. T. W. Davis, 'Treaty Revision, National Security and Regional Cooperation' in H. Conroy, S. T. W. Davis and W. Patterson (eds), *Japan in Transition, Thought and Action in the Meiji Era, 1868–1912*, p. 170.
73. Sir Frederick Bruce, the third son of the 7th Earl of Elgin's second family, began his career (1842) as an attaché to Ashburnham's special mission to Washington; then became Colonial Secretary in Hong Kong, and Lieutenant Governor in Newfoundland before, being appointed Consul General in Bolivia and *chargé d'affaires* in Uruguay in 1847. In the early 1850s he became agent and Consul General in Egypt before accompanying his brother Elgin to China in 1857; he was Minister in China before serving in Washington as Minister from 1865. He died in Boston in 1867. Despite his aristocratic lineage he never served in a European mission (R. A. Jones, *The British Diplomatic Service*, p. 206).
74. *EL*, Private, Sir F. B. to Earl Russell, Peking, 15 April 1864. The Richardson affair triggered off a series of other events. *Satsuma* were fined a large sum for the presumed offence against a British citizen. When they were reluctant to pay, a British naval squadron proceeded to the *Satsuma* capital, Kogoshima, and bombarded it. As a result the *Satsuma* leaders were forced to face reality. Their policies changed; see Chapter 8, note 10.

## 2 Traders and Bankers

1. British Sessional Papers HC 1859 [2571], vol. XXXIII, p. 1. Instructions from Lord Clarendon to Lord Elgin, Plenipotentiary in China and Japan.
2. The East India Company's tea monopoly had been ended in 1833. See Mui, *The Management of Monopoly*.
3. The text of the Treaty of Edo, of Peace, Amity and Commerce between Great Britain and Japan, 26 August 1858, is given in *Meiji Japan through Contemporary Sources*, Tokyo 1969, vol. I, pp. 4–5.
4. The comments of William Rathbone V (about business in China) could also apply to trade with Japan. Rathbone wrote 'an untried business, entered into recklessly and ignorantly, and sure therefore to be overdone at first, ending in heavy losses, taking time to weed out the unknowing and imprudent'. See S. G. Checkland, 'An English Merchant House in China after 1842', *Bulletin of the Business Historical Society*, vol. XXVII, September 1953, no. 3, pp. 158–89.
5. J. McMaster, *Jardines in Japan*, 1966, p. 9.
6. There is much on these matters in JM.
7. See J. E. Hoare, 'The Japanese Treaty Ports, 1868–1899: A Study of the Foreign Settlements', thesis.
8. Dr Hoare suggests that Sir Harry Parkes decided on Niigata.

9. See R. Alcock, *Capital of the Tycoon*, vol. I, p. 137.
10. See H. S. Williams, *Foreigners in Mikado Land*, Tokyo, 1963.
11. E. M. Satow, *A Diplomat in Japan*, 1921, p. 25.
12. Ibid, p. 22.
13. M. B. T. Paske Smith, *Western Barbarians*, pp. 362–3.
14. See J. P. Mollison, 'Reminiscences of Yokohama', Lecture to Yokohama Literary and Musical Society, 8 January 1909 (copy in Yokohama Archives of History).
15. See D. A. Farnie, *East and West of Suez*.
16. There were heated arguments 'in tea circles, whether the new teas, would stand being shut up in an iron steamer and carried through the tropics'; these fears proved unfounded. See Mollison, 'Reminiscences', p. 17.
17. G. Fox, *Britain and Japan*, p. 327, and pp. 327–42, and Paske Smith, *Western Barbarians*, pp. 229–65.
18. Parkes Papers, ULC, Correspondence, Hammond to Parkes, 26 April 1866.
19. Consular Report, Marcus Flowers, 1868, Accounts and Papers, vol. XIX, p. 1014.
20. Fox, *Britain and Japan*, pp. 342–52.
21. G. A. Lensen, *Korea and Manchuria... Observations of Sir Ernest Satow*, 1966, p. 181.
22. Fox, *Britain and Japan*, pp. 352–61.
23. Ibid, pp. 361–4.
24. The status of the British consul is examined by Peter Byrd, 'Regional and Functional Specialization', pp. 127–45.
25. Consul Vyse of Hakodate got into great trouble in 1866. As Sir Harry Parkes wrote, 'Vyse has made a great botch of a disgraceful case that has occurred at Hakodate in which three Englishmen . . . have gone into the country and rifled Ainus tombs of skulls and skeletons', Parkes papers, ULC, Parkes to Winchester, 31 January 1866.
26. See C. Beresford, *The Break-up of China*, p. 412.
27. During the period when foreigners enjoyed rights of extraterritorality the limits of the treaty ports were as follows:

    Hakodate, ten *ri* in any direction.
    Kanagawa, to the river Hoge and ten *ri* in any direction.
    Hiogo, ten *ri* in any direction, that of Kioto excepted, which city shall not be approached nearer than ten *ri*.
    Ten *ri* = 4275 yards English.

    See F. G. D. Bedford, *The Sailor's Handbook*, p. 315.
28. See B. L. Putnam Weale, *The Re-shaping of the Far East*, vol. I, p. 444.
29. D. Steeds and Nish, I., *China, Japan and Nineteenth Century Britain*, p. 50.
30. One example is that of steam engines ordered 'for Japan' on 12 August and 16 October 1865 from W. & A. McOnie, Glasgow, Scotland through International Credit Corporation, Holland and H. C. & K. de Wit. McOnie were primarily manufacturers of sugar-refining

machinery, eventually incorporated into Mirlees Watson. See GUA, UGD 118, 3/37.

31. O. and S. Checkland, 'British and Japanese Economic Interaction under the early *Meiji*, pp. 139–55, coal-mining at Takashima closed in 1987, see 'Sinking Slowly in the East' *Sunday Times* Magazine, 16 August 1987.

32. For vessels sold in Japan before 1868 see Consular Report, 1868, *Accounts and Papers*, Manufacturers, Commerce, China, Coal, etc., vol. XIX, p. 1014 and T. A. Milne, *Steam Vessels Sold or Reportedly Sold to Japan up to 1870*, for what may be a more comprehensive list. According to T. A. Milne the keenest purchasers were *Satsuma-han* which bought fifteen vessels. *Choshu* bought eight and *Tosa* and *Hizen* (*Saga*) each bought seven. Other clans which bought one or two vessels included *Aki*, *Geishu*, *Kishu*, *Bizen*, *Izumo*, *Tsu*, *Kokura*, *Matsuyama*, *Uajima*, *Kaga*, *Awa*, *Izuhara*, *Higo* and *Okayama*, although *Kirume* and *Chikuzen* each bought three.

33. The engines were used primarily to ease manoeuvrability, especially when entering and leaving harbour. As Lord Elgin explained, 'we have now disconnected our machinery from the paddle wheels, and are gliding along over a smooth sea with a light breeze', *EL*, 1 August 1858.

34. Glover & Co. wrote to Jardine Matheson as follows, 'Under any circumstances it would not be worth her while to come here unless Ship, Engines and Boilers are in perfect order and the latter good for at least three years work without repairs', Glover & Co., Nagasaki, to J. M. & Co., Shanghai, JM, Nagasaki, B/10/4/578, 25 March 1869.

35. See S. Sujiyama, 'Thomas B. Glover: A British Merchant in Japan, 1861–70', *BH*, vol. XXVI, no. 2, July 1984, pp. 115–38. The *Jho-Sho Maru* and the *Ho-Sho Maru* were ordered from Alexander Hall of Aberdeen by Glover through the agency of Glover Brothers, Ship Insurance Brokers of Aberdeen. The City of Glasgow Bank loaned the balance for this work. The remains of the patent slip dock were still there at Nagasaki in 1981. For access to Alexander Hall's records apply to NRA Scotland, Register House, Edinburgh.

36. Glover was involved in the arms trade both legally and illegally. As Joseph Heco remarked, 'the various *daimyo* were now (1867) all eager to . . . acquire steamships, sailing ships, guns and munitions of war generally' (Heco, *Narrative of a Japanese*, p. 82). The American Civil War ended in 1865 when surplus rifles became available for export. Glover was involved in this illicit trade. In the list of Glover's debts, compiled in 1876, credit is claimed for '*Hizen* Officers Balance of Spencer rifles contract'. See also material in Royal Netherlands Archives, The Hague, in File Faillisement Glover & Co. 1870–1877 (hereafter File: *Faillissement*) Netherlandsche Handel–Maatschappij 5935 (hereafter NHM 5935). Spencer rifles, manufactured from 1860, were made for the American Union forces, they had a seven-shot magazine and were heavy and sturdy; when the American Civil War ended in 1864, these guns were available for re-sale; my thanks to Gavin White for his help.

Glover also operated at the official level writing to William Armstrong, Elswick Works, Newcastle upon Tyne as follows, 'Referring to our respects of 15th April bearing reference to a contemplated order for guns on account of the Japanese Government we have now the pleasure to hand you the undermentioned order . . . Muzzle loaders 15, 70 pounders with 15 carriages and slides complete, Breech loaders 10, 12 pounders, 5, 8 pounders, 5, 6 pounders. You will ere this have received through Messrs Matheson & Co., London, the necessary information as to the mode of payment which we hope you may find satisfactory. We have only further to urge you to hasten the execution of this order as the Japanese Government is extremely anxious to have the guns with as little delay as possible', JM, Nagasaki, B/10/4/343, 28 June 1865.

37. K. Yamamura, 'The Founding of Mitsubishi', p. 146.
38. Marcus Flowers, *Consular Report*, 1868, Accounts and Papers, Manufacturers, Commerce, China, Coal, vol. XIX, p. 1014.
39. Inoue attempted to resign in June 1873 but was persuaded to continue at his post, see H. J. Jones, *Live Machines*, pp. 87–90, see also *OM* especially C.162–163 (1871), and C.444 (1873), relating to railway building and to W. W. Cargill.
40. W. W. Cargill, 1813–1894, was the son of an army captain. In Japan 'as an administrator-adviser he seemed to understand how to work with, rather than against the bureaucratic tide' (Jones, *Live Machines*, p. 90). Cargill was railway adviser to the Japanese government between 1872 and 1877: he suggested the appointment of the Railway Commissioner, W. W. Cargill to Okuma, *OM*, C.162, dated 20 April 1871, and addressed from 'Yokohama No 32'; others are C.163, C.164 and C.165.
41. Charles Wirgman reported on the opening but also explained that as the train bearing the Emperor passed 'at the intermediate stations on each side of the line men, women and children were kneeling down', *ILN*, 7 December 1872, p. 546.
42. See P. J. English, *British Made*, pp. 13–14.
43. The North British Locomotive company was formed in Glasgow in 1903 from Sharp, Stewart and Co, Neilson and Co, and Dubs and Co. All three of these companies supplied railway engines to Japan prior to the amalgamation in 1903. After the amalgamation in 1903 the North British Locomotive Company continued to supply Japanese railway companies until 1911, see also Anon, *A History of the North British Locomotive Co Ltd. 1903–1953*.
44. Mrs Margaret Lamb kindly worked on the original records of NBL, GUA.
45. English, *British Made*, p. 14.
46. Ibid, p. 16.
47. *EL*, 12 August 1858.
48. PP, 1866, vol. LXII [3707] Parkes to Clarendon, Yokohama, 16 May 1866, p. 241.
49. See also H. Kawakatsu, 'International Competition in Cotton Goods in the Late Nineteenth Century', thesis; my thanks to H. Kawakatsu.

50. PP, 1878–9, vol. LXII [C2358] CR on Kanagawa, 1878, p. 36.
51. A. O. Hirschman, *Strategy of Economic Development*, p. 100.
52. PP, 1887, LXXXII [C4924] 'On Native Manufactures of Cotton Goods in Japan', p. 10.
53. H. Kawakatsu, 'International Competition in Cotton Goods in the Late Nineteenth Century: Britain versus India and East Asia' in W. Fischer *et al.*, *The Emergence of World Economy*.
54. See D. A. Farnie, *The English Cotton Industry*, Oxford, 1979.
55. T. Hayashi, 'The Automatic Loom and the Automobile', *Entrepreneurship*, no. 5, March 1983, pp. 8–15.
56. Ibid, p. 14.
57. *Manchester Guardian*, 14 July 1891; my thanks to Douglas Farnie for his help.
58. Local newspapers including the *Manchester Guardian* and the *Oldham Chronicle* as well as national surveys like the *Daily Mail Year Book* published fact-finding articles anticipating the demise of the machinery export trade.
59. *Daily Dispatch*, 14 October 1907.
60. The author is indebted to Norio Tamaki, Professor of Banking, Keio University, Tokyo, for advice and guidance; see also H. T. Patrick, 'Section VIII Japan, 1868–1914' in R. Cameron (ed.) *Banking and the Early Stages of Industrialization*, pp. 239–89, and K. Yamamura, 'Japan 1868–1930' in R. Cameron (ed.) *Banking and Economic Development*, pp. 168–98; see also A. S. J. Baster, *The Imperial Banks* and *International Banks*.
61. Osborn's account reads:

> By the old laws of the Japanese Empire, the exportation of their currency, whether gold, silver or copper, is strictly prohibited and to ensure it, no European is allowed to possess native coin. The difficulty therefore of purchasing would be great upon that ground alone; but in addition to this rule, another exists, by which the natives are forbidden to receive our coins either. For a while it seemed there must be a deadlock in the market, but it was explained to us that a government bank existed in the bazaar, where we could obtain paper currency (available only in Nagasaki) in exchange for our dollars. From that bank we came out with bundles of very simple-looking strips of cardboard covered with cabalistic signs, indicative of their value, in lieu of the silver we had given . . . With these Japanese banknotes we paid the tradesmen, whom no amount of persuasion could induce to receive silver; and they again had to present them at the bank and receive the amount in the metallic currency of the country, paying of course a handsome tax for the honour of selling to foreigners (S. Osborn, *A Cruise in Japanese Waters*, 1859, pp. 43–4).

62. Sir Thomas Gresham (c.1519–79) advised Queen Elizabeth in 1558 that debased coins will predominate, and more valuable coins (in terms of actual value of the metal in them) will disappear and either be

hoarded, or exported where coins of different value or metal are both circulating, hence Gresham's Law 'bad money drives out good'.

63. J. H. Longford, a British Consul who had served for many years in Japan explained that

> A silver dollar obtainable for 4*s*. 6*d*. in China, distant only a few days steaming could in Japan be exchanged into a gold token that was worth over 18*s*. in all the rest of the world. Trade conducted under such conditions was in itself sufficiently profitable to dazzle the most extreme optimism (J. H. Longford, *The Evolution of the New Japan*, p. 85).

See also M. Tatemoto, 'Gold, Silver and Paper, money muddles before and after the *Meiji* Restoration'.

64. R. Chalmers, *A History of Currency in the British Colonies*, pp. 375–6. See also T. Hamashita, 'A History of the Japanese silver *yen* and the Hong Kong and Shanghai Banking Corporation, 1871–1913' in F. H. H. King (ed.) *Eastern Banking*, p. 323.
65. See various pamphlets on the history of the Imperial Mint, available from the Imperial Mint, Osaka.
66. S. Mossman, *New Japan*, p. 415.
67. See H. J. Jones, *Live Machines*, p. 36, for the disagreements which arose between the Japanese and the British Mint employees.
68. One contract, dated 15 May 1872 was 'between the Oriental Banking Company of the one part and Roland Finch of the other part', the appointment of manager and other officers was vested 'by such Government in the said Corporation'. I am indebted to Kagitani Norichika, of the University of Tokyo, for a copy of Finch's contract. *Zouheikyoku rokujyunenshi* (Sixty Years of the Imperial Mint) Tokyo 1929, pp. 293–4.
69. Jones, *Live Machines*, p. 36.
70. There are thirty-four letters from Robertson in the *OM*, mostly to Okuma but some to Ito, Inoue and others. The first in English is dated 18 August 1869, C.632.
71. Kinder had the pleasure of showing His Imperial Majesty around the Mint, Mossman, *New Japan*, p. 456.
72. Later, foreigners were employed in the Mint for some years although on Japanese contracts. See Henry M. Napier, 'Recollections of a Visit to Japan', handwritten MS, Napier Collections, GUA, GD 96.
73. T. Hamashita, 'The Japanese silver yen' in F. H. H. King (ed.) *Eastern Banking*, p. 321.
74. G. Fox, *Britain and Japan*, ch. XV.
75. Frank Brinkley wrote:

> To conduct coining operations with thoroughly reliable accuracy and regularity, demands a degree of scientific and practical attainments for which sober-minded persons cannot yet persuade themselves to give the Japanese credit . . . It was no secret that in the matter of the Mint the late Minister of Finance (Okuma) sacrificed

expedience to sentiment and set greater store by the name of independence than by the ability to be independent (*Japan Weekly Mail*, 10 June 1882).

76. Neither the Central Bank of Western India nor the Commercial Bank Corporation of India and the Far East survived the Overend Gurney banking crisis in Britain in 1866.
77. Paske Smith, *Western Barbarians*, p. 364, dates the opening of the banks as follows: Chartered Merchantile Bank of India, London and China, 1863; Commercial Bank of India, 1863; Central Bank of Western India, 1864; Hong Kong and Shanghai Banking Corporation, 1864; Hong Kong and Shanghai Banking Corporation, 1867; Oriental Banking Corporation, 1868.
78. See J. Iddittie, *Marquis Okuma*. Okuma also featured in the row in 1881 when the *London and China Telegraph* wrote, in highly critical vein, of a pamphlet published by Okuma entitled 'A General View of Financial Policy during Thirteen Years (1868–80).' See *OM* C.749, from Baron von Siebold, dated Berlin, 4 August 1881, which includes cuttings from the *London and China Telegraph* of 1881.
79. Alexander Allan Shand was born at Turriff, Aberdeenshire on 11 February 1844, son of James Shand, Surgeon, and Margaret Allan, see International Genealogical Index (Scottish Section) microfiche, Church of Jesus Christ of Latterday Saints (Batch C112476, Serial Sheet 0715), 1984.
80. *OM* C.729, 13 February 1894.
81. Shand had at the end of 1873, submitted a memorandum to Okuma; its recommendations were not accepted in their entirety. A. A. Shand to Okuma, *OM* C.726, 9 November 1873; other Shand to Okuma letters are C.727, 10 November 1873, and C.728, 15 December 1881; my thanks to Y. Komatsu.
82. Shibuzawa Eiichi, 1840–1931, of humble origins, attributed the fall of the *Tokugawa* Regime to the lack of opportunity for social mobility. He was one of the great entrepreneurs of *Meiji* Japan being engaged in founding some 300 enterprises of which the Osaka Spinning Mill, 1882, was the best known.
83. The Alliance Bank and Parr's Bank merged in 1892. Parr's Bank was taken over by the Westminster (now the National Westminster) Bank in 1918.
84. J. J. Gerson, *Horatio Nelson Lay and Sino-British Relations*, gives details of Lay's career in China. Lay – 'an old China crony of Parkes' (R. A. Jones, p. 35) – astounded Parkes with his behaviour.
85. Parr's Bank *Minute Book* no 2, Minutes of Meeting, 29 December 1904, p. 940. Shand received gifts from his employers of at least £7000, usually in units of £1000 for his assistance with the Japanese loans; my thanks to R. H. Reed, the archivist of the National Westminster Bank for his kind help. See also Shand's obituary, *The Times*, 16 April 1930, and *The Morning Post*, 16 April 1930.
86. T. Hamashita, 'A History of the Japanese Silver Yen', in F. H. H. King

(ed.) *Eastern Banking*, pp. 321–49; the London branch of the Yokohama Specie Bank opened in 1884.

87. For the founding of the Bank of Japan, see note 89. The author is indebted to Norio Tamaki, who is himself working on *A History of Banking in Japan, 1859–1959*.

88. John Robertson, the Manager of the Oriental Bank in Yokohama (see note 70) was shocked when the Yokohama Specie Bank was opened, judging correctly that such competition from a Japanese-owned bank would seriously affect his bank. The Oriental Bank ceased business in 1884.

89. In November 1876 Matsukata, as head of a Japanese delegation, visited Paris. There he met Leon Say, the French Finance Minister, and was advised to set up in Japan a strong central bank. Matsukata was much impressed with continental banking, especially that in France and Belgium. On returning to Japan he prepared three reports *Zaiseigi* (On Finance) September 1881; *Nippon Ginko Setsuritsu no Gi* (On the establishment of the Bank of Japan) March 1882, and *Nippon Ginko Soritsu Shishu no Setsumei* (The Prospectus of The Bank of Japan) March 1882. In these Matsukata noted the advantages of the Bank of Belgium partly because it had gained much from the experience of the Bank of France and Bank of England and partly because of its success in redeeming inconvertible currency.

90. See P. Kauch, *La Banque Nationale de Belgique, 1850–1918* (Brussels, 1950), published by the National Bank of Belgium, p. 82, '*en 1850, la Banque Nationale se présentait réelement comme le modile le plus parfait de banque d'émission sur le continent*'. See also p. 327, note 161, '*Voir les declarations du ministre des finances du Japon, comte Matsukata, lors de la réforme monétaire du Japon en 1881*'. 'In point of the perfectness of organisation and the well-regulated conditions of business management, the National Bank of Belgium stands highest'; my thanks to Hermann van der Wee. See also *The Centennial History of the Bank of Japan*, 1982, and K. Ishii, 'Establishment of the Bank of Japan and the Japanese Industrial Revolution', unpublished paper, 1986.

91. M. Matsukata, *Report on the Adoption of the Gold Standard in Japan* and *Report on the Post Bellum Financial Administration of Japan*.

92. See S. G. Checkland review of F. H. H. King, *Eastern Banking* and G. C. Allan, *Appointment in Japan*, *TLS*, 30 March 1984, p. 330.

93. See H. Mui, *The Management of Monopoly*, 1984.

94. Gen-ichiro Fukuchi, a well-known Shogunate official stationed at Yokohama, reported that:

> In those early days of port-opening everyone was groping in the dark, for no one was any wiser than anyone else about how to proceed. In Yokohama the two thoroughfares Honcho and Benten-dori were lined with shops displaying in a haphazard manner, lacquer-ware, porcelain, copperware, fancy goods, piece goods, and what-not somewhat in the manner of a bazaar today. In this respect foreign merchants fared no better. They had a foreign bazaar where

woollen and worsted fabrics, woollen and cotton mixed goods and haberdashery were all on view, so as to get a line on Japanese taste in merchandise (Anon., *Foreign Trade in Japan*, Tokyo, 1975, p. 14).

95. S. Okuma, 'The Industrial Revolution of Japan', *North American Review*, vol. CLXXI, 1900, p. 678 and p. 683.
96. Ibid, p. 684.
97. Putnam Weale, *The Re-shaping of the Far East*, vol. I, p. 444.

## 3 Engineers for Lighthouses, Railways, Telegraphs and Mines

1. See H. J. Jones, 'The Formation of the *Meiji* Government Policy toward the Employment of Foreigners', pp. 9–30; and H. J. Jones, *Live Machines*.
2. P. Francks, *Technology and Agricultural Development in pre-war Japan*.
3. The provision of pure drinking water came somewhat later, see Chapter 12, section 2, a bronze statute to Henry Palmer who helped to provide the first modern water system in 1887, was unveiled in Yokohama (*The Independent*, 1 May 1987).
4. W. W. McLaren, 'Japanese Government Documents'; the bureaux are listed in Imp. Notif. No. 60, 2 December 1880.
5. Note the early bicycle industry in Sakai City, Osaka, where metal workers (blacksmiths) previously involved in making cutlery and matchlocks, turned their attention to bicycle making. See (in Japanese) *Actual State of the Bicycle Industry in Osaka Prefecture – Production*, 1954, pp. 4–15; my thanks to Tetsuro Nakaoka for his help. For links between pre- and post-1868 industry see also Chapter 2, Section 4; Chapter 14, Section 3, and Chapter 15, Section 4.
6. Although not comprehensive, the best source, in English, for detailed information on the salaries and length of service in Japan of British engineers and others is H. J. Jones, 'The *Meiji* Government and foreign employees, 1868–1900', thesis; see also H. J. Jones, *Live Machines*, Appendixes 1 and 2.
7. Richard Henry Brunton (1841–1901) was one of the discontented foreign engineers, see Brunton ms. 'Pioneering in Japan' in W. E. Griffis papers, Special Collections, Rutgers University Library, New Brunswick, New Jersey, USA.
8. Albert Richard Brown (1839–1912) was a contented foreign employee who made a life-time's career out of serving the Japanese. The papers of Brown, MacFarlane and Co. are deposited in Glasgow University Archives (GUA).
9. H. J. Jones, '*Bakumatsu* Foreign Employees', p. 326.
10. R. H. Brunton, 'The Japanese Lights', p. 2.
11. The archives of D. & T. Stevenson are held at the National Library of Scotland, Edinburgh. Thanks to Quentin Stevenson for permitting access and to Patrick Cadell for the arrangements made.
12. Craig Mair, *A Star for Seamen*, p. 189.

13. Stevenson's Out Letter-book, NLS, 29 November 1871, p. 567.
14. Brunton, an Aberdeenshire man, had worked for P. D. Brown and later for John Willett, railway engineers in Aberdeen, before moving in 1864 to London to work in the office of W. R. Galbraith, engineer to the London and South Western Railway. Further details of Brunton's career can be found in the Brunton ms., 'Pioneering Engineering', WEG papers.
15. Munenori Terajima (1832–93) was an influential *Satsuma* man, a Minister for Foreign Affairs; see Appendix for biographical details.
16. Brunton explained:

    Our trip was begun on the 27th of November 1868 . . . although bays were entered and places visited which had not been surveyed, the voyage was completed without accident on 5th January 1869. The sites for fourteen lighthouses were visited and surveyed, their height above sea level measured; notes taken of the building material and labour obtainable at each, and other information procured (R. H. Brunton, 'Pioneering Engineering', WEG papers).

17. See R. H. Brunton, 'The Japan Lights', p. 4.
18. Mair, *A Star for Seamen*, pp. 190 and 191.
19. Stevenson's took care to match the parts sent, writing: 'The different parts have been type-marked and the hold and cornice plates on the dormant side of the lantern have been painted black. A spare cast iron vertical casing and three cross ones have been sent in case of breakage' (Stevenson Out Letter Book, 5 May 1871).
20. 'The three workmen who have been engaged to go to Japan leave on 3 April. Their names are John Russell, who was foreman of joiners at Messrs Milne; Thomas Wallace also from Messrs Milne, who is an iron welder and has been chiefly employed in lighthouse apparatus, and John Mason who is a mason and understands granite dressing etc.' (Stevenson Out Letter Book, 30 March 1869).
21. An early example of French lighthouse building in Japan and a lighthouse keeper's house can be seen at Meiji Mura, near Nagoya, Japan.
22. Lewis, Bush, *The Life and Times of the Illustrious Captain Brown*. See also papers of A. R. Brown MacFarlane, GUA.
23. The *Thabor* had been the first vessel to reach Shanghai after passing through the Suez Canal. See D. A. Farnie, *East and West of Suez*, p. 193.
24. The *Meiji Maru* was ordered from Robert Napier's yard on the Clyde. It was built along sailing-ship lines with auxiliary steam engines. By extraordinary good fortune the vessel has survived and is now being restored as a National Treasure in Japan. It can be seen in dry dock at the Tokyo Maritime University. One of its features is a magnificently decorated cabin for the Emperor.
25. E. G. Holtham, *Eight Years in Japan*, pp. 261–2.
26. Stevenson's Correspondence to, 30 September 1871.
27. See the translators introduction, S. D. Brown, *The Diary of Kido Takayoshi*, Vol. I, 1868–1871, p. XXXVI. Kido understood the importance of 'equating the Emperor with national power'.

28. *The Far East*, vol. V, no. 3, March 1874, p. 206.
29. Brunton was also responsible for the design and building of the first iron bridge in Japan, at Yokohama. This bridge with a memorial plaque (for pedestrians only), now straddles part of a four-lane highway. He also prepared plans for sewers, water supplies and railways.
30. B. H. Chamberlain (1891 edition) *Things Japanese*, pp. 265–6.
31. There was opposition from the enemies of modernisation, as well as from those like palanquin-bearers, pack-horse drivers and innkeepers who lived by the old system of transport.
32. See E. Aoki, 'Edmund Morell, 1841–1871, the Father of Japan's railway', *Look Japan*, 10 December 1984.
33. Enbutsu, *Discover Shitamachi*, p. 161. E. G. Holtham, *Eight Years in Japan*, pp. 209–12.
34. Morell's grave and that of his Japanese wife, who died within days of her husband, is in the foreigners' cemetery in Yokohama. It is tended by the Japanese Railway Association.
35. The Japanese had reason to be grateful to him for he appreciated that the Japanese, with their tender feelings, would have to set up their own training facilities and management systems. Accordingly he urged Okuma and Ito in these directions: they passed his suggestions to the Council of State. The Ministry of Industry was founded within six months; the Imperial College of Engineering set up within a year.
36. E. G. Holtham, *Eight Years in Japan*, p. 104.
37. Learning by copying was an important element in the year-by-year process of technical transfer, the Japanese noted that American machining on the locomotives was 'rather rough' while the British models 'were conservative in design though being excellent in machining'. See T. Nakaoka, 'On Technological leaps of Japan as a developing country, 1900–1940', pp. 1–25; see also F. H. Trevithick, 'Japan's Railway System', pp. 157–80.
38. Inoue understood the long-term importance of the railway as a necessary part of the modernisation process, but rapid progress was not possible. Until the mid-1880s the Japanese government was building only a modest 130 miles of track a year. Later on private companies, required to raise their own capital, were encouraged to enter the field.
39. As late as 1904 K. Inuzuka, then Director of the Imperial Railway Bureau, commented that 'as yet the use made of the railway by our people is still in its infancy', A. Stead, *Japan by the Japanese*, Section on Railways, p. 495.
40. J. H. Longford, 'England's record in Japan', p. 110.
41. J. Morris, 'Telegraphs in Japan', pp. 127–47; and J. L. Kieve, *The Electric Telegraph*.
42. On this occasion the *Nagasaki Express* reported matter-of-factly that 'Telegraphic Communication between this port and Europe through Siberia via Vlodivostock was established on Tuesday last.' *Nagasaki Express*, no. 98, 25 November 1871.
43. R. H. Brunton believed that he, together with G. M. Gilbert, was responsible for this line. See 'Pioneering Engineering' ms., p. 8.

44. E. G. Holtham, *Eight Years in Japan*, p. 57; and J. Morris, 'Telegraphs in Japan', pp. 140–1.
45. Private or government messages could be written in cipher 'such cipher to be either in ordinary figures or Roman letters, but a combination is not admissible'. (Copy of early government telegraph regulations, in *OM*.)
46. J. Morris, 'Telegraphs in Japan', pp. 144–5.
47. Ibid, p. 141.
48. The most useful contemporary account is C. Netto, then Professor of Mining and Metallurgy at the University of Tokyo, who wrote 'On Mining and Mines in Japan', pp. 1–55 in *Memoirs of the Science Department of the University of Tokyo*, Tokio, 1879 (copy in ULC, P.240.1.b.11.1).
49. In one government list of forty-seven mining employees, including those at the Head Office of the Ministry of Industry, twenty-four were French, twelve German and eleven British. See N. Kudo, 'The Modernisation of Japanese Non-ferrous Metal Mining – A Survey of the First Phase, 1868–1885', unpublished paper. My thanks to Norikazu Kudo, Faculty of Business and Commerce, Keio University, Tokyo.
50. As Netto has noted, 'mining and reduction works if they are to have any prospect of success, require much more than any other technical establishment to be adapted to local circumstances', C. Netto, 'On Mining and Mines in Japan', pp. 7–8.
51. Even with J. C. H. Godfrey as Chief Mining Engineer, British personnel played a relatively minor role in Japanese mines. Other Britons included Frederick Hayes who served as Secretary at 260*yen* a month from 1872 to 1876 and William Bell Davis an instructor, at 365*yen* a month over the period, 1873 to 1876.
52. M. Sumiya and K. Taira, *An Outline of Japanese Economic History*, p. 217.
53. C. Netto, 'On Mining and Mines', p. 7.
54. The miners, often conscripted men or convicts, worked in intolerable conditions. But note the report of Mr Furukawa, the owner and developer of Ashio Copper Mine, expressing practical concern for miners' welfare in A. Stead, *Japan by the Japanese*, p. 454.
55. British engineers worked at Sado gold and silver mine, on an island in the sea of Japan, offshore from Niigata. They were closely bound to their place of work and alone apart from the tiny group of compatriots. Of the British managerial staff at Sado, Erasmus H. M. Gower served as Ore Preparation Officer from 1869 to 1873 at 600*yen* a month. James Scott must have found conditions satisfactory for he remained from 1870 to 1881, at 280*yen* a month, as Instrumental Officer. Three British miners are listed at Sado, all recruited in 1873, namely James Dale (at 80*yen* a month) departed in 1874; John Simmons (also at 80*yen* a month) stayed until 1876, and Thomas Treloar, at 120*yen* a month, who remained until 1877. See N. Kudo, 'The Modernisation of Japanese Mines'.
56. O. and S. Checkland, 'British and Japanese Economic Interaction ... the Takashima Coal Mine, 1868–1888', pp. 139–55.

57. Frederick Antony Potter was appointed mining engineer in January 1871: he served for seven years often under hazardous, and occasionally dangerous, circumstances. His managerial position was never easy, as he constantly strove to modernise the mine and increase productivity, while a succession of other interests, both British and Japanese, often in conflict, struggled to obtain possession of what was believed to be an asset of great profit potential, Archives of Netherlands Trading Society, Box No. 5935.
58. For a discussion of the number of 'man-years' employed in the various fields, see H. J. Jones, *Live Machines*.
59. William Walter Cargill (1813–94); see Chapter 2, Note 40 above.
60. Richard Vicars Boyle (1822–1908) was an engineer on the railways earning $1250 per month while Thomas Arthur Binton who was also a chief engineer on the railways received $600 per month. Edmund Gregory Holtham was a civil engineer responsible for railway survey and construction and was earning $550 per month. But some 80 per cent of the men employed in the Ministry of Public Works received $200 or less per month for their services. Altogether the numbers of British being paid during the decade from 1872 to 1882 was a considerable drain on Japan's resources.
61. The series of articles published in *The Engineer* between 1896 and 1898 reveals a remarkable interest by a group of professional men under the heading *Modern Japan, Industrial and Scientific*; 'our special correspondent' reported under the following heads:

| | | |
|---|---|---|
| 27 November | 1896 | 1. Anglo-Japanese Business Relations |
| 11 December | 1896 | 2. The Government Inspection of Machinery |
| 8 January | 1897 | 3. The Yokosuka Dockyard |
| 15 January | 1897 | 4. Japanese Labour and Workmanship |
| 5 February | 1897 | 5. Electrical Work |
| 19 March | 1897 | 6. Locomotive Building and Purchasing with supplement showing 30 types of locomotive |
| 26 March | 1897 | engines for the Imperial Railway, Japan |
| 23 July | 1897 | 7. The Chances of the Foreign Engineer |
| 10 September | 1897 | 8. The Railways: (a) General Remarks |
| 17 September | 1897 | 9. The Representatives of Foreign Engineering Firms |
| 1 October | 1897 | 10. Machinery *versus* Agriculture |
| 8 October | 1897 | 11. Official Trade Commissions and Flying Business Visitors |
| 22 October | 1897 | 12. Bogus Manufacturers |
| 3 December | 1897 | 13. The Training of Engineers |
| 10 December | 1897 | 13. The Training of Engineers (contd.) |
| 28 January | 1898 | 14. The Projects of Engineering in Formosa |
| 4 February | 1898 | 15. The Patenting of Inventions |
| 11 February | 1898 | 15. The Patenting of Inventions (concluded) |
| 25 February | 1898 | 16. Japanese-made Machinery |
| 4 March | 1898 | 17. The Railways: (b) Statistics and forecasts |
| 11 March | 1898 | 18. Two Large Business Concerns |

| | | |
|---|---|---|
| 11 March | 1898 19. | The Foreign Advisers to the Japanese |
| 25 March | 1898 20. | General Summary and Conclusion |

62. *The Engineer*, 25 March 1989, pp. 271–2.
63. As Dyer explained:

> the railways which have been constructed in Japan were fully utilised to convey the materials and the ships to transport them overseas. The telegraphs were used to communicate instructions, and to keep the authorities informed regarding movements and requirements. The dockyards and shipbuilding yards were ready to undertake repairs and the arsenals and machine shops to turn out materials of all kinds as well as appliances which aid operations in the field. Light railways were laid down on the way to battlefields, and wireless telegraphy and telephones to convey instructions to the soldiers; in short all the latest applications of mechanical, electrical, and chemical science were freely and intelligently used, H. Dyer, *Dai Nippon*, 1905, p. 415.

## 4 The Makers and Operators of Ships

1. See C. A. Fisher, 'The Britain of the East: A Study of the Geography of Imitation', pp. 343–76.
2. See A. T. Mahan, *The Influence of Sea-power*. Mahan's works were to be a blueprint for American imperial expansion in the Pacific and in the Caribbean.
3. W. Laird Clowes, *The Royal Navy*, Vol. VII, 1903, p. 68.
4. Mahan refers to this 'In Japan, and as yet in Japan alone, do we find the Asiatic welcoming European culture, in which, if a tree may fairly be judged by its fruit is to be found the best prospect for the human race to realize the conditions most conducive to its happiness', A. T. Mahan, *The Problems of Asia*, p. 150.
5. W. Laird Clowes, *The Royal Navy*, Vol. VII, 1903, p. 84.
6. J. C. Perry, 'Great Britain and the emergence of Japan as a Naval Power', pp. 305–21.
7. There is an interesting and detailed report on the Japanese Imperial Naval College, its students, staff and curriculum in NMM. See NMM NOE 15A, 2 March, n.d. but probably 1905.
8. Seppings Wright, *With Togo*, pp. 15–19.
9. L. N. Pascoe, 'Britain's Contribution to Japanese Hydrography', in D. Shoji (ed.) *Researches in Hydrography and Oceanography*.
10. See Notebook of Admiral Pelham Aldrich written while commanding survey vessel *Sylvia* in Japanese waters, c.1878, NMM, ALD/2.
11. See Fred T. Jane, *The Imperial Japanese Navy*, pp. 234–41.
12. In 1905 the British Naval Attaché reported on Dock no. 4 which 'is now approaching completion' remarking that 'there is a great deal of cutting and slicing of the hillside to find room for any new establishment'. Sir Gerard Henry Ucted Noel (1845–1918) was Commander-in-Chief, China Station, 1904–6; for Yokosuka see NMM/NOE/15A, 2 March 1905.

13. For Kure see NMM/NOE/8A, 31 October 1905.
14. See B. L. Putnam Weale, *The Reshaping of the Far East*, vol. I, p. 396.
15. See Jentschura, H. *et al.*, *Warships of the Imperial Japanese Navy*; and A. J. Marder, *British Naval Policy, 1880–1905*.
16. There was intense competition in the 1880s and 1890s to produce high-quality armour-plate. Hayward Augustus Harvey produced a new type of armour-plate, accepted by the US Navy in 1891. The Harvey process consisted of enclosing a low-carbon steel plate at a high temperature between a mass of carbonaceous and non-carbonaceous material, the plate was then hardened on the carburised size and quenched in running water. John Browns, steel-makers in Sheffield, had simultaneously produced something similar which was more generally used in British shipyards. Krupp armour, made in Germany, was slightly different but also highly regarded.
17. The *Dreadnought* was nearly 18 000 tons, powered by the new steam turbines and fuelled with oil instead of coal to achieve a speed of 21 knots. Although many continued to think in terms of coal-fired ships, 'Oil is the very soul of future sea-fighting' as Tennyson D'Enycourt wrote in 1912, see *A Shipbuilders Yarn*, p. 79. They were armed with ten heavily protected 12-inch guns as well as with 12-pounder quick-firing anti-torpedo-boat guns. See A. J. Marder, *From the Dreadnought to Scapa Flow*, 1961.
18. NMM, Cover 274, Adm 138/336.
19. See A. Preston, *The Ship: Dreadnought to Nuclear Submarine*, HMSO, 1980. See pp. 33–6.
20. See W. D. Wray, *Mitsubishi and the NYK*, on which this section relies heavily.
21. For Yataro Iwasaki, see Wray, *Mitsubishi*, pp. 22–3.
22. R. C. Clark, *The Japanese Company*, 1979, pp. 22–3.
23. During the post-1868 interregnum, Yataro as a domain official, was operating a carrier's business with domain steamships. Later, in return for taking over the domain's debts, he was granted its assets, including steamships and camphor and silk-reeling enterprises. Iwasaki emerged as an astute business dealer accustomed to working closely with government authorities and foreign merchants.
24. Wray, *Mitsubishi*, p. 27.
25. By the end of 1874, the expedition's 'ships had made 24 voyages, transported three battalions as well as 5600 civilians, 45 000 bales of rice, large quantities of munitions and currency, including the idemnity of 500 000 *taels* (from the Chinese)', Wray, *Mitsubishi*, p. 51.
26. L. Bush, *The Illustrious Captain Brown*.
27. Sir Harry Parkes, the British Minister deplored the involvement of either British ships or British citizens in a punitive campaign mounted by the Japanese, Wray, *Mitsubishi*, pp. 51–2.
28. Toshimichi Okubo, then Minister of Home Affairs, was clearly won over, reporting that, Yataro Iwasaki 'operates a completely self-reliant enterprise', Wray *Mitsubishi*, p. 77.
29. Anon., *The Golden Jubilee of NYK*, 1935, p. 164.
30. See Wray, *Mitsubishi*, Part II, formation of NYK.

31. 'Report to President of NYK', 1886, A. R. Brown papers, GUA, UGD/172.
32. In the final phase of British service to NYK long-serving officers were often seconded to run the NYK London Office. *Golden Jubilee History of NYK*, pp. 164–5.
33. Henry Napier, shipbuilder on the Clyde, left an interesting description of a Japanese junk in 1886, in his 'Recollections of a Visit to Japan', handwritten ms, GUA, GD96.
34. In 1899 Admiral Lord Charles Beresford, a distinguished naval expert, reported on the Mitsubishi yards in Nagasaki, C. Beresford, *The Break-up of China*, pp. 410–11.
35. See S. Broadbridge, 'Shipbuilding and the State in Japan since the 1850s', pp. 601–13.
36. James Blair, 'The Japanese Mercantile Marine', p. 40.
37. The Glasgow connection with Mitsubishi at Nagasaki was then strong. It was noted on a visit in September 1981 that the archives at the yard held a remarkable contemporary collection of books on engineering and shipbuilding dating from the 1870s, including much by J. M. Rankine, and on the dock-side stood a large crane marked 'Appleby Ltd. No. 200, Glasgow 1909, load 150 tons'.
38. S. Broadbridge, p. 606.
39. The Osaka Iron Works started by building wooden vessels but soon graduated to iron and later steel ships. The firm together with the industry, suffered booms and slumps, these related to the wars with which Japan became involved, notably the Sino-Japanese war of 1894–5 and the Russo-Japanese war of 1904–5. The works flourished and with the introduction of shipping subsidies in 1896, Hunter felt sufficiently confident to expand to a works at Sakurajima in 1899 where he planned and built steel vessels. In 1911 despite a depressed state of trade, the Osaka Iron Works absorbed the nearby Innoshima Dock. Although the principal interest of the company remained shipbuilding, E. H. Hunter and his son, Ryotaro Hunta, were keen to diversify. By 1900 they were making cast-steel tubes for water mains, steel bridges and other steel components. The Company was reorganised as part of the Hitachi group in 1914. By 1915, as a limited company, it had contracted to build thirty-three ships with an aggregate weight of 147 700 gross tons. Hunter's drive and ambition made the Osaka Iron Works one of the success stories of the *Meiji* shipbuilding industry. For advice on Edward Hazlitt Hunter, 1843–1917, my thanks to Yukio Yamashita.
40. Craftsmen included James Fowler Mitchell (1829–1903) of Aberdeen, Scotland, 'Master Shipbuilder, for 44 years a resident of Japan' who had served in the shipyards of both Nagasaki and Kobe, and John Hill 'a native of Scotland and for many years an employee of the Mitsubishi Company' who died in 1900 at Nagasaki. See the gravestones in the foreigners cemeteries at Nagasaki and Kobe and Yokohama.
41. In 1888 J. G. Reid became Chief Engineer at Osaka Zhosen, responsible for planning and drawing. During his three-year service he succeeded in designing and supervising the building of steel ships of

7000 tons each. These included the *Chikugogawa Maru*, *Kisogawa Maru* and *Shinano Maru*. Mitsubishi recruited J.S. Clark as chief engineer; he was responsible for, among others, *Hitachi Maru*. (*Iwasaki Yanosuke Den* (*The life of Iwasaki Yanosuke*)) vol. 2, pp. 301 and 307.

42. J.F.C. Conn, *The Glasgow University Department of Naval Architecture 1883–1983*.
43. F. Elgar, 'Japanese Shipping', pp. 59–82.
44. Although Biles held the chair for thirty years, retiring in 1921, he had set up a consultancy in Naval Architecture in Westminster in 1907 and rarely lectured in Glasgow in person in later years. See entry for (Sir) John H. Biles in *Who Was Who, 1929–1940*, p. 111.
45. For example, the principal shipbuilding yards in Japan were attempting to make workable triple expansion reciprocating steam-engines during the second half of the *Meiji* period, as the table below shows. The vessels were all very small.

| *Shipyard* | *First iron vessel* | *First steel vessel* | *First construction of triple-expansion engine* |
|---|---|---|---|
| Mitsubishi Nagasaki | 1887 *Yugao-maru* 206 gross tons Double Expansion engine | 1890 *Chikugogawa-maru* 610 gross tons Triple Expansion engine | 1890 483 horse power |
| Kawasaki | 1886 *Yoshinogawa-maru* 380 gross tons Double Expansion engine | 1890 *Tamagawa-maru* 576 gross tons Triple Expansion engine | 1893 440 horse power |
| Osaka-Tekko | 1888 *Taiko-maru* 134 gross tons Double Expansion engine | 1890 *Kumagawa-maru* 558 gross tons | 1893 367 horse power |
| Ishikawajima | 1888 *Chokai* 731 gross tons Double Expansion engine gunboat | 1890 *Kamikawa-maru* 60 gross tons paddle steamer | 1902 |

*Source*: T. Nakaoka, 'On Technological Leaps of Japan as a Developing Country, 1900–1940', p. 6. The author is indebted to T. Nakaoka for his kind help.

46. Y. Fukasaku, 'Technology Imports and R&D at Mitsubishi Nagasaki Shipyard in the Pre-war Period', in *Silkworms, Oil & Chips* (ed. E. Pauer) (Bonn 1986).
47. S. Broadbridge, 'Shipbuilding and State', p. 607. See also detailed report of the Japanese Shipbuilding industry in *Japan Chronicle*, 3 August 1917 (copy in Diet Library, Tokyo).
48. On 15 May 1905 one of the British naval attachés, A.T. Jackson, wrote to report on the Tsushima action:

> I called on Admiral Togo at Sasebo and congratulated him on the great victory he had won for his country and said how proud I was at having been permitted to be present on such an occasion. I have never seen anyone so thoroughly happy. He sat and chuckled delightedly and . . . Admiral Kato also talked freely and I was able to get a good deal of information on points that I either knew nothing of or very little. I think the Japanese admirals were only too pleased to get someone to talk to. With their own officers so much 'strict Service' they may not be able to talk freely. Anyway they unbent to me. (A. T. Jackson, Naval Attaché, at sea aboard HIJNS Azuma.)

Although the British naval attachés *were* at sea with the IJN Captain John de M. Hutchinson reminded Noel 'the Japanese still wish the farce that no attachés are with the fleet to be kept up', Hutchinson to Sir Gerard Noel, NMM, NOE/15A, 21 January 1905.

49. Papers by Captain Hutchinson, 2 June 1905 and 4 August 1905, NOE/15A.
50. F. Elgar, 'Japanese Shipping', *JSL*, vol. III, 1893–5, p. 81.
51. G. N. Curzon, *Problems of the Far East*, p. 413.

## 5 Educators for Engineers

1. See C. R. Boxer, *Jan Compagnie in Japan, 1600–1817* and *The Dutch Seaborne Empire*, and J. J. Jones, '*Bakumatsu* Foreign Employees', pp. 9–30.
2. See H. J. Jones, 'The Formulation of *Meiji* Policy towards the Employment of Foreigners', pp. 305–27.
3. In theory the Japanese government liked the idea of help coming from scholars of different nationalities for it lessened their dependence on any one nation, but in practice, confusion over the foreign language in which subjects were taught led to conflict and duplication of courses in any one institution, K. Koizumi, 'Japan's First Physicists', p. 33.
4. See also J. R. Bartholomew, 'Japanese Modernisation and the Imperial Universities, 1876–1920', pp. 251–71 where the author writes:

> nor can the predominance of German professors in the Japanese Universities before 1900 be seriously challenged . . . During the *Meiji* period of the 120 foreign academics at Tokyo 46 [38 per cent] were German by origin . . . 30 faculty members were British and 12 were American [25 per cent and 10 per cent] . . . of 19 foreign professors of medicine 16 [85 per cent] were German, in Agriculture the Germans were 63 per cent of the total [12 out of 19]. They were also the largest bloc in law [7 of 23] and ranked second in letters and engineering [6 of 25 and 3 of 13 respectively]. Only in basic Science – where the British and Americans dominated – were the Germans poorly represented [2 among 21], p. 263.

5. A. Salam, *Address* (on Development).
6. The origins of the Imperial University of Tokyo are complex but are to be found in the following institutions: (a) *Daigaku* or University

founded (1630s) to offer a curriculum of the Chinese Classics and Confucian Studies. Later there was strife over what ought to be taught. This aspect of the university collapsed; (b) *Daigaku Nanko*, originally the descendent of the Institute for the Investigation of Barbarian books, and later was renamed the Institute for Enlightenment (*Kaiseisho*) University, South division in 1870 and was to specialise in Western Studies, this became a flourishing and important college; (c) Tokyo *Igakko* or Medical School was also part of the new foundation.

7. Tanakadate Aikitsu, an early physicist, recorded that W. K. Röntgen commented in 1898, 'It was certainly far-sighted of your country to class the engineering school on a level with the University. Although we are about to set up that sort of organisation [in Germany] obstinate old men of theology and law object to it as if they understand everything, and so we have been hindered by them', Koizumi, in *Historical Studies in the Physical Sciences*, vol. 6 (1975), pp. 3–100.
8. R. H. Smith was educated at the University of Edinburgh, won a class prize in Engineering but did not graduate. He was well regarded by Fleeming Jenkin, his Professor of Engineering. After 1878 Smith became Professor of Engineering at Mason's College, later the University of Birmingham. He failed in his application for the Chair of Engineering at Cambridge in 1890. See *Testimonials in Favour of Robert Henry Smith* (GUL Stack Y2 c.14, 1890). In 1894 he resigned from his Chair of Engineering 'without succeeding in convincing the council of the necessity of a more liberal policy toward the Engineering Department', see The Mason Science College, Birmingham, Minutes of Council, 1894 (University College 4/1/24). He subsequently took up consultancy work in London.
9. See R. H. Smith, *Testimonials* (GUL Stack Y2 c.14, 1890).
10. Professor R. W. Atkinson was an assiduous member of the Asiatic Society of Japan, see Bibliography for details of papers written for *TASJ*.
11. See the obituaries for Robert William Atkinson in *The Institute of Chemistry of Great Britain and Ireland*, *Journal and Proceedings*, February, 1930, p. 56, and *Journal of the Chemical Society* 1931, p. 1024.
12. It was Ewing's special gift to involve his students in his research, especially into magnetism and seismology, thus influencing the first generation of Japanese physicists. According to Aikitsu Tanakadate, one of a distinguished group attached to Ewing, this research commitment enabled Japanese, for the first time, to realise that they could themselves make original contributions to international learning. Ewing had a notable group of students, including Dr Ryintaro Nomaro, later director of the South Manchurian Railway, Dr Rynsaki Godai, a distinguished mining engineer, Tetso Tsuchida, Dr Shohei Tanaka and Dr Aikitsu Tanakadate. The two last-named later represented the Imperial Academy of Science in the House of Lords. See A. W. Ewing, *The Man of Room 40*, pp. 76–7.
13. J. A. Ewing, *An Engineer's Outlook*, [1933], p. XIII. See also A. W.

Ewing, *The Man of Room 40*; and *Proceedings of the Royal Society*. Obituary notices of FRS 1, 1932–5, James Alfred Ewing, 1855–1935, pp. 475–91. Ewing's Obituary was written by R. T. Glazebrook who quoted Ewing speaking of his Japanese students 'To an inexperienced teacher there was stimulus and help in pupils whose polite acceptance of everything put before them was no less remarkable than their quick intelligence and receptiveness . . . For quite half a century two or three of these Japanese youths of 1880 have kept in touch with me as a friend', p. 476.

14. Knott was awarded (1897) the Keith Prize of the Royal Society of Edinburgh for original work on magnetic strains. His publications included work on Electricity and Magnetism, and Physics of earthquake phenomena. Knott subsequently became General Secretary of the Royal Society of Edinburgh which placed him at the heart of the Edinburgh establishment. In this way academics from the University of Edinburgh served in important scientific posts for almost twenty years. Knott's *magnum opus* was his *Life and Scientific Work of Peter Guthrie Tait*. See *Who Was Who, 1916–1928*, p. 594.
15. Although the title 'The Imperial College of Engineering' (*Kobu dai Gakko*) is used here throughout, other translations were 'College of Engineering' or 'College of Technology'. There is a useful contemporary account of the College in *Nature*, vol. XVI, May 1877, p. 44.
16. It was noted that:

> This Engineering College with its substantial buildings, noble central hall, lecture rooms and laboratories has always been, and still is a source of envy on the part of Tokiyo Dai Gakko, or University which includes engineering and the branches of mining, metallurgy, chemistry, telegraphy as within its scope; but has to put up with a lot of rickety wooden shanties, crammed together in a corner, for its accommodation (E. G. Holtham, *Eight Years in Japan*) p. 220.

17. The functions of the Ministry of Public Works (*Kobusho*) were taken over in December 1885 by the Ministry of Communications (*Teishinsho*).
18. Imperial College of Engineering, General Regulations.
19. 7 *yen* per month was a substantial sum for many families. Even the lowliest British teacher at ICE received ¥130 per month, while Dyer's salary was ¥660 per month, see Table 5.1.
20. Henry Dyer (1848–1918) the son of John Dyer, was born in Bothwell near Glasgow. Perhaps his father later worked for Shotts Iron Works in Lanarkshire. Henry attended Wilson's School at the Works where Robert McNab his schoolmaster regarded him highly praising his 'uncommon perseverance and industry'. When he left school, after carrying off all the first prizes, he entered the offices of the Shotts Iron Company. Perhaps the family moved to Glasgow to give Henry more opportunities, at any rate he was apprenticed to James Aitken & Co., Foundrymen of Cranstonhill, Glasgow, in 1863 for five years. During this period Dyer also attended evening classes, incidentally at the same

time as Yozo Yamao, at Anderson's College in Glasgow. The College provided scientific and technical classes for artisans in Glasgow to supplement their practical knowledge with theory.

After his apprenticeship ended in the summer of 1868 Dyer applied to the University of Glasgow where John McQuorn Rankine, Professor of Civil Engineering and Mechanics, encouraged him to work for the Certificate of Proficiency in Engineering Science, originally introduced in 1862 and carrying the qualification CE which Dyer obtained in 1871. He then proceeded to qualify for the Glasgow MA and the newly introduced BSc degree which Sir William Thomson and Professor Rankine had been advocating and which was introduced for the first time in 1872.

In 1870 Dyer was successful in winning one of the Whitworth Scholarships, awarded by the Science and Art Department of the Committee on the Council of Education in London as a result of competitive examination, the first Scot to do so. It should be noted that Dyer won in the category for 'workmen' not 'student', see D. A. Low, *The Whitworth Book* (1926) p. 34.

During the later months of 1872 Ito, in the United Kingdom with the Iwakura Mission, was busy arranging for the appointment of staff for the projected Imperial College of Engineering to be opened in Tokyo. According to Laurence Hill, shipbuilder and marine engineer, and former partner to Rankine, Rankine chose Dyer 'as the fittest man for the post' to be Principal and Professor of Engineering. Testimonials were prepared by February 1873 to support his application. They came from Sir William Thomson (Lord Kelvin) (natural philosophy), Hugh Blackburn (mathematics), John Young (natural history), Thomas Anderson (chemistry) all from the University of Glasgow. Dyer had to make do with a warm tribute from McQuorn Rankine, dated May 1871, for Rankine had died suddenly, apparently of diabetes, in December 1872. It was claimed that Kelvin expressed doubts about Dyer's suitability for the principalship, see T. Constable, *Memoir of Lewis D. B. Gordon*, p. 225.

Dyer was appointed to head the ICE before he had taken the degree examinations. A special dispensation was given and early in 1873 he graduated BSc, the first Glasgow student ever to do so, having taken papers specially set for him. He sailed from Southampton for Japan in April 1873.

See Henry Dyer, *Testimonials*, Court Papers, GUA, and Henry Dyer papers, Mitchell Library, Glasgow; D. A. Low, *The Whitworth Book*, p. 151; Obituary in *Nature* (signed C. G. K. which must be Cargill Gilston Knott) 10 October 1918, pp. 109–10.

21. Dyer matriculated at the University in 1868, subsequently his classes were 1868–9 – in *classe physica*, in *classe mathematica*; 1869–70 – in *classe graeca*, in *classe scientiae machinalis*; 1871–2 – in *classe latina*, in *classe graeca*, in *classe physica*; natural history, class 1 zoology, 2 geology; 1872–3 – in *classe logica*, English language and literature class. (Note the entries in Latin.) See Class Lists, GUA.
22. Henry Dyer, as principal of the College was the primary designer of

the curriculum and the organiser of the courses. Yozo Yamao who had also experienced Glasgow academic courses almost certainly had a strong voice in the decisions, especially on the institution of a 'sandwich' course of theory and practice. Ito probably also advised. Hugh Matheson, who was friendly with Lewis Gordon, himself educated at the Royal Mining Academy in Freiburg and Ecole Polytechnique in Paris, certainly gave advice. Other staff, who with Tadeshi Hayashi, travelled out to Japan with Dyer, were also consulted. The Hochschule at Zurich which Dyer visited in 1882 on his return from Japan, was said to have been the inspiration of the ICE but surely the Glasgow pattern, the only one he knew from his own experience, was strong in Dyer's mind. The British staff were able to create a model engineering college in Tokyo. See also Lewis Gordon's letter to Hugh Matheson (T. Constable, *Memoir of Lewis Gordon*, 1877, pp. 225–8).

23. From the Dyer Collection, Mitchell Library, Glasgow. Letter to Dyer, 25 May 1882, from the Department of Public Works.
24. Divers was a Londoner, educated at the City of London School and then at the College of Chemistry (1852–3). At the age of 17, in 1854 he had been appointed assistant to Professor Rowney at the University College of Galway where he remained for twelve years, graduating MD there in 1860. Before being appointed to the staff of ICE as Professor of Chemistry, he had had a variety of stop-gap jobs as a lecturer. See J. Sakurai, obituary in *Journal of the Chemical Society transactions*, pp. 746–55.
25. William Edward Ayrton, 1874–1908, FRS. Ayrton read mathematics at UCL, and entered the Indian Government service; after a year with Kelvin in Glasgow he became Electrical Superintendent in the Indian Telegraph Department. Ayrton returned to London in 1878 to be Professor of Physics first at Finsbury Technical College then at City and Guilds of London Institute, and later still (1907) at Imperial College, the University of London.
26. Craigie left Japan in poor health in February 1876 and died shortly after returning to Scotland.
27. W. G. Dixon's book *Land of the Morning*, is inscribed 'to the present and former students of the Kobu *dai Gakko*, Tokiyo, this book is affectionately dedicated' and contains some useful insights into the College. W. G. features in *Clara's Diary* written by Clara Whitney. W. G. Dixon lived and worked subsequently as a Presbyterian Minister in Victoria, Australia and in Dunedin, New Zealand.
28. James Main Dixon, MA, St Andrews (1856–1933) travelled widely in the interior of Japan and wrote extensively in *TASJ*. J. M. Dixon took up the professorship of English at ICE at the beginning of 1880; he transferred to the College of Literature at the University of Tokyo in 1886 and remained there until 1892 when he left Japan. While in Japan he wrote *A Dictionary of Idiomatic English Phrases – Specially Designed for the Use of Japanese Students*. He was awarded the Fourth Order of Merit in 1888. J. M. Dixon later taught English and Far Eastern Literature Courses at Washington University, St Louis and

Southern California University at Los Angeles. He retired in 1911 having earlier become an American citizen, for further information refer to the Keeper of the Muniments, The University Library, St Andrews, Fife, Scotland.

29. John Perry, 1850–1930, graduated as Bachelor of Engineering (BE) at Queen's University, Belfast, 1870. He had also been a research assistant to Kelvin at Glasgow. Like Ayrton, Perry left Japan to return to teach at Finsbury, later the City and Guilds College and eventually at Imperial College, the University of London, 1907.
30. See L. K. Herbert-Gustar and P. A. Nott, *John Milne, Father of Modern Seismology*.
31. Fleeming Jenkin (1833–85) first Professor of Engineering in the University of Edinburgh, formed part of the network of those who advised the Japanese on the appointment of British scholars to engineering and scientific posts. He was a broadly cultured man, part of the intelligentsia of Edinburgh and a close friend of the Stevenson family, the lighthouse builders. R. L. Stevenson found him congenial company.
32. Thomas Alexander (1848–1933) was born in Glasgow and educated first at the Normal School. He studied at the University under J. M. Rankine, winning prizes in mathematics, mechanics, geology and civil engineering. He was granted a Certificate of Proficiency in Engineering Science (CE) in 1870. Alexander remained in Tokyo for seven years. In 1887 he was appointed Professor of Civil Engineering at Trinity College, Dublin, a post which he retained for thirty-four years. See *'School Record Volume'* of the *Engineering School of Trinity College, Dublin*, pp. 4–7.
33. Arthur Watson Thomson (BSc, Glasgow 1874) was recruited to fill Alexander's place in Tokyo but served less than three years before returning to Glasgow to become first Professor of Engineering at the re-organised Glasgow and the West of Scotland College. But Thomson became Professor of Engineering at the College of Science in Poona in 1891. A. W. Thomson and T. Alexander published textbooks jointly over many years.
34. Thomas Gray, CE, BSc, FRSE (1850–1908) held the position of Demonstrator of Physics and Instructor of Telegraphy at ICE for a period of three years, 'My duties were to lecture on Experimental Physics, on Electricity and to conduct the work of the Physical Laboratory.' See *Testimonials* in favour of Thomas Gray, BSc, FRSE as a candidate (i) for the Cavendish Professorship of Physics in the Yorkshire College, Leeds, (ii) for the Professorship of Natural Philosophy in the Queen's College, Galway, Ireland, Glasgow, 1885 (GUL, Kelvin Collection, Y2.C.13); also *Testimonials* ... for the Chair of Mathematics, Auckland, New Zealand, Glasgow, n.d. (GUL Kelvin Collection, Y1–m.20).
35. Joji Sakurai, a distinguished Japanese chemist, in his obituary of Edward Divers, comments 'Divers did not publish anything during his first seven years in Japan' because 'his professional duties (at ICE) were very heavy, he was constantly asked by Department of Public Works to undertake analysis of minerals, valuation of ores, assay of gold and sliver. He was

also constantly consulted about the chemical industry in Japan'. J. Sakurai, Obituary in *Journal Chemical Society*, pp. 746–55.

36. The details come from Henry Dyer, *Imperial College of Engineering*, General Report by the Principal 1873–7 (Tokei, 1877) held with other Dyer papers in the Mitchell Library, Glasgow.
37. Natsume Soseki made a sharp comment on J. M. Dixon's teaching 'I was often reproved by Professor Dixon for my wrong pronunciation in reading English poems or prose or for my dropping articles in writing an English composition. He asked such examination questions as "In what years was Wordsworth born and when did he die?" "How many kinds of Shakespeare folios are there?" and "Mention the works of Scott in chronological order". Such questions are of no use in the study of English literature', quoted in *The Introduction of Western Culture into Japan in the Age of her Modernisation*, supplement to *Tokyo Municipal News*, 1967, p. 7.
38. During the first year the series of books called *The Scientific Reading Book* was prescribed as being 'useful as familiarizing the students with not only facts but also words and expression which they will be frequently meeting with in their after studies'. Collier's *History of the British Empire* was adopted 'being from its subject matter calculated to awaken and sustain interest'. The senior class studied Goldsmith's *The Vicar of Wakefield* which 'unites a large number of excellences as a continuous prose composition', together with Sir Walter Scott's *The Lady of the Lake* which appealed because of the simplicity of its poetry. H. Dyer, *General Report by the Principal* (Tokyo, 1877). In this extensive report each professor wrote fully about his own department.
39. H. Dyer, *General Report* (Tokyo, 1877). E. Diver's report on chemistry teaching, p. 35.
40. There is some doubt as to when the laboratory was completed and available for service. Ayrton in his report of 1877 is critical of the laboratory facilities available to him. Yet Perry, his close friend and associate, refers to Ayrton's marvellous laboratory as existing in 1875.
41. J. Perry, *Central*, 7, 1910, 708. Note that Perry was writing in 1910 some thirty-five years after the time when the laboratory was built. See W. H. Brock, 'The Japanese Connexion, Engineering in Tokyo, London and Glasgow at the End of the Nineteenth Century' (Presidential Address, 1980), *British Journal for the History of Science*, vol. 14, no 48 (1981) pp. 229–43.
42. Perhaps the best explanation for the reasoning behind the demand for laboratory training comes from J. A. Ewing who, in his inaugural lecture on taking over the chair of Mechanism and Applied Mechanics at Cambridge in 1891, explained that

> the idea that the student should be brought face to face with things . . . laboratory training to tell how it stimulates interest, how it fosters exactness, how it creates habits of observation and of independent thought, how it makes the dry bones of a science start into life. Facts and principles learnt from the textbook or the lecture

table are colourless and dull: in the laboratory they become vivid and memorable' (J. A. Ewing, *The University Training of Engineers*) p. 14.

43. The Akabane Engineering Works (*Akabane seisakusho*) although founded with Dyer's advice and guidance may always have been intended as a government, rather than a College facility. George Cawley employed as a General Assistant at ICE from 1873 to 1878 referred to his activities 'at the workshops attached to the college and also at the Government Arsenal at Akabane', *Wood and its Application*, pp. 194–232.

44. The works were situated at the north-west corner of Shiba Park near Zojyoji Temple on land formerly occupied by the *Kurume-fief's yashiki*.

45. When completed the works consisted of:

| | |
|---|---|
| 1. Drawing office<br>2. Counting house | at present in part of the former *yashiki* |
| 3. Pattern shop | 65′ × 60′ |
| 4. Foundry | 120′ × 60′ |
| 5. Brass foundry | 40′ × 70′ |
| 6. Smithy no 1 | 55′ × 60′ |
| 7. Smithy no 2 | 76′ × 18′ |
| 8. Machine shop no. 1 | 200′ × 50′ |
| 9. Machine shop no. 2 | 120′ × 100′ |
| 10. Fitting shop | 200′ × 50′ |
| 11. Erecting shop | 280′ × 35′ |
| 12. Boiler shop | 100′ × 60′ |

H. Dyer, *General Report by the Principal* (Tokyo, 1877) the section on the Akabane Engineering Works, pp. 39–45, gives details of the establishment at that time.

46. There were also some forty workmen in the engineering laboratory in the College. Although Dyer was much involved with all aspects of the College, which, at least by some visiting Scots, was referred to as 'Dyer's College', his first love may have been the Engineering Workshops. Although many machines were imported he took special delight in those they made for themselves. As he reported 'In the foundry, for example, we made the cupolas from two old boilers, we had to use wooden moulding boxes until we could make iron ones, and all the ladles and other gear had to be made on the premises. Among our first castings was the gearing for two foundry cranes, and these were afterwards fitted and erected and have since been constantly in use.' It was a special pleasure for Dyer to report that Mr Henry Maudsley 'the well-known engineer' had earlier visited the works at Akabane and 'was quite astonished at the work we carried on'. Dyer, *General Report*, Section on Akabane Engineering Works, p. 39.

47. Professor Kenji Imazu, Department of Humanities, the University of Kobe, most kindly provided a copy of the Catalogue which he located in the Cabinet Library, Tokyo.

48. G. S. Brindley was engineering workshop manager at Akabane. His son, Henry Samuel Bickerton Brindley (1867–1920) was brought up in Japan and attended ICE as a student before returning to Japan as an engineer between 1895 and 1907, *Dictionary of Business Biography*, vol. I, 1984, pp. 448–50.
49. In 1881 the Akabane Engineering Works were prepared to make vertical marine engines which were described as 'small Double Cylinder Engines', fire engines, portable hand-cranes, stone breakers and ore crushers, light hand-winches, improved boring tools, foot lathes, improved timber frames (for sawmill use), hand and force pumps, hydraulic presses (for pressing linseed, cotton rape and other oil-seed) and ornamental gates and railings. See *Catalogue, Akabane Engineering Works*. Notwithstanding the apparent achievements, Japanese historians are more sceptical of the quality of the work at Akabane. M. Kobayashi writes 'but Akabane Machine Factory of the Industrial Department, with which an order was placed to manufacture 10 spinning frames each with 2000 spindles, had to suspend manufacture after completing one frame, as it turned out to be poor in quality', M. Kobayashi, 'Policy of Encouraging Industry', p. 35.
50. There is some doubt as to the status of the Akabane Engineering Works in 1880. From a translation *History of the Ministry of Works* [*Kobusho Enkakushi*] in T. Tsuchiya and H. Onchi (eds) *Collection of Materials of Economic and Financial History in the early Meiji* (*Meiji Zenki Zaisei Keizai Shiryo Shusei*) vol. 17 (Tokyo, 1931). 'The Workshops ceased to operate in March 1880', p. 307; 'Akabane Branch of the Workshops were closed and transferred to the Ordnance Department of the Navy', p. 308. The confusion and changeover may reflect the political power struggle going on in Japan in 1880 and 1881 during which Okuma was ousted by Ito and his Choshu faction. Making the Akabane Engineering Works into a political football may have strengthened Dyer's determination to leave Japan, which he did in the summer of 1882.
51. My thanks to Norio Tamaki and his colleagues at Keio University for interpreting the data for this map. The place of origin of each student is given in the reports on ICE.
52. W. G. Dixon, *Land of the Morning*, p. 365.
53. S. Hirokawa, 'Changing Japanese attitudes', p. 145.
54. In 1873, when chronically short of money for his education he enquired at:

    the School of Engineering and got a copy of their catalogue. Looking at it I found that there was not a word on how to govern the nation, which was what I had been learning through Chinese studies. There was nothing mentioned but such things as how to build a lighthouse or how to construct a bridge, or, say, how to put up electrical wires. 'It is meaningless to learn nothing but this sort of thing' I said to myself and lost all interest in matriculating (K. Koizumi, 'Japan's first physicists', p. 75).

55. Although engineers are not as a category differentiated, see S.

Yonekawa, 'University Graduates in Japanese Enterprises before the Second World War', pp. 193–218.

56. *ICE Calendar*, Session 1874–5, p. 13, Dyer papers, Mitchell Library, Glasgow.
57. One professor commented:

> Not content with attending classes most of the day, making their study encroach on the hours for recreation, and sitting in the common hall of the dormitory until the lights were put out, the more zealous would retire with their books to their rooms and when these also were left in darkness, crouch under the lights in the passages, dressed in their overcoats and mufflers to resist the cold night air (Dixon, *Land of the Morning*) p. 364.

58. Dyer, *General Report*, p. 33.
59. Graduates from the other Colleges of the University of Tokyo, 1890–1900 were: law, 1041; medicine, 352; literature, 530; and agriculture, 192. See A. Stead (ed.) *Japan by the Japanese*, p. 253.
60. W. H. Brock, 'The Japanese Connexion', pp. 229–43.
61. *Engineering Education in the British Dominions*, published by the Institution of Civil Engineers (1891) gives a useful survey of what was available.
62. A. Whitworth (ed.) *A Centenary History: A History of the City and Guilds College, 1885 to 1985*, pp. 95 and 96.
63. See D. Bell, *The Coming of Post-Industrial Society*, pp. 115–16 and 229–32.
64. Proclamation on Education issued in July 1872 by the Administrative Council, Tokyo, Japan.

## 6 British Life in Japan

1. Probably the best material on life in the Treaty Ports is in the Paul C. Blum Collection held by the Yokohama Archives of History, the kind help accorded there both in 1981 and 1984 was much appreciated. Two books help to set the scene, C. T. Marshall, *Letters from Meiji Japan* and Clara Whitney, *Clara's Diary*.
2. See J. E. Hoare, 'The Japanese Treaty Ports, 1868–1899: A Study of the Foreign Settlements', thesis.
3. For an American missionary's views see R. B. Peery, *The Gist of Japan*.
4. The Chinese soon made themselves a vigorous presence in the treaty ports.
5. W. G. Dixon, *The Land of the Morning*, ch. 5.
6. Hoare, 'The Japanese Treaty Ports', p. 7.
7. Glover & Co., Nagasaki, to Jardine's at Shanghai, 25 March 1869, JM, Nagasaki, B/10/4/578.
8. Hoare, 'The Japanese Treaty Ports' remarks that only the missionaries, the employees of the Japanese and various diplomats attempted to learn Japanese, p. 56.
9. Thomas Blake Glover became a trusted employee of Mitsubishi

bringing Western expertise and business acumen to their service in Tokyo and Nagasaki. Edward Hazlitt Hunter, after a hesitant start as a young man in Yokohama settled in Kobe where he became a pillar of the foreign establishment. His firm was the Osaka Iron Works. For E. H. Hunter, Shipbuilder, see Chapter 4, note 39.

10. John Reddie Black (1827–80) became a controversial figure editing the *Japan Herald* and starting up his own *Japan Gazette*. But as Altman has explained, 'Japan's new leaders used the press as an adjunct of government.' See A. A. Altman, 'The Press and Social Cohesion', p. 866.
11. Guide books in English, like *Murray's Handbook of Japan* are a mine of information.
12. S. Osborn, *A Cruise in Japanese Waters*, p. 24.
13. Hoare, 'The Japanese Treaty Ports', p. 57.
14. The steeply sloped cobbled streets are called the *Oranda–Zaka* or Dutch slopes. Glover's house, now the most famous of the foreigners' residences, is designated a National Treasure.
15. Foreigners claimed that 'the Guard houses erected last year, are unworthy attempts to restore the old Desima system'. *Nagasaki Express*, no. 80, 22 July 1871, Prefecture Library, Nagasaki.
16. Lady Lawson, *Highways and Homes of Japan*, p. 26.
17. E. J. Reid, *Japan*, Vol. 2, p. 3.
18. For some years British consular reports were addressed from Kanagawa although they were coming from an office in Yokohama.
19. W. G. Dixon, *Land of the Morning*, gives a vivid account of Yokohama in the 1870s, p. 244.
20. Signor Beato was a photographer sometimes employed by Wirgman to take pictures for the *ILN*, see 7 December 1872, p. 546.
21. J. Conder, 'Report on the Teaching of Architecture' in H. Dyer, *General Report of ICE*, 1877, p. 13.
22. 'Public-spirited Smith' for a time commanded the British detachment of Marines.
23. J. P. Mollison, 'Reminiscences of Yokohama', Lecture, 8 January 1909, p. 7 (copy in Yokohama Archives of History).
24. Ibid, pp. 4–5.
25. See Dresser, *Japan*, p. 4.
26. There are detailed accounts of maps and plans available (in Japanese) of town-planning and development of Yokohama.
27. D. W. Smith, *European Settlements in the Far East*, 1900, p. 31.
28. Westerners' houses, *Ijinkan*, usually featured a veranda, bay windows, and a red brick chimney. One of the grandest is that of Edward Hazlitt Hunter, with its delicate wooden pillars framing elaborate patterns on the astragals of the windows, see Chapter 14, Section 4.
29. The latter housed British, American and German families in Western-style houses with gardens. It was a convenience to take over *Yashiki* premises, for these former clan establishments were often large and provided buildings and grounds which could be relatively easily protected. See also C. T. Marshall, p. 4.
30. St Luke's Hospital is still on its original site. Nearby there is a

memorial set in a small garden to the first school established by Yukichi Fukuzawa (1835–1901), originally the *Okudaira* clan school, which later became Keio University.

31. E. Seidensticker, *Low City, High City*, pp. 36–42, the English architect T. J. Waters, designed the Ginza brick street.
32. Ishizaka, H., 'The Slum-dwellings and Urban Renewal', pp. 169–93.
33. Seidensticker, *Low City*, p. 59, it was hoped that the new brick-built Ginza would be more resistant to fire.
34. During his service in Japan he learned of the custom of Japanese peasants to seal a document with their thumb-print. His system, using the unique human fingerprint, of personal identification was adopted by the Japanese police on 1 April 1911. The memorial reads, 'Dr Henry Faulds (1843–1930) Pioneer in fingerprint identification lived here from 1874–1886'. Henry Faulds, Licentiate Faculty of Physicians and Surgeons, Glasgow, 1871 (Anderson's College, Glasgow); superintendent Tsukiji Hospital, Tokyo, 1874–86; author of *Nine Years in Nippon* (1885), *Guide to Fingerprint identification*, 1905; see also the *Medical Directory*, 1910, p. 621.
35. Niigata 'was a failure from the beginning'. Hoare, 'The Japanese Treaty Ports', p. 40.
36. Thomas Wright Blakiston, an English timber merchant, arrived in Hakodate in 1861. He was an invaluable contact for those whose curiosity, especially about the indigenous Ainu people, took them to the Northern Island. John Milne, Professor of Mineralogy, Geology and Mining at ICE, was a regular visitor to Hakodate. See L. K. Herbert Gustav, *John Milne*, pp. 110–11, and see bibliography for Blakiston's own articles.
37. The *Daily Advertiser*, Yokohama, 13 September 1875. Copies in the Yokohama Archives of History.
38. See the *Daily Advertiser*, no. 236, 8 October 1875. The *Japan Punch* also reported in November 1874, 'St Andrews Day, the Banquet wi' neeps', after which he of Islay sang a song in Gaelic which drew tears from the eyes of the editor of the '*Mail*', to conclude in the words of Burns, 'the taties was gran', the neeps were fine and we a' got fu'' (the potatoes were grand, the turnips were fine and we all got drunk).
39. *Japan Weekly Mail*, 10 November 1883.
40. *Daily Advertiser*, Yokohama, no. 162, 14 July 1875, and *Daily Advertiser*, no. 271, 18 November 1875.
41. Dresser, *Japan*, p. 9.
42. As W. G. Dixon explained, 'So continual were the removals, that auctions came to be an important feature in the foreign life of the city' (W. G. Dixon, *Land of the Morning*, p. 265).
43. C. T. Marshall, *Letters from Meiji Japan*, p. 75.
44. Prince Kitashirakawa drew admiring glances, as one lady noted, 'his jaunty moustache, such lively eyes and his black Hussar's uniform' so 'delightfully becoming to his elegant figure'. Marshall, *Letters from Meiji Japan*, p. 78.
45. Ibid, pp. 112–13 and A. W. Ewing, *The Man of Room 20*, p. 59.

46. But even on holiday the foreigners offended:

> The landlord, Mr Saiko does not like Europeans or Americans ... he sets his face against having them as guests in his hotel, because, while he takes great pride in having it clean and bright and in perfect Japanese order, they have not the good manners to take their boots off and behave as becomes the place (E. J. Reed, *Japan*, vol. 2, p. 307.

47. Lady Parkes was the first woman to climb Fujiyama, F. V. Dickens, *Life*, p. 287, but this may also have caused offence for mountains were regarded as deities and women, believed unclean, were forbidden to climb them.
48. G. Lowes Dickinson, *Appearances*, p. 120; see pp. 120–3 for a vivid account of Dickinson's ascent of Fujiyama.
49. A. W. Ewing, *The Man of Room 20*, pp. 60, 61.
50. The origin of the story has attracted much speculation, some believe the original 'Butterfly' was Tsuru Yamamura who married Thomas Glover, see M. Carnes, *Puccini*, 1974, pp. 125–6, see also J. P. Lehmann, 'Images of the Orient', English National Opera/Royal Opera House *Guide to Madam Butterfly*, 1984, pp. 7–14; and J. P. Lehmann, *Japan and the West in the Shadow of Madam Butterfly*, in Scottish Opera Programme for *Madam Butterfly* 1987; the author is indebted to Roger Witts for his help.
51. J. P. Mollison, 1909, p. 8.
52. Ernest Satow after his move to Japan refers to *musume* (girls) and *onna gochiso* (woman feasts) and how without these he became 'badly screwed'. G. A. Lensen, *The Russian Push towards Japan* etc., p. 19. See also the Catalogue of Exhibition on Satow in the Yokohama Archives of History.
53. Lensen, *The Russian Push towards Japan*, p. 6.
54. Francis Brinkley (1841–1912), see *The Introduction of Western Culture*, supplement to *Tokyo Municipal News*, 1967, p. 104.
55. The prefectural library at Nagasaki contained, in 1981, several photograph albums of the Glover family, other albums have since been deposited, see *Asahi Shimbun*, October 1986.
56. They were buried together in the foreigners' cemetery at Kobe where the headstone commemorates:

Edward Hazlitt Hunter
a native of Ireland,
Born December 3, 1843
Died June 1, 1915
For over fifty years a resident in Japan

Also his beloved wife
Ai Hunter
Born December 4, 1851
Died October 31, 1939.

E. H. Hunter built a fine house in Kita-nu, Kobe. It was removed to the corner of the Zoological Park and has been restored there. The original island site of Hunter's House can only now be distinguished by the cast iron letter H set at regular intervals into the small wall surrounding the property.

57. Tone was the daughter of the Abbot of the Hakodate Temple of Ganjo-ji, Hoikawa Jokyo, one of the pioneers of the development of Hokkaido. He, together with nearly 400 followers, had arrived in Hakodate to settle and found a temple. Apparently the marriage took place in 1881 in Rananza-ku Church, Tokyo. *John Milne*, p. 112 and Teiko Morimoto, *Tone Milne*, Tokyo, 1981.

58. The Conders were buried together at Gokokuji Temple, Tokyo. The simple memorial stone reads:

    Josiah Conder FRIBA
    Born 28 September 1852
    Died 21 June 1920

    and of his wife
    Kume Conder
    Born 16 December 1854
    Died 10 June 1920

    'Life's work well done, loving and true'

    This memorial was erected by Helen, their only child.

59. Satow's biographer, B. M. Allen, does not mention marriage; as far as the *Dictionary of National Biography* were concerned, Satow 'never married'. Yet Satow's dilemma was that of hundreds of other young men. In his case it would have been unthinkable for him to have continued in his chosen career as diplomat had knowledge of his Japanese wife become public. See *DNB, 1922–1930*, p. 748, *Yokohama Archives of History Catalogue of Exhibition on Ernest Satow*, 1984, which gives further detail on O'Kane Takeda (1853–1932); the author is indebted to Nobutashi Hagihara for his help.

60. Some left Japan. Josiah Conder's daughter, Helen, married a Swedish diplomat and lived mostly in Germany. T. B. Glover's daughter, Hana, married an Englishman and probably lived in London. Satow's son Eitaro, visited his father in England but because of chest trouble, settled in La Sal near Denver in the USA. There he changed his name to Alfred Satow, married Lucy and died in 1926. Ernest Satow is believed to have visited Eitaro at least once. Satow's second son, Hisayoshi (1883–1972) became Dr Takeda, a well-known botanist and a founding member of the Japan Mountain Climbers Association.

61. See E. H. Hunter, Shipbuilder, ch. 4, note 39.

62. J. P. Mollison, 'Reminiscences', p. 8; and C. T. Marshall, 'Letters', p. 55. Sadly, Lady Parkes went home to die, see *London and China Telegraph*, 26 November 1879.

63. See C. Haffner, *The Craft in the East* and various other papers. Despite the secrecy which is endemic in the Freemasons, help has kindly been given by the Right Honourable Earl of Elgin and Kincardine and Dr Charles Munn.

64. The first Japanese Freemason appears to have been Viscount Tadeshi

Hayashi, who was initiated into the Order at the end of the century while Minister in London.

65. The Hyogo and Osaka (Lodge No 498) (Scottish Constitution) in 1870, had twenty founding members. There were twenty-four founding members of the Star in the East (Lodge No 640) which was chartered in Yokohama on 1 May 1897. Other members were American or Canadian. These two lodges remain in existence today.
66. The Foreign Secretary insisted that the Japanese government's prohibition was 'aimed at political conspiracies and other analogous criminal efforts', and that this would not affect the activities of the Freemasons, whose 'benevolent efforts' he himself had judged during his residence in Berlin.
67. *London and China Express*, 25 July 1984.
68. Alexander Michie was sharply critical. A. Michie, *An Englishman in China*, vol. 2, p. 125.
69. J. E. Hoare, 'Japan undermines extraterritoriality', I. H. Nish and C. Dunn (eds) *European Studies on Japan*, pp. 125–9.
70. 'The system does not work well', H. Faulds, *Nine Years in Nippon*, p. 301.

## 7 The Iwakura Mission

1. C. Blacker, 'The first Japanese Mission to England'; see also *The Times*, 30 August 1865.
2. W. G. Beasley, 'The Iwakura Mission in Britain, 1872'; M. J. Mayo, 'Rationality in the Meiji Restoration, the Iwakura Embassy'; and A. A. Altman, 'Guido Verbeck and the Iwakura Mission'.
3. The British referred to 'the loud and fussy hospitality of America', *The Times*, 29 July 1872, and 'the bombastic reception given to the Japanese in America', *The Times*, 2 August 1872; see also Note 10 below.
4. Tomomi Iwakura, 1825–83, see biographical details in Appendix B, and *The Times*, 2 August 1872.
5. These men were all government ministers, Iwakura being Minister for Home Affairs, Kido being in the Ministry of the Imperial Household, and Ito, Minister of Public Works and Yamaguchi, Assistant Minister of Foreign Affairs. See also biographical details in Appendix B.
6. Other senior figures in the delegation included the former feudal lords of Choshu, Saga, Fukuoka and Kanazawa as well as two court nobles. For a list of the names and ranks of the officials of the Embassy see S. Mossman, *New Japan*, pp. 430–1.
7. As was noted 'the five young ladies represent five distinct families, aristocracy and wealth combined', S. Mossman, *New Japan*, p. 434.
8. M. J. Mayo, 'The Western Education of Kume Kunitake, 1871–6'.
9. J. E. Hoare, 'Japan Undermines Extraterritoriality: Extradition in Japan 1885–1899', in Nish and Dunn, *European Studies on Japan*.
10. See M. J. Mayo, 'A Catechism of Western Diplomacy: The Japanese and Hamilton Fish, 1872', pp. 389–410.

11. Kido wrote, 26 March 1872, 'We have already lost this round', S. D. Brown and A. Hirota (eds) *The Diaries of Kido Takayoshi,* vol. II, 1871–1874, p. 143.
12. It was unfortunate timing, the British ruling classes were in general on holiday, on the grouse moors of Scotland, *The Times*, 17 August 1872.
13. This is the caption on large picture showing Queen Victoria's farewell to the Embassy in Diplomatic Archives, Tokyo.
14. William G. Aston (1841–1911), interpreter at the British legation from 1862. Along with Satow and B. H. Chamberlain, Aston was regarded as one of the influential foreign scholars in *Meiji* Japan. He translated the *Nihongi* (1896) and wrote works on Japanese literature and Shinto.
15. Major General Alexander may have been Sir Claude Alexander (1831–99) of Ballochmyle, Ayrshire and Southburn, Renfrewshire, MP for South Ayrshire, 1874–85.
16. Lord Blantyre (1818–1900), seats at Erskine House, Renfrewshire and Lennoxlove, Haddingtonshire, Scotland, succeeded father, 1830, owned about 14 000 acres. See *Glasgow Post Office Directory*, 1881–2.
17. Kido, *Diary*, vol. II, p. 231.
18. The *Glasgow Herald* reported the visit of the ambassadors on 8, 9, 10, 11, 12 and 14 October 1872 and the *Scotsman*, 11 October 1872.
19. M. J. Mayo, 'The Western Education of Kume Kunitake', p. 30.
20. The *Scotsman*, 12 October 1872.
21. See Craig Mair, *A Star for Seamen*, pp. 133–4.
22. Commissioners for Northern lights, Edinburgh. Extracts from Board Meetings, 9, 14 and 17 October and 27 November 1872.
23. Kido, *Diary*, vol. II, 5 October, p. 226.
24. *Manchester Guardian*, 9 October 1872.
25. *ILN*, 1 October 1853. At the opening of 'the stupendous model mill' in 1853 the Mayor of Bradford eulogised the 'palaces of industry equal to the palaces of the Caesars'.
26. *The Times*, 28 April 1986.
27. As Brunton explained, 'Ito put himself under my wing', Brunton, 'Pioneering Engineering', WEG Papers, pp. 116–17.
28. Another small group, under the guidance of Provost Swan of Kirkcaldy, visited floor-cloth manufacturers and linen works. The visit of 'these distinguished Orientals caused a good deal of sensation in the district', the *Scotsman*, 12 October 1872.
29. Takato Oshima's career was remarkable. He worked on the problems of the reverberatory furnace before the restoration, examined the mining industry in Britain, as part of the Iwakura Mission, and subsequently struggled with the problems of iron-smelting at Kamaishi Iron Works, see Chapter 15 below, and E. Pauer, *Japan's Industrielle Lehrzeit*, p. 534, and S. Oshima, *Oshima Takato Gyojitsu (Life and Work of Oshima Takato)*.
30. S. Oshima, *Oshima Takato Gyojitsu*; my thanks to Kazuhiko Uejima for his work on the translation. *The Times*, 27 September 1872 (report from *Western Morning News*).
31. Kido commented particularly on the telegraph office, in London 'where 400 men and 700 girls crowd in to work daily . . . and this year's

profit amounts to £300 000. We saw metal tubes for sending messages and telegraphic equipment of a sort we had not previously observed.' On the post office, he noted that '2000 workers handle the business every morning and 800 come to work in the afternoons ... and its annual profit amounts to £1 410 000,' S. D. Brown, *Diary of Kido Takayoshi*, vol. II, pp. 217–18.

32. W. G. Beasley, 'The Iwakura Mission in Britain, 1872', p. 30.
33. *The Times*, 16 September 1872.
34. S. D. Brown, *Diary of Kido Takayoshi*, vol. II, 20 October 1872, p. 238.
35. Before the Restoration, 'The prohibition of Christianity is the first rule of the Tokugawa House ... the *Bakufu* can never ignore or overlook the evils of Christianity,' Tokugawa Nariaka to *Bakufu*, 14 August 1853; see D. J. Lu, *Sources of Japanese History*, p. 10.
36. *The Times*, 22 March 1870, and 6 and 16 March 1872. The reports of 6 March consist of a gruesome description of torture and crucifixion of Japanese Christians in Nagasaki and that of 16 March 1872 an apparent reference to the earlier report as inaccurate.
37. W. G. Beasley, 'The Iwakura Mission in Britain', October 1981, p. 30.
38. J. Pittau, *Political Thought in early Meiji Japan, 1868–1889*, p. 37.
39. Ibid, p. 42.
40. Marlene Mayo believes that over 200 industrial visits were made in all, M. Mayo, 'Western Education', p. 38.
41. Kido's *Diary*, translator's introduction, vol. II, XXVI.

## 8 Towards an Educational Philosophy

1. C. R. Boxer, *Jan Compagnie in Japan, 1600–1817*; and *The Dutch Seaborne Empire*.
2. Useful books include: M. Jansen, *Sakamoto Ryoma and the Meiji Restoration*; R. Dore, *Education in Tokugawa Japan*; R. F. Hackett, *Yamagata Aritomo in the Rise of Modern Japan, 1838–1922*; H. Passin, *Society and Education in Japan*; and J. Pittau, *Political Thought in early Meiji Japan, 1868–1889*.
3. See W. G. Beasley, 'Politics and the Samurai Class Structure in Satsuma 1858–1868', pp. 47–58; W. G. Beasley, 'Political Groups in Tosa 1858–1868'.
4. A. M. Craig, *Choshu in the Meiji Restoration*; and A. M. Craig, 'The Restoration Movement in Choshu' in Hall and Jansen, *Studies*.
5. There is material on the Foreign Office and the *Satsuma* clan in FO papers, PRO; in Sir Harry Parkes papers, ULC; see also Chapter 1, Section 4 above.
6. I. P. Hall, *Mori Arinori*, is the important source for this section.
7. For Mori's views as his career developed see Pittau, *Political Thought in early Meiji Japan*, especially, pp. 52–4, pp. 178–81 and pp. 260–1.
8. Hall, *Mori Arinori*, p. 54.
9. Ibid, p. 33.
10. See Chapter 1, section 8, note 74. The British also suffered casualties, see the memorial plaque in the Yokohama Archives of History,

formerly the British Consulate General, Yokohama. For an anti-British polemic, see E. H. House, *The Kagoshima Affair*.

11. When Mori was accepted into the school he became eligible for a clan stipend, thereafter he and others, who later emerged as *Meiji* leaders, were being supported by the clan.
12. Tomoatsu Godai (1835–85) – see biographical details, Appendix B.
13. Munenori Terajima (1832–93) – the commitment of Terajima to Western learning had been much strengthened when, before the attack on Kagoshima, he had been taken prisoner by the British and had subsequently been forced to watch the bombardment and resultant burning of Kagoshima from the relative safety of a British warship, see biographical details, Appendix B.
14. See Chapter 1, Section 4, Note 28.
15. See A. Taylor, *Laurence Oliphant*, pp. 57 and 129–30.
16. F. V. Dickens, a lawyer and old 'Japan hand', wrote vol. II of *The Life of Sir Harry Parkes*, being Parkes's life in Japan.
17. Hall, *Mori Arinori*, p. 80.
18. Ibid, p. 105.
19. W. P. Swainson, *Thomas Lake Harris, Mad or Inspired?*
20. Anne Taylor, the latest biographer of Laurence Oliphant describes Harris as an 'evil charlatan', p. 258.
21. See H. Schneider and G. Lawton, *A Prophet and a Pilgrim*.
22. Hall, *Mori Arinori*, p. 104.
23. Ibid, p. 114.
24. The Japanese government could not afford to dispense with the services of such men who were conversant with the West and spoke good English. Their interpretative skills later ensured relatively smooth relations with the outside world.
25. H. Mutsu, 'The Diplomatic and Consular Service of Japan'.
26. M. J. Mayo, 'A Catechism of Western Diplomacy'.
27. Kido commented that Mori's behaviour was 'the height of discourtesy'. See S. D. Brown and A. Hirota, *The Diary of Kido Takayoshi*, vol. II, 7 April 1872, and 15 April 1872.
28. Tatsui Baba (1850–88) publishing in London, in 1873, his *Elementary Grammar of the Japanese Language* deplored Mori's suggestion, writing 'There is not the slightest proof, about the impossibility of establishing popular education through our native speech.'
29. The *Japan Weekly Mail* fulminated, 'Mr Mori has proved himself so impractical and reckless a missionary in his educational views, that little apology need be offered for our having paid no attention in England to his vagaries', *Japan Weekly Mail*, 19 July 1873.
30. Hall, *Mori Arinori*, p. 251; this marriage however, was not successful.
31. See Appendix C and T. R. H. Havens, *Nishi Amane and Modern Japanese Thought*.
32. The founder-members of the Meirokusha included Yukichi Fukuzawa. In 1875 Fukuzawa had the *Enzetsukan* (*enzetsa* means public speech) built at the Mita Campus of Keio University. The *Enzetsukan* still stands, embellished with traditional *namako-kabe* black tile plates

set with white-mortar in criss-cross form. The interior is pure New England Meeting House.

33. The *Seiyoken* restaurant, mentioned in Griffis's *Tokyo Guide* of 1874, provided Western food. The restaurant survives but was moved long ago to Ueno Park.
34. See A. A. Altman, 'The Press and Social Cohesion during a Period of Change'.
35. E. Shimao, 'Darwinism in Japan, 1877–1927'.
36. See D. Duncan, *Life and Letters of Herbert Spencer.*
37. Mill published *Logic* (1843) and *The Principles of Political Economy* (1848). These were followed with *On Liberty* (1859) which emphasised the importance of the individual. These issues posed problems in Japan where conformity and consensus were believed to have higher value. In addition Mill's writing *On the Subjection of Women* (1869) secured for him an honoured place among those from all countries, including Japan, who sought to raise women's status in society.
38. Adam Smith's arguments were difficult for Japanese to understand and interpret at this time. It was the relatively simple work by John Hill Burton (1809–81) on *Political Economy* which Yukichi Fukuzawa incorporated into *Seiyo jijo* (*Conditions in the West*); see A. M. Craig, 'John Hill Burton and Fukuzawa Yukichi', Fukuzawa Memorial Center for Modern Japanese Studies, Keio University, Tokyo, 1984.
39. See S. Yamashita, 'Herbert Spencer in Meiji Japan' in H. Conroy *et al.*, *Japan in Transition*, p. 80.
40. J. D. Pierson, *Tokutomi Soho, 1863–1957*, ch. 4.
41. During his Harvard years as a law student in the 1870s Kentaro Kaneko was influenced by John Fiske, a former Professor of Philosophy. Through Fiske, who argued Spencer's theory of social evolution sympathetically, Kaneko came to understand Spencer's objectives. See also Kodansha, *Encyclopedia of Japan*, vol. 4, p. 138.
42. D. Duncan, *The Life and Letters of H. Spencer*, p. 161.
43. Ibid, quoting letters of 21 and 23 August 1892 (pp. 319 and 321) to Kaneko Kentaro.
44. *Pall Mall Gazette*, 26 February 1884.
45. This was a controversial posting, many senior men regarding Mori as a 'Westerniser Reprehensible'. Only Ito, with the Emperor's backing, was able to push the appointment through.
46. Hall, *Mori Arinori*, p. 397.
47. Graduates from the Imperial University unique until 1897 in having 'university status' were permitted to enter without further examination the ranks of the higher civil service.
48. All the attendance problems with which the Japanese struggled from 1872 had been experienced in Western countries during the nineteenth century.
49. The idea of bringing order and discipline into young lives was also popular in the West. But here the inspiration came from Sunday School teachers. The Boys Brigade and similar organisations which brought leisure and outdoor pursuits to countless youths were run through the Christian Church.

## 9 Students

1. The Emperor's 'Charter Oath' of April 1868, see R. Tsunoda, W. T. de Barry and D. Keene, *Sources of Japanese Tradition*, p. 644. See also D. Kikuchi, 'Sketch of Japanese National Development', PRSE vol. XXVII, part IV, 1907.
2. For the purpose of this study records have been searched at UCL King's and Imperial College, the University of London; the Universities of St Andrews, Glasgow, Aberdeen and Edinburgh in Scotland; the Universities of Manchester and Newcastle upon Tyne, several Colleges in Cambridge and Balliol College, Oxford. Because of the nature of the records kept, the University of Glasgow (GUA) has proved the most fruitful source. All the archivists are thanked for their kind help.
3. See Mr Kadono's comments during discussion, H. J. Edwards, 'Japanese Undergraduates at Cambridge University', *JSL*, vol. VIII, p. 56.
4. At Pembroke College, Cambridge, Koyata Iwasaki, the eldest son of Baron Yanosuke Iwasaki gave the name of his guardian as Viscount Hayashi, the Japanese Ambassador in London.
5. A. B. Mitford (Lord Redesdale) *Garter Mission to Japan*, 1906 pp. 255–6.
6. The third son of Tomomi Iwakura, who was staying in America and Europe between 1870 and 1878, attended at Balliol in the Hilary Term of 1874, but did not graduate. Tomotake Minami-Iwakura, 1st Baron – in Oxford for several years in the 1890s – graduating BA in 1895 and taking his MA in 1899. See *Balliol College Register*, pp. 81, 208 and 187.
7. The portrait as the frontispiece to J. H. Gubbins, *The Making of Modern Japan*, is of Prince Iwakura.
8. J. H. Gubbin's appointment as lecturer in Japanese was confirmed by a Decree before Congregation of the University of Oxford, 25 May 1909. His appointment had been preceded by that of J. H. Longford who had been Professor of Japanese at King's College, London, between 1903 and 1916/17. Longford had earlier served for many years in Japan as a Consular official.
9. See J. A. A. Stockwin, *Why Japan Matters*, Inaugural Lecture, University of Oxford, 27 January 1983; and G. Bownas, 'From Japanology to Japanese Studies', Inaugural Lecture, University of Sheffield, 14 December 1966.
10. The *Japanese Club at Cambridge*, Seventh, Eighth and Ninth Meetings, May and Michaelmas Term, 1891, and Lent Term, 1892, Cambridge, n.d. (GUL, Stack, Education R5-1916-C). *Japanese Club at Cambridge*, 1890–3, 6 issues (transactions of the 4th–11th meetings) bound in one volume, *Yokohama Archives of History* (Paul C. Blum Collection) 1226 [K.IV.35].
11. See E. F. B. Macalister, *Sir Donald Macalister of Tarbert*, p. 261. It is almost certainly Sir Donald's copies of the reports of the Society which are in Glasgow University Library.
12. See M. Sanderson, *The Universities in the Nineteenth Century*, 1975, p. 70, where under the heading 'Scottish Philosophy versus Cambridge Mathematics, 1836', Sanderson remarks that 'While philosophy was *a forte* in Scottish Universities, its study of mathematics was far behind

that of Cambridge and excessively philosophical rather than quantative in character. This held back Scottish mathematics-based sciences.'

13. J. Howarth, 'Science Education in late Victorian Oxford: A Curious Case of Failure?'.
14. D. Bennett, *King without a Crown*, p. 152.
15. James Stuart (1843–1913) the first occupant, resigned from the Chair 'after much quarrelling and discord'. Stuart advised, when Cambridge was looking for a replacement 'Try Ewing at Dundee, I can think of no one better, or so good.' See T. J. N. Hilken, *Engineering at Cambridge*, p. 105.
16. James Alfred Ewing (1855–1935) a Dundee man, had been educated at the University of Edinburgh. He came to Cambridge from Dundee where he had established engineering as a teaching subject. See J. A. Ewing, *An Engineer's Outlook*; and A. W. Ewing, *The Man of Room 40*.
17. J. Perry, 'Oxford and Science', *Nature*, 31 December 1903, pp. 208–14.
18. Dairoku Kikuchi (1855–1917); in England 1866–8 and 1870–7; attended University College Preparatory School; graduated BA at UCL in 1875. After returning from Cambridge in 1877 Kikuchi was appointed to the University of Tokyo, President of the university between 1898 and 1901; 1901–3 Minister of Education.
19. Suyematsu was elected to the Japanese Diet in 1890 and created Baron in 1895 and Viscount in 1907. He served in the government of 1900 as Minister of the Interior. Suyematsu wrote of his tutor at Cambridge 'who took much pains during my stay at Cambridge in teaching me English and Roman laws, as well as the law of nations'. Kencho Suyematsu, *The Risen Sun*, p. ix.
20. Manjiro Inagaki (1861–1908) from Hirado; attended University of Tokyo, had matriculated as a non-Collegiate student at the Michaelmas Term 1886, and was admitted to Caius College, January 1888, graduated BA 1889; Japanese Minister in Madrid and died there 26 November 1908. A copy of *Japan and the Pacific* is in the library of Gonville and Caius College, Cambridge; my thanks to Jeremy Prynne.
21. Paper by Alon Kadish (of the Hebrew University of Jerusalem), 'Schools of Economics at Cambridge c.1885', for section on Soyeda see pp. 34–6. Thanks to Professor Watarai, Meiji Gakuin University, for a copy of this paper.
22. Henry Fawcett had been appointed to the Cambridge chair of Political Economy in 1863. When he died in 1884 Alfred Marshall succeeded.
23. Juichi Soyeda (1864–1929). On his return home he became private secretary to the Minister of Finance and then at the age of 35, Vice-Minister. Later he served as President of the Bank of Formosa (1899) and then as founding President of the Industrial Bank of Japan (1902). He served in Okuma's cabinet in 1915. From 1893 he acted as Foreign Correspondent of the Royal Economic Society in London. See T. Johnes's *Obituary* in *EJ*, September 1929.
24. C. R. Ashbee's *Journal*, 1 November 1885, King's College Modern Archives, Cambridge.

25. For one volume of papers of the Cambridge Economic Club see Camb. C291.283 ULC, see also large brown box, Marshall papers, Marshall Library, Cambridge.
26. J. Soyeda, 'The Study of Political Economy in Japan', *EJ*, June 1893, pp. 334–9.
27. Nagotoshi Kuroda, was admitted to King's College in October 1907 but had to write to his tutor, Oscar Browning, 'I am terribly ashamed of the results of the Mays.' He spent the summer 'up in Cambridge and coached with Mr Mitchell' before taking the exams again – 'the Additionals' – in September. Unlike his older brother Nagashige Kuroda, who graduated BA in 1887, and MA in 1891, the younger Kuroda did not graduate. See Kuroda Correspondence, King's College Modern Archives, King's College, Cambridge, 28 August 1908.
28. *Japan Society 4th Annual Report*, Cambridge, 1888, frontispiece (copy in Yokohama Archives of History, cat. no. K.IV.35).
29. The *Independent*, 1 April 1987.
30. The University of London was founded by Royal Charter in 1836 with two constituent Colleges, University College (1828) and King's College (1831). The University as such was an examining and degree-awarding body. In 1898 the University of London's status changed and other suitable institutions were allowed to join. One important development was the formation in 1907 of Imperial College of Science and Technology which was created from elements of the old City and Guilds College, Finsbury, as well as the School of Chemistry, the Royal School of Mines and the Royal College of Science. The London School of Economics and Political Science was established in 1895.
31. Yakichi Nomura was known in Japan as Masaru Inoue.
32. For details of individual Satsuma students see T. Inuzuka, *Satsuma-han, Eikokuryugakusei* (*Satsuma students to England*), Tokyo, 1974, p. 174; the author is indebted to Tamotsu Nishizawa for his help.
33. On this occasion Williamson wrote 'These young men cannot avail themselves of the full laboratory course but wish to enter the laboratory as students for one year working three to four hours a day', UCL College Correspondence, 24 July 1865.
34. See 'The Japanese at the Copper Mines at Alderly Edge', the *Courier and Herald*, Macclesfield, 16 September 1865, and for the visit to the Britannia Ironworks in Bedford, *The Times*, 2 August 1865.
35. Sakurai's impressive performance was crowned in 1879 when he won the Companies Exhibition. Their clerk wrote:

> The Court has accepted Mr J. Sakurai nominated for the Companies Exhibition in connection with University College, London for 1879. The number of candidates is noted to continue small – it is strange that a Japanese should succeed as against English youths in a competition in Chemistry and Physics (College Collection, Letters, 20 August 1879, UCL).

36. See T. Inoue, 'The Story of the Introduction of Modern Economics to

Japan: W. S. Jevons and Seven Japanese Students', *Osaka Commercial University Review*, no. 54, 1979, pp. 95–115.

37. G. E. Davie, *The Democratic Intellect, Scotland and her Universities in the Nineteenth Century*.
38. Kanae Nagasawa (1852–1934) had been at school in Aberdeen, see A. Shewan (compiler) *Aspirat Adhuc Amor*, Aberdeen, 1923, p. 364; Nagasawa was also involved with Thomas Lake Harris, see P. Kagan, *New World Utopias*.
39. William Thomson is referred to throughout at Kelvin. Thomson was knighted in 1866 and became Baron Kelvin of Largs in 1892. Lord Kelvin's papers are held in the University of Cambridge Library (see D. B. Wilson, *Catalogue of Manuscript Collections*; also at the University of Glasgow, in the Library and in the Department of Natural Philosophy). Kelvin was a Scot by adoption, born in Belfast of Scottish parents. See S. P. Thompson, *The Life and Work of William Thomson*; A. G. King, *Kelvin the Man*, and J. I. Sharlin, *Lord Kelvin, the Dynamic Victorian*.
40. M. Sanderson, *The Universities in the Nineteenth Century*, p. 84.
41. A. G. Clement and R. H. S. Robertson, *Scotland's Scientific Heritage*, p. 127.
42. 'The appointment of Professor Lewis D. B. Gordon', University of Glasgow, Faculty of Engineering, privately printed, n.d., c.1980.
43. The Regius Chair of Engineering at the University of Glasgow was established in 1840. See G. J. N. Hilken, *Engineering at Cambridge University 1783–1965*. Regius Chairs were Crown appointments, now proudly held by Universities, but then imposed by government on conservative senates.
44. Founded as Anderson's Institution (1796) by Professor John Anderson it became Anderson's University (1828), Anderson's College (1877), then reorganised as Glasgow and the West of Scotland Technical College (1886). In 1912 it became the Royal Technical College, Glasgow, and then in 1956 the Royal College of Science and Technology. Its final metamorphosis came in 1964 when the Royal College of Science and Technology merged with the College of Science to become the University of Strathclyde.
45. Yozo Yamao (1837–1917) studied science and technical subjects at UCL London and Glasgow. He served in the *Meiji* government.
46. H. Dyer, *Dai Nippon*, 1905, p. 2.
47. For a discussion of the Royal School of Naval Architecture and Marine Engineering at South Kensington (1864) see *TINA*, vol. XVIII, 1877, pp. 361–78.
48. J. F. C. Conn, University of Glasgow, Department of Naval Architecture and Ocean Engineering, 1883–1983, privately printed, Glasgow, 1983.
49. Personal correspondence from Mr Koichi Katsura, Tokyo, 24 February 1987.
50. The Yamao family treasure planes and saws used by Yozo Yamao at Napier's Yard; my thanks to Shinichi Yamao for his kind help.
51. Class Prize Lists, 1881–2, GUA.

52. Court Minutes, 7 February 1901, GUA, the candidates in March/April 1901 were Sampachi Yukuzawa, Tatsuzo Kajima and Konji Satow, in September/October 1901, Tomochika Iwanae; Natsume Soseki was the examiner.
53. During his leisure hours 'he habitually rode on a modern motor cycle all over Scotland as a hobby, which at that time only rich and adventurous people could do'. Personal correspondence from Mr Koichi Katsura, Tokyo, 24 February 1987.
54. The University of Edinburgh did not attract Japanese students as did Glasgow. Fleeming Jenkin became the first holder of the Chair of Engineering in 1868. Koichiro Sugi studied there, learning Engineering Drawing after 1872. See Chapter 5, section 3 above.
55. The federal Victoria University originated in Manchester in 1880. Liverpool joined in 1884 and Leeds in 1887.
56. Armstrong College was the scientific and technical College in Newcastle but was part of the University of Durham. See E. M. Bettinson, *The University of Newcastle, 1834–1971*.
57. The English believed that engineers should be trained in the works and on the job, see Sanderson, *Universities in the Nineteenth Century*, p. 110.
58. Sir Henry Enfield Roscoe (1833–1915) a chemist; educated in London and Heidelberg; close friend of Bunsen; Professor of Chemistry at Owens College, Manchester, from 1857 to 1887; author with Schorlemmer of standard treatise on Chemistry; knighted in 1884. H. E. Roscoe, *The Life and Experiences of H. E. Roscoe*; see also M. Sanderson, *Universities*, pp. 79–80; Roscoe's book, *Lessons in Elementary Chemistry* (1871) was translated into Japanese in 1876, as *Rosuko Shikagaku*; see K. Fujii, 'Atomism in Japan', p. 154.
59. M. Sanderson, *Universities*, p. 109.
60. H. E. Roscoe, *The Life*, pp. 113 and 114.
61. On 18 February 1879 Professor Roscoe presented a paper by one of his Japanese students, Mr Sadama Ishimatsu, 'On the Chemical Investigation of Japanese Laquor (sic) or Urushi', see *Memoirs and Proceedings of Manchester Literary and Philosophical Society*, 1882, pp. 249–61. Another Manchester student 'Ichikawa, who studied Physics under the late Professor Balfour Stewart in Manchester, was a man of much originality', S. Okuma, *Fifty Years of New Japan*, vol. II, p. 255.
62. See *Durham University Journal*, 23 May 1885, quoted in Sanderson, *Universities*, pp. 166–7, for a list of the remarkable range of technical experts produced at the Newcastle College.
63. M. Sanderson, *Universities*, pp. 215–16, for Joseph Chamberlain's role in achieving the Faculty of Commerce, see B. M. D. Smith, *Education for Management*, p. 1.
64. British Universities resisted the idea of formal 'doctoral programmes', wherever research students were accepted it was done informally.
65. Koizumi, 'Japan's First Physicists', p. 77.
66. See *Japan Biographical Encyclopaedia*, 1961, p. 1832 and B. Baker, *The Forth Bridge*.
67. Kelvin papers, NB168, ULC, 25 June 1904.

68. Shida's correspondence with Kelvin, Kelvin papers, S126–S130, UCL.
69. See Y. Markino, *A Japanese Artist in London*, 1910, for the most revealing study of a Japanese student's life.
70. Quoted in *Entrepreneurship: The Japanese Experience*, Electronics Industries Association of Japan, no. 3, Tokyo, June 1982, p. 10.
71. T. J. N. Hilken, *Engineering at Cambridge*, p. 97.
72. J. A. Ewing, *Inaugural*, 1891, p. 15.
73. Baelz believed that the Japanese thought of Western science as 'a machine which can without further ado be transported from the West to any other part of the world there to continue its labours', S. Hirakawa, 'Changing Japanese Attitudes to Western Learning', *Contemporary Japan*, vol. XXIX, September 1968, pp. 145–50.
74. See Hirakawa, vol. XXIX, 1968, p. 140; and Koizumi, 'Japan's First Physicists', p. 98.
75. A. K(uwaki), *Nagaoka Anniversary Volume*, p. iii.
76. In 1911 when Rutherford proposed the nuclear atom he had not 'looked up' the paper or heard of the model which Nagaoka had prepared in 1903, K. Koizumi, 'Japan's First Physicists', p. 94.
77. For a self-evaluation of modern Japanese science see Anon., 'Japan (1): On the Threshold of an Age of Big Science', *Science*, 2 January 1980, p. 32.
78. S. Hirakawa, 'Changing Japanese Attitudes to Western Learning', vol. XXVIII, *Contemporary Japan*, vol. XXVIII, no. 3, May 1966, p. 560.


## 10 In the Shipyards


1. A. J. Marder, *British Naval Policy 1880–1905*: A. J. Marder, *Old Friends; New Enemies*.
2. S. Pollard and P. L. Robertson, *The British Shipbuilding Industry, 1870–1914*.
3. M. S. Moss and J. R. Hume, *Clyde Shipbuilding from old Photographs*, 1975; *Workshop of the British Empire*.
4. D. Dougan, *The History of North-East Shipbuilding*.
5. F. E. Hyde, *Liverpool and the Mersey*.
6. M. S. Moss and J. R. Hume, *Shipbuilders to the World, Harland & Wolff*.
7. See A. Slaven, *The Development of the West of Scotland, 1750–1960*; J. L. Carvel, *Stephen of Linthouse*; Moss and Hume, *Workshop of the British Empire*; J. Burrow (ed.) *Denny, Dumbarton*; G. B. Hunter and E. W. De Rusett, '60 years of Merchant Shipbuilding on the North-east Coast', *TIESS*, vol. 52, 1908–9, pp. 323–46, *Scientific Survey of North-eastern England*; M. Dillon, *Palmer's Shipbuilding and Iron Company Limited*.

8. Captain J. M. James, sent as 'the Mikado's Navigating Lieutenant' to guide HIJMS *Takachiho Kan* in 1886 from the Tyne to Japan, 'flatly refused to take her to sea without sails'; the shipbuilders agreed to 'rig stay sails' and the vessel steamed away, S. Mavor, *Memories of People and Places*, pp. 236–7.

9. D. L. Burn, *The Economic History of Steel-making, 1867–1939*, 1940, and P. L. Payne, *Colvilles and the Scottish Steel Industry*.
10. E. C. Smith, *A Short History of Naval and Marine Engineering*; J. Guthrie, *A History of Marine Engineering*.
11. J. Briggs, *Naval Administration*, p. 306.
12. R. Appleyard, *Charles Parsons*.
13. As J. A. Ewing wrote, 'The *Turbinia*'s performance at Queen Victoria's Diamond Jubilee was as amazing as it was audacious'. J. A. Ewing, *The Man of Room 40*, p. 106.
14. I. Jung, *The Marine Turbine*, Part I, *The days of Coal and Steam, 1897–1927*, p. 15.
15. See A. J. Marder, *Fear God and Dread Nought*, and *From Dreadnought to Scapa Flow*.
16. W. Ashworth, 'Economic Aspects' pp. 499 and 504; and E. W. H. Tennyson D'Eyncourt, *A Shipbuilders Yarn*, on Jacky Fisher, Chapter IX.
17. F. E. Hyde, *Cunard and the North Atlantic, 1843–1973*.
18. The name of 'K. Kawada serving from January 8 to March 2, 1915' does appear in the Apprentice Time Book of Simon Lobnitz, but this is exceptional, GUA, UCS 4/7/1.
19. The only reference, in English, to Yamao's studies in Glasgow comes from Henry Dyer, *Dai Nippon*, p. 2.
20. In the case of the father, Riokichi Kawada, the following commendation has been found:

> Lobnitz & Co. — Slip Dock, Renfrew
> Engineers & Shipbuilders — Scotland
> Renfrew — 24 May 1884
>
> This is to certify that Mr Kawada Riokichi has served us as an Engineering Apprentice, from September 1877 to this date, and has gone through all the various branches of Patternmaking, Engineering as well as Drawing Office departments. He has during all this period always given us the greatest satisfaction, both as to character and ability.
>
> We consider him a first rate workman, as well as a very good draughtsman, with a very good knowledge of all branches connected with Marine Engineering, and he has always performed the work entrusted to his care, with great ability and to our entire satisfaction.
>
> As he is now leaving us in order to join a Steamer as junior Engineer, going to the East, he carries with him our very best wishes, and we can confidently recommend him as a most trustworthy, honourable, intelligent and industrious young man, and feel sure he will give the greatest satisfaction to any one that may require his Services or any place of trust.
>
> LOBNITZ & CO.

My thanks to Michio Amano, historian, of Hakodate, Japan, for this reference. In addition Rio Kitch Kawada [*sic*] attended the Engineering Department of the University of Glasgow (Matriculation no 1826) in Office and Field Work in Engineering from November 1878 to May 1879, the Certificate states that 'he attended with great regularity, that he behaved with propriety in the class; that he showed great ability . . .', GUA.

21. For this type of training see E. W. H. Tennyson D'Eyncourt, *A Shipbuilder's Yarn*, p. 29.
22. See W. D. Wray, *Mitsubishi and the NYK, 1870–1914*, pp. 26 and 487.
23. Taizo Shoda spent seven years in Glasgow. His father (writing 26 March 1919) to 'Mr Brown' (A. R. Brown's son) 'how much I appreciate the value and guardianship and direction' accorded to Taizo (A. R. Brown papers, GUA, UGD 172/5/1/3).
24. Haramiishi subsequently worked for Mitsubishi at Kobe, also served at Shimonoseki and in Tokyo. Obituary, *TNECIES*, vol. 52, 1935, pp.142–3, J. Clarke, believes there may have been Japanese apprentices (possibly Wadagaki?) and suggests apprenticeships of three or four years at a cost of 450. Personal letter to the author, 16 June 1986.
25. Douglas Vickers noted:

    > Captain Iwamoto visited these works today with a party, five of his officers and inspectors, and made himself extremely pleasant . . . he also told me that the number of men he would want to place in Works is very limited, in fact only ten altogether . . . we could no doubt take say four of the men here.

    But Vickers adds 'before we decide I should like to have your private opinion in the matter', Vickers Archive, ULC, Vickers Film, Reel no. 307.
26. On 10 March 1912 William Weir wrote to Admiral Fujii at the Admiralty, Tokyo, Japan:

    > I have to acknowledge receipt of your wire of 16th requesting us to allow Lieutenant Yoshihara to come here as an Apprentice. I have discussed this matter fully last week with Commander Makihara, and arranged that your friend will come here for a certain length of time and then we will give him further experience in other Marine Engineering Works, as you can understand we have a large number of your Countrymen now in the Works, and this is entailing a very large amount of trouble to our Foremen to properly instruct them, as we are anxious that they should learn as much as possible. Accordingly, it is difficult for us to extend this practice, and in addition, the apprentices here do not obtain very much experience as they are kept largely at one particular job. We will accordingly see that your friend has a year of apprenticeship in this country which will be of real value and service to him, and trust that this will be satisfactory (Sir William Weir papers, GUA, D3/5/16), p. 2.

27. See W. J. Reader, *The Weir Group*.
28. Diplomatic Archives, Tokyo; my thanks to Sakae Tsunoyama for this reference.
29. Hume and Moss, *Beardmore*, p. 104.

30. P. Fitzgerald, *Memories of the Sea*, pp. 289–91.
31. See G. Blond, *Admiral Togo*.
32. The *Fuso*, a 3714 ton battle cruiser, with Togo on board, left London in February 1878.
33. S. Pollard and P. L. Robertson, *The British Shipbuilding Industry*, p. 131.
34. J. Russell, *Very Large Ships*.
35. K. C. Barnaby, *The Institution of Naval Architects, 1860–1960*.
36. D. K. Brown, *A Century of Naval Construction*.
37. Copy of draft contract for 'an Unarmoured Ship of War', contract, Sir W. G. Armstrong, Mitchell & Company Limited; my thanks to Tyne & Wear Archives Service for the use of these records.
38. J. H. Biles, memo on visit to Japan and China, October 1895, GUA, ASRS, UCSI/21/85.
39. J. D. Scott, *Vickers: A History*; and R. C. Trebilcock, *The Vickers Brothers*.
40. Vickers Archives, ULC, Reel No 307.
41. GUA, William Denny, Contract Envelopes, Ship no 796–797.
42. Dr S. Yokota in correspondence with William Denny's, Dumbarton, ASRS, GUA, UGD 3/5/0422.
43. Vickers Archive, ULC, Reel no 307, 24 September 1903.
44. One member of the firm wrote:

    > I am especially pleased because such a visit will give the Japanese officers a real insight into what Vickers really are and what they can do and . . . I feel certain that if you treat them well all the reports which these fellows make to their masters here and to their people in Japan will have great weight on the Japanese authorities and that your kindness and attention will not be thrown away (Vickers Archive, ULC, Reel No 307, 29 June 1903).

45. See Marder, *Old Friends, New Enemies*, ch. 1, p. 32.
46. Direction for Naval Construction, Cover Number 4, Cover Number 175, Admiralty Collection 138/20, Ships, NMM; my thanks to D. J. Lyon for advice and help.
47. After the Russo-Japanese War naval decisions were increasingly made on political grounds. Marder, *From Dreadnought to Scapa Flow*, vol. I, *The Road to War, 1904–1914*, p. 234.
48. Admiral of the Fleet Sir John Fisher (First Sea Lord from 21 October 1904 to 25 January 1910) apparently objected to the Anglo-Japanese Alliance, 'the very worst thing England ever did for herself.' Quoted in Marder, *From Dreadnought to Scapa Flow*, vol. I, *The Road to War*, p. 235.
49. Marder, *From Dreadnought to Scapa Flow*, vol. I, *The Road to War, 1904–1914*, Admiralty Mss, pp. 235–6.
50. The governments of Australia, New Zealand and Canada, disliked the Anglo-Japanese Alliance fearing the threat of the 'Yellow Peril', of Japanese arriving as immigrants.
51. Quoted in Marder, *The Road to War, 1904–1914*, p. 238.
52. Marder, *The Road to War, 1904–1914*, p. 239.

## 11 Japanese Life in Britain

1. Most accounts in English of the experience of Japanese in Victorian and Edwardian Britain are guarded and reticent, but for a frank account see Y. Markino, *A Japanese Artist in London*, and *My Recollections and Reflections*.
2. *The Mikado* was given in Yokohama once only (under a different title) and was never performed again in Japan before the Second World War. For the Japanese response to the opera see Y. Kurata, *1952, Nen London Nihonjin Mura* (*The Japanese Village in London, 1885*) Tokyo, 1983, pp. 151–7. My thanks to Takeshi Hamashita and Naoki Watanabe for their help.
3. W. S. Gilbert, *Original Plays*, 1928 edition, p. 177.
4. In 1844 parliament had passed a law requiring railway companies to run one train a day, each way, at a cost of 1 penny a mile, to enable working people to travel cheaply.
5. Military bands in Britain were instructed not to play catchy arrangements of *Mikado* tunes in the presence of visiting Japanese dignitaries.
6. Soseki Natsume, distinguished Japanese writer in London between 1900 and 1912, was unhappy; for his time in Pitlochry, Perthshire see M. Inagaki, *Soseki and his Journey in England* (in Japanese) Tokyo, 1987.
7. A. Lloyd, *Everyday Japan*, p. 268.
8. King's College on the Strand was judged by Hammond to be in a less salubrious part of London.
9. Parkes papers, ULC, Correspondence, Hammond to Parkes, 9 December 1866.
10. Ibid, 20 August 1867.
11. Barr & Stroud Visitor's Book at Barr & Stroud, Anniesland, Glasgow.
12. F. T. Jane, *The Imperial Japanese Navy*, pp. 284 and 255.
13. Information kindly provided by his granddaughter, Professor Hide Ishiguro, Barnard College, USA.
14. See cover of M. Kita, *Pioneers of Making Japan International*.
15. Sir Edward Holden, *Diary*, Midland Bank Archives, 26/8, 5 March 1909; my thanks to Edwin Green for this information.
16. Midland Bank Archives, ref. Y61/11, York City and County Bank, Ossett Branch, annual report 1904. Mungo was the waste produced in a woollen mill from felted cloth, or from tearing up old clothes. It was used in making cheap cloth.
17. H. Mutsu, 'The Diplomatic and Consular Service of Japan'.
18. See Kurata, *1885, Nen London Nihonjin Mura* (*The Japanese Village in London, 1885*).
19. *The Times*, 10 January 1885.
20. *ILN*, 21 February 1885.
21. *ILN*, 9 May 1885.
22. A. R. Brown Papers, GUA, UGD/172.
23. Ibid, UGD/172/1/2.
24. Professor K. Mitsukuri to Professor D'Arcy W. Thompson, FRS, University College, Dundee, correspondence dated 1 August 1896 to 21 February 1901, nos 16230–16241 Special Collections, St AUL.

25. Obituary Dr Motoreru Haramiishi, *TNECSS*, vol. 52, 1935, pp. 142–3.
26. H. J. Edwards, 'Japanese Undergraduates at Cambridge University', *JSL*, vol. VII, 1904–7, 1908, p. 54.
27. H. J. Edwards, p. 54.
28. Private correspondence, copy in GUA.
29. Masataka Taketsuru was very proud of his Glasgow University connections; he studied organic chemistry in 1919. He founded Nikka Whisky company in 1934 and established a malt whisky distillery, stone-built and red-roofed, at Yoichi, Hokkaido.
30. Dr Samuel Cowan (1871–1918) had graduated MB, ChB, from the University of Glasgow in 1903.
31. See 'Love Letters of a Japanese' edited by Marie Stopes, under the pseudonym 'G. N. Mortlake'; M. C. Stopes, *A Journal from Japan*; R. Hall, *Marie Stopes: A Biography*, 1977.
32. Buyata Iwata (BSc, 1893) and Riotaro Hunter (BSc, 1893) both lived for some years with Miss Jessie Strickland at 4 Vinicombe Street, Hillhead. In the early 1880s Naomoto Takayama, Kiyoshi Miname as well as Rinzaburo Shida all lived at 18 Markland Terrace, Hillhead (now Oakfield Avenue), with Gavin Whitelaw as landlord. My thanks to Masami Kita who searched the archives for these addresses.
33. Unfortunately no citation for Dr Sakurai has been found in GUA.
34. See *TIESS* for 1902 and *Report and Abstracts of International Engineering Congress*, Glasgow, 1901 (GUL I1.q16).
35. The Japanese representatives were Viscount Vice-Admiral Enomoto, Tokio [*sic*], I. Fujiko, 56 Tiamokubo, Azabo, Tokio, H. Hara, Tokio University, Admiral S. Sasoa, The Admiralty, Tokio. See *Report and Abstracts of International Engineering Congress*, 1901.
36. Yozo Yamao, the first Japanese, as student and apprentice in Glasgow, may have been consigned by Hugh Matheson in London to Colin Brown with whom he lived at 5 West Regent Street, Glasgow.

## 12 Networks, Commercial and Academic

1. If the Japanese had no trustworthy network they were in danger of being deceived by rogues and charlatans. See *The Engineer* (1896–8) no 12, 'the use of the engineering catalogue to deceive' and the 'Bogus Manufacturers' (22 October 1897); no 11, 'Official Trade Commissioners and Flying Business Visitors' (8 October 1897), and no 19, 'The Foreign Advisers to the Japanese' (11 March 1898).
2. To use the middle man in this way was no new thing, see Chapter 2, note 36.
3. See Chapter 10, note 39.
4. There could be problems of bribery and industrial espionage, see Chapter 13 below.
5. See M. M. Matheson, *Memorials of Hugh M. Matheson*, 1889.
6. Glenfield & Company, *Minute Books*, Strathclyde Regional Archives, TD 500.
7. Waterworks whether in Tokyo, Yokohama or elsewhere in Japan,

were undertaken in the 1880s and 1890s partly because of the impact of fever epidemics on increasingly crowded urban areas.

8. Charles Scott Meik (1853–1923); born and educated Edinburgh; employed by T. F. Sharp, a harbour construction engineer; passed the national public surveyor examination. He went to Japan in 1887 and was employed as Harbour Engineer by the Japanese government. Meik prepared two important reports, on *Hokkaido Harbours* (November 1887) and on *Ishikari Navigation* (October 1889); the latter included a note on the transport of coal from Sorachi. Both these reports are held in Sapporo Prefecture Archive. My thanks to Akio Ishizaka. See also C. S. Meik, 'Around the Hokkaido'.
9. The firm were in a close working relationship with Kennedy's Patent Water Meter of Kilmarnock who paid one-third of Mr James's salary and expenses. *Glenfield Minute Book*, 8 December 1892, pp. 300–1, Strathclyde Regional archives, TD 500.
10. Glenfield's arrangements were made with Mitsui & Co. in London on 9 January 1893.
11. Was the inspection 'extremely rigorous and unreasonable'? see *The Engineer*, 'Modern Japan, Industrial and Scientific, no. 2, The Government Inspection of Machinery' (11 December 1896).
12. See W. K. Burton, 'Sanitation in Japan'. Dr John Henry Tudsberry, BSc (1889), DSc (1895) was Chief Assistant Engineer of the Yokohama Waterworks for the Imperial Japanese Government between 1885 and 1888, see Addison, *Roll of Graduates*, p. 617.
13. During the disagreements Mr Meik suggested that Mr Trevithick of the Japanese railways, should be appointed as arbitrator. This suggestion was not taken up. *Glenfield Minute Book*, 4 July 1895.
14. *Glenfield Minute Book*, December 1900, p. 270, gives the principal features of the agreement with Mr Kawakami.
15. John Brown & Company Limited, GUA, UCS1/21/85b (letter 6).
16. See *Kodansha Encyclopedia of Japan*, vol. 6, p. 98.
17. See *The Engineer*, 'Modern Japan', no. 9, 'The Representatives of foreign engineering firms' (17 September 1897) where it is stated that 'Government work ... is nearly all in the hands of a small clique of wealthy Japanese merchants' (p. 267). See also Anon., *The 100 Year History of Mitsui & Co. Ltd.* (Tokyo, 1977) p. 32.
18. The information on Messrs Takata is scrappy and comes from archives other than those of the company itself.
19. See Chapter 10, note 42.
20. William Denny Contract Envelopes for *Hirafu Maru*, no 796, and *Yamura Maru*, no 797, GUA, ASRS UGD3/5/0422 and UGD3/5/0423 respectively.
21. Alexander Stephen's were sometime associates of William Denny and made the ships' engines.
22. The Imperial government of Japan appointed Honorary Consuls in Liverpool (1 August 1889) and Glasgow (25 May 1889) 'in consequence of the increasing importance of the commercial relations between Japan and Britain'. See*Kakkoku-chuzai-Teikoku-Meiyoryoji-ninmen-kankei-Satsussen* (miscellaneous papers relating to appointments and

dismissals of honorary consuls in various countries) – Glasgow File, M2-1-0, 14-30, Diplomatic Archives, Tokyo. There was also for a time an Honorary Consul for Japan in Middlesbrough. See H. Matsu, 'The Diplomatic and Consular Service of Japan', *JSL*, vol. VII, 1907, p. 448.

23. A. R. Brown's papers, GUA, UGD 172/5, following Brown's death in 1913, two other members of the firm served as consul. They were A. Scott Younger, BSc, MINA, 1913–35, and Urquhart F. Burrell, 1935–41.
24. In 1900 the ship-designing side of the firm was strengthened by the recruitment of George McFarlane, a consulting engineer and naval architect. Thereafter the firm was called A. R. Brown, McFarlane. See newspaper clipping obituary C.1908 in A. R. Brown papers, GUA, UGD 172/5.
25. A. R. Brown, McFarlane Sales Catalogue, C.1912. A. R. Brown papers, GUA, UGD 172/5.
26. See Ward's *Directory of Darlington ... Middlesbrough*, Newcastle, 1899, p. 611 and Kelly's *Directory of Middlesbrough*, 1887, p. 31.
27. James Lord Bowes (1834–99) whose hobby was to collect Japanese art and artefacts. He became known as 'Japanese Bowes'. G. A. Audsley and J. L. Bowes published books illustrating a high quality collection. This was dispersed shortly after his death, being sold at auction by Branch and Lecte of Liverpool in May 1901. The sale raised about £10 000; for further information, B Guinness Orchard, *Liverpool's Legion of Honour*, 1893, privately printed (copy in the University Library, Liverpool); 'An interview with "Japanese Bowes"', *Pall Mall Gazette*, 1889; and Baedeker, *Great Britain for Travellers*. My thanks to Mrs Sylvia Lewis, Honorary Secretary of the Gateacre Society, Liverpool.
28. *Manchester City News*, 8, IV, 3 January 1920; my thanks to Douglas Farnie for his help.
29. *The Times*, 30 August 1865.
30. As Hirubumi Ito said, 'Yes, I was one of Mr Matheson's boys. I owe him a great deal and I shall never forget his home at Hampstead though it is thirty-one years since I saw it', *Westminster Gazette*, 4 March 1895.
31. Letter from Rinzaburo Shida to Kelvin, 28 July 1880, Kelvin Correspondence, ULC.
32. J. Harris and W. H. Brock, 'From Giesson to Gower Street: Towards a Biography of Alexander William Williamson (1824–1904)'.
33. *The Times*, 30 August 1865.
34. Harris and Brock, 'Giesson to Gower Street', p. 125. See note 105, Mrs Williamson's Journal, 20 February 1874.
35. Report of *Fellows Dinner* speech by Dr Sakurai, 3 April 1937, pp. 3–4, UCL Archives.
36. Notwithstanding Sakurai's testimony, Williamson did not remain a productive scholar. As Harris and Brock have explained:

    The session ending with his appointment to the Chair of General Chemistry (1855) was the last in which he published papers upon the results of investigations by himself, or carried out at his instigation with the notable exception of those carried out by Sakurai in 1880 (J. Harris and W. H. Brock, 'From Giessen to Gower Street', pp. 117 and 125).

37. Herbert-Gustar and Nott, *John Milne*, p. 144.
38. 'William Thomson, Lord Kelvin', *Dictionary of Scottish Business Biography*, pp. 190–2.
39. *Kelvin Centenary Oration and Addresses Commemorative* (Glasgow, 1924) pp. 69–70, GUL 18.a.25.
40. Quoted in S. P. Thompson, *The Life and Work of William Thomson*, p. 18; for Kelvin's patents see pp. 1275–7.
41. James White was closely associated with Kelvin producing many of the latter's patent instruments and developing prototypes. He held an appointment as instrument-maker to the University of Glasgow. In 1900 the firm's name became Kelvin & James White Ltd; see also Stratten's, *Glasgow and its Environs*, pp. 108–9.
42. D. J. Bryden, *Scottish Scientific Instrument Makers 1600–1900*, p. 15.
43. Thompson, *The Life and Work of William Thomson*, p. 19.
44. Alfred Ewing, already employed in Japan, had written privately to Kelvin to advise him of the intended request. Kelvin papers, K2, ULC, from T. Kato, 27 January 1883.
45. The appointment was through Arinori Mori, then Japanese Minister in London. After dealing with the Knott matter Mori continued his correspondence with Kelvin. One letter (22 July 1884) requested Kelvin to receive Baron Dairoki Kikuchi who was about to visit the United Kingdom. Kelvin papers, 11 April 1883 and 22 July 1884, Add 7342, M165 and M166, ULC.
46. Kelvin papers, 28 July 1880, ref. S.126, 8 July 1881, ref. S.127, 10 March 1883, ref. S.128 and 16 May 1883, ref. S.129 ULC.
47. Koizumi, K., 'Japan's First Physicists', p. 78.
48. Kelvin papers, R. Taguchi, President of the Lord Kelvin Association, Utsunomiya Middle School, Japan, 17 November 1906, T1 and T2, Add MS 7342, ULC.
49. Hugh B. Sutherland, 'Rankine, his Life and Times', Rankine Centenary Lecture, the Institution of Civil Engineers.
50. W. J. M. Rankine, *Manual of Applied Mechanics*, [1858], pp. 8–10.
51. See W. J. M. Rankine, *Memoir of John Elder*.
52. In 1878 Dyer had submitted a paper entitled 'The Education of Civil and Mechanical Engineers' to the Institute of Civil Engineers in London. The paper gave the substance of Dyer's experience at the Imperial College of Engineering in Tokyo and by inference praised the achievement there. Dyer also recommended that the money for such education should 'come from the Imperial Exchequer' (p. 41). The paper was perhaps an attack indirectly not only on the piecemeal provision of technical education in the UK but also on those in the Institute who were anxious to maintain the pupillage system. The Institute declined to hear Dyer's paper. Subsequently, in 1880, he published it, prefacing the paper with an attack on the Insititute which would he hoped be awakened 'to a proper sense of its duty'.

53. Chapter 9, Section 4, note 49.
54. The printed *Testimonials* prepared for Dyer's applications for the Chair of Naval Architecture in 1883 and 1886 are in the Court Minutes, 21 September 1886, GUA.
55. See *Testimonials*, pp. 31–2; extract from *Glasgow Herald*, 15 May 1886.
56. See A. R. Buchan (ed.) *A Goodly Heritage: A Hundred Years of Civil Engineering at Strathclyde University, 1887–1987* (Glasgow, 1987).
57. From Professor Sakuro Tanabe, 'a distinguished graduate of Kobu-dai-Gakko', Dyer and his family received many kindnesses. Tanabe was in Glasgow in August 1904 talking to Dyer about editing 'The History of Industry in the *Meiji* Era'. Professor Tanabe also wrote the obituary in October 1918 for the *Osaka Mainichi News*. Fragments of Tanabe Correspondence, University of Tokyo Archives.
58. Japanese students continued to take the preliminary entrance paper in Japanese in subsequent years. Those taking this option included Konji Satow (1902); Edward Hunter (1905); Shigeya Kondo (1905) and Taizo Shoda (1912). This list is not comprehensive, material from GUA.
59. Dyer, *Evolution of Industry*, p. 182.
60. There is no reason to doubt that it would be possible to build up a fuller picture of the Japanese connections in other 'skill centres'. For example, at Newcastle upon Tyne where there were:

    > immense stores of bituminous coal, as well as Armstrong Whitworth & Co, Swan Hunter, Wigham Richardson & Co. The turbine manufacturing enterprise of Charles Parsons was situated adjacent to the Newcastle upon Tyne Electric Supply Company's (NESCO) Carville A power station. Blast furnaces, engineering works, chemical plants and brick and tile works all added to the industrial activity of the region (T. P. Hughes, *Networks of Power*, p. 454).

61. Sir Henry Enfield Roscoe (1833–1915); see chapter 9, note 64.
62. See Chapter 14, note 33.

## 13 Licencers and Licensees

1. See Ian E. Inkster, 'Meiji Economic Development in Perspective'; Inkster, *Japan as a Development Model?*; and Inkster, *Science Technology and Late Development Effect*.
2. H. J. Jones, *Live Machines*, pp. 12–14.
3. See Chapter 2, Section 5.
4. Ito, in 1872, in Glasgow, requested Rankine to supply 'a key person to give assistance to Japan to build a steel works where weapons could be manufactured'. Rankine explained 'that what Japan needs are iron ore exploitation specialists, steelwork experts and processors and that an independent nation should have an institute which would train these men'. The Imperial College of Engineering resulted. See S. Fujita, *Gojuikunen mae no Kobu Daigaku ni tsuite no Kioku* (*Recollections of the Institute of Technology some Fifty Years Ago*).

5. D. Dougan, *The History of North-East Shipbuilding*; P. McKenzie, *W. G. Armstrong: The Life and Times of Sir William George Armstrong, Baron Armstrong of Cragside*; R. C. Trebilcock, *The Vickers Brothers: Armaments and Enterprise, 1854–1914*; J. D. Scott, *Vickers: A History*.
6. The material used here comes from 'Memorandum on Japanese Business', 5 June 1909 (Tyne & Wear Archives Service ref. 31/7772) and 'Report on the condition of the KKN *Seikosho*' (TWAS, ref. 31/7806). Other Armstrong references come from the Armstrong Minute books (AMB); my thanks to Richard Potts for his help.
7. The *Meiji* government invested heavily in Hokkaido, partly to give resettlement opportunities to displaced *samurai* and partly to forestall the Russians.
8. I. L. Bird, *Unbeaten Tracks in Japan*, Letter XXXV, p. 221.
9. The works were laid out as far as possible on level ground, although the hills encroached. Smithy, hammer shop, power shop, steel-smelting furnaces and a press house were all planned.
10. W. G. Armstrong became Sir W. G. Armstrong and then Sir W. G. Armstrong, Mitchell & Co. Ltd (1883); later, in 1897, with the takeover of the Manchester engineering firm of Sir James Whitworth, the firm became known as Armstrong, Whitworth & Co. Ltd.
11. Vickers, Sons & Co. Ltd, became Vickers Sons & Maxim Ltd (1897) and Vickers Ltd (1911); Vickers & Armstrongs amalgamated in 1927.
12. AMB, 8 October 1908 (ref. 130/1267). Report on the condition of the KKN *Seikosho*, ref. 31/7806.
13. By October 1908, when Lord Rendel was himself about to depart for Japan, the Directors of Armstrong's asked 'that Mr John Noble be requested to prepare a return showing the nature and extent of our financial arrangements in Japan', TWAS, ref. 31/7806.
14. The British were critical of the naval arsenal at Kure.
15. Report, F. B. Trevelyan, Report on KKN *Seikosho*, TWAS, ref. 31/7806, n.d.
16. My thanks to Yukiko Fukasaku for the use of her paper 'Technology Imports and R&D at Mitsubishi Nagasaki Shipyard in the pre-war Period', presented to the European Association of Japanese Studies, Paris, September 1986, p. 17. The firm of 'Nesdrum and Co.', boiler-makers, has not been traced.
17. W. J. Reader, *The Weir Group: A Centenary History*. Some of the Weir papers, including Sir William Weir's letter books, are held in GUA.
18. Kawasaki was a major manufacturer of ships and machinery. It was originally Kawasaki Tsukiji Shipyard (1878); the Kawasaki Hyogo Shipyard was opened in Kobe in 1886. The two firms merged in 1896.
19. It was James Weir who first became involved in heating feed-water for the ship's boiler Reader, (*The Weir Group*, pp. 4–5). James George Weir (born 1886) studied in Germany working at Nord Deutsche Maschinen and Armaturen Fabrik, Bremen, and later at Freiburg Academy (Reader, *The Weir Group*, p. 27).
20. See Reader, *The Weir Group*, p. 8.

21. William Douglas Weir (1877–1959), First Viscount Weir of Eastwood. The papers of Lord Weir of Eastwood, post-1918, are held at Churchill College, Cambridge.
22. E. C. Smith, *A Short History of Naval and Marine Engineering*, p. 220.
23. Reader, *The Weir Group*, p. 33.
24. Ibid, pp. 34–5.
25. W. Weir to Noltenius 27 December 1911, GUA, DC/96/1/7; Noltenius worked for Nord Deutsche Maschinen und Armaturen Fabrik, Bremen.
26. W. Weir to G. D. Irving, 17 January 1912, GUA, DC/96/1/7.
27. W. Weir to J. R. Richmond, 19 February 1907, GUA, DC/96/1/7.
28. W. Weir to Captain Fujii, 18 December 1907, GUA, DC/96/1/7.
29. W. Weir to G. D. Irving, 17 January 1912, GUA, DC/96/1/7.
30. See R. Appleyard, *Charles Parsons: His Life and Work*.
31. For the *Turbinia*'s triumph see Chapter 10, Note 13.
32. Some of the archives of Parsons Marine Steam Turbine Co. Ltd. (now NEI Parsons) are now held at TWAS, Blandford House, Newcastle upon Tyne.
33. Parson's marine steam turbines fitted to ships for Japanese owners, 1906–1918.

| *Design No.* | *Shipbuilder or agent* | *Ship Type/Name etc.* | *Date* |
|---|---|---|---|
| 9 | Mitsubishi Co. | | n.d. (1905) |
| 22 | Mitsubishi Co. Brown McFarlane | *Ten-yo Maru* and *Chi-yo Maru* | 1906 |
| 43 | Mitsubishi Brown McFarlane | Japanese torpedo boat destroyers, *Umikase, Yamakase* | 1908 |
| 105 | Brown McFarlane for Mitsubishi | Messrs Toyo Kiseu Kaishka's S. American liner *Auyo Maru* | 1911 |
| 130 | Cdr. Toshida and Mitsubishi | Japanese battleship *Hyuza* | 1913 |
| 135 | Mitsubishi *per* Mr Esaky | NYK Steamers No 242 *Toysaka Maru* No 243 *Toyama Maru* | 1913 |
| 18 | Mitsubishi yard | Volunteer steamer 194 *Sakura Maru* | 1906 |
| 21 | Brown McFarlane for Mitsubishi | Model for Imperial Japanese Naval Academy at Etajima | 1908 |
| 23 | Denny & Co. | 'Japanese (*Hirafis Maru Jamura Maru* pencilled) | 1907 |
| 25 | Mitsubishi | Volunteer steamer for the Imperial Marine Association (*Umsyaka Maru* pencilled) | 1908 |
| 26 | Mitsubishi | *Shinyo Maru* | 1908 |
| 34 | Mitsubishi | Japanese cruiser 2nd class *Yahagi* | 1909 |
| 47 | Mitsubishi | 'Combination' NYK European liner *Katori Maru* | 1911 |
| 79 | Mitsubishi | 550 ton light cruiser no 291 (?*Tanca* pencilled) | 1917 |
| 80 | Mitsubishi | *Sawakaze, Minekaze, Hakaze* | 1917 |

(*continued*)

| Design No. | Shipbuilder or agent | Ship Type/Name etc. | Date |
|---|---|---|---|
| 81 | Mitsubishi | 2nd class torpedo boat destroyers *Kaki* and *Toza* | 1918 |
| Engine 43 | Mitsubishi | Japanese despatch vessel *Mogami* | 1906 |
| Engines 44 & 45 | Mitsubishi | TSS *Tenyo Maru* and *Chinyo Maru* | 1906 |

*Source*: TWAS, Parsons Marine Steam Turbine Co. Ltd, 1361/7, 1361/8 and 1361/9; my especial thanks to Richard Potts for extracting this material.

34. Two of the turbines were intended for Mitsubishi at the Takashima Colliery, one was for Mitsubishi at Namadzuta Colliery (both on Kyushu Island), another for Mitsubishi's own powerhouse, one was for Shinnen Colliery and one for Sado Mine, one for Lamazata Colliery, one for Futasi Colliery of the Imperial Steel Worls, Kyushu. Finally, one was for Nikkan Gas Kabushiki Kaisha, Maho, Korea.
35. The amount of royalty payable on each dynamo seems to have varied between £12 10*s* and £25. No other detail of the licensing arrangements has been found.
36. Reader, *The Weir Group*, p. 25.
37. W. Weir, *Letter Books*, GUA, W. Weir to J. Latta, 26 February 1907.
38. Vickers Film, R.307, UCL, Letter from Admiral Yamanouchi, Japanese Steel Works Ltd, 5 July 1911.
39. Vickers Film, R.307, UCL, 11 July 1903.
40. *The Times*, 17 February, 17 April, 5 & 7 May and 20 July 1914.
41. Barr & Stroud papers, Barr to Harold Jackson, 9 May 1907; my thanks to Iain Russell.

## 14 Exhibitions, Designers and Architects

1. See C. Yamada (ed.) *Japonisme in Art*.
2. See B. H. Chamberlain and W. B. Mason, *A Handbook for Travellers in Japan*, gave advice on the 'purchase and shipment of goods' and listed a wide range of 'curio dealers' in various Japanese towns.
3. Japanning was originally the art of lacquering as practised in Japan and China, the lacquer being made from the sap of *rhus vernicifera*. But in the West Japanning meant varnishing metal objects followed by heating or stoving; bastardised Japanese designs were used usually on a black background.
4. R. West, *The Fountain Overflows*, Virago Edition, 1983, p. 173.
5. Mortimer Menpes (1855–1938) an Australian who settled in London, published in 1901, in A. and C. Black's Beautiful Books Series, *Japan: A Record in Colour* with 100 of his original coloured plates; see also C. Inman, 'A and C Black's 20/- Series', *Antiquarian Book Monthly Review*, October 1987, pp. 372–8.

6. See 'Mr Mortimer Menpes House, 25 Cadogan Gardens', *The Studio*, vol. 17, 1899, pp. 170–8. The house is now the north-west corner of the premises of Messrs Peter Jones, Department Store, Sloane Square, London.
7. See W. Buchanan, 'Japanese Influences on the Glasgow Boys and Charles Rennie Mackintosh', C. Yamada (ed.) *Japonisme in Art*, pp. 291–301, and W. Buchanan, *Mr Henry and Mr Hornel Visit Japan*.
8. R. Spencer, 'Whistler and Japan: Work in Progress' in C. Yamada (ed.) *Japonisme in Art*, pp. 57–81; note also D. Harbron, *The Conscious Stone*. Godwin's widow Beatrice married Whistler in 1888. Godwin was one of the earliest collectors of Japanese art.
9. M. Menpes, *Whistler as I Knew Him*.
10. Kawanabe Kyosai (1831–89); see W. Anderson, 'A Japanese artist, Kawanabe Kyosai', *The Studio*, vol. XV, 1898, pp. 29–38. M. Menpes, 'A personal view of Japanese Art', and M. Menpes, *Japan*, ch. III.
11. See obituary of Dr Josiah Conder (1852–1920) *Japan Times and Mail*, 23 June 1920 (a copy in Meiji Shimbun, Zaishi Bunko, University of Tokyo).
12. See C. Dresser, *Japan, its Architecture, Art and Art Manufacture*, and W. Halen, 'Christopher Dresser and the Cult of Japan', a lecture for the Society for the Studies of Japonisme, Tokyo, 4 December 1983.
13. In the Shuhogahara Foreign Cemetery in Kobe there are the graves of Christopher Dresser (born 3 July 1857, died 20 November 1903) and Charles Dresser (born 1881, died 1932). These, it is assumed, would be Dresser's son (and grandson?) who settled in Kobe; my thanks to C. C. Duncan of Lipton, Japan KK Kobe.
14. M. Menpes, 'A Letter from Japan', *The Studio*, vol. XI, 1897, pp. 32–6 and vol. XII, 1898, pp. 21–6.
15. D. Bennett, *King without a Crown*, pp. 198–211; C. H. Gibbs- Smith, *The Great Exhibition of 1851*, and E. Bonython, *King Cole*.
16. Gibbs-Smith, *The Great Exhibition*, p. 7.
17. Y. Fukuzawa, *Seiyo Jiyo* (*Conditions in the West*), *Collected Works*, Tokyo, 1985, p. 312.
18. In Japan, Charles Wirgman the correspondent of the *ILN*, reported on local Japanese exhibitions, *Hakurankai*, *ILN*, 19 October 1872.
19. Bonython, *King Cole*, p. 7.
20. Kido, *Diaries*, vol. II, p. 322.
21. See R. Alcock, *Art and Art Industries in Japan*, p. 291.
22. My thanks to Peter Kornicki for the use of his material.
23. Part of the Japanese Collection held at the Glasgow Museums and Art Galleries was an exchange for engineering exhibits to be exhibited in Tokyo, organised by R. H. Smith in the 1870s when he was Professor of Engineering at Tokyo.
24. G. A. Audsley and J. L. Bowes, *Ceramic Art of Japan*. (This copy in St.AUL NK 4167.A8B7, 2 vols.) See also Chapter 12, note 27, and R. L. Wilson, 'Tea Taste in the Era of *Japonisme*: A Debate'.
25. P. Fitzgerald, *Memories*, p. 116.
26. In 1901 in the Japanese pavilion there were 5000 square feet of display,

see *Catalogue and Guide, Glasgow International Exhibition*, Glasgow, 1901.

27. Christopher Dresser's role as designer is described in J. Heskett, *Industrial Design*, Oxford, 1980, pp. 9–10, 24–6.
28. See Halen, 'Christopher Dresser and the Cult of Japan', a lecture for the Society of the Studies of Japonisme, Tokyo, 4 December 1983. The author is grateful for his help.
29. John C. Robinson, *Catalogue of the Museum of Manufactures*, 1856, p. 92.
30. National Archives, Tokyo, Official Records of the Ministry of the Interior (free translation), January (*Meiji* 10), 1877.
31. Dresser's itinerary was as follows: visited: the Shiba Mausoleum of the *Tokugawa* family (29 December); Toshu-gu at Ueno (6 January); Confucian temple in Tokyo (16 January); Daibatsu, Kamakura; theatre in Tokyo (18 January); the Kofuku-ji, Todai-ji, Great Buddha Hall, Shosoin (the treasures) and the Grand Kasaja Shrine in Nara and pagoda in Osaka (3 February); Ki Mii-dera Temple (15 February); the Koya-san region; several temples in the Kyoto environs (18 February); Ise Shrine, Nagoya Castle and temples in and near Nagoya (7 March); the Shiba mausoleum of the Tokugawas (return visit) (25 March); the region of the Toshu-gu at Nikko (30 March); sailed from Yokohama (3 April). Diary of the Interior Department (*Meiji* 10), 1877, p. 2764, quoted in Halen, 'Christopher Dresser and the Cult of Japan'.
32. Halen, 'Christopher Dresser and the Cult of Japan', p. 17.
33. Ibid, p. 21.
34. He started designing for Linthorpe Art Pottery and James Couper and Sons, makers of Clutha Glass, as well as designing items for Wedgwood and Mintons. For one year in 1880 he was Art Editor for *Furniture Gazette* and for the Art Furnishers Alliance he became Art Manager. At the same time he ran his own design studio and lectured widely, particularly in London and Glasgow; Dresser, *Japan*, p. 353.
35. Halen, 'Christopher Dresser and the Cult of Japan', p. 24.
36. Dresser, *Japan*, preface, p. V.
37. *Architectural Japan: Old, New*, Tokyo, 1936, and 'The search for "Japanese architecture" in Modern Ages', *The Japan Foundation Newsletter*, vol. XV, no 3, December 1987, pp. 1–9.
38. De Boinville, who arrived in Glasgow after the Franco-Prussian war in 1871, was recruited from Glasgow for service in Japan. Charles Alfred Chastel de Boinville (1850–97) obituary, *Journal Royal Institute British Architects*, vol. IV, 3rd Series, 1897, pp. 359–60.
39. 'The History of Shimizugumi', *Architectural Japan* pp. 221–2.
40. See Chapter 6, Section 2, and K. Abe, 'Early Western Architecture in Japan'.
41. C. T. Marshall, *Letters from Meiji Japan*, p. 75.
42. C. Whitney, *Clara's Diary*, p. 255.
43. In Osaka he was responsible for the design and construction of the Royal Mint. See Chapter 2, Section 5.
44. E. Seidensticker, *Low City, High City*, pp. 59–60.

45. Hansell was responsible for the following buildings, almost all of which were commissioned by Westerners: Bishop Poole's School, Osaka (for girls) (1888–9); Bishop Poole's School, Osaka (for boys) (1890) both for the Christian Missionary Society; 'Harris School of Science' for the Doshisha College at Kyoto, to accommodate 300 chemistry students, with laboratories (1889–90); exclusive premises for the Kobe Club House, Kobe (1892); Hong Kong and Shanghai Bank, Kobe; enlargement of the Oriental Hotel, No. 80 Kobe; works on godowns and other commercial premises for the principal firms of Kobe (1892); Chartered Bank of India, Australia and China, Kobe (1912); Kobe International Hospital, Kobe (1916). Alexander Nelson Hansell (1856–1940), biographical details and transcription of A.N. Hansell's Fellowship Statement, 1890, from the Librarian, the Royal Institute of British Architects, Portland Place, London, to whom my thanks are due.
46. See Chapter 6, section 4.
47. William Burges (1827–81); best-known work was the restoration of Cardiff Castle for the Marquis of Bute. See Robert Furneaux Jordan, *Victorian Architecture*, 1966, p. 100.
48. See H. Dyer, *Report on Imperial College of Engineering 1873–1877*, Tokyo, 1877, Conder's report on the teaching of Architecture, pp. 64–5.
49. See P. Barr, *The Deer Cry Pavilion*, pp. 179–80.
50. Seidensticker, *Low City, High City*, pp. 69–70.
51. See J. Conder, *A Few Remarks on Architecture*, pamphlet to be found at the Institute of Architecture, Minato-Ku, Tokyo.
52. Dr Tatsuno Kingo (1854–1919) an early student of Conder's at ICE, was responsible for the original Bank of Japan building in Tokyo which is still in use. Kingo was also responsible for the Bank of Japan building in Kyoto (1903), Tokyo Station (1914) and Osaka City Public Hall. See also S. Sakamoto, 'Railway Station architecture', *Architectural Japan*, pp. 81–9.
53. Obituary, J. Conder, *Japan Times and Mail*, 23 June 1920.
54. See Chapter 6, note 58; his grave was tended and his memory kept alive by the artist, Kusumi Kawanabe.
55. *Memorial Albums* can be seen at The Architectural Institute of Japan (Shiba 5-26-20, Minato-Ku, Tokyo, Japan 108).
56. See *West Meets East*, the Japanese introduction to Western Architecture in nineteenth century and twentieth century, vol. 2.
57. Of the buildings which were designed and built directly under Conder's own eye, the following remain and can still be seen today in Tokyo: the Iwasaki house (Yushima 4-6, Bunkyo-Ku); another Iwasaki house and garage (both at Takanawa, 4-25-33 Minato-Ku and the Iwasaki tomb (Okamoto 2-23, Setagaya-Ku). There is also a Furukawa house (Nishigakana 1-27-29 Kita-Ku); the Mitsui Club (Mita 2-3-7 Minato-Ku) and Shimazu House, now the administrative building of Seisen Women's College, (Higashi-Gotanda 3-16-21, Shinagawa-Ku). The only large-scale public building which remains – not designed by Conder but built under his supervision – is the Greek Orthodox Church at Kanda (Surogodai 4-1-3 Chiyoda-Ku, Tokyo).

58. J. Conder, ICE, class reports of the professors, 1873–7, Tokei, pp. 64–5; see also J. Conder's articles in the *Japan Gazette*, 2, 10, 13 and 15 March, 1877.
59. Dresser, *Japan*, preface, 1882.

## 15 A Copartnery: On Japanese Terms?

1. For a simple contemporary Western account of the Emperor Mutsu Hito (Gentle Pity) see J. H. Longford, *The Evolution of New Japan*, ch. X, pp. 142–57.
2. Although German interests in Japan were powerful, the German Emperor's attempts to organise the European powers against the 'yellow peril' made an alliance in that quarter less likely. See I. Nash, *The Anglo-Japanese Alliance*, pp. 285, 309, 377.
3. Navies were equipped with Barr & Stroud Rangefinders to focus the guns to the correct range. The Japanese crews had practised with the equipment for months. There is a story – perhaps apocryphal – that Admiral Togo in after years assured the people at Barr & Stroud in Glasgow that their rangefinders had won the Battle of the Japan Sea for him. Seppings Wright commented 'By this great victory the Japan Sea becomes the moat of Tokyo' (Seppings Wright, *With Togo*, p. 273).
4. The term feudalism is used for convenience although Japanese feudalism, *hoken sei*, was markedly different from any kind of feudalism in Europe.
5. As Dyer remarked, 'the highest ambition of all the officials with whom I came into contact, and also of my own students, was that their country might become the Britain of the East', and he added 'and they not infrequently got laughed at by foreigners for what was considered their conceit', H. Dyer, *Dai Nippon*, p. 342.
6. Masahaga Yazu's *Universal Regional Geography for Middle Schools*, quoted in C. A. Fisher, 'Britain of the East', p. 344.
7. G. N. Curzon, *Problems of the Far East*, pp. 395–6.
8. G. S. Graham, *The politics of naval supremacy*, p. 125.
9. S. G. Checkland, *The Elgins*.
10. Fitzgerald, *Memories*, p. 113.
11. Translation of a letter, written by an unknown Japanese, transcribed by J. M. Whistler, BP.1136/45 8pp Whistler Collection, GUL, quoted by kind permission.
12. *Iwakurako Jikki* (A true record of Prince Iwakura) (Tokyo, 1927) quoted in H. D. Harootunian, 'The Progress of Japan and the Samurai Class', p. 258.
13. See S. D. Brown and A. Hirota, 'Okubo Toshimichi, his Political and Economic Policies in early Meiji Japan'; M. Iwata, *Okubo Toshimichi*; and S. D. Brown and A. Hirota, *The Diary of Kido Takayoshi.*
14. B. S. Silberman and H. D. Harootunian, *Modern Japanese Leadership*, p. 412.
15. B. S. Silberman, *Ministers of Modernisation*, p. 73.
16. E. I. Sugimoto, *A Daughter of the Samurai*, p. 5.

17. A. J. Toynbee, *A Study of History* (abridged by D. C. Somervell), Oxford, 1946, pp. 372–3.
18. Y. Fukuzawa, 'On de-Asianisation' in *Modern Japan through Contemporary Sources*, vol. III, 1869–94, Tokyo, 1972, p. 129.
19. W. T. Stead (ed.) *Review of Reviews*, vol. IX, January to June 1894, p. 271.
20. E. Pauer, 'Japan's Industrial Apprenticeship', pp. 1184–200; Pauer, *Japans Industrielle Lehrzeit*.
21. E. Pauer, 'Japan's Industrial Apprenticeship', p. 1186.
22. The plans for the reverberatory furnace complexes built in Saga (after 1850) and Kagoshima (1857) can be reconstructed. At Nirayama (c. 1856) near Shimoda, the layout was planned as on a Western model. At Miyako, but only in the planning stage, the Japanese succeeded in putting the various production processes into a line of continuous manufacture.
23. For a facsimile of the title page see Pauer, *Japans Industrielle Lehrzeit*, p. 19.
24. T. Terakawa and W. H. Brock, 'The Introduction of Heurism into Japan'.
25. Takato Oshima was involved with the reverberatory furnace movement before the Restoration, see S. Oshima, *Oshima Takato gyojitsu*; for his itinerary in Britain as a member of the Iwakura Mission see Chapter 7, section 3 and note 29 above.
26. I. Ken'ichi, 'The Early Steel Industry, successes and failures', *Entrepreneurship, the Japanese Experience*, no 3, Tokyo, June 1982, pp. 7–16, T. Nakaoka, 'On Technological Leaps of Japan'.
27. At the end of the 1880s Japan was importing some 80 per cent of the annual demand for iron and steel, for rails and locomotives, factory machinery and ships; see Chapter 2, Section 3 above.
28. Although Kamaishi has remained a steel city, the wheel has come full circle, as Nippon Steel contracts its operation at Kamaishi to cut company losses. See 'Sunset in the East', *The Observer Magazine*, 2 August 1987, pp. 23–7.
29. From our Special Commissioner, 'The training of Engineers, Modern Japan – Industrial and Scientific', XIII, *The Engineer*, 3 & 10 December 1897, pp. 567–9. For a list of these articles see Chapter 3, note 62.
30. K. Koizumi, 'Japan's First Physicists', p. 87. The original letter is in the Tanakadate Papers, National Science Museum, Tokyo, Japan.
31. B. M. Allen, *Sir Ernest Satow*, p. 38.
32. R. Minami, 'Mechanical Power in the Industrialisation of Japan', p. 935; see also A. Gerschenkron, *Economic backwardness in historical perspective*, ch. 1, p. 27.
33. *Sunday Times*, 21 February 1988, and C. G. Ryan, *The Marketing of Technology*.
34. The *Daily Telegraph*, 1 November 1858, see also *The Times*, 10 November 1858.
35. P. J. Cain and A. G. Hopkins, 'Gentlemanly Capitalism and British Expansion Overseas II: New Imperialism, 1850–1945', *EcHR*, 2nd series, 1986, vol. XL, no 1, pp. 1–26.

36. Between 1896 and 1899 of the 131 million *yen* spent abroad 111 million *yen* was spent on warships. See H. Saito, 'The Formation of Japanese Specie Abroad', Chiba University of Commerce, 1988.
37. See D. J. Lyon, 'The Thornycroft List'; my thanks to David Lyon, curator, Naval Ordnance, Department of Ships and Antiquities, NMM. See also K. C. Barnaby, *100 Years of Specialised Engineering and Shipbuilding*.
38. S. Terano and M. Yukawa, 'The Development of Merchant Shipbuilding in Japan', *TINA*, 1911 (Jubilee Volume), p. 146 (contribution to discussion by Dr S. J. P. Thearle).
39. The *Zosen Kio Kui*, or Society of Naval Architects in Japan was founded in 1897; see F. P. Purvis, 'Japanese Ships', p. 81.
40. *TINA*, 1911 (Jubilee Volume) Rear Admiral Kondo, pp. 50–60; Dr S. Terano, pp. 133–48; Dr S. Terano and Professor Baron Shiba, pp. 184–92, and Engineer Rear-Admiral T. Fujii, pp. 193–200.
41. For details of Admiral Miyabara's boilers and the tests used on them see *TINA*, 1911 (Jubilee Volume) p. 195. J. M. Allan (of Hawthorn Leslie on the Tyne) commented 'We have all heard of the boiler that was invented by Admiral Miyabara; he was a very old friend of ours and I am very pleased to know that the boiler he designed has given such satisfactory results' (p. 200).
42. *TINA*, 1911 (Jubilee Volume) A. E. Seaton, p. 199.
43. Inaugural Address of the President of the Institute of Bankers, *Journal of the Institute of Bankers*, December 1905, pp. 535–6; my thanks to Edwin Green.
44. Allen, *Sir Ernest Satow*, p. 110.
45. From material shown at Yokohama Archives of History, in the autumn of 1984, as part of exhibition on Jardine, Matheson in Japan; my especial thanks to Hisako Ito.
46. R. H. Bruce Lockhart, *My Scottish Youth*, p. 348.
47. See M. B. Jansen, 'Monarchy and Modernisation in Japan'; and J. W. Hall, 'A Monarch for Modern Japan'.
48. S. Tsunoyama, 'Watching the Clock'.
49. See O. Saito, *Purota-kogyoka no jidai: Sei-o to Nihon no hikakushi* (*The Age of Proto-industrialisation: Western Europe and Japan in Comparative and Historical Perspective*) (Tokyo, 1985) and 'Changing Structure of Urban Employment and its Effects on Migration Patterns in Eighteenth- and Nineteenth-century Japan', March 1986, Institute of Economic Research, Hitotsubashi University, Tokyo.
50. M. Matsukata, *Report on the Adoption of the Gold Standard in Japan*, p. XIV.
51. J. H. Gubbins, *The Progress of Japan, 1853–1871*, p. 224.
52. See J. E. Hoare, 'Japan undermines Extraterritoriality . . . 1885–1899' in I. Nish and C. Dunn (eds) *European Studies in Japan*, pp. 125–9.

# Select Bibliography

*Place of publication given if not London.*


ABE, K., 'Early Western Architecture in Japan', *Journal of the Society of Architectural Historians*, XIII, 2 (1950–4) pp. 13–18.

ABERCONWAY, 1st Baron, *The Basic Industries of Great Britain* (1927).

ADAMS, F. O., *The History of Japan*, 2 vols (1875).

ADDISON, W. I., *Roll of Graduates of the University of Glasgow* (Glasgow, 1913).

ALCOCK, Sir Rutherford, *The Capital of the Tycoon: A Narrative of Three Years Residence in Japan*, vols I and II (1863).

ALCOCK, Sir Rutherford, *Art and Art Industries in Japan* (1878).

ALDCROFT, D. H. (ed.), 'The Entrepreneur and the British Economy, 1870–1914', *EcHR*, n.s. 17 (1964) pp. 113–34.

ALDCROFT, D. H., 'The Depression in British Shipping 1901–1911', *Journal of Transport History*, 7.1 (May, 1965) pp. 14–23.

ALDCROFT, D. H., *The Development of British Industry and Foreign Competition, 1875–1914* (1968).

ALDCROFT, D. H., 'Technical Progress and British Enterprise, 1875–1914', *BH*, 8, 1963. Reprinted in D. H. Aldcroft and H. W. Richardson, *The British Economy 1870–1939* (1969).

ALDCROFT, D. H., 'McCloskey on Victorian Growth', *EcHR*, n.s. 27 (1974) pp. 271–4.

ALEXANDER, K. J. W. and JENKINS, C. L., *Fairfields* (1970).

ALLEN, B. M., *Sir Ernest Satow: A Memoir* (1933).

ALLEN, C. J., *A Century of Scientific Instrument Making* (1953).

ALLEN, G. C., *A Short Economic History of Modern Japan* (1946).

ALLEN, G. C., *Appointment in Japan, Memories of Sixty Years* (1983).

ALLEN, G. C. and DONNITHORNE, A. G., *Western Enterprise in Far Eastern Economic Development: China and Japan* (New York, 1954).

ALTMAN, A. A., 'Guido Verbeck and the Iwakura Mission', *Japan Quarterly* (1966) vol. XIII, no. 1, pp. 54–62.

ALTMAN, A. A., '*Shimbushi*: The Early *Meiji* Adaptation of the Western-Style Newspaper' in W. G. Beasley, *Modern Japan, Aspects of History, Literature and Society* (1975).

ALTMAN, A. A., 'The Press and Social Cohesion during a Period of Change: The Case of Early Meiji Japan', *MAS*, 15, 1 (1981) pp. 865–76.

AMES, E. and ROSENBERG, N., 'Changing Technological Leadership and Industrial Growth', *Economic Journal*, 73 (1963) pp. 13–31.

AMES, E. and ROSENBERG, N., 'The Progressive Division and Specialization of Industries', *Journal of Development Studies*, 1 (1965).

ANDERSON, W., 'A Japanese Artist, Kawanabe Kyosai', *The Studio*, vol. XV, 1898, pp. 29–38.

ANETHAN, E. M., *Fourteen Years of Diplomatic Life in Japan* (1912).

ANON., *Papers relative to the principalship of Henry Dyer* (printed for private circulation) (1886, GUA) Court Papers.

ANON., *Engineering Education in the British Dominions*, published by the Institution of Civil Engineers (1891).
ANON., *Japanese Club at Cambridge*, 7th, 8th and 9th meetings (Cambridge, 1892) (GUL Educ, R5. 1916-G).
ANON., *Japanese Club at Cambridge* (Cambridge, 1893) (Yokohama Archives of History).
ANON., *Lord Kelvin's Jubilee* (Glasgow, 1896).
ANON., 'Mr Menpes Japanese Drawings', *The Studio*, vol. IX (1897) pp. 165–77.
ANON., 'Mr Mortimer Menpes' House, 25 Cadogan Gardens', *The Studio*, vol. 17 (1899) pp. 170–8.'
ANON., *An Engineering Record of the Glasgow Exhibition* (1901).
ANON., *Imperial University of Tokyo* (Tokyo, 1904).
ANON., *The Fairfield Shipbuilding and Engineering Works* (1909).
ANON., *Mining in Japan* (Bureau of Mines) (Tokyo, 1909).
ANON., 'Obituary notice: Admiral of the Fleet Lord Fisher of Kilverstone', *TINA*, vol. 62 (1920).
ANON., *Jardine, Matheson and Company, afterwards Jardine, Matheson and Company Ltd, an Outline of the History of a China House for a Hundred Years 1832–1932*, privately printed (1934).
ANON., *Golden Jubilee History of Nippon Yusen Kaisha 1885–1935* (Tokyo, 1935).
ANON., *Architectural Japan, Old and New* (Tokyo, 1936).
ANON., *A History of the North British Locomotive Co. Ltd, 1903–1953* (Glasgow, 1953).
ANON., *Jardine's Centenary in Japan 1859–1959*, 'privately printed' (Tokyo, 1959).
ANON., *Iwasaki Yanosuke Den* (The Life of Iwasaki Yanosuke) (Tokyo, n.d.).
ANON., *The Introduction of Western Culture into Japan in the Age of her Modernization*, supplement to *Tokyo Municipal News* (Tokyo, 1967).
ANON., *Barr and Stroud Limited* (Glasgow, 1968).
ANON., *Foreign Trade of Japan* (Tokyo, 1975).
ANON., *The 100 year history of Mitsui & Co. Ltd, 1876–1976* (Tokyo, 1977).
ANON., *The Centennial History of the Bank of Japan* (Tokyo, 1982).
ANON., *The Museum Meiji Mura* (Aichi, Japan, n.d.).
ANON., *West meets East, the Japanese Introduction to Western Architecture* (in Japanese) (Tokyo, 1983).
ANON., *Nagasaki in Colour* (Nagasaki, n.d.).
AOKI, E., 'Edmund Morell' in *Look Japan*, 10 December 1984.
APPLEYARD, R., *Charles Parsons: His Life and Work* (1933).
APPLEYARD, R., *History of the Institution of Electrical Engineers* (1939).
ARCHER, R. L., *Secondary Education in the Nineteenth Century* (Cambridge, 1921).
ARCHIBALD, E. T. H., *The Metal Fighting Ship in the Royal Navy* (1971).
ARGLES, M., *South Kensington to Robbins, English Technical Education since 1851* (1964).
ARIMA, S., 'The Western Influence on Japanese Military Science, Shipbuilding and Navigation', *MN*, XIX (1964), 3–4, pp. 119–45.
ARMSTRONG, H. E., *Royal College of Science* (1921).

ARMYTAGE, W. H. G., *A. J. Mundella, 1825–1897: The Liberal Background to the Labour Movement* (1951).
ARMYTAGE, W. H. G., *A Social History of Engineering* (1961).
ARMYTAGE, W. H. G., *The Rise of the Technocrats: A Social History* (1965).
ARNOLD, Sir E., *Japonica* (1891).
ASAKAWA, K., *The Russo-Japanese Conflict* (Boston, 1904).
ASHWORTH, W., 'Economic Aspects of Late Victorian Naval Administration', *EcHR*, vol. XXII (1969) pp. 491–505.
ASHWORTH, W., 'Backwardness, Discontinuity and Industrial Development', *EcHR*, vol. XXIII, no. 1 (1970) pp. 163–9.
ATKINS, J. L., *Industrial Espionage and Trade Secrets: A Bibliography* (Coventry, 1972).
ATKINSON, R. W., 'The Water Supply of Tokio', *TASJ*, vol. 6, pt I (1878) pp. 87–105 (graph).
ATKINSON, R. W., 'Notes on the Manufacture of Oshiroi (white-lead)', *TASJ*, vol. 6, pt II (1878) pp. 277–83.
ATKINSON, R. W., 'The Chemical Industries of Japan', *TASJ*, no. 2, vol. 7, pt IV (1879) pp. 318–28 (tables).
ATKINSON, R. W., 'Notes on the porcelain industry of Japan', *TASJ*, vol. 8, (1880) pt II, pp. 267–76; tables pp. 126–35.
ATKINSON, R. W., *The Chemistry of Saki Brewing* (Tokio, 1881) (GUL C.1882).
AUDSLEY, G. A., *Notes on Japanese Art* (Liverpool, 1874).
AUDSLEY, G. A. and BOWES, J. L., *Ceramic Art of Japan* (Liverpool, 1875).
AYRTON, W. E. and PERRY, J. L., 'The Importance of a General System of Simultaneous Observations of Atmospheric Electricity', *TASJ*, vol. 5, pt I (1877) pp. 131–41 (4 pts).
BADEN, E. M., *A Manual of Ship Subsidies* (Chicago, 1911).
BAELZ, E., *Awakening Japan: Diary of a German Doctor*, reprint (Bloomington, 1974).
BAKER, B., *The Forth Bridge* (1882).
BANBURY, P., *Shipbuilders of the Thames and Medway* (1971).
BANCROFT, H. H., *The New Pacific* (New York, 1900).
BARD, B., *Applications and Limitations of the Patent System*, Licensing Executives Society (November 1974).
BARNABY, K. C., *The Institution of Naval Architects, 1860–1960* (1960).
BARNABY, K. C., *100 years of Specialised Shipbuilding and Engineering: John I. Thornycroft Centenary* (1964).
BARNABY, N., *Naval Development in the Century* (Edinburgh, 1902).
BARNABY, S. W., *Marine Propellers* (1921).
BARR, A., *The Engineer of the Future* (Leeds, 1888).
BARR, A., 'Testimonials for the Regius Professorship of Civil Engineering and Mechanics in the University of Glasgow' (Kelvin Collection) (n.p., 1889) (GUL, Y.1.m.20).
BARR, A., 'James Watt and the Application of Science to the Mechanical Arts; An Inaugural Address' (Glasgow, 1889) (GUL Educ R5, 1891-K).
BARR, A., 'Glasgow University Engineering Society Inaugural Address, 12 January 1892' (Kelvin Collection) (Manchester, 1892).

BARR, A. and STROUD, W., *Some New Telemeters and Range-Finders for Naval and Other Purposes* (1891) (GUL I9-aly).
BARR, A. and STROUD, W., *Telemeters and Range-Finders for Naval and Other Purposes* (1896) (GUL I9.a.20).
BARR, P., *The Coming of the Barbarians: A Story of Western Settlement in Japan 1853–1970* (1967).
BARR, P., *The Deer Cry Pavilion: A Story of Westerners in Japan 1868–1905* (1968).
BARR, P., *A Curious Life for a Lady: The Story of Isabella Bird* (1970).
BARTHOLEMEW, J., 'Japanese Culture and the Problem of Modern Science' in A. Thackray and E. Mendelsohn (eds) *Science and Values* (New York, 1974).
BARTHOLEMEW, J. R., 'Japanese Modernization and the Imperial Universities 1876–1920', *JAS*, vol. XXXVII, no. 2 (1978) 31, pp. 251–71.
BASTER, A. S. J., *The Imperial Banks* (1929).
BASTER, A. S. J., *International Banks* (1935).
BATES, L. F., *Sir Alfred Ewing* (1946).
BAXENDALL, M., *Patterns of Invention* (Yale, 1985).
BAXTER, J. P. III, *Introduction of the Ironclad Warship* (Cambridge, Mass., 1933).
BEASLEY, W. G., *Great Britain and the Opening of Japan 1834–1858* (1951).
BEASLEY, W. G., *Select Documents on Japanese Foreign Policy 1853–1868* (Oxford, 1955).
BEASLEY, W. G., 'Councillors of Samurai Origin in the Early *Meiji* Government', *BSOAS*, no. 20 (1957) pp. 89–103.
BEASLEY, W. G., 'Feudal Revenue in Japan at the time of the *Meiji* Restoration', *JAS*, 19 (1960) pp. 255–72.
BEASLEY, W. G., *The Modern History of Japan* (1963).
BEASLEY, W. G., 'Political Groups in Tosa 1858–1868', *BSOAS*, no. 30 (1967) pp. 382–90.
BEASLEY, W. G., 'Politics and the Samurai Class Structure in Satsuma, 1858–1868', *MAS*, vol. 1 (1967) pp. 47–58.
BEASLEY, W. G., *The Meiji Restoration* (1973).
BEASLEY, W. G., *Modern Japan: Aspects of History, Literature and Society* (BSOAS Studies on Modern Asia and Africa II) (1975).
BEASLEY, W. G., 'The Iwakura Mission in Britain 1872', *History Today*, vol. 31 (October 1981) pp. 29–33.
BEASLEY, W. G., *Japanese Imperialism 1895–1945* (Oxford, 1987).
BEASLEY, W. G. and PULLEYBLANK, E. G. (eds) *Historians of China and Japan* (1961).
BEAUCHAMP, E. R., 'Griffis in Japan: the Fujui Interlude 1871', *MN*, vol. XXX, no. 4 (winter, 1975).
BECK, C. L. and BUCKS, A. W. (eds) *Aspects of Meiji Modernization* (New Brunswick, 1983).
BECKMANN, G. M., *The Making of the Meiji Constitution, the Oligarchs and the Constitutional Development of Japan, 1868–1891* (Westport, Conn., reprint, 1975).
BEDFORD, F. G. D., *The Sailor's Handbook* (1906).
BELL, D., *The Coming of Post-Industrial Society* (New York, 1976).
BELLOT, H. H., *University College London 1826–1926* (1929).

BENEDICT, R., *The Chrysanthemum and the Sword* (1946).
BENNETT, D., *King without a Crown, Albert Prince Consort of England, 1819–1861* (1977).
BERESFORD, C., *The Break-up of China* (1899).
BETTINSON, E. M., *The University of Newcastle, 1834–1971* (Newcastle, 1971).
BEVERIDGE, A. J., *The Russian Advance* (New York, 1903).
BIGOT, G., *Albums Humoristiques de la Vie Japonaise* (Yokohama, 1899).
BILES, J. H., 'Fifty Years of Warship-building on the Clyde', *TIESS*, 52 (1808–9) pp. 347–70.
BILES, J. H., *Design and Construction of Ships* (1908 and 1911).
BIRD, I. L., *Unbeaten Tracks in Japan, An Account of Travels in the Interior including Visits to the Aborigines of Yezo and the Shrine at Nikko*, vols I and II, 1880 (reprinted Virago Press, 1984).
BIRSE, R. M., *Engineering at Edinburgh University: A Short History 1673–1983* (Edinburgh, 1983).
BLACK, J. R., *Young Japan, Yokohama and Yedo: A Narrative of the Settlement, and the City from the Signing of the Treaties in 1858 to the Close of the Year 1879*, 2 vols (Yokohama, 1880–1) (reprinted Oxford, 1969).
BLACKER, C., 'The First Japanese Mission to England', *History Today*, vol. 7 (1957) pp. 840–7.
BLACKER, C., *The Japanese Enlightenment: A Study of the Writing of Fukuzawa Yukichi* (Cambridge, 1964).
BLAIR, J., 'The Japanese Mercantile Marine', *JSL*, vol. XVI (1917–18), pp. 38–55.
BLAKISTON, T. W., 'A Journey in Yezo', *Journal of the Royal Geographical Society*, vol. 42 (1872) pp. 77–142.
BLAKISTON, T. W., 'A Journey in North East Japan', *TASJ*, vol. II (1874) pp. 198–222.
BLAKISTON, T. W. and PRIOR, H., 'Catalogue of the Birds of Japan', *TSAJ*, vol. VIII (1880) pp. 29–99.
BLOND, G., *Admiral Togo* (1961) trans. Edward Hyams.
BONAR, H. A. C., 'On Maritime Enterprise in Japan', *TASJ*, vol. 15, pt I, (1887) pp. 103–5.
BONYTHON, E., *King Cole: A Picture Portrait of Sir Henry Cole, KCB, 1808–1882* (n.d.).
BORROWMAN, W. C., 'Some Considerations Affecting the Training of Young Engineers', *TNECIES*, 16 (1899–1900).
BORTHWICK, A., *Yarrow, 1865–1965* (Edinburgh, 1965).
BORTON, H., *Japan's Modern Century* (New York, 1955).
BOXER, C. R., *Jan Compagnie in Japan, 1600–1817: An Essay on the Cultural, Artistic and Scientific Influence Exercised by the Hollanders from the Seventeenth to the Nineteenth Century* (The Hague, 1950).
BOXER, C. R., *The Dutch Seaborne Empire, 1600–1800* (Harmondsworth, 1973).
BRAY, R. A., 'The Apprenticeship System', *Economic Journal*, 19 (September 1909) pp. 404–515.
BRIGGS, Sir J., *Naval Administration 1827–1892; The Experience of Sixty-five Years* (1897).

BRINKLEY, F., *History of the Empire of Japan* (Tokyo, 1893).
BRINKLEY, F., *The Art of Japan* (Boston, 1901).
BRINKLEY, F., *Japan and China* (Boston, 1902).
BROADBRIDGE, S., 'The Economic Development of Japan 1870–1920', *Journal of Development Studies*, vol. 4 (January 1968) pp. 268–87.
BROADBRIDGE, S., 'Shipbuilding and State in Japan since the 1850s', *MAS*, 11, pt 4 (October 1977) pp. 601–13.
BROCK, W. H., *H. E. Armstrong and the Teaching of Science 1800–1930* (Cambridge, 1973).
BROCK, W. H., 'The Japanese Connexion: Engineering in Tokyo, London and Glasgow at the End of the Nineteenth Century (Presidential Address 1980) *British Journal for the History of Science*, vol. 14, no. 48 (1981), pp. 229–43.
BRONFENBRENNER, M., 'Some Lessons of Japan's Economic Development, 1853–1938', *Pacific Affairs*, vol. 34 (1961) pt 1, pp. 7–27.
BROOKS, V. W., *Fenellosa and his Circle, with Other Essays in Biography* (New York, 1962).
BROWN, A. R., 'Winds and Currents in the Vicinity of the Japanese Islands', *TASJ*, vol. 2 (1874) pp. 139–51.
BROWN, D. K., *A Century of Naval Construction: A History of the Royal Corps of Naval Constructors, 1883–1983* (1983).
BROWN, M., *On the Theory and Management of Technical Change* (1968).
BROWN, S. D., 'Kido Takayoshi, Japan's Cautious Revolutionary', *Pacific Historical Review* 15.2 (1956), pp. 151–62.
BROWN, S. D. and HIROTA, A., 'Okubo Toshimichi, His Political and Economic Policies in Early Meiji Japan', *JAS*, 21.2 (February 1962) pp. 183–97.
BROWN, S. D. and HIROTA, A., 'The Self Image of an early *Meiji* Statesman through the Diary of Kido Takayoshi 1868–1877', *selected papers in Asian Studies*, W. Conference Association, 1 (1976).
BROWN, S. D. and HIROTA, A. (eds) *The Diary of Kido Takayoshi*, vol. I, 1868–71 (Tokyo, 1983), vol. II, 1871–4 (Tokyo, 1985), vol. III, 1874–7 (Tokyo, 1986).
BRUCE, A. B., *Life of William Denny, Shipbuilder, Dumbarton* (1889).
BRUCE, LOCKHART, R. H., *My Scottish Youth* (1937).
BRUNTON, R. H., 'Constructive Art in Japan', *TASJ*, vol. 2, pt I (1874) pp. 56–75.
BRUNTON, R. H., 'Constructive Art in Japan', *TASJ*, vol. 3, pt II (1875) pp. 18–27.
BRUNTON, R. H., 'Notes Taken on a Visit to Okinawa, Shima-Loochoo Islands', *TASJ*, vol. 4 (1876) pp. 66–77.
BRUNTON, R. H., 'The Japan Lights', *MPICE* (1876–7) pt I, pp. 1–41.
BRYDEN, D. J., *Scottish Scientific Instrument Makers 1600–1900* (Edinburgh, 1972).
BUCHAN, A. R. (ed.) *A Goodly Heritage: A Hundred Years of Civil Engineering at Strathclyde University* (Glasgow, 1987).
BUCHANAN, W., *Mr Henry and Mr Hornel visit Japan* (Edinburgh, 1979).
BUELL, R. L., *Japanese Immigration*, World Peace Foundation (1924) VII, nos 5–6.

BURKS, A. W. and COOPERMAN, J., 'The William Elliot Griffis Collection', *JAS*, vol. 20 (November 1960–1) pp. 61–71.
BURN, D. L., *The Economic History of Steel-making, 1867–1939* (Cambridge, 1940).
BURROW, J. (ed.) *Denny, Dumbarton* (1932).
BURTON, J. H., *Political Economy* (Edinburgh, 1852).
BURTON, W. K. (ed.) 'Abstract of a Lecture on Sanitation in Japan', *TASJ*, vol. XVII, pt III (1889) pp. xvi–xvii.
BUSH, L., *The Life and Times of the Illustrious Captain Brown* (Tokyo, 1970).
BUXTON, N. K., 'The Scottish Shipbuilding Industry between the Wars: A Comparative Study', *BH*, 13 (1968) pp. 101–20.
BYATT, I. C. R., *The British Electrical Industry, 1875–1914* (Oxford, 1979).
BYRD, P., 'Regional and Functional Specialization in the British Consular Service' in *JCH*, vol. 7, no. 3–4 (July–October 1972) pp. 127–45.
BYRES, T. J., 'Entrepreneurship in the Scottish Heavy Industries, 1870–1900', in P. L. Payne (ed.) *Studies in Scottish Business History* (1967).
CABLE, B., *A Hundred Year History of the P. & O., Peninsular and Oriental Steam Navigation Company 1837–1937* (1937).
CAIN, P. J. and HOPKINS, A. G., 'Gentlemanly Capitalism ... 1850–1945', *EcHR* 2nd series, 1986, vol. XL, no 1.
CAMERON, R., *Banking in the Early Stages of Industrialization* (New York, 1967).
CAMERON, R., *Banking and Economic Development: Some Lessons of History* (1972).
CARDWELL, D. S. L., *From Watt to Clausius, the Rise of Thermodynamics in the early Industrial Age* (1971).
CARDWELL, D. S. L., *The Organisation of Science in England* (1972).
CARDWELL, D. S. L., *Turning Points in Western Technology* (New York, 1972).
CARDWELL, D. S. L., *Artisan to Graduate, University of Manchester Institute of Science and Technology (UMIST)* (Manchester, 1974).
CARNES, M., *Puccini* (1974).
CARVEL, J. L., *Stephen of Linthouse* (Glasgow, 1950).
CAWLEY, G., 'Some Remarks on Constructions in Brick and Wood and their Relative Suitability for Japan', *TASJ*, vol. 6, pt II (1878) pp. 291–317.
CAWLEY, G., 'Wood and its Application to Japanese Artistic and Industrial Design', *JSL*, vol. II (1892–5) pp. 194–224.
CHALMERS, R., *A History of Currency in the British Colonies* (1893).
CHAMBERLAIN, B. H., *Things Japanese* (1891).
CHAMBERLAIN, B. H. and MASON, W. B., *A Handbook for Travellers in Japan* (1907).
CHANCE, J. T., *An Optical Apparatus used in Lighthouses* (1867).
CHANDLER, A. D., Jr, *Strategy and Structure: Chapters in the History of the Industrial Enterprise* (Cambridge, Mass., 1962).
CHANDLER, A. D., Jr, *The Visible Hand: the Managerial Revolution in American Business* (Cambridge, Mass., 1967).
CHANG, Chung-fu, *The Anglo-Japanese Alliance* (Baltimore, 1931).

CHANG, R., 'General Grant's 1879 Visit to Japan', *MN*, vol. XXIV, no. 4 (1969) pp. 373–92.

CHAPMAN, J. W. M., *The Price of Admiralty: The War Diary of the German Naval Attaché in Japan, 1939–1943* (Ripe, 1981).

CHECKLAND, O., 'Scotland and Japan, 1860–1914, A Study of Technical Transfer and Cultural Exchange', in I. Nish (ed.) *Bakumatsu and Meiji: Studies in Japan's Economic and Social History* (ICERD, LSE International Studies 1981–2).

CHECKLAND, O., 'The Scots in Meiji Japan, 1868–1912', in R. A. Cage (ed.) *The Scots Abroad, labour, capital, enterprise, 1750–1914* (1984).

CHECKLAND, O. and S. G., 'British and Japanese Economic Interaction under the early *Meiji*: The Takashima Coal Mine 1868–88', *BH*, vol. XXVI, no. 2 (July 1984) pp. 139–55.

CHECKLAND, S. G., *The Elgins: A Tale of Aristocrats, Proconsuls and their Wives, 1766–1917* (Aberdeen, 1988).

CHECKLAND, S. G. and O., *Industry and Ethos: Scotland 1832–1914* (1984).

CHEONG, W. E., *Mandarins and Merchants, Jardine Matheson & Co.: A China Agency of the Early Nineteenth Century* (Malmö, 1979).

CHIKAYOSHI, K., 'The Role Played by the Industrial World in the Progress of Japanese Science and Technology', *JWH*, vol. 9, pt 2 (1965) pp. 400–21.

CHIROL, V., *The Far East Question* (1896).

CLARK, R. C., *The Japanese Company* (New Haven, 1979).

CLARKE, J. F., *A History of R. & W. Hawthorn Leslie: Power on Land and Sea, 160 years of Industrial Enterprise on Tyneside* (n.p., n.d.).

CLARKE, J. F., *A History of the North East Coast Shipbuilders Association* (n.p., n.d.).

CLEMENT, A. G. and ROBERTSON, R. H. S., *Scotland's Scientific Heritage* (Edinburgh, 1971).

CLINARD, O. J., *Japan's Influence on American Naval Power* (1947).

CLOWES, W. L., *The Royal Navy: A History* (1897–1903).

CLYDE Shipbuilders' and Engineers' Association and Clyde Associated Shipwrights, *Arbitration Proceedings, 1877* (Glasgow, 1878).

COCHRANE, A., *The Early History of Elswick* (Newcastle upon Tyne, 1909).

COLE, A. B., *A Scientist with Perry in Japan: the Journal of Dr James Morrow* (Chapel Hill, North Carolina, 1947) p. xviii.

COLLIS, M., *Wayfoong: The Hongkong and Shanghai Banking Corporation* (1965).

COLQUHOUN, A. R., *English Policy in the Far East* (1895).

COLUMB, P. H., *Naval Warfare* (1891).

CONDER, J., *A Few Remarks on Architecture* (Tokyo, 1878).

CONDER, J., 'The History of Japanese Costume', *TASJ*, vol. VIII (1880) p. 333 and vol. IX (1881) p. 254.

CONDER, J., 'The Art of Landscape Gardening in Japan', *TASJ*, vol. XIV (1886) p. 119.

CONDER, J., 'The Theory of Japanese Flower Arrangement', *TASJ*, vol. XVII (1890) pp. 1–96 + 68 plates of illustrations.

CONN, J. F. C., *University of Glasgow, Department of Naval Architecture 1883–1983* (Glasgow, 1983) privately printed.

CONROY, H., DAVIS, S. T. W. and PATTERSON, W. (eds) *Japan in Transition: Thought and Action in the Meiji Era, 1868–1912* (Toronto, 1985).

CONSTABLE, T., *Memoir of Lewis D. B. Gordon* (Edinburgh, 1877) (GUL Mul-e.37).

CONSULAR REPORTS, see individual references.

CORLETT, E. C., *The Iron Ship* (Bradford-on-Avon, 1975).

CORTAZZI, H., 'The Pestilently Active Minister', *MN*, Summer 1984, vol. XXXIX, no. 2.

CORTAZZI, H., *Victorians in Japan, in and around the Treaty Ports* (1987).

COSENZA, M. E., *Complete Journal of Townshend Harris, First American Consul and Minister to Japan* (New York, 1930).

COTGROVE, S. F., *Technical Education and Social Change* (1958).

COWAN, C. D. (ed.) *The Economic Development of China and Japan* (1964).

COWPE, A., 'The RN and the Whitehead Torpedo' in Bryan Ranft (ed.) *Technical Change and British Naval Policy 1860–1939* (1977).

CRAIG, A. M., *Choshu in the Meiji Restoration* (Cambridge, Mass., 1961).

CRAIG, A. M., 'John Hill Burton and Fukuzawa Yukichi', Fukuzawa Memorial Center, Kindai Nihon Kenkyu, Keio University, Tokyo (1984) vol. 1, pp. 238–218.

CRAIG, A. M. and SHIVELY, D. (eds) *Personality in Japanese History* (Berkeley, California, 1970).

CRAMMOND, E., *The British Shipping Industry* (1917).

CRAMP, C. H., 'The Coming Sea Power', *North American Review*, vol. CLXV (October, 1897) pp. 444–51.

CRAWCOUR, S., 'The Tokugawa Period and Japan's Preparation for Modern Economic Growth', *Journal of Japanese Studies*, vol. I (Autumn, 1974).

CRIGHTON, R. A., *The Floating World: Japanese Popular Prints, 1700–1900* (1973).

CRUMP, J. D., *The Origins of Socialists Thought in Japan* (1984).

CURZON, G. N., *Problems of the Far East* (Westminster, 1896).

DALBY, W. E., 'The Training of Engineers in the United States', *TINA*, vol. 45 (1903).

DALLIN, D. J., *The Rise of Russia in Asia* (1950).

DANIELS, G., 'The Japanese Civil War. 1868: A British View', *MAS*, vol. I (1967) pp. 241–64.

DANIELS, G., 'The British Role in the *Meiji* Restoration: A Re-interpretive Note', *MAS*, vol. II (1968) pp. 291–313.

DAVIE, G. E., *The Democratic Intellect: Scotland and her Universities in the Nineteenth Century* (Edinburgh, 1961).

DAVIS, G. T., *A Navy Second to None* (1940).

DAYER, R., *Finance and Empire* (1988).

DEAKIN, B. M., *Shipping Conferences: A Study of their Origins, Development and Economic Practices* (Cambridge, 1973).

DENNY, W., 'The Trial of Screw Steamships', *British Association Reports* (1875).

DEVINE, W. D., Jr, 'From Shafts to Wires; Historical Perspective on Electrification', *Journal of Economic History*, vol. XLIII (June 1983) no 2, pp. 347–72.
DICKENS, F. V., *The Life of Sir Harry Parkes, KCB. GCMG, sometime Her Majesty's Minister to China and Japan*, vol. II *Minister Plenipotentiary* (1894).
DICKENSON, G. LOWES, *Appearances* (1914).
DICKSON, W. G., *Gleanings from Japan* (Edinburgh, 1889).
DILLON, M., *Palmer's Shipbuilding and Iron Company Limited* (Newcastle upon Tyne, 1904).
DIOSY, A., *The New Far East* (1898).
DIVERS, E., Obituary of Alex. Williamson, *PRS*, vol. 78A, pp. XXIV–X/IV (1907).
DIXON, J. M., 'Konodai and its Spots of Interest', *TASJ*, vol. 10, pt I (1882) pp. 39–47.
DIXON, J. M., 'The Tsuishikari Ainos', *TASJ*, vol. 2, pt 1 (1874) pp. 39–50.
DIXON, J. M., 'Voyage of the Dutch Ship *Grol*, from Hirado to Tong King', *TASJ*, vol. 11, pt II (18) pp. 180–215.
DIXON, J. M., 'Japanese Etiquette', *TASJ*, vol. 13, pt I (1885) pp. 1–21.
DIXON, J. M., 'Christian Valley', *TASJ*, vol. 16, pt III (1888) pp. 207–14.
DIXON, J. M., 'Habits of the Blind in Japan', *TASJ*, vol. 19, pt III (1891) pp. 578–82.
DIXON, J. M., 'Chomei and Wordsworth: A Literary Parallel', *TASJ*, vol. 20, pt II (1893) pp. 193–204.
DIXON, J. M., 'A Description of My Hut', *TASJ*, vol. 20, pt II (1893) pp. 205–15.
DIXON, W. G., 'Some Scenes between the Ancient and Modern Capitals of Japan', *TASJ*, vol. 6, pt III (1878) pp. 401–31.
DIXON, W. G., *Land of the Morning* (Edinburgh, 1882).
DOLBY, J., *The Steel Navy* (1962).
DORE, R., *Education in Tokugawa Japan* (1965).
DORE, R., *British Factory: Japanese Factory* (1973).
DOUGAN, D., *The History of North East Shipbuilding* (1968).
DOUGAN, D., *The Great Gun-makers, The Story of Lord Armstrong* (Newcastle, 1971).
DOUGLAS, A. C., 'The Genesis of Japan's Navy', *JSL*, vol. XXXVI (1938–9) pp. 19–28.
DRESSER, C., *Unity in Variety, as Deduced from the Vegetable Kingdom* (1859).
DRESSER, C., *The Art of Decorative Design* (1862).
DRESSER, C., *The Principles of Decorative Design* (1873).
DRESSER, C., *Japan: its Architecture, Art and Art Manufactures* (1882).
DU CANE, F., *The Flowers and Gardens of Japan* (1908).
DUNCAN, D., *Life and Letters of Herbert Spencer* (1908).
DUNN, C. J., *Everyday Life in Traditional Japan* (Tokyo, 1969).
DUUS, P., 'Whig History, Japanese Style: the *Min'yusha* historians and the *Meiji* Restoration', *JAS*, XXXIII, no. 3 (May 1974) pp. 415–36.
DYER, H., *General Report by the Principal* (Tokyo, 1877).

DYER, H., *The Education of Engineers*, Imperial College of Engineering (Tokei, 1879). (GUL, Y4.f.25).
DYER, H., *The Education of Civil and Mechanical Engineers* (1880).
DYER, H., *Valedictory Address to the Students of the Imperial College of Engineering* (with letter from A. Yoshikawa, Assistant Minister of Public Works) (Tokei, 1882). (GUL, I15, d.8).
DYER, H., *Technical Education, with Special Reference to the Requirements of Glasgow and the West of Scotland* (Glasgow, 1883).
DYER, H., *On Energy and Entropy, with their Applications to the Theories of Air and Steam* (Glasgow, 1885).
DYER, H., *The Development of the Marine Engine* (Glasgow, 1886).
DYER, H., *On the Present State of the Theory of the Steam Engine and Some of its Bearings on Current Marine Engineering Practice* (Glasgow, 1886).
DYER, H., *On the Education of Engineers* (Glasgow, 1887).
DYER, H., 'The Technical Schools (Scotland) Act, 1887, and Some of its Relations to Elementary and Higher Education', *PGPS*, vol. 19 (Glasgow, 1888).
DYER, H., 'The First Century of the Marine Engine', *TINA*, vol. 30 (1889) pp. 86–112.
DYER. H., On the Horse Power of Marine Engines', *TIESS*, vol. 32, 1888–9 (Glasgow, 1889) pp. 1–36.
DYER, H., *The Efficiency of Steamships from the Owners' Point of View* (Glasgow, 1889).
DYER, H., *The Foundations of Social Politics* (Glasgow, 1889).
DYER, H., *A Modern University with Special Reference to the Requirements of Science* (Perth, 1889).
DYER, H., *Notes on Some Recent Steam Engine Trials* (1889).
DYER, H., *The Steam Engine since the Days of Watt* (Greenock, 1889).
DYER, H., 'The Training of Architects', *PGPS*, vol. 20 (Glasgow, 1889).
DYER, H., 'On a University Faculty of Engineering . . . with Discussion', *TIESS*, vol. 33 (1889–90) (Glasgow, 1890) pp. 15–54.
DYER, H., *Christianity and Social Problems* (Glasgow, 1890).
DYER, H., 'The Science Curriculum in the Universities', *Scots Magazine* (May 1890).
DYER, H., 'Memoir of Henry Muirhead, M.D., Ll.D.', *PGPS*, vol. 22 (1890–2) pp. 22–30.
DYER, H., *The Influence of Modern Industry on Social and Economic Conditions* (Manchester, 1892).
DYER, H., *Science Teaching in Schools*, an Address (1893).
DYER, H., 'Technical Education in Glasgow and the West of Scotland. A Retrospect and a Prospect', *PGPS* (November 1893).
DYER, H., 'Education in Citzenship', in Cooperative Wholesale Socieites Ltd, England and Scotland, Annual for 1894.
DYER, H., *The Evolution of Industry* (1895).
DYER, H., *Dai Nippon, the Britain of the East: A Study in National Evolution* (1905).
DYER, H., 'Education and National Efficiency in Japan', *Nature*, vol. 71, letter to the Editor (1905–6).

DYER, H., *Introductory Address on the Training and Work of Engineers in their Wider Aspects* (Glasgow, 1905).
DYER, H., *Japanese Industries and Foreign Investments* (Popular Financial Booklets, IX) (1906).
DYER, H., *The Continuation Classes of the School Board of Glasgow* (Glasgow, 1906).
DYER, H., *Education and Work: A Lecture* (Dunfermline, 1906).
DYER, H., *Glasgow Technical College Scientific Society: An Introductory Address on the Training and Work of Engineers in their Wider Aspects* (Glasgow, 1906).
DYER, H., 'Some Lessons from Japan', in Cooperative Wholesale Societies Ltd, Annual for 1908, pp. 146–66.
DYER, H., 'Western teaching for China', *Nature*, vol. 80 (1909) pp. 99–100.
DYER, H., *Japan in World Politics: A Study in International Dynamics* (1909).
DYER, H., *Education and National Life* (1912).
DYER, H., *Education and Industrial Training of Boys and Girls* (1913).
DYER, H., *Missions and Missionaries* (n.p., n.d.).
EARDLEY-WILMOT, Sir J. E., *Reminiscences of the late Thomas Assheton Smith* (1960).
EARLE, J., *An Introduction to Japanese Prints* (1980).
EDWARDS, H. J., 'Japanese Undergraduates at Cambridge University', *JSL*, vol. III (1905–7) pp. 46–58.
EHRLICH, E., *Japan: A Case of Catching Up* (Budapest, 1984).
ELGAR, F., 'Japanese Shipping', *JSL*, vol. III (1893–5) pp. 59–82.
ELLIOTT, I., *The Balliol College Register*, 1833–1933 (Oxford, 1934) 2nd edn.
EMERSON, G. S., *Engineering Education: A Social History* (Newton Abbot, 1973).
EMERSON, G. S., *John Scott Russell: A Great Victorian Engineer and Naval Architect* (1977).
ENBUTSU, S., *Discover Shitamachi* (Tokyo, 1984).
ENGLISH, P. J., *British Made: Industrial Development and Related Archaeology of Japan, Rail Transportation* (Aaalst Waalre, Nederland, 1982).
ERICSON, M. D., 'The *Bakufu* Looks Abroad', *MN*, vol. XXXIV, no. 4 (Winter 1979) pp. 383–407.
EWING, A. W., *The Man of Room 40: A Life of Sir Alfred Ewing* (1939).
EWING, J. A., 'Notes on Some Recent Earthquakes', *TASJ*, vol. 9, pt I (1881) pp. 40–7.
EWING, J. A., *The University Training of Engineers: An Introductory Lecture* (Cambridge, 1891) (ULC Cam C 891.22).
EWING, J. A., *The Steam Engine and Other Heat Engines* (Cambridge, 1897).
EWING, J. A., *An Engineer's Outlook* (1933).
EYRE, J. V., *H. E. Armstrong 1848–1937* (1938).
FAIRBANK, J. F. *et al.*, 'The Influence of Modern Western Science and Technology on Japan and China', *Explorations in Entrepreneurial History*, vol. 7 (1955) pp. 189–204.
FAIRBANK, J. F. *et al.*, *East Asia: the Modern Transformation* (Boston, 1965).

FALK, E. A., *Togo and The Rise of Japanese Sea Power* (1936).

FARNIE, D. A., *East and West of Suez: The Suez Canal in History 1854–1956* (Oxford, 1969).

FARNIE, D. A., *The English Cotton Industry and the World Market, 1815–1896* (Oxford, 1979).

FAULDS, H., *Nine Years in Nippon* (1885).

FAULDS, H., *Guide to Finger-Print Identification* (Hanley, 1905).

FAYLE, C. E., *A Short History of the World's Shipping Industry* (1933).

FINN, D., *The East*, Tokyo, vol. XIII, pt 1–2 (December 1976) pp. 84–8.

FISCHER, W. *et al. The Emergence of a World Economy, 1500–1914* (Wiesbaden, 1986).

FISHER, C. A., 'The Britain of the East: A Study of the Geography of Imitation', *MAS*, vol. 2 (1968) pp. 343–76.

FISHER, Lord J. A., *Memories* (1919).

FISHER, Lord J. A., *Records* (1920).

FITZGERALD, P., *Memories of the Sea* (1913).

FOX, G., 'The Anglo-Japanese Convention of 1854', *Pacific Historical Review*, vol. 10 (1941) pp. 411–34.

FOX, G., *Britain and Japan 1858–1883* (Oxford, 1969).

FRANCKS, P., *Technology and Agricultural Development in Pre-war Japan* (New Haven, 1984).

FRASER, A., 'The Expulsion of Okuma from the Government in 1881', *JAS*, vol. 26, pt 2 (February 1967) pp. 213–36.

FRASER, A., 'Komuro Shinobu (1839–1898): A *Meiji* Politician and Businessman', *Papers on Far Eastern History*, 3 (March 1971) pp. 61–83.

FRASER, M. C., *A Diplomat's Wife in Japan* (1899) new edition edited by Hugh Cortazzi (New York, Tokyo, 1982).

FUJII, K., 'Atomism in Japan, 1868–1888', *Japanese Studies in the History of Science*, no. 14 (1975) pp. 141–56.

FUJII, T., 'Progress of Naval Engineering in Japan', *TINA*, vol. LIII (1911).

FUJITA, S., (in Japanese) *Recollections of the Institute of Technology* (Tokyo, January 1930).

FUKUZAWA, Y., *The Autobiography of Fukuzawa Yukichi*, translated by Eiichi Kiyooka (Tokyo, 1960).

FUKUZAWA, Y., *An Encouragement of Learning (Gakomon no susume, 1872–6)* translated by D. A. Dilworth and U. Hirano (Tokyo, 1969).

FUKUZAWA, Y., *An Outline of a Theory of Civilization (Bummeiron no Gairyaku, 1875)* translated by D. A. Dilworth and G. C. Hurst (1973).

FUKUZAWA, Y., *An Education: Selected Works*, translated and edited by E. Kiyooka (Tokyo, 1985).

FUKUZAWA, Y., *Seiyo Jiyo* (*Conditions in the West), Collected Works* (Tokyo, 1985).

FURUYA, H., *Toko Yoyei* (Tokyo, 1910).

FYNN, R., *British Consuls Abroad* (1846).

GERSCHENKRON, A., *Economic Backwardness in Historical Perspective* (Cambridge, Mass., 1962).

GERSCHENKRON, A., *Europe in the Russian Mirror* (Cambridge, 1970).

GERSCHENKRON, A., *An Economic Spirit that Failed: Four Lectures in Austrian History* (Princeton, 1977).

GERSON, J. J., *Horatio Nelson Lay and Sino-British Relations, 1854–1864* (Cambridge, Mass., 1972).
GIBBS-SMITH, C. H., *The Great Exhibition of 1851* (Victoria & Albert Museum, 1950).
GILL, E. M., *British Economic Interests in the Far East* (1943).
GLAZEBROOK, R. T., 'James Alfred Ewing, 1855–1935', *Obituary Notices of Fellows of the Royal Society* (1932–5) pp. 475–92.
GOOCH, G. P. and MASTERMAN, J. H. B., *A Century of British Foreign Policy* (1917).
GORDON, A., *The Evolution of Labour Relations in Japan: Heavy Industry, 1853–1955* (Harvard, 1985).
GRAHAM, G. S., *The Politics of Naval Supremacy* (Cambridge, 1965).
GRANT, A., *Steel and Ships: The History of John Browns* (1950).
GRAY, T., *Testimonials* (GUL Kelvin Collection, Y2.c.13 and Y1-m.20).
GREEN, E. and MOSS, M., *A Business of National Importance: the Royal Mail Shipping Group, 1902–1937* (1982).
GREEN, G. and LLOYD, J. T., *Kelvin's Instruments and the Kelvin Museum* (Glasgow, 1970).
GREEN, J., *On the Nature and Character of the Consular Service* (1848).
GREENBERG, M., *British Trade and the Opening of China 1800–1842* (Cambridge, 1951).
GREENHILL, R., 'Shipping, 1850–1914' in D. C. M. Platt, *Business Imperialism, 1840–1930* (Oxford, 1977).
GREY, E., *Twenty-five years 1892–1916* (1916).
GRIFFIS, W. E., *The Mikado's Empire* (New York, 1876).
GRIFFIS, W. E., *Townshend Harris, First American Envoy in Japan* (Boston, 1895).
GRIFFIS, W. E., *Verbeck of Japan* (New York, 1900).
GRIFFIS, W. E., 'British and American cooperation in Asia', *Landmark VII* (1925).
GUBBINS, J. H. (translator) *The Civil Code of Japan* (Yokohama, 1897).
GUBBINS, J. H., *The Progress of Japan 1853–1871* (Oxford, 1911).
GUBBINS, J. H., *Japan*, HMSO, no. 73 (1920).
GUBBINS, J. H., *The Making of Modern Japan, 1853–1871: An Account of the Progress of Japan from Pre-feudal days to Constitutional Government and the Position of a Great Power, with chapters on religion, the complex family system, education, etc.* (1922).
GUTHRIE, J., *A History of Marine Engineering* (1971).
HAACK, R., 'The Development of German Shipbuilding', *Engineering Magazine* (August 1899).
HACKER, B. C., 'The Weapons of the West Military Technology and Modernization in Nineteenth Century China and Japan', *Technology and Culture*, vol. 18, no. 1, January 1977, pp. 43–55.
HACKETT, R. F., *Yamagata Aritomo in the Rise of Modern Japan 1838–1922* (Cambridge, Mass., 1972).
HAFFNER, C., *The Craft in the East* (Hong Kong, 1979).
HAGEN, E. E., *Theories of Economic Growth and Development* (1962).
HALL, A. R., 'Scientific Method and the Progress of Techniques', in E. E.

Rich and Charles H. Wilson (eds) *Cambridge Economic History of Europe*, vol. IV (Cambridge, 1967).
HALL, I. P., *Mori Arinori* (Cambridge, Mass., 1973).
HALL, J. W., 'A Monarch for Modern Japan', in R. E. Ward (ed.) *Political Development in Modern Japan* (1968).
HALL, J. W. and JANSEN, M. B., *Studies in the Institutional History of Early Modern Japan* (Princeton, 1968).
HALL, R., *Marie Stopes: A Biography* (1977).
HALLIDAY, J., *A Political History of Japanese Capitalism* (New York, 1975).
HAMADA, K., *Prince Ito* (1936).
HAMAOKA, I., *A Study on the Central Bank of Japan* (Tokyo, 1902).
HANE, M., 'The Sources of English Liberal Concepts in early Meiji Japan', *MN*, vol. XXIV, no. 3 (1969) pp. 259–72.
HANE, M., 'Early Meiji Liberalism: An Assessment', *MN*, vol. XXIV, no. 4 (1969) pp. 353–71.
HARBRON, D., *The Conscious Stone: A Life of E. W. Godwin* (1949).
HARCOURT, L. F. V., *Achievements in Engineering in the Last Half Century* (1891).
HARDY, A. C., *From Ship to Sea* (Glasgow, 1926).
HAROOTUNIAN, H. D., 'The Progress of Japan and the Samurai Class', *Pacific Historical Review*, 28 (1959) pp. 255–66.
HAROOTUNIAN, H. D., 'The Economic Rehabilitation of the Samurai in the Early Meiji Period', *JAS*, vol. XIX, no. 4 (August 1960) pp. 433–44.
HARRIS, J. and BROCK, W. H., 'From Giessen to Gower Street: Towards a Biography of Alexander William Williamson (1824–1904)', *Annals of Science* (1974) vol. 31 no. 2, pp. 95–130.
HARRISON, P., *Oliphant* (1956).
HAVENS, T. R. H., 'Comte, Mill and the Thought of Nishi Amane in Meiji Japan', *JAS*, vol. XXVII (1968) pp. 81–94.
HAVENS, T. R. H., 'Scholars and Politics in Nineteenth Century Japan: The Case of Nishi Amane', *MAS*, vol. 2 (1968) pp. 315–24.
HAVENS, T. R. H., *Nishi Amane and Modern Japanese Thought* (Princeton, 1970).
HAYASHI, T., *The Secret Memoirs of Count Hayashi*, edited by A. M. Pooley (1915).
HEARN, L., *Glimpses of Unfamiliar Japan* (1903).
HEARNSHAW, F. J. C., *Centenary History of King's College, London, 1828–1928* (1929).
HECO, J., *Narrative of a Japanese*, 2 vols (Yokohama, 1899).
HEINZ, M. and MIYOKO, S., 'The Blue-eyed Storyteller', *MN*, vol. XXXVIII, no. 2 (summer 1983) pp. 133–62.
HENDERSON, Sir J., *MacQuorn Rankine* (Glasgow, 1932).
HENDERSON, P., *Laurence Oliphant* (1956).
HENDERSON, W. O., *The Rise of German Industrial Power, 1834–1914* (Berkeley, 1975).
HERBERT-GUSTAR, L. K. and NOTT, P. A., *John Milne, Father of Modern Seismology* (Tenterden, 1980).
HESKETH, E., *J. & E. Hall Ltd, 1785–1935* (Glasgow, 1935).

HESKETT, J., *Industrial Design* (Oxford, 1980).
HEWAT, E. G. K., *Vision and Achievement* (Edinburgh, 1960).
HILKEN, T. J. N., *Engineering at Cambridge University, 1783–1965* (Cambridge, 1967).
HILLS, R. L., *Power in the Industrial Revolution* (Manchester, 1970).
HIRAKAWA, S., 'Changing Japanese Attitudes toward Western Learning: A Study on the Rise and Fall of Western Learning by Rintaro (Ogai) Mori, 1862–1922', *Contemporary Japan*, vol. XXVIII, no. 3 (May 1966) pp. 550–66.
HIRAKAWA, S. 'Changing Japanese Attitudes ... Is Study Abroad Meaningless?' *Contemporary Japan*, vol. XXVIII, no. 4 (May 1967) pp. 789–806.
HIRAKAWA, S., 'Changing Japanese Attitudes ... Dr Erwin Baelz and Mori Ogai', *Contemporary Japan*, vol. XXIX, no. 1 (1968) pp. 138–57.
HIROSIGE, T., 'The Role of the Government in the Development of Science', *JWH*, vol. 9 (1965–6) pp. 320–39.
HIRSCHMANN, A. O., *The Strategy of Economic Development* (New Haven, 1959).
HIRSCHMEIER, J., *Origins of Entrepreneurship in Meiji Japan* (Cambridge, Mass., 1964).
HIRSCHMEIER, J., 'Shibusawa Eiichi: Industrial Pioneer', in W. W. Lockwood (ed.) *The State and Economic Enterprise in Japan* (Princeton, 1965).
HIRSCHMEIER, J. and YUI, T., *The Development of Japanese Business, 1600–1973* (Cambridge, Mass., 1975).
HODGSON, C. P., *A Residence at Nagasaki and Hakodate 1859–60* (1860).
HOLMES, H., *My Adventures in Japan* (1859).
HOLTHAM, E. G., *Eight Years in Japan 1873–1881* (1883).
HOOK, E., *A Guide to the Papers of John Swire & Sons Ltd* (1977).
HOELITZ, B. F., *The Progress of Underdeveloped Areas* (Chicago, 1952).
HOUGH, R., *The Big Battleship* (1966).
HOUSE, E. H., *The Japanese Expedition to Formosa* (Tokyo, 1875).
HOUSE, E. H., *The Kagoshima Affair* (Tokyo, 1875).
HOUSE, E. H., *The Shimonoseki Affair* (Tokyo, 1875).
HOUSE, E. H., 'Martyrdom of an Empire', *Atlantic Monthly* (April 1881) pp. 610–23.
HOWARTH, J., 'Science Education in late-Victorian Oxford: A Curious Case of Failure?, *English Historical Review*, vol. CII, no. 403 (April 1987) pp. 334–67.
HOWARTH, T., *Charles Rennie Mackintosh and the Modern Movement* (1952).
HUBBARD, J. E., *British Far Eastern Policy* (New York, 1943).
HUDSON, G. F., *The Far East in World Politics: A Study in Recent History* (Oxford, 1937).
HUDSON, G. F., 'The Far East' in vol. X of *The New Cambridge Modern History* (Cambridge, 1957–60).
HUGHES, T. P., *Networks of Power, Electrification in Western Society 1880–1930* (Baltimore, 1983).
HUGUENIN, U., *Het Gietwezen in Srijks Ejzer-Goschutzieterij te Link* (*Casting in the State Iron (Cannon) Foundry in Liege*), (Te's Gravenhage, 1826).

HUMBLE, R., *Before the Dreadnought* (1976).
HUME, J. R. and MOSS, M. S., *Clyde Shipbuilding from Old Photographs* (1975).
HUME, J. R. and MOSS, M. S., *Beardmore: The History of a Scottish Industrial Giant* (1979).
HUNTER, G. B. and de RUSETT, E. W., '60 Years of Merchant Shipbuilding', *TIESS*, vol. 52, 1908–9.
HURD, A. S., 'Japan's Ascendancy and Her Naval Development', vol. LXII, *Nineteenth Century and After* (London, July–December, 1907) pp. 365–77.
HUTCHINS, J. G. B., *The American Maritime Industries and Public Policy, 1789–1914* (Cambridge, Mass., 1941).
HYDE, F. E., *Blue Funnel: A History of Alfred Holt and Company of Liverpool from 1865–1914* (Liverpool, 1957).
HYDE, F. E., *Liverpool and the Mersey: An Economic History of a Port, 1700–1970* (Newton Abbot, 1971).
HYDE, F. E., *Far Eastern Trade, 1860–1914* (1973).
HYDE, F. E., *Cunard and the North Atlantic, 1843–1973: A History of Shipping and Financial Management* (1975).
IDDITTIE, J., *Marquis Okuma: A Biographical Study in the Rise of Democratic Japan* (Tokyo, 1956).
IKE, N., *The Beginnings of Political Democracy in Japan* (Baltimore, 1950).
IMAZU, K., 'The Beginning of Electrical Engineers in Japan', *Japanese Studies in the History of Science*, no. 17 (1978) pp. 13–26.
IMPERIAL College of Engineering (Tokyo) (Tokyo, 1873–4).
INAGAKI, M., *Japan and the Pacific*, 1890.
INGLIS, J., *The Apprenticeship Question* (Glasgow, 1894).
INKSTER, I. E., 'Meiji Economic Development in Perspective: Revisionist Comments upon the Industrial Revolution in Japan', *Developing Economics*, XVII, pt I (March 1979) pp. 45–67.
INKSTER, I. E., *Japan as a Development Model? Relative Backwardness and Technological Transfer* (Bochum, 1980).
INKSTER, I. E., *Science Technology and the Late Development Effect: Transfer Mechanisms in Japan's Industrialisation, circa 1850–1912* (Tokyo, 1981).
INMAN, C., 'A. and C. Black's 20/- Series', *Antiquarian Book Monthly Review* (October 1987).
INOUYE, K., *Commemoration Volume Dedicated to Konosuke Inouye* (Ryojun, 1934).
INUZUKA, T. (in Japanese) *Satsuma Students in England* (Tokyo, 1974).
IRVIN, J. C., 'Scotland's Contribution to Chemistry', *Journal of Chemical Education*, vol. 7 (1930).
IRVING, R. J., 'New Industries for Old? Some Investment Decisions of Sir W. G. Armstrong Whitworth & Co., Ltd, 1900–14', *BH*, 17, no. 2 (July 1975).
ISHII, R., *Japanese Legislation in the Meiji Era* translated by W. J. Chambliss (Tokyo, 1958).
ISHII, R., *A History of Political Institutions in Japan* (Tokyo, 1980).
ISHIZAKA, H., 'The Slum-Dwellings and Urban Renewal Schemes in Tokyo 1868–1923', *Developing Economies*, vol. XIX, pt 2 (June 1981) pp. 169–93.

ITO, H., *Ito Ko Zenshu*, edited by M. Komatsu (Tokyo, 1928).
ITO, H., *Ito Hirobumi* (Tokyo, 1929–30).
ITSUO, H., *A Study of the Central Bank of Japan* (1902) (GUL.Y9.c.20).
IWAO, S., *A List of Foreign Office Records Preserved at the PRO, London, relating to China and Japan* (Tokyo, 1959).
IWATA, M., *Okubo Toshimichi: The Bismarck of Japan* (Berkeley, 1964).
JAMIESON, A., 'On the Technical Education of our Young Engineers, Shipbuilders and Artisans', *TIESS*, 24 (1880–1).
JANE, F. T., *All the World's Fighting Ships* (1898).
JANE, F. T., *The Imperial Japanese Navy*, 1904 (reprinted 1984).
JANSEN, M. B., *Sakamoto Ryoma and the Meiji Restoration* (Princeton, 1961).
JANSEN, M. B., *Changing Japanese Attitudes towards Modernisation* (Princeton, 1965).
JANSEN, M. B., 'Monarchy and Modernisation in Japan', *JAS*, vol. 36 (August 1977) pp. 611–22.
JANSEN, M. B. and ROZMAN, G. (eds) *Japan in Transition: From Tokugawa to Meiji* (Princeton, 1986).
JENKIN, F., *A Lecture on the Education of Civil and Mechanical Engineers* (Edinburgh, 1868).
JENKIN, F., *The Papers of Fleeming Jenkin*, 2 vols, with Memoir by R. L. Stevenson (1887).
JENNINGS, E., *Cargoes: A Centenary Story of the Far Eastern Freight Conference* (Singapore, 1980).
JENTSCHURA, H., JUNG, D., and MICKEL, P., *Warships of the Imperial Japanese Navy 1869–1945* (Annapolis, 1977) translated by A. Preston and J. D. Brown.
JOHN, T. G., 'Shipbuilding Practice of the Present and Future', *Engineering* (10 July 1914) pp. 68–71.
JOHNSON, H. H. and BARWELL, F. T., *The Whitworth Register*, published by the Whitworth Society (n.d., c. 1960).
JONES, F. C., *Extra Territoriality in Japan* (New Haven, 1931).
JONES, H. J., 'The Formulation of Meiji Policy towards the Employment of Foreigners', *MN*, vol. 23, 1–2 (1968) pp. 9–30.
JONES, H. J., '*Bakumatsu* Foreign Employees', *MN* vol. 29, 3 (1974) pp. 305–27.
JONES, H. J., *Live Machines* (Tenterden, Kent, 1980).
JONES, R. A., *The Nineteenth Century Foreign Office: An Administrative History* (1971).
JONES, R. A., *The British Diplomatic Service 1815–1914* (Gerrards Cross, 1983).
JONES, S. H., 'Early Industrialization in Japan, the Example of the Saga Clan', *Columbia University East Asian Institute Studies*, no. 6 (New York, 1959) pp. 16–19.
JONES-PARRY, E., 'Under-Secretaries of State for Foreign Affairs, 1782–1855', *English Historical Review*, vol. 49 (1934) pp. 308–20.
JORDAN, G., *Naval Warfare in the Twentieth Century* (1977).
JORDAN, R. F., *Victorian Architecture* (1966).
JUNG, I., *The Marine Turbine: A Historical Review by a Swedish Engineer,*

*Part I, The Days of Coal and Steam 1897–1927*, Maritime Monographs and Reports, no 50 (1982).
KADONO, C., 'Japanese Railways', *JSL*, vol. V (1898–1901) pp. 28–37.
KAGAN, P., *New World Utopias* (New York, 1975).
KAJIMA, M., *A Brief Diplomic History of Modern Japan* (Rutland, Vermont, 1968).
KAJU, N., *Prince Ito* (New York, 1910).
KANO, H., *Banking in Japan: An Outline of its History* (Tokyo, 1953).
KAPLAN, E. J., *Japan: the Government Business Relationship* (Washington, DC, 1972).
KARGON, R. H., *Science in Victorian Manchester* (Johns Hopkins, Baltimore, 1978).
KEENE, D., *The Japanese Discovery of Europe, 1720–1830* (Stanford, 1969).
KEENLEYSIDE, H. L. and THOMAS, A. F., *A History of Japanese Education* (Tokyo, 1937).
KEIZO, S., *Japanese Society in the Meiji Era* (Tokyo, 1958).
KELLEY, A. C. and WILLIAMSON, J. G., 'Writing History Backwards, Meiji Japan revisited', *Journal of Economic History*, vol. 31, no 4 (December 1971) pp. 729–76.
KELLEY, A. C. and WILLIAMSON, J. G., *Lessons from Japanese Development* (Chicago, 1974).
KELVIN, LORD, *Kelvin Centenary Oration and Addresses Commemorative* (Glasgow, 1924).
KEMBLE, J. H., 'A Hundred Years of the Pacific Mail', *American Neptune*, 10, pt 2 (April 1950).
KEMP, P. K. (ed.) *The papers of Admiral Sir John Fisher* (Greenwich, 1960).
KENGI, H., *Prince Ito* (Tokyo, 1936).
KEN'ICHI, I., 'The Early Steel Industry', *Entrepreneurship*, no 3, June (Tokyo, 1982).
KENNEDY, M. D., *The Estrangement of Great Britain and Japan 1917–35* (Manchester, 1969).
KESWICK, M., *The Thistle and the Jade* (1982).
KIEVE, J. L., *The Electric Telegraph* (Newton Abbot, 1973).
KIKUCHI, D., *Sketch of Japanese National Development more Especially with Reference to Education* (Edinburgh, 1907).
KIKUCHI, D., *Japanese Education* (1909).
KING, A. G., *Kelvin the Man* (1925).
KING, F. H. H., *Eastern Banking: Essays in the History of the Hong Kong and Shanghai Banking Corporation* (1983).
KING, J. W., *The Warships and Navies of the World* (Boston, 1880).
KINMONTH, E. H., 'Nakamura Keiu and Samuel Smiles, a Victorian Confucian and a Confucian Victorian', *American Historical Review*, vol. 85, no. 3 (June 1980), pp. 535–56.
KINMONTH, E. H., *The Self-made Man in Meiji Thought: From Samurai to Salary-man* (Berkeley, California, 1981).
KITA, M., *Kokusai Nippon wo Kirihiraita Hitobito, Nippon to Scotland no Kizuna* (*Pioneers of Making Japan International*) (Tokyo, 1984).
KITA, M., *Kindai Scotland Shakaikeizaishi Kenkyu* (*Studies of Social and Economic History of Scotland*) (Tokyo, 1985).

KNOTT, C. G., 'The Abacus, in its Historic and Scientific Aspects', *TASJ*, vol. 14, pt I (1886) pp. 18–71.
KNOTT, C. G., 'Ino Chukei, the Japanese Cartographer and Surveyor', *TASJ*, vol. 16, pt II (1888) pp. 173–8.
KNOTT, C. G., 'Remarks on Japanese Musical Scales', *TASJ*, vol. 19, pt II (1891) pp. 373–91.
KNOTT, C. G., 'Notes on the Summer Climate of Kamizawa', *TASJ*, vol. 19, pt III (1891) pp. 565–77.
KNOTT, C. G., *The Life and Scientific Work of Peter Guthrie Tait* (Cambridge, 1911).
KNOTT, C. G. and TANAKADATE, A., 'A Magnetic Survey of all Japan', *Journal of the College of Science*, Imperial University, Japan, vol. II (Tokyo, 1887) pp. 163–262.
KOBAYASHI, M., 'Policy of Encouraging Industry', *Kanto Gakuin University Economic Review* (Tokyo, 1978).
KOBAYASHI, U., *Military Industries of Japan* (New York, 1922).
KODANSHA, *Encyclopedia of Japan* (Tokyo, 1983).
KOIKE, S., 'The Evolution of Industrial Design in Japan as an Expression of Cultural Values', *JWH*, vol. 9, pt 2 (1965) pp. 380–99.
KOIZUMI, K., 'The Emergence of Japan's First Physicists, 1868–1900', *Historical Studies in the Physical Sciences*, vol. 6 (1975) pp. 3–108.
KONDO, M., 'Progress of Naval Construction in Japan', *TINA*, vol. LIII (1911) pt 2, pp. 50–60.
KOSAKA, M. and ABOSCH, D. (eds) *Japanese Thought in the Meiji Era* (Tokyo, 1958).
KUBLIN, H., 'The Modern Army of early Meiji Japan', *Far Eastern Quarterly*, 9, pt 1 (1949) pp. 20–41.
KUME, K., *Tokumei zenken taishi bei-O Kairan Jikki* (true account of the special embassy in America and Europe) (Tokyo, 1878).
KURATA, Y., *1885, Nen London Nihonjin Mura* (*The Japanese Village in London*) (Tokyo, 1985).
KUWABARA, K., *Japan and Western Civilization* (Tokyo, 1983).
LANDES, D. S., 'Entrepreneurship in Advanced Industrial Countries: The Anglo-German Rivalry', paper presented to the Conference on Entrepreneurship and Economic Growth (Cambridge, Mass., 1954).
LANDES, D. S., *The Unbound Prometheus* (Cambridge, Mass., 1969).
LANE, R., *Images from the Floating World* (Oxford, 1978).
LANE-POOLE, S. and DICKENS, F. V., *The Life of Sir Harry Parkes, KGB, GCMG, sometime Her Majesty's Minister to China and Japan* (1894) vol. II, *Japan*, by F. V. Dickens.
LANMAN, C., *Leading Men of Japan* (Lothrop, 1883).
LARNER, C., 'The Amalgamation of the Diplomatic Service with the Foreign Office', *JCH*, vol. 7, 1–2 (1972) pp. 107–26.
LAWSON, Lady, *Highways and Homes of Japan* (1910).
LEACH, B., *Beyond East and West, Memoirs, Portraits and Essays* (1978).
LEBRA, J. C., *Okuma Shigenobu, Statesman of Meiji Japan* (Canberra, 1973).
LEHMANN, J. P., *The Japanese Image* (1979).
LEHMANN, J. P., *The Roots of Modern Japan* (New York, 1982).

LEHMANN, J. P., *Guide to Madam Butterfly* (1984).
LENSEN, G. A., *Korea and Manchuria, Between Russia and Japan 1895–1904: The Observations of Sir Ernest Satow, British Minister to Japan (1895–1900) and China (1900–1906)* (Tallahassee, Florida, 1966).
LENSEN, G. A., *Report from Hokkaido: The Remains of Russian Culture in Northern Japan* (Hakodate, 1954).
LENSEN, G. A., *The Russian Push towards Japan, Russo-Japanese Relations, 1697–1875* (Princeton, 1959).
LERSKI, H., 'Josiah Conder's Bank of Japan, Tokyo', *Journal of the Society of Architectural Historians*, vol. XXXVIII, no. 3 (October 1979) pp. 271–4.
LEVINE, A. L., *Industrial Retardation in Britain 1880–1914* (New York, 1967).
LEVY, M. J., Jr, 'These are only hypotheses but . . .', *TASJ*, 3rd series, vol. 12 (Tokyo, 1975) pp. 70–101.
LLOYD, A., *Every-day Japan Written after Twenty-five Years Residence and Work in the Country* (1909).
LOCKWOOD, W. W., *The Economic Development of Japan: Growth and Structural Change 1868–1938* (Princeton, 1968).
LONGFORD, J. H., 'The Growth of the Japanese Navy', *The Nineteenth Century and After*, vol. LIV (July–December 1903).
LONGFORD, J. H., 'England's Record in Japan', *JSL*, vol. VII (1904–7) pp. 82–118.
LONGFORD, J. H., *The Evolution of New Japan* (Cambridge, 1913).
LOW, D. A., *The Whitworth Book* (1926).
LOWE, P., *Great Britain and Japan, 1911–1915: A Study of British Far Eastern Policy* (1969).
LU, D. J., *Sources of Japanese History*, vol II (New York, 1973).
LUBBOCK, B., *China Clippers* (Glasgow, 1916).
LUBBOCK, B., *Colonial Clippers* (Glasgow, 1924).
LUBBOCK, B., *Last of the Windjammers* (Glasgow, 1927).
LUBBOCK, B., *Opium Clippers* (Glasgow, 1933).
LYON, D. J. (compiler) *The Denny List*, pts I, II, III and IV (Greenwich, 1975).
LYON, D. J., *The Ship, Steam, Steel and Torpedoes: the Warship in the Nineteenth Century* (NMM, 1980).
MACALISTER, E. F. B., *Sir Donald Macalister of Tarbert* (1935).
McCLELLAND, C. E., *State, Society and University in Germany 1700–1914* (Cambridge, 1980).
McCLOSKEY, D. N., 'Did Victorian Britain Fail?' *EcHR*, n.s.23 (1970) pp. 446–59.
McCLOSKEY, D. N., *Essays on a Mature Economy: Britain after 1840* (1971).
McCLOSKEY, D. N., *Economic Maturity and Entrepreneurial Decline: British Iron and Steel 1870–1913* (Cambridge, Mass., 1973).
McCLOSKEY, D. N., 'Victorian Growth: A Rejoinder', *EcHR*, 27 (1974) pp. 275–7.
MacDONAGH, O. O. M., *A Pattern of Government Growth: The Passenger Acts and their Enforcement* (1961).
MacGREGOR, J. G., *Research in the Scottish Universities* (Edinburgh, 1901).

McKAY, J. P., *Pioneers for Profit, Foreign Entrepreneurship and Russian Industrialization, 1885–1913* (Chicago, 1970).
MacKAY, S. and ALLEN, M., *Bridge across the Century: The Story of the Forth Road Bridge* (Edinburgh, 1985).
McKENZIE, C., *Realms of Silver: One Hundred Years of Banking in the East Chartered Bank of India, Australia and China* (1954).
McKENZIE, P., *W. G. Armstrong: The Life and Times of Sir William George Armstrong, Baron Armstrong of Cragside* (Newcastle, 1983).
McLAREN, W. W., 'Japanese Government Documents', *TASJ*, vol. XLII, pt 1 (May 1914).
McLAREN, W. W., *Political History of Japan during the Meiji Era, 1867–1912* (1916).
McLEAN, R. A., 'The Finances of Japan', *JSL*, vol. VI (1901–4) pp. 206–24.
MacLEOD, R. and COLLINS, P., *The Parliament of Science: The British Association for the Advancement of Science 1831–1981* (Northwood, 1981).
MacLEOD, R. M., 'Resources of Science in Victorian England: The Endowment of the Science Movement, 1868–1900', in P. Mathias (ed.) *Science and Society 1600–1900* (Cambridge, 1972).
McMASTER, J., 'The Japanese Gold Rush of 1859', *JAS*, vol. 19, no. 3 (May 1960) pp. 273–87.
McMASTER, J., 'The Takashima Mine: British Capital and Japanese Industrialization', *BHR* (1963) vol. XXXVII, pp. 217–39.
McMASTER, J., *Jardines in Japan 1859–67* (Groningen, 1966).
McMASTER, J., *British Trade and Traders to Japan, 1859–1869* (1969).
MAGNUS, P., *Educational Aims and Efforts 1880–1910* (1910).
MANN, A. T., *The Influence of Sea-power upon the French Revolution and Empire 1793–1812* (1892).
MAHAN, A. T., *The Interest of America in Sea Power, Present and Future* (1897).
MAHAN, A. T., *The Problems of Asia and its Effects upon International Policies* (1900).
MAHAN, A. T., 'Reflections, Historic and Other, Suggested by the Battle of the Japan Sea', *United States Naval Institute Proceedings* (June 1906).
MAHAN, A. T., *Naval Strategy* (1911).
MAIR, C., *A Star for Seamen: The Stevenson Family of Engineers* (1978).
MANNARI, H., *The Japanese Business Leaders* (Tokyo, 1974).
MANNING, F. L., *The Life of Sir William White* (1923).
MANSFIELD, E., 'Technical Change and the Rate of Imitation', *Econometrica*, vol. 29, no. 4 (October 1961).
MARDER, A. J., *British Naval Policy, 1880–1905: The Anatomy of British Sea Power* (1941).
MARDER, A. J., *Fear God and Dread Nought: The Correspondence of Admiral of the Fleet Lord Fisher of Kilverstone*, 3 vols (1952–9).
MARDER, A. J., *From the Dreadnought to Scapa Flow: The Road to War, 1904–1914,* vol. I (1961).
MARDER, A. J., *Old Friends, New Enemies: The Royal Navy and the Imperial Japanese Navy, Strategic Illusions, 1936–1941* (Oxford, 1981).
MARKINO, Y., *A Japanese Artist in London* (1912).

MARKINO, Y., *My Recollections and Reflections* (1913).
MARRINER, S. and HYDE, F. E., *The Senior: John Samuel Swire 1825–1898* (Liverpool, 1967).
MARSHALL, C. T. with BOWERS, J. Z., *Letters from Meiji Japan: Correspondence of a German Surgeon's wife 1878–1881* (New York, 1980).
MARSHALL, D. H., 'Notes of a Trip from Yedo to Kioto via Asama-Yama, the Hokurokudo, and Lake Biwa', *TASJ*, vol. 4 (1876) pp. 152–74.
MARSHALL, D. H., 'Notes on some of the Volcanic Mountains in Japan', *TASJ*, vol. 6, pt II (1878) pp. 321–45.
MASAAKI, K. (ed.) *Japanese Thought in the Meiji Era* (1958).
MASAJIMA, R., 'Modern Japanese Legal Institutions', *TASJ*, vol. XVIII (1890) pp. 229–58.
MASON, W. B., 'Thomas B. Glover: A Pioneer of Anglo-Japanese Commerce', *The New East*, vol. 2 (Tokyo, 1918).
MASSON, D., *Edinburgh Sketches and Memories* (1892).
MASUDA, T., *Japan: its Commercial Developments and Prospects* (n.d. but c. 1910).
MATHESON, H. M., *Memorials of Hugh M. Matheson* (1899).
MATHIAS, P. and PEARSALL, A. W. H., *Shipping: A Survey of Historical Records* (Newton Abbot, 1971).
MATHIAS, R., *Industrialisierung und Lohnarbeit, der Kohlebergbau in Nord Kyushu und sein Einfluss auf die Heraus bildung einer Lohnarbeiterschaft* (Vienna, 1978).
MATSU, H., 'The Diplomatic and Consular Service of Japan', *JSL*, vol. VII, 1907.
MATSUKATA, M., *Report on the Adoption of the Gold Standard in Japan* (Tokyo, 1899).
MATSUKATA, M., *Report on the Post Bellum Financial Administration of Japan* (Tokyo, 1900).
MATTHEW, S. N. and WAINWRIGHT, M. D. (edited by J. D. Pearson) *A Guide to the Ms and documents in the British Isles relating to the Far East* (Oxford, 1977).
MAVOR, S., *Memories of Peoples and Places* (1940).
MAYO, M. J., 'The Iwakura Mission to the US and Europe 1871–1873', *Researches in the Social Sciences in Japan*, 6, Columbia University East Asian Institute Studies (1959) pp. 28–47.
MAYO, M. J., 'Rationality in the Meiji Restoration: The Iwakura Embassy' in B. S. Silberman and H. D. Harootunian (eds) *Modern Japanese Leadership* (Tucson, Arizona, 1966).
MAYO, M. J., 'A Catechism of Western Diplomacy: The Japanese and Hamilton Fish 1872', *JAS*, vol. XXVI, no 3 (May 1967) pp. 389–410.
MAYO, M. J., 'The Western Education of Kume Kunitake 1871–6', *MN*, vol. 28, 1 (spring, 1973) pp. 3–67.
MEEKER, R., *History of Shipping Subsidies* (New York, 1905).
*Meiji Japan through Contemporary Sources, The*, vols I, II, III (Tokyo, 1969–72).
MEIK, C. S., *Hokkaido Harbours* (Sapporo, 1887).
MEIK, C. S., *Ishikari Navigation* (Sapporo, 1889).

MEIK, C. S., 'Around the Hokkaido', *TASJ*, vol. XVI (1889) pp. 151–72.
MENPES, M., 'A Personal View of Japanese Art', *Magazine of Art* (1888) pp. 192–9, 255–61.
MENPES, M., 'A Letter from Japan', *The Studio*, vol. XI (1897) pp. 165–77.
MENPES, M., 'A Letter from Japan', *The Studio*, vol. XII (1898) pp. 21–6, 32–6.
MENPES, M., *Japan, A Record In Colour* (1901).
MENPES, M., *Whistler as I Knew Him* (1905).
MICHIE, A., *The Englishman in China during the Victorian Era, as illustrated in the career of Rutherford Alcock*, 2 vols (Edinburgh, 1900).
MICHIE, A., 'Anglo-Japanese Alliance', *Blackwoods Magazine* (Edinburgh) vol. CLXXI (1902) p. 444.
MICHIO, N., 'Herbert Spencer in early Meiji Japan', *Far Eastern Quarterly*, 14, 1 (November 1954) pp. 55–64.
MILLARD, W., 'The Late Dr Conder', *JRIBA*, XXVII, series III (25 September 1920) p. 474.
MILNE, J., 'Journey across Europe and Asia', *TASJ*, vol. 7, pt I (1879) pp. 1–72.
MILNE, J., 'Notes on Stone Implements from Otam and Hakadate, with a Few General Remarks on the Pre-historic Remains of Japan', *TASJ*, vol. 8, pt 1 (1880) pp. 61–91.
MILNE, J., 'Evidences of the Glacial Period in Japan', *TASJ*, vol. 9, pt I (1881) pp. 53–86.
MILNE, J., 'Notes on Koro-Pokgura or Pit-dwellers of Yezo and the Kurile Islands', *TASJ*, vol. 10, pt II (1882) pp. 187–98.
MILNE, T. A., *Steam Vessels Sold or Reportedly Sold to Japan up to 1870* (Tokyo, 1964) (copy in NMM Library).
MINAMI, R., 'Mechanical Power in the Industrialization of Japan', *Journal of Economic History*, vol. 37, no. 4 (December 1977) pp. 935–58.
MITFORD, A. B. F. (Lord Redesdale) *Tales of Old Japan* (1871).
MITFORD, A. B. F., *Garter Mission to Japan* (1906).
MITFORD, A. B. F., *Memories*, vols I and II (1915).
MOLLISON, J. P., 'Reminiscences of Yokohama', Lecture to Yokohama Literary and Musical Society (8 January 1909).
MORGAN, A., *Scottish University Studies* (Oxford, 1933).
MORIKAWA, H., 'The Organizational Structure of the Mitsubishi and Mitsui Zaibatsu, 1868–1922, a Comparative Study', *BHR* (spring 1970) 44, 1, pp. 622–83.
MORISHIMA, M., *Why has Japan 'Succeeded'? Western Technology and the Japanese Ethos* (1982).
MORISON, J. L., *The Eighth Earl of Elgin: A Chapter in Nineteenth Century Imperial History* (1928).
MORLEY, J. W., *Japan's Foreign Policy 1868–1941: A Research Guide* (New York, 1974).
MORRIS, J., 'Telegraphs in Japan', *Telegraphic Journal*, vol. 1 (1872–1873) (copy from Institution of Electrical Engineers, London).
MORRIS, J., *Advance Japan: A Nation Thoroughly in Earnest* (1896).
MORRIS, J., *Makers of Modern Japan* (1906).

MORRISON, G. E. (ed.) Lo Hui-min, *The Correspondence of G. E. Morrison*, 2 vols (Cambridge, 1976–8).

MORSE, E. S., *Japanese Houses and their Surroundings* (Boston, 1886).

MORSE, E. S., *Japan: Day by Day 1877, 1878–9, 1882–3*, 2 vols (Boston, 1917).

MORSE, H. B. and MacNAIR, H. F., *Far Eastern International Relations* (Shanghai, 1928).

MORTLAKE, G. N. (ed.) *Love Letters of a Japanese* (n.d.).

MOSES, J. A. and KENNEDY, P. M., *Germany in the Pacific and Far East, 1870–1914* (St Lucien, Queensland, 1977).

MOSS, M. S. and HUME, J. R., *Workshop of the British Empire: Engineering and Shipbuilding in the West of Scotland* (1977).

MOSS, M. S. and HUME, J. R., *Shipbuilders to the World: Harland & Wolff* (Belfast, 1986).

MOSSMAN, S., *New Japan, the Land of the Rising Sun* (1873).

MOTOSADA, Z., 'Journalism in Japan', *JSL*, vol. VI (1904) pp. 108–22.

MOUNSEY, A. H., *The Satsuma Rebellion: An Episode of Modern Japanese History* (1879).

MUI, H. and L. H., *The Management of Monopoly* (Vancouver, 1984).

MUNESHIGE, N., *The Japanese Print: Its Evolution and Essence* (Tokyo, 1966).

MURAMATSU, T., 'Venture into Western Architecture', *Dialogue in Art* (Tokyo and New York, 1976).

MURDOCH, J., *History of Japan*, 2 vols (1903 and 1910).

MUTSU, H., 'The Diplomatic and Consular Services of Japan', *JSL*, vol. VII (1907) pp. 434–57.

NAGAI, M., 'Herbert Spencer in early Meiji Japan', *Far Eastern Quarterly*, vol. 14, 1 (1954) pp. 55–64.

NAGAOKA, H., *Anniversary Volume dedicated to Professor Hantaro Nagaoka by his Friends and Pupils on the Completion of Twenty-five years of his Professorship* (Tokyo, 1925).

NAKAGAWA, K. (ed.) *Strategy and Structure of Big Business*, vol. 1 of *International Conference on Business History* (Tokyo, 1976).

NAKAGAWA, K. (ed.) *Marketing and Finance in the Course of Industrialization*, vol. 3 of *International Conference on Business History* (Tokyo, 1978).

NAKAMURA, J., *Agricultural Production and the Economic Development of Japan, 1873–1922* (Princeton, 1966).

NAKAMURA, J., *Economic Growth in pre-war Japan* (New Haven, 1982).

NAKAMURA, K., *Lord II Naosuke and New Japan* (translated by S. Akimoto) (n.p., 1905).

NAKAMURA, K., *Prince Ito* (New York, 1910).

NAKAMURA, N., *Okuma Shigenobu* (Tokyo, 1961).

NAKAMURA, T., 'The Contribution of Foreigners' (Special Issue on History of Science, *JWH*, vol. 9, no 2 (June 1965) pp. 294–319.

NAKAOKA, T., 'On Technological Leaps of Japan as a Developing Country, 1900–1940', *Osaka City University Economic Review*, no. 22 (1987) pp. 1–25.

NAKASIMA, Commander G., 'The Japanese Navy in the Great War', *JSL*, vol. 17 (1920).
NAKAYAMA, I., *Industrialization of Japan* (Tokyo, 1962).
NAKAYAMA, S., 'The Role Played by Universities in Scientific and Technological Development in Japan', *JWH*, vol. 9, pt 2 (1965–6) pp. 340–62.
NAPIER, D. D., *Autobiographical Sketch of David Napier, Engineer, 1790–1869* (Glasgow, 1912).
NAPIER, J., *The Life of Robert Napier of West Shandon* (Edinburgh, 1904).
NAPIER, J. R., 'A Memoir of David Elder', *TIESS*, vol. IX (1865–6).
NETTO, C., 'On Mining and Mines in Japan', *Memoirs of the Science Department of the University of Tokyo, Japan*, vol. II (Tokyo, 1879).
NISH, I. H., 'Japan reverses the Unequal Treaties: The Anglo-Japanese Commercial Treaty of 1894', *Papers of the Hong Kong International Conference on Asian History*, no. 20 (1964).
NISH, I. H., *The Anglo-Japanese Alliance: The Diplomacy of Two Island Empires, 1894–1907* (1966).
NISH, I. H., *Alliance in Decline: A Study in Anglo-Japanese Relations 1908–1923* (1972).
NISH, I. H., *China, Japan and Nineteenth Century Britain* (Dublin, 1977).
NISH, I. H., *Japanese Foreign Policy, 1869–1942* (1977).
NISH, I. H., *Anglo-Japanese Alienation 1919–1952* (Cambridge, 1982).
NISH, I. H., *Origins of Russo-Japanese War* (1985).
NISH, I. H. and DUNN, C., *European Studies on Japan* (Tenterden, 1979).
NITOBE, I. O. *et al.*, *Western Influences in Modern Japan* (Chicago, 1931).
NORMAN, E. H., *Japan's Emergence as a Modern State: Political and Economic Problems of the Meiji Period* (New York, 1940; reprinted Westport, Connecticut, 1973).
NORMAN, H., *The Real Japan* (New York, 1893).
OBATA, K., *The Interpretation of the Life of Viscount Shibusawa* (Tokyo, 1939).
OKOCHI, A. and UCHIDA, H., *Development and Diffusion of Technology: Electrical and Chemical Industries* (Tokyo, 1980).
OKUMA, S., 'The Industrial Revolution of Japan', *North American Review*, vol. CLXXI (1900).
OKUMA, S., *Fifty Years of the New Japan* (Tokyo, 1910) English version edited by M. B. Huish.
OLIPHANT, L., *Narrative of the Earl of Elgin's Mission to China and Japan in the Years 1857, 58 and 59*, 2 vols (Edinburgh, 1859).
OLIPHANT, L., 'The Attack on the British Legation', *Blackwood's Magazine*, vol. CXLI (January 1887).
OLIPHANT, M. O. W., *Memoir of the Life of Laurence Oliphant and of Alice Oliphant his Wife*, vols I and II (Edinburgh, 1891).
ORAM, H. J., 'Fifty Years Change in British Warship Machinery', *TINA*, LIII, pt 2 (1911) pp. 96–101.
ORCHARD, J. E., *Japan's Economic Position* (New York, 1930).

OSBORN, S., *A Cruise in Japanese Waters* (Edinburgh, 1859).
OSHIMA, S., *Oshima Takato gyojitsu* (Life and work of Oshima Takato) (Tokyo, 1938).
OWEN, R. and SUTCLIFFE, R. (eds) *Studies in the Theory of Imperialism* (1972).
PAGE, J., *Japan: Its People and Missions* (n.d.).
PAPINOT, E., *Historical and Geographical Dictionary of Japan* (1910).
PARKES, O., *British Battleships* (1957).
PASKE SMITH, M. B. T., *Western Barbarians in Japan and Formosa in Tokugawa Days, 1603–1868* (Kobe, 1930).
PASSIN, H., *Society and Education in Japan* (New York, 1965).
PATRICK, H. 'Japan, 1868–1914' in R. Cameron, *Banking in the Early Stages of Industrialization* (Oxford, 1967).
PATRICK, H., (ed.) *Japanese Industrialisation and its Social Consequences* (Berkeley, 1976).
PAUER, E., 'Japan's Industrial Apprenticeship: A Case Study on the Initiative Role of the Reverberatory Furnace for the Japanese Industrial Revolution', *Rivista internazionale di Science Economiche e Commerciali*, Anno XXIX Dicembre (1982) no. 12.
PAUER, E., *Japans Industrielle Lehrzeit, die Bedeutung des Flammofens in der Wirtschaftlichen und technischen Entwicklungen Japans Für den Beginn der Industriellen Revolution* (Bonn, 1983).
PAUER, E., *Silkworms, Oil and Chips* (Bonn, 1986).
PAYNE, P. L., *Studies in Scottish Business History* (1967).
PAYNE, P. L., *British Entrepreneurship in the Nineteenth Century* (1974).
PAYNE, P. L., *Colvilles and the Scottish Steel Industry* (Oxford, 1979).
PEERY, R. B., *The Gist of Japan* (Edinburgh, 1904).
PELCOVITS, N. A., *Old China Hands and the Foreign Office* (1948).
PERRY, J., 'Oxford and Science', *Nature*, 3 December 1903, pp. 208–14.
PERRY, J. and AYRTON, W. E., 'On a Neglected Principle that may be Employed in Earthquake Measurements', *TASJ*, vol. 5, pt I (1877) pp. 181–202 (graph).
PERRY, J. and AYRTON, W. E., 'The Specific Inductive Capacity of Gases', *TASJ*, vol. 5, pt 7 (1877) pp. 116–30.
PERRY, J. C., 'Great Britain and the Emergence of Japan as a Naval Power', *MN*, XXI, 3–4 (1966) pp. 305–21.
PERRY, M. C., *Narrative of the Expedition of an American Squadron to China Seas and Japan . . . 1852, 1853 and 1854* (Washington, 1854).
PEVSNER, N., 'Christopher Dresser, Industrial Designer', *Architectural Review*, vol. 4 (1937) pp. 184–6.
PEVSNER, N., *Pioneers of Modern Design* (Harmondsworth, 1960).
PEVSNER, N., *Some Architectural Writers of the Nineteenth Century*, vol. I (1972).
PIERSON, J. D., *Tokutomi Soho, 1863–1957: A Journalist for Modern Japan* (Princeton, 1980).
PITTAU, J., *Political Thought in early Meiji Japan, 1868–1889* (Cambridge, Mass., 1967).
PLATT, D. C. M., 'The Role of British Consular Service in Overseas Trade', *EcHR* (1963) no 3, pp. 494–512.

PLATT, D. C. M. (ed.) *Business Imperialism, 1840–1930* (Oxford, 1977).

POLLARD, S., 'The Decline of Shipbuilding on the Thames', *EcHR*, n.s. 3 (1950) pp. 72–89.

POLLARD, S., '*Laissez-faire* and Shipbuilding', *EcHR*, n.s.5 (1952) pp. 98–113.

POLLARD, S., 'Barrow-in-Furness and the seventh Duke of Devonshire', *EcHR*, n.s. 8 (1955) pp. 213–21.

POLLARD, S., 'British and World Shipbuilding, 1890–1914: A Study in Comparative Costs', *Journal of Economic History*, 17 (1957) pp. 426–44.

POLLARD, S. and ROBERTSON, P. L., *The British Shipbuilding Industry, 1870–1914* (Cambridge, Mass., 1979).

POLLOCK, D., *Modern Shipbuilding and the Men Engaged in it* (1884).

POOL, B., *Navy Board Contracts* (1966).

POOL, B., 'Navy contracts after 1832', *Mariners Mirror*, vol. 54 (1968).

POOLEY, A. M., *Hayashi* (1915).

POPE HENNESSY, J., *Verandah: Some Episodes in the Crown Colonies, 1867–1889* (1964).

PRESTON, A., *The Ship, Dreadnought to Nuclear Submarine*, HMSO (1980).

PULESTON, W. D., *Mahan: The Life and Work of Captain A. T. Mahan* (1939).

PURDIE, T., *The Relations of Science to University Teaching in Scotland* (St Andrews, 1885).

PURVIS, F. P., 'Japanese Ships of the Past and Present', *JSL*, vol. XXIII (1925–6) pp. 51–87.

PUTNAM WEALE, B. L., *The Re-shaping of the Far East* (New York, 1905).

PUTNAM WEALE, B. L., *The Coming Struggle in the Far East* (1908).

PUTNAM WEALE, B. L., *An Indiscreet Chronicle from the Pacific* (New York, 1922).

PYLE, K. B., *The New Generation in Meiji Japan: Problems of Cultural Identity, 1885–1895* (Stanford, 1969).

RANFT, B., *Technical Change and British Naval Policy, 1860–1939* (1977).

RANIS, G., 'The Financing of Japanese Economic Development', *EcHR*, vol. XI, no 3 (1959).

RANKINE, W. J. M., *Introductory Lecture on the Science of the Engineer* (1857).

RANKINE, W. J. M., *Manual of Applied Mechanics* (1858).

RANKINE, W. J. M., 'On the Resistance of Ships', *PGS*, vol. 16 (1858) pp. 238–9.

RANKINE, W. J. M., *Civil Engineering* (1862).

RANKINE, W. J. M., 'On the Mechanical Principles of the Screw Propeller', *TINA*, vol. 6 (1865) pp. 13–39.

RANKINE, W. J. M., *Shipbuilding, Theoretical and Practical* (1866).

RANKINE, W. J. M., *A Memoir of John Elder* (Edinburgh, 1871).

RANKINE, W. J. M., *Miscellaneous Scientific Papers including Memoir by P. G. Tait* (1881) edited by W. J. Millar.

RANSOME, S., *Japan in Transition* (New York, 1899).

READER, W. J., *Professional Men: The Rise of the Professional Classes in Nineteenth Century England* (1966).
READER, W. J., *Architect of Air Power* (1968).
READER, W. J., *The Weir Group: A Centenary History* (1970).
REDESDALE, Lord (see MITFORD, A. B. F.).
REED, E. J., *Japan, its History, Traditions and Religion* (1880).
REID, J. M., *James Lithgow, Master of Work* (1964).
REISCHAUER, E. O., *Japan, Past and Present* (1946).
REISCHAUER, E. O., 'Modernization in Nineteenth Century China and Japan', *Japan Quarterly* (July 1963).
REISCHAUER, E. O., *The Japanese* (Cambridge, Mass., 1977).
REISCHAUER, H. M., *Samurai and Silk: A Japanese and American Heritage* (Harvard, 1985).
RINGER, F. K., *Education and Society in Modern Europe* (Bloomington, 1979).
ROACH, J., *Public Examinations in England* (Cambridge, 1971).
ROBB, A. M., 'Shipbuilding', in Charles Singer *et al.*, *A History of Technology*, vol. V (Oxford, 1958).
ROBERTS, J. G., *Mitsui: Three Centuries of Japanese Business* (Tokyo and New York, 1973).
ROBERTS, W. P., 'The Formation of the Society of Naval Architects and Marine Engineers', *Transactions of the Society of Naval Architects and Marine Engineers* (1945).
ROBERTSON, D. H. and MORISON, D. C., 'Shipping and Shipbuilding', in *London and Cambridge Economic Service* (1923).
ROBERTSON, P. L., 'Shipping and Shipbuilding: The Case of William Denny and Brothers', *BH*, 19 (1974).
ROBINSON, J. C., *Catalogue of the Museums of Manufactures* (1856).
RODERICK, G. W. and STEPHENS, M. D., *Scientific and Technical Education in Nineteenth Century England* (Newton Abbot, 1972).
RODERICK, G. W. and STEPHENS, M. D., *Education and Industry in the Nineteenth Century* (1978).
ROSCOE, H. E., *The Life and Experiences of Sir H. E. Roscoe* (1906).
ROSEN, R., *Forty Years of Diplomacy*, 2 vols (1922).
ROSENBERG, N., *Perspectives on Technology* (Cambridge, 1976).
ROSOVSKY, H., *Capital Formation in Japan, 1868–1910* (Glencoe, 1961).
ROSOVSKY, H., 'Japan's Transition to Modern Economic Growth 1868–1885' in *Industrialization in Two Systems* (New York, 1966).
ROSTOW, W. W., *The Process of Economic Growth* (Oxford, 1953).
ROSTOW, W. W., *The Stages of Economic Growth* (Cambridge, 1960).
ROSTOW, W. W. (ed.) *The Economic Take-off into Sustained Growth* (New York, 1963).
RUSSELL, J. S., 'On the Education of Naval Architects in England and France', *TINA*, 4 (1863) pp. 163–76.
RUSSELL, J. S., *The Fleet of the Future, Iron or Wood* (1863).
RUSSELL, J. S., *Very Large Ships, their Advances and Defects* (1863).
RUSSELL, J. S., *A Modern System of Naval Architecture* (1865).
RUSSELL, J. S., *Systematic Technical Education for the English People* (1869).

RUSSELL, O. D., *The House of Mitsui* (Boston, 1939).
RYAN, C. G., *The Marketing of Technology* (1984).
SAITO, M., 'Britons in the Japanese Navy', *The New East*, vol. I (August 1917) p. 51.
SAKATA, Y. and HALL, J. W., 'The Motivation of Political Leadership in the Meiji Restoration', *JAS*, vol. XVI (November 1956) p. 46.
SAKURAI, J., 'Obituary of Edward Divers', *Journal of the Chemical Society* (1913) vol. 103, pp. 746–55.
SALAM, A., *Address*, Inaugural Session on Development, 'The Human Dimension' (Istanbul, 1985).
SANDERSON, M., *The Universities and British Industry, 1850–1970* (1972).
SANDERSON, M., 'The University of London and Industrial Progress 1880–1914', *JCH* (July/October 1972).
SANDERSON, M., *The Universities in the Nineteenth Century* (1975).
SANDHAM, H., 'On the History of Paddle Wheel Steam Navigation', *Proceeding of Institute Mechanical Engineers* (1885) pp. 121–59.
SANSOM, G. B., *The Western World and Japan: A Study in the Interaction of European and Asiatic Cultures* (New York, 1950).
SATOW, E. M. (translation) *Japan 1853–1864*, or *Genji Yume Monogatari* (Tokyo, 1905).
SATOW, E. M., *A Guide to Diplomatic Practice* (1917).
SATOW, E. M., *A Diplomat in Japan: The Inner History of the Critical Years in the Evolution of Japan When the Ports were Opened and the Monarchy Restored* (1921).
SAUL, S. B., 'The Engineering Industry', in D. H. Aldcroft (ed.) *The Development of British Industry and Foreign Competition, 1875–1914* (1968).
SAUL, S. B., *The Myth of the Great Depression, 1873–1896* (1969).
SAUL, S. B., 'The Machine Tool Industry in Britain to 1914', *BH*, vol. X, 1, (1968) p. 29.
SAXONHOUSE, G., 'A Tale of Japanese Technological Diffusion in the Meiji period', *Journal of Economic History*, 34, 1 (March, 1974) pp. 149–65.
SCHAIBLE, C. H., *The State and Education: An Historical and Critical Essay* (1884).
SCHNEIDER, H. W. and LAWTON, W., *A Prophet and a Pilgrim, being the Incredible History of Thomas Lake Harris and Laurence Oliphant* (New York, 1942).
SCHWANTES, R. S., *Japanese and Americans: A Century of Cultural Relations* (New York, 1955).
SCOTT, J. D., *Vickers: A History* (1962).
SCOTT, W. R. *et al.*, *An Industrial Survey of the South West of Scotland* (1932).
SEARLE, G. R., *The Quest for National Efficiency* (Oxford, 1971).
SERGE, E., *From X-Rays to Quarks: Modern Physicists and their Discoveries* (Berkeley, 1980).
SEIDENSTICKER, E., *Low City, High City, Tokyo from Edo to the Earthquake* (1983).
SEPPINGS WRIGHT, H. C., *With Togo* (1905).
SHADWELL, A., *Industrial Efficiency: A Comparative Study of Industrial Life in England, Germany and America* (1906).

SHARLIN, H. I., *Lord Kelvin: The Dynamic Victorian* (Penn. State, 1979).
SHARP, W. H., *The Educational System of Japan* (Bombay, 1906).
SHELDON, C. D., *The Rise of the Merchant Class in Tokugawa Japan, 1600–1868: An Introductory Survey* (New York, 1958).
SHEWAN, A. (compiler) *Aspirat Adhuc Amor* (Aberdeen, 1923).
SHIBUSAWA, K., *Japanese Society in the Meiji Era* (Tokyo, 1958).
SHIELDS, J., *Clyde Built* (Glasgow, 1949).
SHIMAO, E., 'Darwinism in Japan 1877–1927', *Annals of Science*, 38 (1981) pp. 93–102.
SHIVELY, D. H. (ed.) *Tradition and Modernisation in Japanese Culture* (Princeton, 1971).
SHOJI, D. (ed.) *Researches in Hydrography and Oceanography: In Commemoration of the Centenary of the Hydrographic Department of Japan* (Tokyo, 1972).
SILBERMAN, B. S., *Ministers of Modernization: Elite Mobility in the Meiji Restoration 1868–1873* (Tucson, 1964).
SILBERMAN, B. S., 'Bureaucratic Development and the Structure of Decision-making in the Meiji period: The Case of the Genro', *JAS*, vol. XXVII (February, 1968) pp. 81–94.
SILBERMAN, B. S., 'Ringisei-traditional Values and Organisational Imperatives in the Japanese Upper Civil Service 1868–1945', *JAS*, vol. XXXII, no. 2 (February, 1973) pp. 251–64.
SILBERMAN, B. S. and HAROOTUNIAN, H. D., *Modern Japanese Leadership: Transition and Change* (Arizona, 1966).
SILBERMAN, B. S. and HAROOTUNIAN, H. D., *Japan in Crisis: Essays on Taisho Democracy* (Princeton, 1974).
SKZYPCZAK, E., *Japan's Modern Century* (Tokyo and Vermont, 1968).
SLAVEN, A., *Development of the West Scotland 1750–1960* (1975).
SMILES, S. *Lives of the Engineers* (1861).
SMILES, S., *Self-Help* (1866).
SMILES, S., *Thrift* (1875).
SMILES, S., *Men of Invention and Industry* (1884).
SMITH, B. M. D., *Education for Management: Its Conception and Implementation in the Faculty of Commerce at Birmingham mainly in the 1900s*, Centre for Urban and Regional Studies, University of Birmingham, Research Memorandum, no. 37 (October 1974).
SMITH, D. W., *European Settlements in the Far East* (1900).
SMITH, E. C., *A Short History of Naval and Marine Engineering* (Cambridge, 1938).
SMITH, E. L., *A History of Industrial Design* (Oxford, 1983).
SMITH, E. W. F., 'The Future of British Engineering and Shipbuilding', *TNECI*, 31 (1914–15).
SMITH, J. W. and HOLDEN, T. S., *Where Ships are Born, Sunderland 1846–1946* (Sunderland, 1946).
SMITH, L. and HARRIS, V., *Japanese Decorative Arts from the Seventeenth Century to the Nineteenth Century*, B. M. (1982).
SMITH, R. H., *Testimonials* (n.p. 1890) GUL Stack Y2.c.14.
SMITH, T. C., *Political Change and Industrial Development in Japan: Government Enterprise 1868–1880* (Stanford, 1955).

SMITH, T. C., *The Agrarian Origins of Modern Japan* (Stanford, 1959).
SOVIAK, E., 'On the Nature of Western Progress: The Journal of the Iwakura Embassy', in D. H. Shively (ed.) *Tradition and Modernisation in Japanese Culture* (Princeton, 1971).
SOYEDA, J., 'The Study of Political Economy in Japan', *Economic Journal*, June 1893, pp. 334–9.
SOYEDA, J., 'The Adoption of Gold Monometallism by Japan', *Political Science Quarterly*, vol. XIII, no. 1 (Boston, 1898) pp. 60–90.
SPENCER, D. L. and WORONIAK, A. (eds) *The Transfer of Technology to Developing Countries* (New York, 1967).
SPINKS, C. N., 'The Background to the Anglo-Japanese Alliance', *Pacific Historical Review*, vol. 8 (1939) pp. 317–39.
SPRATT, H. R., *Science Museum Handbook of the Collections Illustrating Marine Engineering* (HMSO, n.d.).
STATLER, O., *Shimoda Story* (Tokyo, 1971).
STEAD, A., *Review of Reviews*, vol. IX, January to June 1894.
STEAD, A., *Japan, Our New Ally* (1902).
STEAD, A., *Japan by the Japanese* (1904).
STEEDS, D. and NISH, I., *China, Japan and Nineteenth Century Britain* (Dublin, 1977).
STEPHEN, A., *A Shipbuilding History, 1750–1932* (Cheltenham, 1932).
STERN, H. P., *Master Prints of Japan* (New York, 1969).
STEVENSON, D. A., 'Our Lighthouses', *Good Words* (1864).
STEVENSON, D. A., *Lighthouses* (Edinburgh, 1865).
STEVENSON, D. A., 'Description of the Electric Light on the Isle of May', *Proceedings of the Institution of Mechanical Engineers* (1887) pp. 347–72.
STEVENSON, T., *Lighthouse Illumination: being a Description of the Holophotal System* (1859).
STOCKWIN, J. A. A., *Why Japan Matters* (Oxford, 1983).
STOPES, M. C., *A Journal from Japan* (1910).
STORRY, R., *A History of Modern Japan* (1960).
STORRY, R., *Japan and the Decline of the West in Asia, 1894–1943* (1979).
STORRY, R. (*Festschrift*), *Themes and Theories in Modern Japanese History*, edited by S. Kenny and J. P. Lehmann (1987).
STRANG, J., *The Progress, Extent and Value of Steamboat Building and the Marine Engine Making on the Clyde* (Glasgow, 1852).
STRANGE, E. F., 'The Art of Kyosai', *JSL*, vol. IX (1909–11) pp. 264–76.
STRATTEN'S *Glasgow and its Environs* (Glasgow, 1891).
STURMEY, S. G., *British Shipping and World Competition* (1962).
SUGIMOTO, E. I., *A Daughter of the Samurai* (New York, 1927).
SUGIYAMA, C., 'The Development of Economic Thought in Meiji Japan', *MAS*, vol. 2 (1968) pp. 315–41.
SUGIYAMA, C. (ed.) *Political Economy Comes to Japan* (Tokyo, 1988).
SUGIYAMA, S., 'Glover & Co., a British Merchant in Nagasaki, 1861–70', I. Nish (ed.) *Bakumatsu and Meiji Studies in Japan's Economic and Social History* (ICERD, LSE) (1981–2).
SUGIYAMA, S., 'Thomas B. Glover; A British Merchant in Japan, 1861–70', *BH*, vol. XXVI, no 2 (July 1984) pp. 115–38.

SUGIYAMA, S., *Japan's Industrialization in the World Economy 1859–99, Export Trade and Overseas Competition* (1988).
SUMIYA, M. and TAIRA, K., *An Outline of Japanese Economic History 1603–1940* (Tokyo, 1979).
SUTHERLAND, H. B., 'Rankine, his Life and Times', *Institution of Civil Engineers* (1973).
SUYEMATSU, Baron Kencho, *The Risen Sun* (1905).
SWAINSON, W. P., *Thomas Lake Harris, Mad or Inspired* (Croydon, 1895).
TAKAHASHI, K., *The Rise and Development of Japan's Modern Economy* (Tokyo, 1969).
TAKESHI, N., 'The Contributions of Foreigners', *JWH*, vol. 9, no 2 (1965–6) pp. 294–319.
TANAKA, T., 'Meiji Government and the Introduction of Railways', *Contemporary Japan* (2 parts) 28 (1966–7) pp. 567–88, and 750–88.
TARRING, J. C., *British Consular Jurisdiction in the East* (1887).
TATEMOTO, M., 'Gold, Silver and Paper Money Muddles before and after the Meiji Restoration', ICERD, LSE (1981).
TAUEBER, B., *The Population of Japan* (Princeton, 1958).
TAYLOR, A., *Laurence Oliphant 1829–1888* (1982).
TENNYSON D'EYNCOURT, E. W. H., *A Shipbuilders Yarn* (n.d., *c.* 1949).
TERAKAWA, T. and BROCK, W. H., 'The Introduction of Heurism into Japan', *History of Education*, vol. 7, no. 1 (1978) pp. 35–44.
TERANO, S. and YUKAWA, M., 'Development of Merchant Shipbuilding in Japan', *TINA*, 53, pt 2 (1911).
TEZUKA, T., 'Alien Contributions to the Modernization of Japan in the Meiji Period', *Supplement to Tokyo Municipal News* (1965).
THOMAS, J., *The Springburn Story* (Newton Abbot, 1964).
THOMPSON, J. L., *One Hundred Years, 1846–1946* (Sunderland, 1946).
THOMPSON, S. P., *The Life and Work of William Thomson, Baron Kelvin of Largs* (1908).
TIEDEMANN, A. E., 'Japan's Economic Foreign Policies, 1868–1893', in J. W. Morley (ed.) *Japan's Foreign Policy, 1868–1941: A Research Guide* (New York, 1974).
TIRPITZ, A. von, *My Memoirs* (New York, 1919).
TOMLINSON, B. R., 'Writing History Sideways: Lessons for Indian Economic Historians from Meiji Japan', *MAS*, vol. 19, pt 3 (1985) pp. 669–98.
TOWLE, P., *Estimating Foreign Military Power* (1982).
TOYNBEE, A. J., *A Study of History* (abridged by D. C. Somervell) (Oxford, 1946).
TOYNBEE, A. J., *The World and the West* (Oxford, 1952).
TREBILCOCK, R. C., 'A "Special Relationship" – Government Rearmament and Cordite Firms', *EcHR*, 19 (1966) pp. 364–79.
TREBILCOCK, R. C., 'Spin-off in British Economic History: Armaments and Industry, 1760–1914', *EcHR*, n.s. 22 (1969) pp. 474–90.
TREBILCOCK, R. C., 'Legends of the British Armament Industry, 1890–1914: A Revision', *Journal of Contemporary History*, 5 (1970) pp. 3–19.
TREBILCOCK, R. C., 'British Armaments and European Industrialization 1890–1914', *EcHR*, n.s. 26 (1973) pp. 254–72.

TREBILCOCK, R. C., *The Vickers Brothers: Armaments and Enterprise 1854–1914* (1977).
TREBILCOCK, R. C., *The Industrialisation of the Continental Powers 1780–1914* (1981).
TREVITHICK, F. H., 'Japan's Railway System', *JSL*, vol. IX (1909–11) pp. 158–80.
TREVOR-ROPER, H., *Hermit of Peking: The Hidden Life of Sir Edmund Blackhouse* (1976).
TSOUKALIS, L. and WHITE, M., *Japan and Western Europe Conflict and Cooperation* (1984).
TSUCHIYA, T. and ONCHI, H. (eds) (in Japanese) *Collection of Materials on Economic and Financial History in the early Meiji* (Tokyo, 1931).
TSUNODA, R., de BARRY, W. T. and KEENE, D., *Sources of Japanese Tradition* (New York, 1958).
TSUNOYAMA, S., 'Watching the Clock: Time and Japan's Industrialization', *Look Japan* (10 December 1984) p. 7.
TSURU, S., 'The Take-off in Japan, 1868–1900' in W. W. Rostow, *The Economic Take-off* (1963).
TURNER, R. S., 'The Growth of Professional Research in Prussia 1818–1848: Causes and Context', *Historical Studies in the Physical Sciences*, vol. III (1971) pp. 137–82.
TUBSON, E. W. A., *The British Consul's Manual* (1856).
TYLER, D. B., *The American Clyde* (n.p., 1958).
TYLER, D. B., *Steam Conquers the Atlantic* (New York, 1939).
UNESCO, *History of Industrial Education in Japan* (Tokyo, 1959).
UYEHARA, C. H., *Checklist of Archives in the Japanese Ministry of Foreign Affairs: Tokyo, Japan 1868–1945* (Washington, 1945).
UYEHARA, S., *The Industry and Trade of Japan* (1926).
VARGAS, E. J., *Henry Edward Armstrong 1848–1937, the Doyen of British Chemists and Pioneer of Technical Education* (1958).
VARLEY, H. P., *Japanese Culture: A Short History* (New York, 1973).
VENN, J. A., *Alumni Cantabrigiensis* (1954).
VICKERS, Son and Maxim, *Vickerstown Souvenir* (1903).
von SIEBOLD, A., *Japan's Accession to the Comity of Nations* (1901).
von SIEBOLD, A., 'Personal Reminiscences of Prince Ito Hirubumi', pamphlet (May 1910).
von SIEBOLD, A., *Manners and Customs of the Japanese*, reprint (Vermont, 1973).
WALROND, T., *Letters and Journals of James, 8th Earl of Elgin* (1872).
WARD, D., 'The Public Schools and Industry in Britain after 1870', in W. Lacquer and G. Mosse (eds) *Education and Social Structure in the Twentieth Century, JCH*, no. 6 (New York, 1967).
WARD, R. E. (ed.) *Political Development in Modern Japan . . .* (1968).
WARNER, O., *The British Navy: A Concise History* (1977).
WARNABY, J., 'The Early Scientific Work of John Milne', *Japanese Studies in the History of Science*, vol. 8 (Tokyo, 1969) pp. 77–124.
WATANABE, M., 'Japanese Students Abroad and the Acquisition of Scientific and Technical Knowledge', *JWH*, 9 (1965) pp. 254–93.

WATSON, W. P., *Japan: Aspects and Destinies* (1904).
WATSON, W. P., *The Future of Japan, with a Survey of Present Conditions* (1907).
WELCH, J. J., 'The Scientific Education of Naval Architects', *TNECIES*, 25 (1908–9) pp. 177–98.
WEST, R., *The Fountain Overflows* (Virago, 1983).
WHITE, L. T., *The Medieval Roots of Medicine, Technology and Science* (Oxford, 1963).
WHITE, W. H., 'On the Course of Study in the Royal Naval College, Greenwich', *TINA* (1877).
WHITE, W. H., 'The Cult of the Monster Warship', *Nineteenth Century* (June 1908).
WHITNEY, C. A. W., *Clara's Diary: An American girl in Meiji Japan* (Tokyo and New York, 1979).
WHITWORTH, A. (ed.) *A Centenary History: A History of the City and Guilds College, 1885–1985* (1985).
WILL, J. B. (edited by LENSEN, G. A.) *Trading under Sail off Japan* (Tokyo, 1968).
WILLIAMS, H. S., *Shades of the Past* (Tokyo, 1959).
WILLIAMS, H. S., *Tales of Foreign Settlements in Japan* (Tokyo, 1963).
WILLIAMS, H. S., *Foreigners in Mikado Land* (Tokyo, 1963).
WILLIAMSON, J., *Clyde Passenger Steamers 1812–1901* (Glasgow, 1890).
WILMOT, S. M. E., *Our Fleet Today* (1900) 2nd edn.
WILSON, D. B., *Catalogue of the Manuscript Collections of Sir C. G. Stokes and Sir William Thomson, Baron Kelvin of Largs, in Cambridge University Library* (Cambridge, 1976).
WILSON, G., *What is Technology? An Inaugural Lecture in the University of Edinburgh*, 7 November 1855 (Edinburgh, 1855).
WILSON, G., *The Industrial Museum of Scotland and its Relation to Commercial Enterprise* (Edinburgh, 1858).
WILSON, R. A., *Genesis of the Meiji Government in Japan 1868–1871* (1957).
WILSON, R. L., 'Tea Taste in the Era of *Japonsime*: A Debate', *Chanoyu Quarterly*, vol. 50 (1987) pp. 23–39.
WOOD, W., *The Battleship* (1912).
WRAY, William D., *Mitsubishi and the NYK 1870–1914: Business Strategy in the Japanese Shipbuilding Industry*, sub-series on the history of Japanese Business and Industry, Harvard East Asian Monographs, no. 108 (Cambridge, Mass., 1984).
YAMADA, C., *Japonisme in Art: An International Symposium* (Tokyo, 1980).
YAMAGUCHI, K., 'The Leaders of Industrial and Economic Development in Modern Japan', *JWH*, vol. 9, pt 2 (1965–6) pp. 179–86.
YAMAMURA, K., 'The Role of the Samurai in the Development of Modern Banking in Japan', *Journal of Economic History*, vol. 27, no 2 (June, 1967) pp. 198–220.
YAMAMURA, K., 'The Founding of Mitsubishi: A Case Study in Japanese Business History', *BHR*, 41.2 (Summer 1967) pp. 141–60.

YAMAMURA, K., 'Japan, 1868–1930: A Revised View' in R. Cameron (ed.) *Banking and Economic Development* (Oxford, 1972).

YAMAMURA, K., *A Study of Samurai Income and Entrepreneurship*, Harvard East Asian Series 76 (Cambridge, Mass., 1974).

YAMAMURA, K., 'Entrepreneurship, Ownership and Management in Japan' in P. Mathias and M. M. Postan (eds) *Cambridge Economic History of Europe*, vol. VII, pt 2 (Cambridge, 1978).

YAMAWAKI, H., *Japan in the Beginning of the Twentieth Century* (Tokyo, 1903).

YAMAZAKI, T. 'Japan's Contribution to the Modern History of Technology', *Japan Studies in the History of Science*, no 1 (Tokyo, 1962) pp. 45–7.

YANAGA, C., *Japan since Perry* (New York, 1949).

YARROW, Lady, *Alfred Yarrow, His Life and Work* (1923).

YASUBA, Y., 'Freight Rates and Productivity in Ocean Transportation for Japan 1875–1943', *Explorations in Economic History*, vol. 15, no. 1 (January 1978) pp. 11–39.

YAZU, M., *Chugaku Bankoku Chishi* (*Universal Geography for Middle Schools*) (Tokyo, 1896).

YETARO, K., *The Past and Present in Japanese Commerce* (New York, 1902) (GUL Y9.c20).

YOKOYAMA, T., *Japan in the Victorian Mind: A Study of Stereotyped Images of a Nation, 1850–1880* (1987).

YONEKAWA, S., 'University Graduates in Japanese Enterprises before the Second World War', *BH*, vol. XXVII, no 2 (July 1984) pp. 193–218.

YONEMARA, A., *Japanese Lacquer* (1979).

YONEYAMA, U., *A Bankers Reminiscences*, with introduction by A. A. Shand (1902).

YOSHIDA, S., *Japan's Decisive Century 1867–1967* (New York, 1967).

YOUNG, P., *Power of Speech, 1883–1983. Standard Telephone and Cables* (1983).

YUASA, M., 'Scientific Revolution in Nineteenth Century Japan', *Japanese Studies in the History of Science*, no. 2 (1963) pp. 119–26.

YUASA, M., 'The Scientific Revolution and the Age of Technology', *JWH*, vol. 9, no. 2 (June 1965) pp. 187–207.

YUASA, M., 'The Growth of Scientific Communities in Japan', *Japanese Studies in the History of Science*, no. 9 (1970) pp. 137–58.

YUASA, M., 'The Role of Science and Technology in the Economic Development of Modern Japan' in *XII Congrès Internationale D'Historie des Sciences*, vol. 6 (Paris, 1971).

## THESES

ANDERSON, M. A., 'Edmund Hammond, Permanent Under-Secretary of State for Foreign Affairs', Ph.D. (University of London, 1955).

CHANG, C. F., 'The Anglo-Japanese Alliance', D.Phil. (Johns Hopkins University, Baltimore, 1931).

DANIELS, GORDON, 'Sir Harry Parkes, British Representative in Japan 1865–1883', D.Phil. (University of Oxford, 1967).
GOW, I., 'Admiral Kato Kanji and the Inter-war Naval Arms Limitation, the Japanese Navy in Politics and Politics in the Japanese Navy', Ph.D. (University of Sheffield, 1985).
HOARE, J. E., 'The Japanese Treaty Ports 1868–1899; A Study of the Foreign Settlements', Ph.D. (London, 1971).
HOOVER, W. D., 'Godai Tomoatsu, 1836–185: An Economic Statesman of Early Meiji Japan', Ph.D. (University of Michigan, 1973).
JONES, HAZEL, J., 'The Meiji Government and Foreign Employees, 1868–1900', Ph.D. (University of Michigan, 1967).
KAWAKATSU, H., 'International Competition in Cotton Goods in the Late Nineteenth Century', D.Phil. (University of Oxford, 1984).
KENNISON, G., 'Robert Napier as a Businessman', M.Litt. (University of Strathclyde, 1975).
KOIZUMI, K., 'The Development of Physics in Meiji Japan, 1868–1912', Ph.D. (University of Philadelphia, 1973).
McMASTER, J., 'British Trade and Traders to Japan, 1859–1869', Ph.D. (University of London, 1961).
MAYO, MARLENE, J., 'The Iwakura Mission and the Unequal Treaties', Ph.D. (University of Columbia, 1961).
SIMS, R. L., 'French Policy towards Japan, 1854–1894', Ph.D. (University of London, 1968).
SUGIYAMA, S., 'Japan's Export Trade, 1859–1899, with Special Reference to Silk, Tea and Coal', Ph.D. (University of London, 1981).
WRAY, W. D., 'Mitsubishi and the NYK Line 1870–1894: The Beginnings of the Modern Japanese Shipping Industry', Ph.D. (Harvard University, 1976).

# Index